Erik Satie
A Parisian Composer and his World

Erik Satie
A Parisian Composer and his World

Caroline Potter

THE BOYDELL PRESS

© Caroline Potter 2016

All Rights Reserved. Except as permitted under current legislation no part of this work may be photocopied, stored in a retrieval system, published, performed in public, adapted, broadcast, transmitted, recorded or reproduced in any form or by any means, without the prior permission of the copyright owner

The right of Caroline Potter to be identified as the author of this work has been asserted in accordance with sections 77 and 78 of the Copyright, Designs and Patents Act 1988

First published 2016
The Boydell Press, Woodbridge
Paperback edition 2026

ISBN 978 1 78327 083 5 (hardback)
ISBN 978 1 83765 320 1 (paperback)

The Boydell Press is an imprint of Boydell & Brewer Ltd
and of Boydell & Brewer Inc.
website: www.boydellandbrewer.com

A catalogue record for this book is available from the British Library

The publisher has no responsibility for the continued existence or accuracy of URLs for external or third-party internet websites referred to in this book, and does not guarantee that any content on such websites is, or will remain, accurate or appropriate

Designed and typeset in Scala and Scala Sans Pro by
David Roberts, Pershore, Worcestershire

To Paul, with love

Contents

List of Illustrations viii

List of Music Examples ix

Preface x

Acknowledgements xviii

Personalia xx

Chronology and Worklist xxx

CHAPTER 1 Satie in Montmartre: Mechanical Music in the Belle Epoque 1

CHAPTER 2 Futurism, the New Avant-Garde and Mechanical Music 47

CHAPTER 3 Satie's Texted Piano Works 98

CHAPTER 4 Repetition and Furniture Music 138

CHAPTER 5 Science, Society and Politics in Satie's Life 177

CHAPTER 6 The Provocative Satie and the Dada Connection 206

CHAPTER 7 Satie's Death and Musical Legacy 236

Select Bibliography 254

Index of Names 261

Index of Works by Satie 268

Illustrations

Map of Paris, *c.* 1900	xxxiv
1.1 Organ grinder in Paris, 1898–9, photograph by Eugène Atget	9
1.2 Pianista advert (*Chat noir*, 18 April 1891, p. 1734)	19
1.3 Satie's title page for *Jack in the Box* (Erik Satie papers, bMS Mus 193 (28), Houghton Library, Harvard University)	33
2.1 Erik Satie, 'Le Golf' (*Sports et divertissements*). Satie's score. Typ. 915.14.7700, Houghton Library, Harvard University	70
2.2 Bouteillophone	78
2.3 Photo of Satie by Henri Manuel (April 1917) dedicated 'à Jean Cocteau, son gros vieil ami' (Archives de la Fondation Erik Satie, Paris)	84
2.4 Photo taken on 4 October 1923 at Théâtre des Champs-Elysées on the occasion of the filming of *L'inhumaine*. Left to right: Darius Milhaud, Erik Satie, Georgette Leblanc, Fernand Léger, Marcel L'Herbier (Archives de la Fondation Erik Satie, Paris)	96
3.1 Wooden head looking out of 23 rue de l'Homme de Bois, Honfleur	116
4.1 Santiago Rusiñol (1861–1931), *Una romanza* (1893). Museu de Arte Moderno, Barcelona (Archives de la Fondation Erik Satie, Paris)	140
5.1 Galerie des Machines	185
6.1 Photo of Satie by René Clair (1924) in front of 'Soirée de Paris' poster, dedicated by René Clair to his future wife Bronja Perlmutter (Archives de la Fondation Erik Satie, Paris)	223

Music Examples

Ex. 1.1	Satie, *Gymnopédies*, no. 1: bars 1–12	7
Ex. 1.2	(a) Satie, *Jack in the Box*: sketch 'L'orgue de barbarie du compère Wegg le fou'; (b) Satie, *Jack in the Box*: opening of 'Entr'acte'	36
Ex. 1.3	Satie, *Jack in the Box*, Final: bars 23–34	40
Ex. 1.4	Satie, *Jack in the Box*: Prélude, bars 17–24	41
Ex. 2.1	(a) Satie, *Les Pantins dansent*: first version, piano, bars 5–16; (b) Satie, *Les Pantins dansent*: second version, piano, bars 1–12	57
Ex. 2.2	Satie, *Avant-dernières pensées*, 'Idylle': 'Mais mon cœur est tout petit'	71
Ex. 2.3	Ranges of bouteillophone and xylophone in 'Acrobates' (*Parade*, third dance)	77
Ex. 2.4	*Parade*, 'Prélude au rideau rouge': piano duet version	81–2
Ex. 3.1	Satie, *Embryons desséchés*, 1 ('d'Holothurie'): 'Ne me faîtes pas rire, brin de mousse'	102
Ex. 3.2	Satie, 'Le chapelier' (*Trois mélodies*, no. 3): bars 1–6	109
Ex. 3.3	*Chapitres tournés en tous sens*, 1 ('Celle qui parle trop'): top of p. 2, printed score	121
Ex. 3.4	*Chapitres tournés en tous sens*, 1 ('Celle qui parle trop'): end	121
Ex. 3.5	Satie, *Avant-dernières pensées*, I ('Idylle'): 'The trees look like big odd-shaped combs'	122
Ex. 3.6	(a) Satie, *Heures séculaires et instantanées*, 3 ('Affolements granitiques'): opening of sketch (BNF 9593); (b) Satie, *Heures séculaires et instantanées*, 3 ('Affolements granitiques'): opening of final version	132
Ex. 4.1	Satie, *Carrelage phonique*	147
Ex. 4.2	Satie, *Tapisserie en fer forgé*	148
Ex. 4.3	Satie, *Carrelage pour cabinet noir de luxe*	149
Ex. 4.4	Satie, 'Chez un bistrot': final four bars	166
Ex. 4.5	(a) Saint-Saëns, *Danse macabre*: solo violin, second theme, bars 32³–41¹; (b) Satie, 'Un salon': bars 13–20	167
Ex. 4.6	*Tenture de cabinet préfectoral*: bars 1–4	173
Ex. 6.1	(a) Satie, *Mercure*, 4 ('Signes du Zodiaque'): bars 1–8; (b) Satie, *Parade*, 'Petite fille américaine': bars 59–62	226
Ex. 7.1	Satie, 'La mort de Socrate': bars 278–end	240–1

Preface

ERIK Satie is known to audiences around the world as the composer of three *Gymnopédies* (1888), piano pieces which are more popular than any others of his place and time, the Paris of the late nineteenth and early twentieth centuries. He has always been a 'crossover' composer who appeals well beyond classical music audiences. But Satie is more than a composer of short, memorable and technically unchallenging piano pieces. He was also embedded in the social milieu and artistic environment of Paris and he collaborated with some of the best-known artists and writers of his day. A highly experimental artist and a radical in both art and politics, he often concealed his views behind an ironic or jokey surface. This book situates Satie firmly in the Paris of his time and focuses both on well-known pieces and works which are barely known at all. Some of these rare pieces are available as recordings that accompany this book.

Satie witnessed cataclysmic change in his lifetime. From abject defeat in the Franco-Prussian war of 1870–1, France re-emerged as one of the most dynamic, innovative and artistically vibrant countries in Europe. Sound recording was a concept dreamed up by the Montmartre poet and amateur scientist Charles Cros, though Thomas Edison patented the phonograph and was the toast of the 1889 Exposition Universelle in Paris. Street lighting by electric arcs coexisted with gaslight by the turn of the century and eventually superseded gas; Paris' nickname 'the City of Light' might have originally derived from its status at the centre of the Enlightenment, but the nineteenth and twentieth centuries saw it take a literal turn. The telephone was introduced to France in 1879 and the first transatlantic calls were made from Arlington, Virginia to Paris in October 1915. In 1892, Léon Bouly patented the film camera (*cinématographe*), though the Lumière brothers were the first to exploit the new invention. And the Paris Métro opened in July 1900, during the other major Exposition Universelle in the city during Satie's lifetime. While he was not always an active or willing participant in these changes – for instance, Satie hated the telephone, preferring the beautifully calligraphed written word – the Paris he knew as a child was transformed by developments in communications, technology, transport and society. He first moved to Paris as a four-year-old in 1870: his father, Alfred, sold his shipbroking business on his return from active service in the Franco-Prussian War and was offered a job as a translator in Paris thanks to his friend, the historian Albert Sorel.[1] But following the death of Satie's mother in 1872, the future composer and his brother Conrad were sent back to Honfleur to live with

---

[1] See Robert Orledge, 'The Musical Activities of Alfred Satie and Eugénie Satie-Barnetche, and Their Effect on the Career of Erik Satie.' *Journal of the Royal Musical Association*, vol. 117 no. 2 (1992): pp. 270–97, at pp. 271–2.

relatives until their grandmother's death in a drowning accident in 1878, when they returned to Paris.

Little about Erik Satie was conventional (not least the spelling of his first name, which he changed as an adult), and he resists classification under easy headings such as 'classical music'. He studied at the Paris Conservatoire, though was dismissed without obtaining a diploma, and at the time of the *Gymnopédies* he was working sporadically as a pianist in the cafés and cabarets of Montmartre, accompanying singers and shadow plays and performing in the background to everyday activity. Understanding these popular roots is key to understanding Satie's music.

La musique des pauvres – music of poor people – is an expression that crops up time and again in French literature and the journalism of Satie's lifetime, the late nineteenth and early twentieth centuries. *La musique des pauvres* was synonymous with music played on the barrel organ: music which was free (unless the listener deigned to give their spare change to the performer) and played on the street by tramps or ex-servicemen scraping a living by turning the handle of a hired instrument. The Parisian barrel organ grinder was therefore a marginal figure, and as such he was an inspiration for poets and artists who wished to express sympathy with people outside the bourgeois norm. Satie's music is often short but repetitive, simple in texture and harmony and sometimes based on popular tunes – all characteristics shared with barrel organ music. It is irresistible to place Satie, often described by his Montmartre acquaintances as 'Monsieur le Pauvre', in this sonic landscape.

The many technological innovations in the Belle Epoque were coupled with an artistic interest in machines as one aspect of the self-conscious modernity of the period. Beyond the Belle Epoque, the rapid pace of technological change was mirrored in artistic enthusiasm which often surfaced as admiration for everything new coming out of the United States: praise for everything from the motorcar to skyscrapers was commonplace in art of the 1910s and 1920s. As a participant in both the cabaret music scene and in new artistic movements of the first decades of the twentieth century – usually heralded by manifestos and small-circulation art magazines – Satie was at the centre of this Parisian bohemian and avant-garde milieu.

Technological advances engendered fear as well as excitement. Satie much admired the artist Pierre Puvis de Chavannes, creator of many large scale frescos including those in the Panthéon; in 1889 Puvis was taken to the Galerie des Machines, one of the exhibits at the 1889 Exposition Universelle in Paris. Maurice Raynal claims 'he never would have set foot there on his own' and, on seeing the exhibits, he 'exclaimed: "Oh! My children, *there is no more art to be done!* How could a painter, a poet, fight such social influence, such power over the imagination? Let's get out of here! What will become of us artists in the face of that invasion of engineers and mechanics?"'[2] Raynal, by contrast, believed that 'the modern artist must live with his era and know how to extract the beautiful, the curious, and the sensitive from everything that happens, to extract the pretexts for diversions of the mind and of the imagination'.[3] Satie's attitude to innovation is far closer to Raynal's than Puvis'. The Exposition Universelle was the most prominent event in Paris in 1889: the Eiffel Tower served as the entrance arch for the exhibition, which was held on the Champ de Mars. While the impact on musicians of the colonial display part of the exhibition – which included a Javanese gamelan and Annamite theatre – is well known, that of the Galerie des Machines has been little explored. The Galerie des Machines, which was designed by the architect Ferdinand Dutert and the engineer Victor Contamin, was 111 metres long – the longest interior space in the world at the time. It was reused in the 1900 Exposition Universelle and included a giant projection screen.

Satie's music is indivisible from the sonic environment of Paris: whatever his interest in daring innovations, he rarely travelled beyond Paris and Arcueil, the suburb where he lived from 1898. I propose that mechanical musical instruments had a strong impact on Satie's music because of their repertoire (which focused largely on popular tunes), their sonic qualities and the repetitive nature of mechanical performance. Mechanistic repetition with surprise interjections is also a key component of humour, a quality so often associated with Satie. The popular view of the composer is of someone who gave his works odd titles, whose scores feature peculiar texts or performance directions, and who collaborated in absurdist multimedia works such as René Clair's film interlude 'Entr'acte', part of the ballet *Relâche* (1924) whose title translates as 'no performance'. The philosopher Henri Bergson, a contemporary of Satie, wrote that 'all that is serious in life comes from our freedom. [...] What, then, is needed to transform all this into a comedy? Realising that our apparent freedom conceals the strings of a puppet master and that we are, as the poet said, "humble marionettes/ Whose strings are held in the hands of Necessity".'[4] (Bergson is here quoting Diderot.)

---

[2] Article by Maurice Raynal, 'L'Exposition de la "Section d'Or"'; originally published in *La Section d'Or*, vol. 1 no. 1 (9 October 1912), ed. Pierre Dumont. Reprinted in Mark Antliff and Patricia Leighten (eds), *A Cubism Reader*. Chicago: University of Chicago Press, 2008, pp. 332–40 (translated by Jane Marie Todd), at p. 335.

[3] Cited in Antliff and Leighton (eds), *A Cubism Reader*, pp. 335–6.

[4] Henri Bergson, *Le rire. Essai sur la signification du comique* (1900); originally published in three numbers of the *Revue de Paris* (1 February, 15 February and 1 March 1900), and in book form by Editions Alcan, 1924, p. 39: 'Tout le sérieux de la vie lui vient de notre liberté. [...] Que faudrait-il pour transformer tout cela en comédie? Il faudrait se figurer que la liberté apparente recouvre un jeu de ficelles, et que nous sommes ici-bas, comme

The texts that accompany Satie's piano music from around 1912–17 were the main feature of his work noted by contemporary audiences. Who could possibly forget the in-text annotation on 'd'Holothurie', the first of his *Embryons desséchés* (1913): 'Comme un rossignol qui aurait mal aux dents' ('Like a nightingale with toothache')? Indeed, humour became the only quality that audiences recognised: even *Socrate*, which is based on Plato's account of the death of Socrates, elicited laughter from audience members who feared not being in on the joke. While *Socrate* is unequivocally a serious work, there is far more to Satie's piano pieces of the period than their texts (which are not always funny, far from it). Satie's ironic, mocking, playful and paradoxical style, which often incorporates parody, is summed up in a word often used in the Paris of his day: *blague*.

Satie was too old to be called up during World War I but he was affected by the absence of friends and patrons, and especially by shortages. He received charitable assistance during the war years from the Comité Franco-Américain, an organisation set up by Nadia and Lili Boulanger and the American composer and diplomat Blair Fairchild. Set up with financial assistance from both French and American sources, the charity supported musicians both on the front and at home who were struggling. The singer Jane Bathori write to Fairchild seeking support for 'our friend Erik Satie who is going through a difficult time – like many others besides'; a second letter, written in 1918, asks 'I wonder whether you could send him another package in a few days' time; it will be very necessary.'[5] While Satie rarely had money and was never interested in managing it carefully, the privations of the war years added extra pressure to his existence.

In Chapter 1 I explore Satie's musical environment in the late nineteenth and early twentieth centuries and show how his music (and other creative activity) was very much part of its time. Satie's creative life was then focused on Montmartre, where he worked sporadically as a café pianist and accompanied shadow plays on the harmonium. Here, he met artists, writers and unclassifiable eccentrics whose art, opinions and discoveries shaped his creativity. Deborah Menaker Rothschild encapsulates the importance of the cabaret to the avant-garde Parisian artistic scene: 'It was in the cabaret, not the opera house, that performers took risks, bantered with their audiences and responded to current events, ideas and sentiments. Against this, the ballet, opera, and dramatic theatre – where timely or political references were taboo – came to

---

dit le poète, «... d'humbles marionnettes Dont le fil est aux mains de la Nécessité».'

[5] Undated letters (possibly from 1918) housed in the Bibliothèque Nationale de France and cited in Caroline Potter, *Nadia and Lili Boulanger*. Aldershot: Ashgate, 2006, p. 22: 'notre ami Erik Satie qui traverse un moment bien difficile – comme beaucoup d'autres du reste'; 'Je crois que si vous pouvez renouveler un envoi d'ici quelques jours, cela lui sera très nécessaire.'

be viewed as being irrelevant and hopelessly out-of-touch by many Frenchmen.' The Ballets Russes impresario Serge Diaghilev, however, was not impressed by the 'lack of discernment and short attention span' of the music hall audience.[6] Nevertheless, always eager to collaborate with the most fashionable artists, Diaghilev commissioned the circus and music hall themed *Parade* from Satie, Cocteau and Picasso in 1916.

After returning to study as a mature student at the Schola Cantorum from 1905, Satie was bemused that his early piano pieces, such as the *Sarabandes* and *Gymnopédies*, were promoted by major Parisian musical figures including Ravel and the pianist Ricardo Viñes. He was now being talked about as a precursor, not simply as an eccentric figure from the Montmartre café scene. This promotion of his work led to publisher interest in his music and new audiences for his writings. Satie also became a totemic figure of the avant-garde and a rallying point for young composers, notably the Nouveaux Jeunes, many of whom became more celebrated in Les Six. Jean Cocteau's promotion of Satie in his tract *Le coq et l'arlequin* (1918), dedicated to and probably co-written with Georges Auric, gave Satie a similar status to his friend Debussy: he was dragged into artistic polemics whether he liked it or not.

The contemporary obsession with mechanical instruments was explored in every medium: poets as varied as Mallarmé, Verlaine and Baudelaire all explore this topic, and all identified with the marginal, very unbourgeois figure of the street performer. Reflecting technological advances of the period, mechanisms and automata were obsessions of artists, writers and composers active in Paris in the early twentieth century. The many tiny art magazines which sprung up in Paris (often directly imitating New York publications), including *391* and *Le Cœur à barbe*, all show this self-conscious modernity, and Satie was a contributor to these publications. The mechanical is a key theme in the work of George Antheil, Edgard Varèse, Maurice Ravel and Igor Stravinsky, all composers who knew Satie and in various ways were connected to his musical world. The second and sixth chapters show Satie's connections to the futurist and Dada movements and the emergence of surrealism; indeed, the neologism 'sur-réalisme' was coined by Guillaume Apollinaire in his programme note for the premiere of *Parade* in 1917. Connections he had made with artists in Montparnasse during the war were crucial in the last years of his life; his collaborations were genuine multimedia works in which his music is to be heard and understood in relation to another medium.

Satie's writings – particularly his texted piano works of 1912–17 – show multiple references to current events. The textual commentaries he wrote for his piano works tend to be described as surreal, amusing, nonsense or

---

[6] Deborah Menaker Rothschild, *Picasso's 'Parade'*. New York: Sotheby's Publications/The Drawing Center, 1991, p. 38. See also Lisa Appignanesi, *The Cabaret*. New York: Universe Books, 1976.

a combination of these, but my research shows that these texts often have a firm basis in reality. The texted piano works are investigated in detail in Chapter 3, which shows that Satie constantly returned to a narrow range of topics for his texts and used various strategies for integrating (or not) text and music. I am all too aware that there are dangers in taking Satie's words at face value – but also aware that his plays on words and habit of finishing sentences with an amusing twist (which Cocteau called 'finir les mots', 'finishing an expression') depends on being aware of a word's many possible meanings in different contexts. His humour very often hinges on these twists in meaning and I will explore, particularly in Chapter 3, how Satie's texts, which are often considered to be simply witty or ironic, reveal new and unexpected significance when words are understood in a different context.

One topic is important enough to warrant a separate chapter: *musique d'ameublement* (furniture music) is the focus of Chapter 4. Satie's invention of this term means that he has been credited as the precursor of muzak, minimalism, chance music and many other subgenres central to twentieth-century musical, artistic and social culture. While Satie wrote a handful of short pieces which were explicitly designed as furniture music (and only two of these were definitely publicly performed in his lifetime), the concept was applied by him and by Jean Cocteau in other contexts. His multiple artistic connections and collaborations of the 1910s and early 1920s coalesce in his furniture music. This is a period where, in Paris avant-garde art, everyone seemed to know everyone else.

Robert Orledge, in his influential *Satie the Composer*, wrote that

> for so progressive a composer there was a curiously insular and conservative streak in Satie's mentality. He hated travel and upheaval as much as he hated the telephone and other modern inventions. He never sought to record his music for posterity (as Debussy and Fauré did), he never possessed a radio or listened to one, and he even refused to use the Métro. In short, his essential world idealized the medieval past rather than the present or the future, and he showed an unexpected distrust of modern technology and the conventional concept of progress.[7]

I contend, however, that Satie showed a good deal of interest in modern technology, scientific discoveries and contemporary issues, even if he did not personally wish to engage with all of this new technology. This intriguing paradoxical issue is addressed in Chapter 5 together with Satie's interest and involvement in left-wing politics. Satie's life in Arcueil saw him mixing in radical progressive political circles, a little-known facet of his existence which he concealed from most of his Paris connections.

---

[7] Robert Orledge, *Satie the Composer*. Cambridge: Cambridge University Press, 1990, p. 16.

The composer did occasionally use the Métro in later life; indeed, as Ornella Volta states, 'Hearing, in the Métro, the news of the death of Lenin on 21 January 1924, Satie could not hold back tears.'[8]

For everyone interested in Satie, there is a danger in looking only at the dazzling and novel surface of his work. As Ornella Volta wrote, 'Often with Satie, we are stunned by the striking images he offers us and forget to look at the substance. As if it were a magical incantation, we are happy just to contemplate it, even to repeat it and pass it on.'[9] Satie's writings, letters and conversation were intriguing, often amusing, ironic, punning, occasionally touching and almost always baffling. Surely all Satie researchers approach his words with trepidation, always knowing that multiple interpretations are possible and the dividing line between being serious and joking is, with him, indistinct to say the least. Léon-Louis Veyssière, a friend of Satie's who knew him in Arcueil social and political circles for two decades from around 1900, has left perhaps the most telling of all anecdotes about him: 'I got to know Satie about as well as one can get to know someone so strange and odd, who was at the same time chatty and closed-up, constantly contradicting himself; it was often hard to know if he was joking or if he was being serious. It would be unwise of me to say: Satie as I knew him; far more reasonable to say: Satie as I thought I knew him.'[10]

Certainly, contemporary audiences and composers know one side of Satie very well: his early piano pieces, especially the *Gymnopédies* and *Gnossiennes*, are favourites of amateur players and regularly seen in 'relaxing' and 'chillout' recorded classics compilations. Indeed, much of Satie's work is difficult to programme in the concert hall as he had no interest in virtuoso display for its own sake, but it has found its true niche in broadcasting and recording. The intimate quality of Satie's piano music is ideal for home listeners and the composer was comfortable with

---

[8] Ornella Volta (ed.), *Erik Satie: Correspondance presque complète*. Paris: Fayard/IMEC, 2/2003, p. 579: 'En apprenant, dans le métro, la mort de Lénine (21 janvier [1924]), Satie ne peut retenir ses larmes.'

[9] Ornella Volta, 'Le rideau se lève sur un os: Quelques investigations autour d'Erik Satie': 'Erik Satie – L'os à moelle.' *Revue internationale de musique française*, 23 (June 1987): p. 1: 'Il arrive souvent avec Satie que, stupéfait par l'image saisissante qu'il propose, on en oubli de creuser le propos. Telle une formule magique, on se contente de la contempler, voire de la répéter, la transmettre.'

[10] *Réflexions et anecdotes sur Erik Satie par Léon-Louis Veyssière*. Preface by Annette Le Bonhomme-Veyssière. Cachan: Litavis, 2013, p. 13: 'j'ai appris à connaître Satie aussi bien que l'on pouvait connaître un être aussi étrange et aussi bizarre, à la fois loquace et fermé, en constante contradiction avec lui-même, dont il était souvent difficile de savoir s'il plaisantait ou s'il parlait sérieusement. Il me serait imprudent de dire: Satie tel que je l'ai connu, mais beaucoup plus sage de dire: Satie tel que j'ai cru le connaître.'

the notion that his music could be a background to other activities or art forms.

But much of Satie's music remains little known, and one of my aims in this book is to highlight pieces which readers might like to explore. Recordings of his furniture music, including some unavailable elsewhere, by performers from the Royal College of Music may be accessed online at my YouTube channel (Caroline Potter Satie): https://www.youtube.com/channel/UCGfOdIdyBcPCtFlg0UXF0Lw. Satie was at the centre of one of the most exciting periods in the cultural history of Europe, in one of the most exciting cities in the world. While his work raises fundamental questions about the importance of technology in music of his time, the role of the performer in a machine-driven age, and music's place as one of many demands on the audience's attention in a multimedia world, it is also enduringly popular. If this book encourages readers to listen beyond their favourite Satie pieces, it will have succeeded in its aims.

Acknowledgements

Many friends and French music colleagues have supported this project. In particular, I should like to acknowledge *mon cher maître* Professor Robert Orledge, who kindly read the entire manuscript and made many useful suggestions. Any remaining errors are, of course, my own responsibility. I am also grateful to Christopher Dawson, Andrew Hugill, Roger Nichols and various anonymous readers for their assistance and advice. Ornella Volta, the doyenne of Satie research, was extremely helpful in the latter stages of this project and generously permitted me to reproduce images from the collection of the Fondation Erik Satie.

It was my great pleasure and privilege to act as Series Advisor to the Philharmonia Orchestra and Royal College of Music's 2014–15 Paris season, alongside Caroline Rae. I am very grateful indeed to the orchestra staff, supporters and 'other Caroline' for their interest in my work. This connection resulted in the performance of several Satie works and the recording of *musique d'ameublement* by students of the Royal College, recordings which are available online at my YouTube channel: Caroline Potter Satie. I would like to thank the performers for their commitment and enthusiasm, and Steve Harrington and Matt Parkin of the RCM Studio for their expertise and patience. My students at Kingston University London have been unwitting guinea pigs for some of the material in this book: I would like to thank them, particularly the 'Musical Museum' and 'City of Light: Paris 1900–1950' classes, and also Helen Julia Minors for her collegial support.

Marina Vidor of the Philharmonia Orchestra kindly facilitated the reproduction of the front and back cover images. Staff at the Bibliothèque Nationale de France (particularly Anne Mary of the Département des Manuscrits), the Paul Sacher Stiftung, Basel, and the reproduction service of the Houghton Library, Harvard University were most helpful. Parts of this book have appeared in print before. I would like to thank the Lyrica Society, especially Paul-André Bempéchat, for permission to reproduce my article 'Erik Satie's "Obstacles venimeux."' *Ars Lyrica*, 20 (2011): pp. 99–114, which appears in revised form as part of Chapter 3. My article 'Erik Satie's *musique d'ameublement* and Max Jacob's *Ruffian toujours, truand jamais*', published in *Revue de musicologie* vol. 101 no. 2 (2015), is revised in Chapter 4: I would particularly like to thank the editor-in-chief, Yves Balmer, and Thomas Soury for kindly consenting to its reuse in this book.

I am very grateful to the British Academy for funding a research visit to Paris and IMEC (Institut Mémoires de l'édition contemporaine) in Normandy in preparation for this book, and to Kingston University for funding a visit to the Paul Sacher Stiftung, where I studied Arthur Honegger's *musique d'ameublement* – three short pieces composed in the wake of Satie which are discussed in Chapter 4.

At Boydell & Brewer I am extremely grateful to Michael Middeke for his patience and support, to Megan Milan for promptly replying to many queries, and to Monica Kendall, Nick Bingham, David Roberts and Rohais Haughton for assistance in the production of the book. Most of all, I would like to thank Paul Auerbach for his encouragement, suggestions and support.

Personalia

Albert-Birot, Germaine (1877–1931) composed music for Apollinaire's play *Les mamelles de Tirésias*, which had been commissioned by her husband, Pierre. Some reports suggest that Satie was asked to provide unspecified noises for this production.

Albert-Birot, Pierre (1876–1967) founded the avant-garde magazine *SIC* (*Sons, Idées, Couleurs*), which was published from 1916 to 1919. He was closely connected to writers including Apollinaire and to the Italian futurists, especially Gino Severini, and also contributed to two numbers of Tristan Tzara's DADA magazine. He was also a theatre producer and artist.

Allais, Alphonse (1854–1905) was a humorist and journalist born in Honfleur (his father's pharmacy still stands in the town). Editor of the *Chat noir* journal from 1886, he published many amusing poems and short stories and met Satie, a fellow Honfleur native, in the Montmartre café scene.

Antheil, George (1900–59) was born in Trenton, New Jersey and died in New York, but was most celebrated as an avant-garde pianist and composer during his time in Paris in the early 1920s. His works including *Ballet mécanique* (1926) were notorious for their futurist style incorporating sounds such as airline propellers. He later adopted a neoclassical style and composed much film music.

Apollinaire, Guillaume (1880–1918) was one of the great poets of his day and inventor of the calligramme, a poem with visual appeal whose words were shaped into a form appropriate to the theme of the poem. He was the first writer to use the term 'sur-réalisme', which appeared in his programme note for Satie's *Parade*. He died of a head wound he suffered during World War I.

Auric, Georges (1899–1983) was the youngest member of Les Six and author, aged just fourteen, of one of the first detailed critiques of Satie's music. He was particularly close to Cocteau, was the dedicatee of *Le coq et l'arlequin* and later collaborated with Cocteau on several film scores, notably *Le sang d'un poète* (1930), *La belle et la bête* (1946) and *Orphée* (1950). From 1954 to 1978 he was president of SACEM, the French composers' rights collecting society.

Auriol, Georges (1863–1938), born Jean-Georges Huyot, was an illustrator who worked for publishers including Larousse and Hachette. He got to know Satie through the *Chat noir* journal, of which he was secretary from 1885; he also composed cabaret songs.

Bathori, Jane (1877–1970), born Jeanne-Marie Berthier, was the dedicatee and first performer of many of Satie's songs. A great supporter of contemporary music, she also premiered works by Fauré, Debussy and Ravel. She sometimes accompanied herself at the piano.

Beaumont, Etienne de (1883–1956) The Count and his wife **Edith** (1877–1952) were patrons of Satie in the last years of his life. Etienne de Beaumont commissioned *Mercure* for his Soirées de Paris series and mounted a Festival Erik Satie at the Salle Erard on 7 June 1920. He put on the first jazz performance in Paris to feature black performers (1918) and staged Milhaud and Cocteau's *Le bœuf sur le toit* (1920).

Bertin, Pierre (1891–1984) was an actor and singer. He performed the role of Lucien in Max Jacob's *Ruffian toujours, truand jamais* (1920), for which Satie wrote furniture music entr'actes, and the title role in *Le piège de Méduse*. He was later a member of the Comédie-Française company and was briefly married to the pianist Marcelle Meyer.

Bongard, Germaine (1885–1971) was a costume designer (whose couture house was called Jove) who created costumes for the Ballets Russes, including for Prokofiev's ballet *Chout* (1921). Her couture house at 5 rue de Penthièvre also hosted, during World War I, exhibitions, poetry and play readings, and concerts. Bongard was the sister of the couturier Paul Poiret.

Brancusi (Brâncuşi), Constantin (1876–1957) Romanian sculptor who settled in Paris. He was a close friend of Satie: they met in 1910 and Satie often visited his studio in Montparnasse. Brancusi's sculpture *Socrates* (1922, now in MoMA, New York) was created in the wake of Satie's *Socrate*; the sculptor apparently discussed its progress with the composer. Brancusi's nickname for Satie was Socrates.

Caby, Robert (1905–92) was a composer who became close to Satie in the last year of his life. He edited many Satie works for posthumous publication, notably in the Salabert edition of Satie's piano pieces (1968). He was also an active member of the Communist party.

Canudo, Ricciotto (1877–1923) was a poet, dramatist and (with his partner, Valentine de Saint-Point) a salon host, in which context he met Satie in the early 1910s. He also edited the avant-garde magazine *Montjoie!*, which published the Satie/Saint-Point collaborative work *Les Pantins dansent*. In an article for *Le Figaro* published in 1914 he coined the phrase 'la septième art' to signify the developing importance of the cinema as an art form. He established the first ciné-club in Paris in 1921.

Caran d'Ache (1858–1909), born Emmanuel Poiré in Moscow of French origins, was a caricaturist and illustrator who met Satie in the Montmartre cabaret scene. His shadow play *L'épopée* (1886), based on the Napoleonic wars, was one of the most successful of its type, and he drew cartoons for journals including *Le chat noir*.

Carol-Bérard, [Louis] (1881–1942), born in Marseille, was a composer and critic whose particular interests were mechanical music and the fusion of music and colour. He composed a *Symphonie des forces mécaniques* (1908) which is now lost.

Cendrars, Blaise (1887–1961), born Frédéric Louis Sauser, was a Swiss-born writer. He lost his right arm during World War I. His poetry and novels are often based on his many foreign travels. He met Satie at 6 rue Huyghens, the artists' studio used as an art gallery and venue for concerts and readings during World War I. Cendrars also founded the publishing house La Sirène, which published several Satie works including *Socrate*, with the financier Paul Laffitte.

Clair, René (1898–1981), born René Lucien Chomette, was a film director and author who collaborated with Satie and Francis Picabia in *Entr'acte*, created for the ballet *Relâche* (1924). Satie appears in the first five minutes of this film. Picabia and Clair staged a new production of the ballet in 1970.

Cocteau, Jean (1889–1963) was a polymath, best known as an author and poet though he also drew and directed films. Although not a musician, he set himself up as the spokesman for avant-garde composers through his tract *Le coq et l'arlequin*, in which he promoted Satie as a role model for younger composers. He collaborated with Satie, Picasso and Massine in *Parade*.

Contamine de Latour, Patrice (1867–1926) was a poet, mystic and friend of the young Satie in Montmartre. His poem *Les antiques* may have been the inspiration for Satie's *Gymnopédies* (1888).

Cros, Charles (1842–88) was a poet in the Montmartre cabaret scene, founder of the Hydropathes group and a visionary amateur scientist who in 1877 invented the paléophone – a machine which could reproduce sounds. Although his patent preceded Edison's patent for the phonograph, which was deposited in December 1877, Cros' lack of financial resources ensured that it was Edison's invention which changed the sonic world.

Darty, Paulette (1871–1939), born Pauline Joséphine Combes, was a singer, 'Queen of the Slow Waltz', who premiered Satie's *Je te veux*, *Tendrement* and *La Diva de l'Empire*. Her reputation ensured the success of these songs at a very difficult time in Satie's career.

Debussy, Claude (1862–1918) may have met Satie in a Montmartre café. The two composers were friends for almost 30 years, meeting weekly for lunch (typically mutton cutlets and a glass of white Bordeaux). Debussy orchestrated the first and third of Satie's *Gymnopédies*, contributing to the younger composer's increasing reputation in Paris.

Delgrange, Félix (?–?) was a cellist turned conductor and impresario who co-promoted concerts at venues including 6 rue Huyghens. He conducted the first concert performance of *Parade* in 1919, and the furniture music entr'actes Satie composed for Max Jacob's play *Ruffian toujours, truand jamais*. He founded the Concerts Delgrange series.

Dépaquit, Jules (1869–1924) was an illustrator, known for his round-figured cartoons published in humorous newspapers such as *Le Rire*. He got to know Satie in Montmartre and was one of few people who remained friends with him; they collaborated on the pantomime *Jack in the Box* (1899). Dépaquit was the first Mayor of the 'free commune of Montmartre' in 1920, standing on an anti-skyscraper ticket (*antigrattecieliste*).

Depaw, Georges (1871–1938) Born in Sedan, like his close friend, Dépaquit, Depaw left Sedan for Montmartre in the company of Dépaquit in 1893. Depaw illustrated Hyspa's *Chansons d'humour* (1903) and tales by Satie's favourite author Hans Christian Andersen, translated by W. A. Guégan and published by Editions de la Sirène in 1920.

Derain, André (1880–1954) was a painter associated with the fauviste movement. He and Satie had many friends in common, including Picasso, and planned several joint works in 1923–4, though none of these came to fruition.

Désormière, Roger (1898–1963) Conductor who started his musical career as a composer associated with L'Ecole d'Arcueil (together with Maxime Jacob, Henri Sauguet and Henri Cliquet-Pleyel). He conducted the premiere of *Relâche* and orchestrated *Geneviève de Brabant* when the manuscript was discovered after Satie's death. Later, Désormière made many significant recordings of French music, most notably of Debussy's *Pelléas et Mélisande* (1941).

Diaghilev, Serge (1872–1929) studied at the St Petersburg Conservatory but is best known as a ballet impresario and founder of the Ballets Russes troupe. He commissioned Satie's *Parade* in 1916.

Duchamp, Marcel (1887–1968) The artist's path crossed Satie's for the first time in 1917, when he co-edited *The Blind Man* with Henri-Pierre Roché: a short text by Satie was published in the second and final number of this magazine, on page 3.

Fragerolle, Georges (1855–1920) was a composer and performer active in the Montmartre café and shadow play scene. Satie performed in his shadow play *La marche à l'étoile* in 1890 at the Auberge du Clou.

Gide, André (1869–1951) was an author, winner of the Nobel Prize for Literature in 1947, who got to know Satie through Adrienne Monnier's La Maison des Amis des Livres (7 rue de l'Odéon). In 1919 he performed *Socrate* as a reciter rather than singer at the home of the Godebski family.

Gleizes, Albert (1881–1953) was a painter and art theorist, one of the founders of Cubism. Gleizes was to have been the set designer for a version by Cocteau of *A Midsummer Night's Dream* to which Satie contributed *Cinq grimaces*, though the complete project did not ultimately materialise.

Guégan, Bertrand (1892–1943) abandoned medical studies in favour of poetry and became best known as a publisher. He founded Les Compagnons de Cocagne and published books combining recipes, art and music; Satie contributed to all three of his *Almanach de Cocagne* series. Active in the resistance, he was deported and killed in Berlin on 28 August 1943.

Honegger, Arthur (1892–1955) was a composer of Swiss parentage who was born and died in France. He was the only member of Les Six to follow Satie's example and compose furniture music (1919), though in later years he distanced himself from Satie's aesthetic.

Hugo, Valentine (1887–1968), born Valentine Marie Augustine Gross, was a painter, designer and close friend of Satie. The first meeting between Cocteau and Satie to discuss their future collaboration, *Parade*, took place at Valentine Hugo's salon.

Hyspa, Vincent (1865–1938) was a comic singer and poet who frequently worked with Satie in Montmartre cabarets. He wrote the words for several Satie songs, including *Tendrement*, *Un dîner à l'Elysée* and *Chez le docteur*, and for Debussy's *La belle au bois dormant*. He published a volume of humorous stories illustrated by Dépaquit, *L'éponge en porcelaine*, with La Sirène in 1921, having been introduced to the publisher by Satie.

Indy, Vincent d' (1851–1931) was a composer who taught Satie at the Schola Cantorum. Despite their considerable social and political differences, he and Satie had a cordial relationship.

Jacob, Max (1876–1944), a poet, painter and critic, was a mainstay of the Montparnasse scene in the 1910s. Satie composed furniture music for the interludes of Jacob's *Ruffian toujours, truand jamais* (1920), a play which has yet to receive a second performance.

Jourdain, Francis (1876–1958) was a painter turned furniture designer known for his left-wing political engagement. In 1913 he was the first set designer for the Théâtre du Vieux-Colombier.

Le Flem, Paul (1881–1984) Breton composer and music critic who taught Satie at the Schola Cantorum. He also collaborated with Max Jacob and is tantalisingly mentioned in the manuscript of Jacob's play *Ruffian toujours, truand jamais*.

Léger, Fernand (1881–1955) French painter and friend of Satie who went through a 'mechanical period' from 1917. In the early 1910s he was influenced by the Italian futurists and was a member of the 'Section d'Or' group with Picabia, Gleizes, Marie Laurencin and others. He designed the set for the laboratory scene in Marcel L'Herbier's *L'inhumaine* and, also in 1924, he produced and directed the film *Ballet mécanique* in collaboration with Dudley Murphy, George Antheil and Man Ray.

Lejeune, Emile (1885–1964)   Swiss painter who owned a studio at 6 rue Huyghens in Montparnasse which was used as a venue for artistic activity of all types during World War I. Satie's music was played at many of these events.

Lhote, André (1885–1962)   Painter who was to have collaborated with Satie and other composers on Cocteau's *Midsummer Night's Dream* project (1915).

Maré, Rolf de (1888–1964)   Swedish art collector and impresario, director of the Ballets Suédois which made a considerable impact on the Parisian artistic scene in the first half of the 1920s. He founded Les Archives internationales de la Danse in Paris in 1933, the first institution of its kind.

Marinetti, Filippo Tommaso (1876–1944) was a poet and polemicist, theorist of the Italian futurist movement which created a stir in Paris from the publication of its first manifesto in 1909.

Méerovitch, Juliette (1896–1920) was one of Satie's favourite pianists. She performed the piano duet version of *Parade* with the composer at 6 rue Huyghens in 1917 and is the dedicatee of Satie's *Sonatine bureaucratique* and the second piece of Tailleferre's *Jeux de plein air* (1917). Poulenc dedicated his piano piece *Napoli* (1922–5) to her memory.

Meyer, Agnes (1887–1970), née Ernst, was an art journalist and patron who founded the avant-garde magazine *291*, to which Satie contributed. She married Eugene Meyer Jr, director of the *Washington Post*; their children included the publisher Katharine Graham. Agnes Meyer was the only commissioner of furniture music from Satie: his *Tenture de cabinet préfectoral* (1923) was written for her Washington home.

Meyer, Marcelle (1897–1958) was one of Satie's favourite pianists; she also worked with Debussy on his *Préludes*. She was briefly married to the actor Pierre Bertin. Meyer is at the centre of Jacques-Emile Blanche's famous group portrait of Les Six (1921) wearing a dress by Germaine Bongard.

Milhaud, Darius (1892–1974)   The extremely prolific French composer, a Jew from Provence, was a loyal friend of Satie who supported him in his last illness and helped to clear his filthy room in Arcueil after his death. He was a member of Les Six; his writings, including the autobiography *Notes sans musique*, are invaluable and entertaining recollections of this period. He completed *Cinq grimaces*, which was premiered after Satie's death in 1926.

Mortier, Jane (?–?) was a pianist who promoted Satie's piano music in France and abroad during Satie's lifetime. She gave US premieres of many of his works in the 1920s and was the dedicatee of 'de Podophthalma' (*Embryons desséchés*; 1913). An important promoter of contemporary music, on 3 May 1911 she gave the first complete performance of the first book of Debussy's *Préludes* in the Salle Pleyel in Paris.

Norton, Louise [née McCutcheon, later Varèse] (1891–1989) Literary translator who met Satie in Paris. She married Varèse in 1922.

Ozenfant, Amédée (1886–1966) Artist whose style changed radically on meeting Le Corbusier in 1917; together they founded 'purism', a rational, post-cubist movement based on mathematics. Ozenfant was also the editor of the journal *L'Elan*. He discussed exhibiting Satie's furniture music scores, though this plan did not come to fruition.

Picabia, Francis (1879–1953), of partly Spanish-Cuban origins, was a painter and collaborator with Satie in *Relâche*. He founded the avant-garde magazine *391* (modelled on the New York publication *291*) and was one of the first painters associated with Dada and surrealism.

Picasso, Pablo (1881–1973) Spanish painter who knew Satie when he was resident in Paris in the 1910s and 1920s. He was the costume and set designer for *Parade* and *Mercure* and had an excellent working relationship with Satie; the composer thought Picasso's ideas for *Parade* were more interesting than those of Cocteau. Overcoming a strong fear of illness and death, Picasso visited Satie during his final months and even changed his bed sheets.

Poiré, Emmanuel. *See* Caran d'Ache

Poiret, Paul (1879–1944) was a fashion designer who promoted artistic events at his workshop and gallery complex in the 8th arrondissement of Paris. This complex included the Galerie Barbazanges, venue of the premiere of Satie's collaboration with Max Jacob, *Ruffian toujours, truand jamais*, and of many other events which combined music with visual art and the spoken word.

Poueigh, Jean (1876–1958), who also wrote under the pseudonym Octave Séré, was a music critic who disliked Satie's music. He sued Satie for responding on a postcard in vulgar terms to a negative review he wrote of *Parade*.

Poulenc, Francis (1899–1963) was a composer, a member of Les Six who knew Satie well in the late 1910s and early 1920s. Satie wrote Poulenc a touching letter on the death of Poulenc's father in 1917. Poulenc's first composition, *Rapsodie nègre* (1917), is dedicated to Satie.

Radiguet, Raymond (1903–23) was a gifted novelist, author of *Le diable au corps* and *Le bal du Comte d'Orgel*; the title character of the latter was modelled on Satie's patron Count Etienne de Beaumont. Cocteau, Radiguet and Satie discussed ideas for an opera based on *Paul & Virginie* around 1922, though the project did not ultimately happen. He died of typhoid fever.

Ravel, Maurice (1875–1937) met Satie in Montmartre as a young man and was instrumental in Satie's increasing reputation in Paris from 1911. While Ravel never criticised Satie, the older composer's friendship with Ravel cooled from around 1919, perhaps influenced by Cocteau and some young composers associated with Les Six.

Ribemont-Dessaignes, Georges (1884–1974) Artist and author active in Montparnasse and Dada circles; some of his works appeared on the same programmes as Satie in the early 1920s. He was also a composer.

Rivière, Henri (1864–1951) was an artist and member of the editorial team on the *Chat noir* journal. He is best known for his shadow plays performed in the cabaret of the same name. Later he produced etchings and watercolours and was a pioneer of photography.

Roché, Henri-Pierre (1879–1959) was a journalist and art collector who was friends with several artists in Montparnasse during the war years, including Satie. He and Marcel Duchamp travelled to New York in 1916; with Beatrice Wood they published two numbers of the Dada magazine *The Blind Man*. Satie contributed to the second of these. Later he was a novelist; his *Jules et Jim* (1953) became a successful film directed by François Truffaut in 1962.

Roland-Manuel (1891–1966), born Roland Alexis Manuel Lévy, was a composer and critic. Satie introduced him to Ravel in 1911; Roland-Manuel became Ravel's pupil and the two composers were lifelong friends. As a composer, Roland-Manuel collaborated with Max Jacob and with the film director Jean Grémillon.

Rusiñol, Santiago (1861–1931) was a Spanish painter whose portrait of Satie at the harmonium is one of the most memorable early images of the composer. Later he was active as a poet and playwright.

Russolo, Luigi (1883–1947) was associated with the Italian futurist movement and is author of the manifesto *L'arte dei rumori* (Art of Noises; 1913). He gave noise concerts in Paris before and after World War I, classified sounds based on their mode of production and designed instruments which he called *intonarumori*. A concert in 1914 featuring these instruments provoked a riot.

Saint-Point, Valentine de (1875–1953), born Anna Jeanne Valentine Marianne Glans de Cessiat-Vercell, was a dancer, choreographer and writer, great-niece of Alphonse de Lamartine. She propounded a theory of unified arts known as Métachorie; her only performances as a dancer and writer included *Les Pantins dansent*, to music by Satie. In 1912 she wrote a Manifesto of Futurist Woman, a response to Marinetti's Futurist Manifesto which she considered misogynist. The last three decades of her life were devoted to Middle Eastern and North African religious and political causes.

Salis, Rodolphe (1851–97) owned the Chat Noir cabaret, which opened in 1881. He contributed many short stories to the cabaret's house journal, and published *Contes du Chat noir* in 1888–91. Satie was employed as second pianist at the Chat Noir until 1891.

Sâr Péladan (Joséphin Péladan; 1858–1918) was a writer associated with the occult who co-founded the Ordre cabbalistique du Rose-Croix in 1888. He split from this group in 1891 and founded l'Ordre de la Rose-Croix catholique et esthétique du Temple et du Graal; Satie was the house composer of this movement. He wrote the text for Satie's *Le Fils des étoiles* (1892).

Schmitt, Florent (1870–1958) was a composer who was acquainted with Satie in his Montmartre days: Schmitt won the Prix de Rome in 1900 and invited Satie to a celebratory banquet (Satie turned down the invitation). Their paths also crossed at Ricciotto Canudo's *Montjoie!* salon. The two composers shared a sense of humour, if not a musical style.

Sivry, Charles de (1848–1900) started his career as an accountant before turning to music. He wrote music for shadow plays at the Chat Noir including *Phryné* (1891) and *Ailleurs* (1891, texts by Maurice Donnay) and was a skilled improviser. He was also interested in early music and alchemy, and was a member of the Hydropathes circle.

Stravinsky, Igor (1882–1971) Satie wrote two articles on the Russian composer, one for *Vanity Fair* which was not published in his lifetime, and a second for *Feuilles libres* (1922). He was especially interested in the mechanical quality of Stravinsky's work. Stravinsky, for his part, enjoyed Satie's company but considered him to be the oddest person he ever met.

Tailleferre, Germaine (1892–1983) was a prolific composer and member of Les Six. Satie was fond of her, calling her his 'fille musicale', and they performed the piano duet score of *Parade*. Tailleferre also played the organ in the premiere of *Ludions* (1923) at Comte Etienne de Beaumont's ball.

Templier, (Pierre-)Alexandre (1867–1932) Architect and father of Pierre-Daniel Templier, author of the first full-length biography of Satie. He lived in Arcueil and met Satie through a shared interest in radical politics.

Tinchant, Albert (1860–92) was a poet and pianist from Normandy associated with the Chat Noir journal and cabaret. He and Satie were both pianists at the cabaret, and Tinchant was secretary of the journal.

Tzara, Tristan (1896–1963), born Samuel Rosenstock, was a Romanian-born Dada pioneer who met Satie in Paris in the early 1920s. He is the author of the play *Le cœur à gaz* (1921) and published a single issue of the magazine *Le Cœur à barbe* (1922) to which Satie contributed.

Varèse, Edgard (1883–1965) was a composer, born in France of Franco-Italian origins. He studied at the Schola Cantorum and encountered Satie when both had finished their studies at that institution. He invited Satie to write incidental music for a Cocteau production of *A Midsummer Night's Dream*, initially conceived as a 'hommage à Satie'; the project did not materialise, though Satie composed *Cinq grimaces* for it. Varèse took American citizenship in 1927 and, after an extended visit to Paris, settled in the United States

Verlaine, Paul (1844–96) was a poet whose path crossed Satie's at the Chat Noir. Many of his late poems were first published in the *Chat noir* journal.

Veyssière, Léon-Louis (1875–1955) Painter and decorator in Arcueil, neighbour of Satie and fellow member of the radical socialist committee. The Veyssière family were friendly with Satie; Léon-Louis was mayor of Arcueil in the early twentieth century, and he and his son André recorded their memories of Satie which were published in full in 2013.

Villiers de l'Isle Adam, Jean-Marie-Mathias-Philippe-Auguste de (1838–89) Poet and novelist, author of the dystopian novel *L'Eve future* (1878, published 1886) and *Contes cruels* (1883). He was also a composer.

Viñes, Ricardo (1875–1943) was a Spanish pianist, a close friend of Ravel who premiered many of Satie's piano works in the 1910s. He was also Francis Poulenc's piano teacher and a decisive influence on him.

Chronology and Worklist

1842 Birth of Jules Alfred Satie, the composer's father
1865 Marriage of Alfred Satie and Jane Leslie Anton at St Mary's Church, Barnes, London
1866 In the words of the birth announcement, 'Monsieur Eric-Alfred-Leslie Satie' born on 17 May in Honfleur, Normandy. He was baptised a Protestant in September.
1868 Birth of sister, Olga
1869 Birth of brother, Conrad
1870 The Satie family moves to Paris.
1872 Death of Satie's mother; Eric and Conrad sent to live in Honfleur with paternal grandparents and were rebaptised as Catholics
1874 Eric starts music studies with Monsieur Vinot, a former pupil of Louis Niedermeyer.
1878 Following his grandmother's death by drowning, Eric returns to Paris to live with his father. Studies Greek and Latin, and attends lectures with father at Collège de France.
1879 Father marries piano teacher and composer Eugénie Barteche, who is ten years his senior; Eric does not get on with his new stepmother. Eric enters Paris Conservatoire as piano student.
1881 Eric described as the 'laziest student in the Conservatoire'
1882 Dismissed from Conservatoire with no qualifications.
1883 Is admitted to Antoine Taudou's harmony class as an auditor
1884 *Allegro*, piano (written during holiday in Honfleur)
1885 Readmitted to Conservatoire piano class, this time in class of Georges Mathias. *Valse-ballet* and *Fantaisie-valse*, piano
1886 Meets Contamine de Latour, a writer of Spanish origin. Volunteers for military service and leaves Conservatoire in November; deliberately contracts bronchitis to get out of military obligations the following month.
1887 Four settings of poems by Contamine de Latour; three *Sarabandes*, piano. Moves to own room in Montmartre. Starts attending Chat Noir café.
1888 *Trois Gymnopédies*, piano; four *Ogives*, piano Nos. 3, 1 orch. Debussy, Exposition de Genève, cond. Gustave Doret, June 1896; Salle Erard, cond. Doret, 20 Feb. 1897; Cercle Musical, cond. Debussy, 25 March 1911
1889 Exposition Universelle in Paris. *Gnossienne* [No. 5], piano

1890 *Trois Gnossiennes* [Nos. 1–3]. Meets Joséphin 'Sâr' Péladan and becomes official composer of his Ordre de la Rose-Croix Catholique, du Temple et du Graal. Moves to tiny room, which he described as a cupboard (*placard*), to escape his creditors.

1891 *Gnossienne* no. 4; [*Trois*] *Sonneries de la Rose + Croix*, 3 fanfares for trumpets and harps (or orchestra); *Le Fils des étoiles*, incidental music for flutes and harps for Joséphin Péladan's 3-act 'Pastorale Kaldéenne'. Becomes second pianist at Auberge du Clou.

1892 *Fête donnée par des Chevaliers Normands en l'honneur d'une jeune Demoiselle (XIe Siècle)*, piano; *Prélude du Nazaréen*, piano; *uspud*, 'Ballet chrétien' in 3 acts by Contamine de Latour and Satie

1893 Relationship with the painter and model Suzanne Valadon lasts from 14 January to 20 June. *Eginhard. Prélude*, piano; *Danses Gothiques*, piano; *Vexations*, piano

1894 *Prélude de La Porte héroïque du ciel*, piano (incidental music for esoteric drama in one act by Jules Bois)

1893–5 *Messe des pauvres*, Mass for organ with small choir of children and men specified in *Kyrie eleison*

1896 *Gymnopédies* nos. 3 and 1 orchestrated by Debussy

1897 *Gnossienne* [No. 6], piano; *Pièces froides*, piano (2×3 pieces: *Airs à faire fuir* and *Danses de travers*); song *Je te veux*

1898 Moves to a room in Arcueil, where he lives for the rest of his life; no human visitors were allowed

1899 *Jack in the Box*, music for 2-act pantomime or 'clownerie' by Jules Dépaquit

1899–1900 *Geneviève de Brabant*, incidental music to 3-act play in prose and verse by Lord Cheminot (Contamine de Latour)

1900 *Verset laïque & somptueux*, piano; *Poudre d'or*, 2 waltzes for piano

1901 *The Dreamy Fish* (*Le Poisson rêveur*), piano; *The Angora Ox* (*Le Boeuf Angora*), piano – both based on tales (which are now lost) by Lord Cheminot (Contamine de Latour)

1902 *Tendrement* [also known as *Illusion*], voice and piano

1903 *Trois Morceaux en forme de poire*, 7 pieces for piano duet, mostly based on earlier compositions

1904 *Le Piccadilly. Marche* (originally titled *La Transatlantique*), piano (later orchestrated)

1905 Enrols in Schola Cantorum. Composed many cabaret songs for Vincent Hyspa over the next few years.

1906 *La Diva de l'Empire*, cabaret song; *Prélude en tapisserie*, piano

1907 [*Nouvelles*] *Pièces froides* [*pour un chien*], 3 pieces for piano

1908 *Aperçus désagréables* [–1912], 3 pieces for piano duet

1911 *En Habit de cheval* (orig. *Divertissement*), 4 pieces for piano duet [*Choral, Fugue litanique, Autre choral, Fugue de papier*]

1912 *Deux Préludes pour un chien*, piano; *Préludes flasques (pour un chien)*, 4 pieces for piano; *Véritables Préludes flasques (pour un chien)*, 3 pieces for piano

1913 *Le piège de Méduse* 'lyric comedy in 1 Act by M. Erik Satie with dance music by the same gentleman'; *Descriptions automatiques* (also referred to as *Vocations éléctriques* in June 1913), 3 pieces for piano; *Croquis et agaceries d'un gros bonhomme en bois*, 3 pieces for piano; *Embryons desséchés*, 3 pieces for piano; *Chapitres tournés en tous sens*, 3 pieces for piano; *Vieux sequins et vieilles cuirasses*, 3 pieces for piano; *L'Enfance de Ko-Quo (Recommandations maternelles)*, 3 pieces for piano; [*Trois Nouvelles Enfantines*], 3 easy pieces for piano; *Menus propos enfantins*, 3 easy pieces for piano; *Enfantillages pittoresques (Enfantines II)*, 3 easy pieces for piano; *Peccadilles importunes (Enfantines III)*, 3 easy pieces for piano; *Les Pantins dansent*, 'poème dansé' for piano or small orchestra to accompany the reading of the poem and a dance by Valentine de Saint-Point (2 versions exist)

1914 *Choses vues à droite et à gauche (sans lunettes)*, 3 pieces for violin and piano (*Choral hypocrite, Fugue à tâtons, Fantaisie musculaire*); *Sports et divertissements*, 21 pieces for piano for set of drawings by Charles Martin, with in-score texts by Satie; *Heures séculaires et instantanées*, 3 pieces for piano; *Les Trois Valses distinguées du précieux dégoûté*, 3 waltzes for piano; *Trois poèmes d'amour*, 3 short songs, text and music by Satie

1915 *Cinq grimaces pour 'Le Songe d'une nuit d'été'*, incidental music for Jean Cocteau's unrealised production of Shakespeare's *A Midsummer Night's Dream* (adapted text lost); *Avant-dernières pensées*, 3 pieces for piano

1916 *Trois Mélodies*, 3 songs for voice and piano (*La Statue de bronze* (Léon-Paul Fargue); *Daphénéo* (Mimi Godebska); *Le Chapelier* (René Chalupt, based on Chapter 7 of 'A Mad Tea-Party' in Lewis Carroll's *Alice in Wonderland*)); *Parade* [–1917], 'ballet réaliste sur un thème de Jean Cocteau'

1917 *Sonatine bureaucratique*, piano; *Musique d'ameublement*, 2 'furnishing' pieces for small ensemble (*Tapisserie en fer forgé; Carrelage phonique*); *Socrate* [–1918], voice (or 4 voices) and piano or small orchestra

1919 *Nocturnes* for piano (5 pieces); *Marche de Cocagne*, march for 2 trumpets in C, later used as the outer sections of the second of the *Trois Petites Pièces montées*; *Trois Petites Pièces montées*, 3 short pieces for piano duet or orchestra (*De l'enfance de Pantagruel (Rêverie), Marche de Cocagne (Démarche), Jeux de Gargantua (Coin de Polka)*)

1920 *Musique d'ameublement* (Sons industriels), 2 short 'entr'actes' for piano duet, 3 clarinets (in E♭, B♭, A) and trombone, written as interludes to Max Jacob's play *Ruffian toujours, truand jamais* (Chez un bistrot, Un salon); *Premier Menuet*, piano; *La Belle Excentrique*. *Fantaisie sérieuse*, written for the dancer Caryathis, for small orchestra, piano duet or piano solo; *Quatre Petites Mélodies*, 4 songs for voice and piano (*Elégie* (Lamartine); *Danseuse* (Cocteau); *Chanson* (anon., 18th century); *Adieu* (Radiguet)

1921 *Sonnerie pour réveiller le bon gros Roi des Singes (lequel ne dort toujours que d'un œil)*, fanfare for 2 trumpets in C

1923 *Divertissement (La Statue retrouvée)*, short piece for organ, with trumpet at end, composed for party at Comte Etienne de Beaumont's home; *Tenture de Cabinet préfectoral*, furniture music for small orchestra; *Ludions*, 5 songs for voice and piano, texts by Léon-Paul Fargue (*Air du Rat, Spleen, La Grenouille américaine, Air du Poète (Papouasie), Chanson du chat*); *Scènes nouvelles* [Recitatives] for Gounod's opéra-comique *Le Médecin malgré lui* [1858], for Diaghilev's Monte Carlo production of Gounod's opéra-comique

1924 *Mercure* [*Les Aventures de Mercure*], ballet based on scenario in 3 'incidents' by Comte Etienne de Beaumont. 'Poses plastiques' by Picasso; *Relâche* [*Ballet instantanéiste*] for Ballets Suédois, based on scenario by Picabia (using some ideas by Cendrars). Includes *Cinéma*, an 'Entr'acte symphonique' to accompany film interlude by René Clair; the opening sequence of the film features Satie and Picabia

1925 Suffering from cirrhosis of the liver and pleurisy, Satie is unable to live in Arcueil and moves to various hotel rooms, paid for by friends. Comte Etienne de Beaumont paid for final hospital stay in Hôpital Saint-Joseph (15 February – 1 July). Satie dies on 1 July 1925.

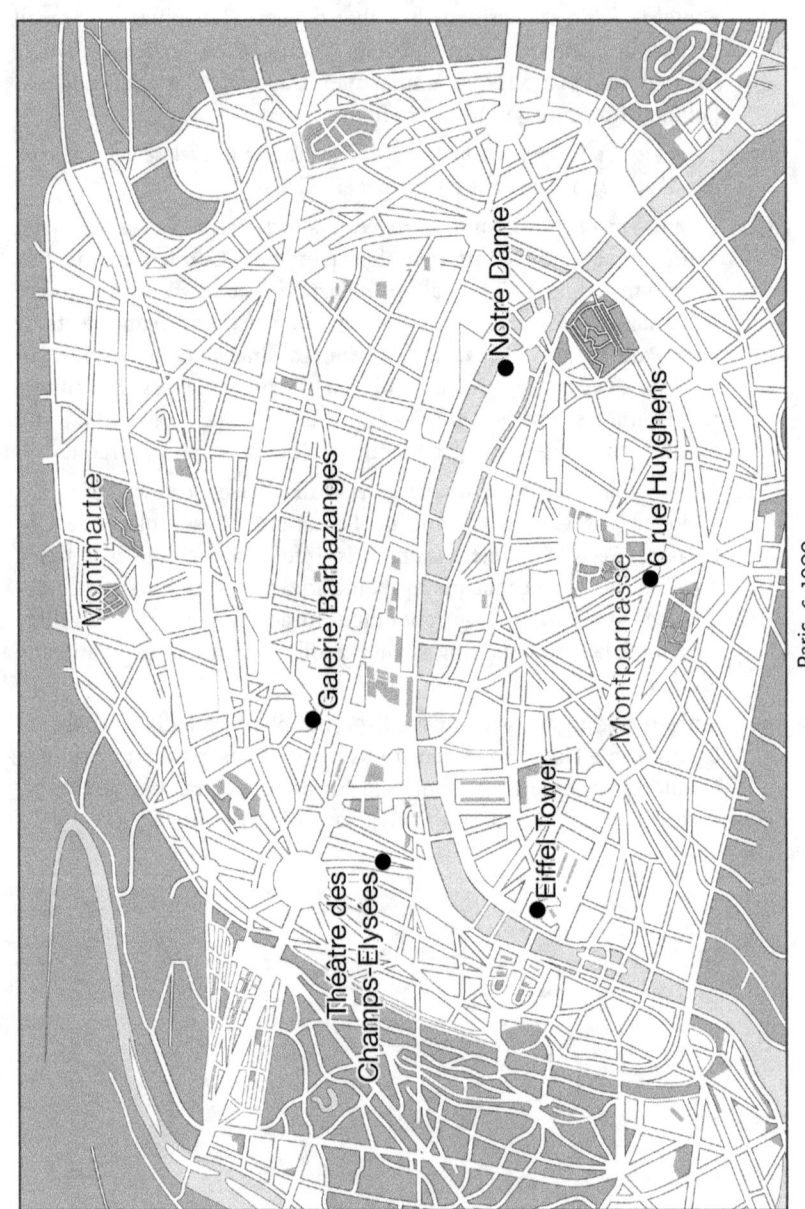

Paris, c. 1900

CHAPTER 1

Satie in Montmartre: Mechanical Music in the Belle Epoque

ERIK Satie, in the early 1890s, was a notorious though not a conspicuously successful figure. He had studied piano at the Paris Conservatoire from 1879 to 1886, doubtless compelled by his stepmother, a salon composer and piano teacher whom he disliked, but was described as 'the laziest student at the Conservatoire' by his teacher Emile Descombes[1] and left the institution without a diploma. Further sporadic study of harmony and piano was no more successful, and in 1886 Satie preferred military service to further education. This dramatic change of focus turned out not to suit him at all: after less than a month with his regiment in Arras, northern France, he deliberately contracted bronchitis to escape the tedium of military life. By this stage he had already written some short piano pieces and songs, and while convalescing he discovered the music of Chabrier and the novels of Flaubert. In September 1887, he wrote his first characteristic set of three piano pieces – the *Sarabandes* – and on 14 November he was discharged from military service.

Satie moved out of his family's flat in the 9th arrondissement of Paris up the hill to Montmartre in 1887, thanks to a gift of 1600 francs from his father. But by 1890 he was obliged to move to a much smaller room to escape his creditors. In July 1896 he was forced into an even tinier room in the same house, which he called his 'placard' (cupboard). Even at this stage, Satie was recognised for his distinctive clothing; in the early 1890s he favoured bohemian garb of a frock coat, hat, long hair and messy beard. Roxanne Classen aptly describes Satie at this period as a 'flâneur' who 'consciously manufactured a public identity through his appearance'.[2] In June 1895 he suddenly changed his image when, having come into money again through a small legacy, he bought seven identical dun-coloured corduroy suits from the department store La Belle Jardinière. His final sartorial shift was to a British-style three-piece business suit, complete with white shirt, tie, bowler hat and cane, which he wore every day from around 1905 when he enrolled at the Schola Cantorum. It is as if repetition and routine had meaning for him, even in his clothing, or perhaps he believed that repetition might instil meaning into his life.

[1] Cited in Robert Orledge, *Satie the Composer*. Cambridge: Cambridge University Press, 1990, p. xx.
[2] Roxanne Classen, 'Satie as Flâneur and Trois morceaux en forme de poire', http://academic.macewan.ca/classenr/satie-as-flaneur-and-trois-morceaux-en-forme-de-poire (accessed 5 April 2015).

Satie's music has a strong sense of time and place. In this chapter, I will explore the sonic environment of Satie's Montmartre, which was dominated by the barrel organ, café music (including shadow plays), the circus and other street musicians. Satie, as a café musician who was intimately associated with cabarets including the Chat Noir, was at the heart of this environment. Poets as varied as Baudelaire, Mallarmé, Verlaine and Apollinaire were also inspired by this milieu and their work shows they identified with the marginal figure of the street performer. The Montmartre period of Satie's musical life, spanning the late 1880s until the early 1900s, also coincided with significant technological innovation and experiment, some of which happened close to the composer's regular haunts. Montmartre is now the 18th arrondissement of Paris, but in this period it was not part of the city and was not subject to city taxes. It was distinct from Paris, on a hill on the northern outskirts of the city; it was also (and is still) the location of a tiny vineyard which in the late nineteenth century was tended by nuns. Its many establishments devoted to drinking were certainly a prime attraction for artists and pleasure seekers.

Technology devoted to the reproduction and repetition of sound was then in its infancy. It is well known that Thomas Edison invented the phonograph in 1877, his aim being to create a reproducing technology whose purpose was to perpetuate the voices of celebrated people. But, geographically closer to Satie, the poet and inventor Charles Cros (1842–88) patented the 'phonautograph' in the same year: he conceived an engraving process onto disc which preserved the trace of a sound. His preferred term for the reproducing instrument was 'paleophone' – literally 'voice of the past': as with Edison, the primary application for this technology was the recording of voices of people before they die. However, as an impoverished poet, Cros did not have the funds to build a prototype. Edison, who was unaware of Cros' patent, built a machine in 1878 and this became the dominant technology.

Cros was also a member of the Hydropathes group of poets founded by Emile Goudeau in the Left Bank of Paris, though in 1881 the group's get-togethers moved north of the river to the Chat Noir cabaret in Montmartre. (Their name means that they feared water, presumably because they preferred stronger beverages.) Cros was also an innovator as a writer: Steven Moore Whiting has said of the poet, 'As early as 1874, Cros had called for poetic forms that measured art syllable by syllable (rather than word by word or image by image): monosyllabic sonnets, palindromes, and *quatrains holorimes*, in which rhyme involved not just final syllables but the entire poetic line.'[3] While there is no evidence that Cros ever met Satie, they had several friends in common (not least

---

[3] Steven Moore Whiting, *Satie the Bohemian*. Oxford: Clarendon Press, 1999, p. 179.

Cros' fellow Hydropathe Alphonse Allais),[4] and later in the 1880s Satie worked at the Chat Noir. While Cros never established a lasting reputation as a poet, in the early 1870s his work was published alongside Mallarmé, Villiers de l'Isle-Adam and Verlaine in the short-lived weekly *Renaissance littéraire et artistique*, edited by Emile Blémont. Cros was also chief editor of *Revue du monde nouveau*, which was described on the masthead as a 'revue littéraire, artistique, scientifique'. An indication of its scope and ambition is that its first number featured an article 'L'Alchimie moderne' by Cros himself, a drawing by Manet, a prose poem by Mallarmé ('Le Démon de l'analogie'), poems by Théodore de Banville and musical works. Sadly, only three numbers were produced, in February, April and May 1874.[5]

From 1888 to 1889, when Satie was emerging as a composer, Cros' poems appeared in *La Lanterne japonaise*, the house magazine of the cabaret Le Divan Japonais. *La Lanterne japonaise* also featured poems by Verlaine and, once, Satie's friend and early collaborator Contamine de Latour. Satie almost certainly contributed some amusing quips to *La Lanterne japonaise* under the pseudonym Virginie Lebeau.[6] One of the first of these, published on 24 November 1888, reads: 'As we approach the cold season, with the arrival of the first showers, we believe we are doing the right thing by exhorting the many readers of *La Lanterne japonaise*, and their families, not to go out without having first packed an umbrella.'[7] Satie was obsessed with remembering to carry an umbrella, even devoting some of his writings to this topic, though acquaintances often noted that he would not use it for its intended purpose. Another short piece in *La Lanterne japonaise*, published on 12 January 1889, includes one of the first mentions of Satie's music in print: 'On 14 [July], the government will put on a lavish celebration of the anniversary of the taking of the Bastille. On this occasion, the grandson of Latude, Charles Levadé, will make speeches on the tomb of his grandfather and will then dance Erik Satie's 3rd Gymnopédie on the ruins of the public reaction, while the band of the Metalworkers of Puteaux plays its best pieces. It'll be a fine sight

---

[4] And Debussy set one of Cros' poems, *L'Archet*, in 1881.

[5] http://camillesourget.com/livres-anciens-revue-monde-nouveau/ (accessed 5 April 2015).

[6] See Whiting, *Satie the Bohemian*, pp. 101–6. On 8 December 1888 Contamine de Latour's poem 'Miroir plein' was published in this magazine.

[7] Reprinted in Ornella Volta (ed.), *Erik Satie: Ecrits*. Paris: Editions Champ Libre, 1979, p. 103: 'A l'approche de la mauvaise saison et en présence des premières ondées, nous croyons bien faire en engageant les nombreux lecteurs de la *Lanterne japonaise*, ainsi que leur famille, à ne pas sortir sans s'être munis préalablement d'un parapluie.'

for those who like that kind of thing.'[8] Steven Moore Whiting points out that 'the author of this prediction evidently knew that Charles Levadé, Satie's old friend from the Conservatoire, was the dedicatee of the Third Gymnopédie and that the original meaning of the title implied dancing in the buff'.[9] This jokey prediction of events on the 100th anniversary of the French Revolution mentions Levadé's alleged grandfather, the writer Jean-Henri Latude, who was notorious for escaping from prisons including the Bastille and wrote an account of his time behind bars.[10] While it would be pleasing if this were true, this could be one of Satie's innumerable plays on words; perhaps Charles Levadé, like his supposed ancestor, was an escape artist as his surname almost suggests (*l'évadé*).

The word which encapsulates the style of Satie's humorous writing is 'blague'. While the term predates the Montmartre café and cabaret scene in which Satie was involved, it is particularly associated with this district. The theatre critic Francisque Sarcey wrote: '*Blague* is a certain taste which is peculiar to Parisians, and still more to Parisians of our generation, to disparage, to mock, to render ludicrous everything that *hommes*, and above all *prud'hommes*, are in the habit of respecting and caring for; but this raillery is characterized by the fact that he who takes it up does so more in play, for a love of paradox, than in conviction: he mocks himself with his own banter, *il blague*.'[11] This is playful and ironic banter, often directed at sensible bourgeois people (*prud'hommes*), at those in positions of power or at fashionable preoccupations. As Jeffrey Weiss puts it, '*blague* and mystification were accessible expressions of critical dissent, the obvious tools with which to perpetrate a parody of contemporary esthetic anxieties'.[12] Satie's verbal humour is pointed and highly topical – the essence of *blague*.

---

[8] Ibid., pp. 107–8: 'Le 14 [juillet], le gouvernement célébrera en grande pompe l'anniversaire de la prise de la Bastille. A cette occasion, le petit-fils de Latude, Charles Lévadé [*recte*: Levadé], prononcera quelques discours sur la tombe de son grand-père, et dansera ensuite, sur les ruines de la réaction, la 3e Gymnopédie d'Erik Satie, pendant que la fanfare des Tôliers de Puteaux mugira ses plus jolis morceaux. En somme, beau coup d'œil pour les amateurs.'

[9] Whiting, *Satie the Bohemian*, p. 102.

[10] Satie was evidently fond of this character; he appears in the title of his texted piano work 'Regrets des enfermés (Jonas et Latude)', the third of his *Chapitres tournés en tous sens* (1913).

[11] Cited in Jeffrey Weiss, *The Popular Culture of Modern Art: Picasso, Duchamp, and Avant-Gardism*. New Haven: Yale University Press, 1994, p. 120. Sarcey (1827–99) was one of the most influential critics of his time, though by the end of his life he had little sympathy for avant-garde work and was mercilessly mocked by Alphonse Allais, who published columns under Sarcey's name (or under the name 'Sarcisque Francey').

[12] Ibid., p. 119.

From his earliest years as a creative artist, Satie expressed himself in writing as well as music and published in both media. In the late nineteenth century his writings were confined to newspaper promotion, polemics against critics and theatre directors he disliked, and occasional eccentric performance indications on his music, but by the twentieth century he wrote articles, public talks, the play *Le piège de Méduse* (1913), and short poems which he set to music as *Trois poèmes d'amour* (1914). His in-score textual commentaries became more extensive in the rich period 1912–15, when he wrote over sixty short piano pieces. Almost all his writing exhibits his characteristic wit, and he was surely inspired in this by his fellow Honfleur native, Alphonse Allais. Nancy Perloff wrote: 'Satie's wit bears a striking resemblance to the satiric tone of the *Chat noir* journal, and particularly to the humour of his friend and colleague at the Chat Noir, Alphonse Allais. Both men delighted in absurd self-portraits which lavished excessive praise or mockery on one's personal situation and achievements, in parodies of pedantry and academicism, and in the adoption of poses as a means of caricaturing certain human types.'[13] Allais was editor of the Chat Noir in-house journal in 1886–92, its heyday, and the journal in this period was another venue for work by Paul Verlaine as well as occasional contributions by Satie and Contamine de Latour.

The proprietor of the Chat Noir, Rodolphe Salis, contributed short stories in cod-medieval style, with 'authentic' antique spelling, to the *Chat noir* journal; the most interesting things about these stories by far were the elaborate illustrations which echo Satie's many Gothic doodlings.[14] The Chat Noir décor was similarly fake medieval in style. Jean Pascal, an early twentieth-century historian of Montmartre, recalls that 'rustic chairs, benches and solid wood tables, a stained-glass window, a tall fireplace, some antique armor, shining brass and copperware made up the Louis XIII establishment'.[15] Satie's enthusiasm for the Gothic extended to its

---

[13] Nancy Perloff, *Art and the Everyday: Popular Entertainment and the Circle of Erik Satie*. Oxford: Clarendon Press, 1991, p. 81.

[14] Caroline Potter, 'Satie as Poet, Playwright and Composer,' in Caroline Potter (ed.), *Erik Satie: Music, Art and Literature*. Farnham: Ashgate, 2013, pp. 67–84, at p. 69.

[15] Madhuri Mukherjee, 'When the Saints Go Marching in: Popular Performances of La *Tentation de Saint Antoine* and *Sainte Geneviève de Paris* at the Chat Noir Shadow Theater', in Elizabeth Emery and Laurie Postlewate (eds.), *Medieval Saints in Late Nineteenth Century French Culture: Eight Essays*. Jefferson, NC: McFarland, 2004, pp. 25–55, at p. 27; citing Jean Pascal, 'Les chansons et poésies du Chat noir.' *Les Chansonniers de Montmartre*, 24 (25 June 1907), p. 2; 'des chaises rustiques, des bancs et des tables en bois massif, un vitrail enluminé, une haute cheminée, quelques armures anciennes, de luisantes pièces de dinanderie, constituaient l'établissement Louis XIII'.

original manifestations, as in this period he frequented Notre-Dame cathedral as well as the Chat Noir. His four *Ogives* for piano (1888) take their title from the pointed arch characteristic of the Gothic cathedral.

Satie's writings for the *Chat noir* journal – we can assume he was the author – were mostly unsigned advertisements for his music. For instance, on 24 November 1888, another advertisement for a *Gymnopédie* appeared: 'The third Gymnopédie by Erik Satie has just come out at 66 boulevard Magenta. It would be impossible for us to recommend too highly to the public this work which is essentially an artistic one, which is considered, quite rightly, one of the most beautiful works of the century which has seen the birth of this unhappy gentleman.'[16] The boulevard Magenta address was the home of his father and stepmother. The multi-talented Alfred Satie, a translator who spoke nine languages, bought out the music publishing firm Wiart in 1882 and used it as a forum for his second wife's music, some of his son's early work and other composers including Vittorio Monti, author of the famous *Csárdás*.[17] Although Satie gave this contact address, Alfred Satie was, oddly, not the publisher of the *Gymnopédies* or the earlier *Ogives*, whose first editions came out under the Imprimerie Dupré imprint.[18] Erik Satie paid privately for these publications.

It is worth pausing to contemplate the extraordinary composition that is the three *Gymnopédies* (1888), extraordinary because of its title, haunting quality and the similar mood of all three pieces. The title is an invented word which has connotations of naked Greek boys doing exercise. All three pieces are slow and they share a triple-time rhythm with a low note on the first beat of the bar followed by a higher-pitched chord sustained on the second and third beats. While one could analyse the opening chords as unresolved sevenths or ninths, they surely arose from Satie fumbling at the keyboard: a simple G–D ostinato in the bass is combined with treble chords which all include F♯, below which the hand wanders down from D–B to C♯–A. The meandering melodic line is rhythmically simple and focuses more on F♯ than the supposed tonic D; the piece only settles on a D major triad in bar 39, and this is approached by a seventh chord with a flattened C. The melodic contour of all three pieces is strikingly similar: creating variety within a set of pieces was never something which concerned Satie. And almost all of Satie's pieces

---

[16] *Chat noir*, p. 1230: 'Vient de paraître, 66, boulevard Magenta, la troisième Gymnopédie de Erik Satie. Nous ne saurions trop recommander au public musical cette œuvre essentiellement artistique, qui passe, à juste titre, pour l'une des plus belles du siècle qui a vu naître ce malheureux gentilhomme.'

[17] See Robert Orledge, 'The Musical Activities of Alfred Satie and Eugénie Satie-Barnetche, and Their Effect on the Career of Erik Satie.' *Journal of the Royal Musical Association*, vol. 117 no. 2 (1992), pp. 270–97.

[18] Ibid., p. 277.

Ex. 1.1 Satie, *Gymnopédies*, no. 1: bars 1–12

are grouped in threes (the four *Ogives* are an exception) suggesting a Trinitarian obsession.

While Satie's advertisements in the *Chat noir* journal and *La Lanterne japonaise* ensured his unusual title came to public attention, no contemporary comments on the musical style of these works survive. This may be because the *Gymnopédies* were not performed as part of a conventional concert programme in an established Paris venue until several years after their composition; together with the three *Sarabandes*, they were promoted by major Parisian musical figures including Debussy and Ravel from 1911. The dissemination of the *Gymnopédies* as sheet music rather than in public performance linked Satie more with the popular salon composers of his day, not that these works were particularly popular in the late nineteenth century. Other piano pieces he published around this time, including *Valse-ballet* and *Fantaisie-valse* (both *c.* 1885–7), are more akin to conventional salon products than the revolutionary *Gymnopédies*, and both these works first appeared in a magazine devoted to home music-making, *La Musique des familles*.

Satie was also acquainted with a plumber and Chat Noir regular, Vital Hocquet (1865–1931), who wrote under the self-absorbed pseudonym Narcisse Lebeau. Indeed, Hocquet claims to have introduced Satie to Debussy at the Chat Noir.[19] In the number of *Chat noir* following the advertisement for the third *Gymnopédie*, this mysterious character published a short story 'Fleurs aujourd'hui fanées ...' (Flowers which are now faded ...) which was dedicated 'A Erik Satie'.[20] Narcisse Lebeau is also the author of a *Chat noir* article about the contemporary press published on 11 March 1893, 'Piquantes révélations, pour que C. Debussy réfléchisse' (Piquant revelations for C[laude] Debussy to ponder).[21] The striking title

---

[19] Whiting, *Satie the Bohemian*, p. 112.
[20] 1 December 1888, p. 1234.
[21] *Chat noir*, p. 2128.

with the adjective before the noun is characteristic of Satie's writing style. More significantly, the first section of the article shows that 'Lebeau' shared Satie's fascination with plays on words and on time:

> *Le Temps* [literally, Time] is decidedly a most unusual newspaper. Each evening at 5.30 – the time noted by the Observatory – it has not yet been distributed, and at 5.35 – with watch in hand – the final number has just been sold.
>
> One must believe that individuals skulking in the shadows of kiosks rush at the porters as soon as they arrive, knock them over, seize the issues shamelessly and rush off to read them in the company of women! But why do these people do that, and who is paying them?
>
> In order to have a clean conscience, the police should be arresting groups of readers of *Le Temps* and should bang them up to make examples of them. But the press would make a fuss.[22]

The humour of 'Narcisse Lebeau' in this article shows distinctively Satiean characteristics; it is also odd to relate that Satie used the pseudonym 'Virginie Lebeau' in his Montmartre years, as if he wanted to give the impression he were related to 'Narcisse'. Satie's humour tends to feature plays on words and jokes based on taking things literally, as evidenced in the article cited above in which the title of the newspaper is taken at face value. Satie observes everyday activities, is alive to their absurdities, and he often takes what appears to be a fact and pushes it to ludicrous consequences. He also has an odd obsession with clocks and time which is still apparent many years later in his texted piano works.

The barrel organ

Satie's Parisian environment in the late nineteenth century was also filled with sound: the piano for indoor music, and the barrel organ for street music (Fig. 1.1). The barrel organ (*orgue de Barbarie*) was a regular fixture on the Paris street scene from the late eighteenth century. Its ancestors included the vielle and the serinette, the latter being a tiny mechanical instrument producing high-pitched short tunes which were supposed to charm birds and encourage them to sing. The vielle, which like the barrel

---

[22] 'Le *Temps* est décidément un bien singulier journal. Chaque soir à 5 h. 30 – heure de l'Observatoire – il n'est pas encore distribué, et à 5 h. 35 – montre en main – le dernier numéro vient d'être vendu. ¶ C'est à croire que des individus tapis dans l'ombre des kiosques se ruent à l'assaut des porteurs dès qu'ils arrivent, les terrassent, se saisissent sans vergogne des numéros et courent les lire avec des femmes! Mais dans quel but et payés par qui, ces individus? ¶ Pour en avoir le cœur net, la police devrait arrêter par-ci, par-là une bande de lecteurs du *Temps*, les coffrer pour faire un exemple. Mais la presse crierait.'

Fig. 1.1 Organ grinder in Paris, 1898–9, photograph by Eugène Atget

organ was associated with beggars, often attracted an audience with the help of a dancing monkey. Various 'Instrumens qu'on fait parler avec une Roue' (Instruments played by turning a wheel) are illustrated in the third volume of Diderot and d'Alembert's *Encyclopédie* (1765). Langwill and Ord-Hume describe the mechanism of the barrel organ:

> The music is provided by a pinned wooden barrel arranged horizontally within the organ case and rotated by a worm gear on a cross-shaft extending outside the case and terminating in a crankhandle. This cross-shaft also carries one or (more usually) two offset bearings like a crankshaft and to these are attached reciprocators which pass to the lower part of the organ where

a simple air bellows and reservoir is provided. Turning the crankhandle thus fulfils two purposes: it pumps wind into the organ chest and it turns the barrel.[23]

The barrel organ was not purely an outdoor instrument, though its unusually loud volume for the period made it particularly suitable for this purpose. It was also used to provide entertainment in private homes and had the advantage over other instruments of not requiring specific training in musical performance. The French Imperial household in the Second Empire discovered other benefits of the barrel organ:

> At Compiègne, where Napoleon and Eugénie usually gave a series of brilliant *fêtes* during November, it was the custom for the guests, after dinner, to enjoy a simple carpet dance to the accompaniment of the *orgue de barbarie*, the hand-organ. This hand-organ of Compiègne, Fontainebleau and Saint-Cloud, its handle turned by cardinals, princes, ambassadors and, on occasion, by the Emperor – who revealed himself the most hopeless of performers, since he had no sense of rhythm – is in itself an indictment of the imperial good taste. [...] For these more intimate dances, as the Emperor said, an orchestra was awkward: 'They talk about what they've seen or have not seen'.[24]

The barrel organ had the advantage of being unable to gossip, though it was perceived by some to have drawbacks as a musical instrument. Earl Cowley, the British ambassador to France from 1852 to 1867, was one guest at Compiègne who did not appreciate its sound. Whether because of Napoleon's rhythmic ineptitude (perhaps surprising in a military man) or for some other reason, Cowley described the 'dancing to a *hand-organ*' as 'a dreadful trial for one's auricular nerves'.[25]

The barrel organ was used for two different types of repertoire: church music and popular entertainment. For the former – barrel organs were often found in small private chapels – there was a selection of hymn tunes which eliminated the need for a human organist; for private parties and public café and street performances, popular tunes, dances and contemporary opera melodies were the staple repertoire. The website of Le Ludion, one of the few surviving French manufacturers of barrel organs, provides a potted history of the instrument: 'The barrel organ (*l'orgue de Barbarie*) is an instrument which is traditionally played

---

[23] Lyndesay G. Langwill and Arthur W. J. G. Ord-Hume, 'Barrel Organ.' *Grove Music Online. Oxford Music Online.* Oxford University Press, accessed 4 April 2015, http://www.oxfordmusiconline.com/subscriber/article/grove/music/02111.

[24] Frederick H. Martens, 'Music Mirrors of the Second Empire – Part II.' *The Musical Quarterly*, vol. 16 no. 4 (October 1930): pp. 563–87, at p. 563.

[25] Ibid., p. 564.

by travelling musicians in the street to catch the attention of curious onlookers and advertise a magic lantern show, a monkey dance (in the Savoy region) or bear dancing act (peasants in the Ariège), or to launch a satirical cabaret singer and therefore to spread seditious texts. The instrument's repertoire is made up of opera arias, fashionable tunes and popular songs.'[26]

The animal accompanying the barrel organ thus varied according to region: bears native to the Pyrenees were presumably tamed and used in the Ariège area. Jacques Attali notes that in the late nineteenth century, both pinned cylinders and perforated cards were used as 'recording' mechanisms for scores, allowing them to be played without the need for a skilled human musician. New instruments such as the pianola and pianista were also developed, using similar technologies. Attali is aware that mechanical instruments created anxiety in performers because they feared redundancy, and new laws were required to regulate potential clashes between the interests of musicians and those who preferred to substitute them with barrel organs. He writes that 'In France, a law dated 16 May 1886 authorised these instruments to be used as orchestra substitutes in dances; more generally, the law permitted "the manufacture and sale of instruments which mechanically reproduce musical works".'[27]

The organ grinder's livelihood was itinerant and precarious, not least because, from its earliest days, the barrel organ was considered a suspect instrument. For some, its sound was uniquely unappealing, and for others, the social status of its performers reflected poorly on the instrument. European barrel organ players were often invalids, immigrants or elderly, in other words people with few other options for making a living. Circus performers sometimes used a barrel organ to attract attention to their arrival in town; again, the association of the instrument with an irregular, marginal lifestyle ensured that 'respectable' people were suspicious of the sound. Picasso's saltimbanque (circus performer) paintings of the early twentieth century often feature a barrel organ. Articles published in the London *Times* in the late eighteenth and

---

[26] http://www.leludion.fr/index.php/creations-orgue-mecanique/orgues-de-barbarie (accessed 5 April 2015): 'Traditionnellement l'Orgue de Barbarie est un instrument de saltimbanques, joué au coin de la rue pour attirer les badauds et annoncer un spectacle de lanterne magique, un numéro de danse de marmotte (*les ramoneurs savoyards*) ou d'ours (*les paysans ariégeois*), lancer un spectacle de chansonniers et ainsi diffuser des textes séditieux. Le répertoire se choisit parmi les grands airs d'Opéra, les ariettes à la mode, ou la chanson populaire.'

[27] Jacques Attali, *Bruits* (revised edition). Paris: Fayard/PUF, 2001, p. 150: 'En France, une loi de 16 mai 1886 autorise leur usage comme substitut aux orchestres dans les bals; plus généralement, elle permet «la fabrication et la vente des instruments servant à reproduire mécaniquement les airs de musique».'

nineteenth centuries invariably mention the barrel organ in the context of police reports: usually the organ grinder was arrested for public order offences, and Charles Dickens was not the only London resident to regularly pay organ grinders to go away.

An article written in 1908 for *Le Petit Journal* tells us a lot about the life of an organ grinder on the streets of Paris at the time when the livelihood was under threat:

> [the barrel organ] was the livelihood of many poor people. In the past, the organ players' central market was at place Maubert. There, many business owners kept a large number of these instruments in their shops and rented them out for 3 francs per day. The organ player collected his instrument in the morning and went out on the streets. When he returned in the evening, he had made, on average, about 100 sous [i.e. 5 francs]. Therefore, his net profit was around 2 francs. And to earn these 2 francs, he had turned the crank handle all day ... Frankly, it wasn't enough money for such a hard day's work.[28]

By 1908, the Préfet de Police of Paris decided no longer to grant new licences for barrel organ players. *Le Petit Journal* criticised this measure:

> Most of these performers are old or disabled people incapable of doing another job. They do this job because they have self-respect and don't want to beg ... But they will end up begging because their livelihood is being taken away. [...] What harm do they do? [...] People are happy to hear them. They echo popular songs; their music might be whining and trembling, but it is a cheerful interlude on a boring long day at work ... The organ player had his place in society. What place will he have now the Préfet de Police has banned him?[29]

---

[28] Anonymous author, 'Un type populaire qui disparaît: Le joueur d'orgue de Barbarie' in *Le Petit Journal*, 26 April 1908, p. 2: '[l'instrument] faisait vivre nombre de pauvres gens. Naguère, la Bourse des joueurs d'orgue se tenait place Maubert. Là, plusieurs industriels avaient en magasin une grande quantité de ces instruments qu'ils louaient trois francs par jour. Le joueur d'orgue prenait son instrument le matin et se mettait en route. Quand il rentrait, le soir, il avait fait en moyenne une recette de cent sous. Son bénéfice net était donc de deux francs environ. Et, pour gagner ces deux francs, il avait roulé sa boîte sonore et tourne la manivelle toute la journée ... Franchement, ce n'était guère pour une telle besogne.'

[29] Ibid.: 'Ce sont, en général, des vieillards ou des infirmes incapables d'exercer un autre métier. Ils prennent celui-là parce que, misérables, ils ont le respect d'eux-mêmes et ne veulent pas tendre la main ... Ils la tendront, désormais, puisqu'on leur enlève leur gagne-pain. [...] Mais quel mal faisaient-ils? [...] Depuis longtemps on les avait chasses des quartiers du centre. Ils ne jouaient plus guère que sous les porches ou dans les

While even the most stalwart supporter of the barrel organ performer did not claim that their instrument made an attractive sound, the organ grinder was part of the sonic landscape of Paris. Many residents of the city were sentimentally attached to the barrel organ and were happy to give the odd coin to the performer.

It is irresistible to place Satie, who was often described by his Montmartre acquaintances as 'Monsieur le Pauvre', in the universe of the barrel organ. He was identified with popular café entertainment and was gaining a reputation as a composer of short, repetitive, oddly haunting music. Street musicians were part of the Parisian urban landscape in the late nineteenth century and, while the sound of instruments such as the barrel organ divided opinion, it could not be ignored. Such a characteristic sight and sound was bound to have an impact on artists of all types, particularly in an age that prized the romantic individual, the urban hero, and the talented person from the margins. The bourgeoisie, in the shape of officials who policed the urban landscape, attempted to control street performers, giving artists a perfect opportunity to oppose officialdom and speak up for the humble barrel organ grinder. While artistic works connected with the barrel organ rarely had an overt political dimension, an implicit sympathy with people at the margins of society is omnipresent. Mechanical music, especially the type heard in Paris streets and public places such as cafés, was a key source of inspiration to poets and musicians of the late nineteenth century.

Street music and poets

Literary and artistic symbols and topics associated with mechanical instruments such as the barrel organ are strikingly consistent. The word/music scholar Florent Albrecht describes the barrel organ as 'a topos in decadent literature for proclaiming urban solitude, pessimism and unhappiness';[30] Albrecht notes its appearance in Baudelaire and Laforgue as well as Verlaine. It is as if the character of the poverty-stricken, down-on-his-luck, isolated street performer transferred directly to the instrument he played. An instrument which required little skill, and no musical training or knowledge, to operate was the perfect vehicle for the

cours de ces maisons des faubourgs qui sont de grandes ruches ouvrières sans cesse en travail. On les y accueillait avec joie. Ils apportaient l'écho de la chanson en vogue: leur musique, toute geignarde et tremblotante qu'elle fût, interrompait d'un peu de gaîté la monotonie des longues journées de labeur ... Le joueur d'orgue avait son petit rôle social. Qui le remplira pour lui, à présent que M. le préfet de police l'a supprimé?'

[30] Florent Albrecht, 'Verlaine l'anti-théoricien: contre la poétique, la musique?' *Revue silène* (2010), http://www.revue-silene.com/f/index.php?sp=liv&livre_id=140, p. 4; 'un topos de l'écriture décadente pour clamer la solitude, le pessimisme et le malheur urbains'.

street musician. No doubt, performance on the barrel organ was also a retort to the bourgeois virtues of practice, hard work and dedication which were inculcated in countless young ladies struggling at the piano. And Baudelaire 'was (famously) *not* a nature poet – one of his great paradigm shifts celebrated the urban environment as a space for poetic epiphany – and he had little use for Romantic reverence of the natural world'.[31]

The composer and poet Charles de Sivry wrote in *Le chat noir* in 1890 on the poetry of street music in terms which typify the response of artists to the barrel organ:

> The songs they play are so haunting, so evocative, that they pass unnoticed among the sounds of the city and, astonished, we think we still hear them when they are not there.
>
> Who are the geniuses who fabricate barrel organ cylinders? ... Who knows? But who has not noted how carefully they select the most banal, obsessive and irritating phrase from a popular song?[32]

Sivry stresses the paradoxical emotional force of music which is experienced in the background and is part of the fabric of life. This is music which appears unconnected to an author and yet is oddly familiar, which is both annoying and strangely haunting. The barrel organ is most unlike the lyre, the traditional musical accompaniment to the poet, and far removed from the ivory tower preoccupations of the Parnassian poetic school.

Other poet contributors to the *Chat noir* newspaper included Paul Verlaine, who was briefly and unhappily married to Mathilde Mauté de Fleurville, Sivry's half-sister. Verlaine's fascination with music included a love of the barrel organ, at least as much for its social milieu as for its sound. The sixth poem of his collection *Epigrammes* (1894), titled '... l'orgue de Barbarie!', was dedicated to the writer Octave Mirbeau, and a much earlier long poem, *Nocturne parisien*, was published in the collection *Poèmes saturniens* in 1866. Like '...l'orgue de Barbarie!', *Nocturne parisien* gives poetic force to everyday language and scenes. Here, Verlaine describes the sound quality and emotional impact of a barrel organ heard in the street:

---

[31] Steven Huebner, 'Ravel's Perfection', in Deborah Mawer (ed.), *Ravel Studies*. Cambridge: Cambridge University Press, pp. 9–30, at p. 20.

[32] Charles de Sivry, 'Les musiciens de rue – Les orgues de Barbarie', *Chat noir*, 6 December 1890, p. 1656: 'Les airs qu'elles jouent sont tellement imposées, tellement des souvenirs, qu'il passent inaperçus parmi les bruits de la ville et que l'âme étonnée croit encore les entendre lorsqu'ils se sont tus. Quels sont les gens de génie qui *piquent* les cylindres des orgues? ... nul ne le sait; mais qui n'a remarqué avec quel soin particulier ces artistes ne choisissent, dans un air *à succès*, que la phrase la plus parfaitement banale, la plus obsédante, la plus irritante?'

> Son cri qui se lamente, et se prolonge, et crie,
> Eclate en quelque coin l'orgue de Barbarie:
> Il brame un de ces airs, romances ou polkas,
> Qu'enfants nous tapotions sur nos harmonicas
> Et qui font, lents ou vifs, réjouissants ou tristes,
> Vibrer l'âme aux proscrits, aux femmes, aux artistes.
> C'est écorché, c'est faux, c'est horrible, c'est dur,
> Et donnerait la fièvre à Rossini, pour sûr;
> Ces rires sont traînés, ces plaintes sont hachées;
> Sur une clef de sol impossible juchées,
> Les notes ont un rhume et les do sont des la,
> Mais qu'importe! l'on pleure en entendant cela!

[Its lament is drawn out, and cries/ It's the barrel organ bursting forth in a corner/ wailing a ballad, romance, or polka/ a tune that as children we bashed out./ Fast or slow, joyful or sad, they make/the souls of outcasts, women, and artists tremble./ It's mispronounced, out-of-tune, horrid, harsh,/ and would, for sure, give Rossini a fever;/ those laughs are dragged out, those laments are chopped;/ the notes on an impossible treble clef are stopped/and bunged up; all the Cs are As/ but who cares! We weep when we hear it.]

If this extract sounds like doggerel, that was no doubt the author's intention. Verlaine describes music which a child could have played and which strikes a chord with marginal people of all types (including women). The sound of the barrel organ is out of tune and wheezy, its songs are derivative and simplistic – and yet the music moves people to tears.

Jules Laforgue (1860–87) wrote two barrel organ themed poems in his collection *Les complaintes*: 'Complainte de l'orgue de barbarie' and 'Autre complainte de l'orgue de barbarie'. He draws on the popular song connections of the instrument, evoking repetitive refrains, sometimes using slang or deliberate mispronunciation ('Je suis-t-il malhûreux!' is one of the refrains of 'Autre complainte'). Like Verlaine in *Nocturne parisien*, Laforgue conjures up a street scene featuring a poor, lonely vagabond – a flâneur, no doubt – and sets his poems in autumn. His tone is more ambiguous than Verlaine's, though: is Laforgue taking the vagabond character entirely seriously, or mocking the conventions of poetry inspired by alienation and misery?

Mallarmé's prose poem *Plainte d'automne* was written in 1863 just before Verlaine's *Nocturne parisien*, and it was reprinted in the *Chat noir* journal under the heading 'Pages oubliées' (Forgotten pages).[33] The mood here is nostalgic and again the season is autumn, and the barrel organ enhances this mood: 'Je lisais donc un de ces chers poèmes ... quand un orgue de Barbarie chanta languissamment et mélancoliquement sous ma

---

[33] *Chat noir*, 26 June 1886, p. 725.

fenêtre' (So I was reading one of those dear poems ... when a barrel organ started singing listlessly and melancholically beneath my window). For Helen Abbott,

> The emotion of sadness that the sound of the instrument creates for Mallarmé is reinforced by a climax of related terms, offset by a series of contrasts. For him, 'l'orgue de Barbarie' sings 'languissamment', 'mélancoliquement' and is later described as 'l'instrument des tristes' ['the instrument of sad people'] which has made him 'désespérément rêver' ['dream despairingly']. The climactic force of the despairing sadness is offset by the contrast created by other instruments: 'L'instrument des tristes, oui, vraiment: le piano scintille, le violon donne aux fibres déchirées la lumière, mais l'orgue de Barbarie, dans le crépuscule du souvenir, m'a fait désespérément rêver.' [The instrument of sad people, yes, in truth: the piano sparkles, the violin gives light to torn fibres, but the barrel organ, in the shadows of memory, made me dream despairingly.][34]

Why are these poetic topoi so consistent? The barrel organ is an instrument of nostalgia because it reproduces something well known, even hackneyed, yet in imperfect form: the tune can never be as good as the original because the technology is imperfect. Carolyn Abbate's suggestive and stimulating article on Ravel and the mechanical recognises that 'a presence from the past is manifested, but in an unexpected register, spectral and greatly mediated';[35] she senses this quality not only in mechanically reproduced music but also in Ravel's neoclassical nostalgia in works such as *Le tombeau de Couperin*. In this, she is inspired by Baudelaire's essay *Morale du joujou* (1853) and Vladimir Jankélévitch's writings on Ravel.[36] Baudelaire notes that children's curiosity about their toys, especially curiosity about the soul of a doll, leads them to attack and destroy the toy, a moment which for Baudelaire 'marks the beginning of stupor and melancholy'. The epigraph to Abbate's article, by Jankélévitch, highlights why automata and mechanical musical instruments can make us uncomfortable: 'Mechanical pianos and mechanical birds, scornful marionettes and wound-up automata [...] do they not evoke a sort of derisory humanity, an automaton humanity midway between the human being and the pendulum?'[37]

---

[34] Helen Abbott, *Between Baudelaire and Mallarmé: Voice, Conversation and Music*. Farnham: Ashgate, 2009, p. 197.

[35] Carolyn Abbate, 'Outside Ravel's Tomb.' *Journal of the American Musicological Society*, vol. 52 no. 3 (Autumn 1999): pp. 465–530, at p. 474.

[36] Particularly his book *Ravel*. Paris: Editions du Seuil, 1959.

[37] Abbate, 'Outside Ravel's Tomb', p. 465. Citing Jankélévitch, *Musique et l'ineffable*, trans. Carolyn Abbate as *Music and the Ineffable*. Princeton, NJ:

Satie uses mechanistic repetitive musical material in most of his works, often deliberately blurring the dividing lines between background and foreground and between mechanical and human. Often quoting familiar tunes, sometimes with satirical intent, it is as if Satie were constructing a barrel organ punched card or cylinder. But he often plays with his mechanisms by purposely introducing flaws, setting up something predictable or familiar and then jolting listeners out of their complacency. And it is surely the lulling, repetitive, self-similar qualities of the *Gymnopédies* that lend them their nostalgic melancholy which appeals to so many listeners.

The barrel organ was also associated with very early forms of multimedia entertainment. A street performer often carried two boxes: a barrel organ and, on his back, a magic lantern. There is documentary evidence that light shows, which often depicted natural phenomena or, in their more sophisticated form, Bible stories, were a regular fixture in Paris from the sixteenth century (though the technology is far older: Mariel Oberthür points out that 'shadow theatre had existed for a long time in China, Egypt and Turkey' before the entertainment was known in Europe).[38] These magic lantern shows 'were presented by itinerant performers wherever they stopped. They were like modern-day film projectors. The public could be "put in a box" with "moving" images which seemed to appear and disappear suddenly. Often, to accompany a story, glass plaques were used: well-known stories were accompanied by specially painted coloured backdrops.'[39] These forerunners of the cinema were often accompanied by music played on the barrel organ, and, as very early examples of son et lumière shows, they are the start of a long French tradition of outdoor entertainment. They are also very clearly the ancestors of shadow play shows in the Montmartre cabaret of the late nineteenth century and of the cinema – both media to which Satie contributed.

Princeton University Press, 2003, pp. 43–4 (her translation): 'Pianos mécaniques et oiseaux mécaniques, marionnettes dérisoires et automates remontés ... n'évoquent-ils pas une sorte d'humanité dérisoire, une humanité automatique intermédiaire entre les hommes et les pendules?'

[38] Mariel Oberthür, *Le Cabaret du Chat noir à Montmartre (1881–1897)*. Geneva: Slatkine, 2007, p. 169; 'le théâtre d'ombres existait depuis longtemps en Chine, en Egypte et en Turquie'.

[39] http://www.vivelafoire.net/html/icon.aspx?id=16&p=3 (accessed 5 April 2015): 'Ils étaient présentés par des forains itinérants aux endroits où ceux-ci s'arrêtaient. Ils étaient comme les projecteurs de diapositives modernes. Le public pouvait être « mis en boîte » (lui aussi) avec des images « mobiles », de soudaines apparitions et disparitions. Souvent, pour raconter les histoires, on recourait à des plaques de verre. Des histoires bien connues étaient illustrées par des séries spéciales de plaques peintes.'

The connection between Satie and a barrel organ performer is immediately evident. Satie initially made a living in Montmartre as a café pianist, accompanying cabaret singers who, to paraphrase the Ludion text quoted above, performed satirical songs which might 'spread seditious texts'. The cabarets in which Satie performed hosted shadow plays which he sometimes accompanied. And walking was always Satie's preferred mode of transport, partly because he was often too poor to afford the train fare when he moved out of Montmartre to the southern suburb of Arcueil in 1898. Walking was, however, not only a practical necessity for Satie. Many commentators have noted the importance of the regular walking pace in his music, from the *Gymnopédies* to the unchanging rhythm of later works. Satie wrote in 1913, 'Before I compose a piece, I walk round it several times, accompanied by myself.'[40] Roger Shattuck, in conversation with John Cage, 'suggested that the source of Satie's sense of musical beat – the possibility of variation within repetition, the effect of boredom on the organism – may be this endless walking back and forth across the same landscape day after day … the total observation of a very limited and narrow environment'.[41] During his walks, Satie would sketch ideas in his notebook. It is as if he were an itinerant street musician – an organ grinder.

New mechanical instruments

The advertisements published on the back page of the *Chat noir* journal are an intriguing insight into the presumed concerns of its readers: widows or orphans seeking marriage (usually with a significant dowry as carrot); purgative medicines (often of Hungarian origin);[42] and, from the early 1890s, the player piano. 'Play the piano with no musical

---

[40] Written at the end of a 1913 publicity document for his publisher Eugène-Louis Demets, cited in Volta (ed.), *Satie Ecrits*, p. 143. 'Avant d'écrire une œuvre, j'en fais plusieurs fois le tour, en compagnie de moi-même.'

[41] Cited in Orledge (ed.), *Satie Remembered*, p. 69; Shattuck's conversation with Cage was published in *Contact*, 25 (1982), p. 25.

[42] An article published in *La Lanterne japonaise* (no. 15, 23 March 1889, p. 3), attributed by Ornella Volta to Satie, reads like a satire of one of these advertisements for miracle health cures: 'M. Erik Satie, compositeur de musique, reçoit la lettre suivante qu'il nous prie d'insérer: "Monsieur, Depuis 8 ans, je souffrais d'un polype dans le nez, compliqué d'une affection du foie et des douleurs rhumatismales. A l'audition de vos *Ogives*, un mieux sensible s'est manifesté dans mon état: quatre ou cinq applications de votre *Troisième Gymnopédie* m'ont radicalement guérie. Je vous autorise, Monsieur Erik Satie, à faire de cette attestation l'usage qu'il vous plaira."'

Fig. 1.2 Pianista advert (*Chat noir*, 18 April 1891, p. 1734)

knowledge,' these advertisements read (see Fig. 1.2);[43] in Satie's position we would surely have been worried about being sacked and replaced by this new technology. While the player piano was itself superseded by recorded music, it went through a creative period in the early 1920s when composers including Stravinsky and Antheil wrote for it.

These new instruments had half-familiar names because their appearance and sonorities were partly familiar and yet also excitingly new. Pianistas or pianolas[44] looked like pianos but were operated with pedals and perforated card rolls; the enormous orchestrion could produce sounds vaguely reminiscent of the orchestral percussion section, though it looked like a bastard hybrid of the organ and the juke box; organinas or organettes were tiny, crank-operated barrel organs with a wooden body like an old-fashioned cash register into which perforated card rolls were inserted. The repertoire of these instruments, as for the barrel organ, was usually popular tunes which had been arranged to suit the capability of the instrument. Songs were, naturally, shorn of their words, and the limited duration capacity of a barrel or perforated card resulted in truncated versions, perhaps focusing just on the chorus or another well-known part of a song. The pianista or pianola had fewer limitations, and indeed some composers took advantage of the ability of the pianola to produce chords and counterpoints which are unplayable by a human performer. We will see in Chapter 2 that Satie found Stravinsky's *Etude pour pianola* appealing for this very reason.

Satie was himself fond of creating imaginary advertisements, an example of his 'exercice de style' approach to writing which shows how familiar he was with advertising slogans and 'puff pieces'. Some of these advertisements focus on the contemporary need to arrange music for different commercial purposes: before the widespread availability of the radio or gramophone, simplified versions of the classics and popular tunes were sold as sheet music which could be played by an amateur pianist in the home, or were rearranged for mechanical instruments and

---

[43] An example of an advertisement of this type can be seen in the *Chat noir* journal, 11 April 1891, p. 1730.

[44] The term 'pianola' was originally the name of a specific brand of player piano, though it eventually became the standard term used for all player pianos.

played in public. One of Satie's texts pokes fun at the incongruous nature of some of these arrangements:

> Spécialité de Marches funèbres.
> Requiem, Messes arrangés pour bals.
> La maison se charge des réparations harmoniques.
> Transformation rapide de symphonies, quatuors etc., etc.
> Musique sérieuse rendue gaie.
> Morceaux les plus difficiles réduits pour un seul doigt.
> Mélodies vocales arrangées à deux pianos.
> Plus de compositions incompréhensibles.
> La Subtilité à la portée de tous.
> Sonates réduites, réharmonisées.
> Notre musique est garantie jouable.

> [Funeral marches are our speciality.
> Requiems and Masses arranged for dances.
> The house can undertake harmonic repairs.
> Rapid transformation of symphonies, quartets, etc. etc.
> Serious music made cheerful.
> The most difficult pieces reduced for a single finger.
> Vocal melodies arranged for two pianos.
> No more incomprehensible compositions.
> Subtlety accessible to all.
> Sonatas reduced, reharmonised.
> Our music is guaranteed playable.]

While of course Satie's *blague* humour lies partly in his exaggeration of contemporary practice ('the most difficult pieces reduced for a single finger'), his text is highly suggestive about how the music business perceived the tastes and desires of the listening public. Concerns about the attention span of the public and its preference for music which is upbeat, simple and approachable rather than serious, long and complicated are evidently not new. Satie mentions that most serious and lengthy musical genres which might be considered 'incomprehensible' – the Requiem or other masses, the symphony, string quartet and sonata – can be efficiently 'rapidly transformed' into a more user-friendly format. At the same time, Satie insinuates that this public is eager to be seen as sophisticated connoisseurs of music ('Subtlety accessible to all'). Interestingly, one of his statements shows that music could be expanded beyond its original bounds as well as reduced and simplified: vocal melodies could be 'arranged for two pianos', no doubt a reference to the production for an opera or ballet of a *monstre*, a demonstration score (from the verb 'montrer', to show) for audition or rehearsal purposes.

Another of Satie's fake advertisements features an imagined conversation between the business and a potential client:

Our customers are advised that we have just bought an extensive range of symphonies. These symphonies, revised & corrected in our workshops, will be tailor-made for the needs of our large client base. Eager to satisfy everyone, the company is responsive to feedback and pays required royalties.
– A symphony? Here it is, madam.
– It doesn't look much fun.
– We can arrange it for you as a waltz, & with words. It's played in all the cafés.[45]

The notion that the symphony – that august, serious Germanic musical form – is a product which can be purchased and arranged at will in popular styles for consumption by the general public shows Satie's humour at its most provocative.

Satie, the café-concert and shadow plays

Satie was linked with the popular music scene in Montmartre as a composer and pianist. He accompanied many well-known singers in the late 1890s and early 1900s, including Paulette Darty (for whom he wrote *La Diva de l'Empire* and the slow waltz *Je te veux*) and collaborated with Vincent Hyspa from 1899 in a number of cabaret songs. Steven Moore Whiting's book *Satie the Bohemian* gives a comprehensive account of this side of Satie's creativity, showing that songs such as *Chez le docteur* (1905) are indivisible from the contemporary political context which inspired them – in this case, the satire is directed at Emile Combes, the serving French Prime Minister who was both a qualified medical doctor and a doctor in theology.[46]

At the start of the 1890s, Satie was employed as second pianist and occasional conductor at the Chat Noir (the regular piano player being his

---

[45] Texts reproduced in Volta (ed.), *Satie Ecrits*, p. 188. The original of the second text is housed in IMEC, SAT 1.18. Like most of Satie's fake advertisements, these texts are undated; the first was transcribed by Pierre-Daniel Templier from an original manuscript which has since disappeared. 'Les clients sont prévenus que nous venons d'acheter un grand choix de symphonies. Ces symphonies, revues & corrigées dans nos ateliers, seront mises au point pour les besoins de notre importante clientèle. Soucieuse de contenter tout le monde, la maison reçoit toutes les observations & y fait droit de suite. ¶ Une symphonie? Voilà, madame. ¶ Elle n'a pas l'air très amusante. ¶ Nous pouvons vous la donner arrangée en valse, & avec paroles. Elle est jouée dans tous les cafés.'

[46] Whiting, *Satie the Bohemian*, pp. 237–8. See also Whiting's article 'Musical Parody and Two "Oeuvres posthumes" of Erik Satie: The *Rêverie du pauvre* and the *Petite musique de clown triste*.' *Revue de musicologie*, vol. 81 no. 2 (1995): pp. 215–34.

fellow Norman, Albert Tinchant (1862–92)).[47] Following an argument with the Chat Noir owner Rodolphe Salis, Satie moved in 1891 to a rival cabaret, the Auberge du Clou, though he also worked and drank at other local venues. Benjamin Ivry claims that in 1893 'Maurice [Ravel] met Erik Satie through his father, who knew the Montmartre composer, then eking out a living as pianist at the Café de la Nouvelle Athènes. Satie gravely consulted with Ravel and Viñes about his plan to set newspaper advertisements to music, writing miniscule [recte: minuscule] orchestrations to texts from the want ads.'[48] While no such piece survives (and, while Satie did indeed meet Ravel through the latter's father, there is no hard evidence of these supposed 'grave consultations'), Satie's fondness for advertisements extended to him writing his own, imaginary advertising.

Satie's name surfaces in stories published in venues such as the *Chat noir* journal. Steven Moore Whiting notes that 'In a story printed on 29 October 1892, George Auriol spins a yarn about a London dowager who has left a fantastic inheritance to her parakeet; "M. Fred Erick Saty" is identified as the narrator's "vieux camarade de chez Routledge, libraire" who has informed him of the particulars in the case. In the next year, Léopold Dauphin (an operetta composer who published verse under the pseudonym Pimpinelli) dedicated a poem to Satie.'[49]

Some of the articles Satie wrote towards the end of his life look back with characteristic humour and irony on the time he spent working in the café-concert and cabaret. In October 1922 he wrote 'Pénibles exemples' for *Catalogue Pierre Tremois* no. 5, in which he expresses the conventional view that one should not be seen at a café ('as Allais told me, "it would be enough to wreck a marriage proposal"') and provides an allegedly factual account of his café habits and a sincere recommendation to young people tempted by café culture. He writes about his 'great-uncle' who drank frequently with Rabelais in the 'Pomme de Pin' cabaret but 'sadly did not know Villon'.[50] Satie ends his article:

> I don't think that going to a café, or to any other establishment of that type, is bad in itself; I admit I have myself worked in these

---

[47] Tinchant is the author of an excellent parody verse, 'Andante', which appeared in the *Chat noir* journal on 5 May 1888: 'J'ai vu fleurir des lys au long des étangs sombres/ A l'heure où l'essaim bleu des elfes fait dodo' (p. 1113).

[48] Benjamin Ivry, *Ravel*. New York: Welcome Rain, 2000, p. 15.

[49] Steven Moore Whiting, 'Erik Satie and Vincent Hyspa: Notes on a Collaboration.' *Music & Letters*, vol. 77 no. 1 (1996): pp. 64–91, at p. 66.

[50] Reprinted in Volta (ed.), *Satie Ecrits*, p. 57: 'comme me le disait Allais, «cela peut vous faire rater un mariage» [...] il vida souvent «moult pots» avec Rabelais, à la «Pomme de Pain» [...] Il est fâcheux qu'il n'ait pu connaître Villon'.

places a lot, and I think that the illustrious characters who spent time there before me did not waste their time. There can be an exchange of ideas in these places which can only be profitable – as long as one is not seen. However, to show that I am a moral person and to give myself a respectable appearance, I say: Young people, do not go to the café: listen to the serious voice of a man who has been there far too much, in his view – but does not regret it, the monster![51]

Again, we see Satie deriving humour from plays on time (Rabelais (c. 1483–1553) and Villon (c. 1431–63) would most certainly not have known his great-uncle!) and toying with bourgeois conventions. Just as Satie wore the uniform of a British businessman but his professional activity was far from the office-bound salary-earning classes, he poses in this article as someone who espouses bourgeois values when these did not at all reflect his lifestyle.

Many Montmartre cafés were not just drinking and meeting venues where music featured as a backdrop to life; they also housed miniature theatres which were venues for experimental work. Steven Moore Whiting notes that experiments with shadow plays in Montmartre started around 1886. He writes that the medium, as experienced in the café,

> originated in a playful experiment by Henri Rivière. While Jules Jouy performed his satire on Parisian cops, 'Les Sergots', Rivière had the room darkened, then marched cardboard cut-outs between a candle and a sheet suspended over the edge of the guignol, to create moving shadows on a miniature screen. [...] Recognising the potential of such spectacles, Salis had Rivière build a permanent theatre into the second floor Salle des Fêtes.[52]

The first show of this type to attract critical attention was *L'épopée* by Caran d'Ache (on the topic of Napoleon's Russian campaign) which premiered on 27 December 1886: 'While Caran d'Ache, Allais and [Georges] Auriol provided sound effects on a variety of percussion instruments, Salis narrated the plot with his usual display of verbal virtuosity.'[53] Caran d'Ache was better known as a cartoonist whose work

---

[51] Ibid., p. 58: 'Je ne crois pas que d'aller au café, ou à tout autre endroit de ce genre, soit mauvais en soi; j'avoue y avoir beaucoup travaillé: et je crois que les illustres personnages qui y furent avant moi n'y ont pas perdu leur temps. Il s'y fait un échange d'idées qui ne peut qu'être profitable – à la condition de ne pas se faire remarquer. ¶ Cependant, pour faire montre de morale et pour me donner un air respectable, je dis: Jeunes gens, n'allez pas au café: écoutez la voix grave d'un homme qui y a beaucoup trop été, à son avis – mais qui ne le regrette pas, le monstre!'

[52] Whiting, *Satie the Bohemian*, p. 47.

[53] Ibid., p. 48.

was often seen in the *Chat noir* journal (his pseudonym is derived from the Russian word for pencil); the subject of his shadow play shows that this new form of entertainment did not lack ambition. Many of these performances featured improvised sound effects or music arranged from other sources. Satie himself attended in 1888 a performance of *La tentation de saint Antoine*, a shadow play based on Flaubert's prose poem.[54] For this production, Rivière experimented with colour, placing paper over glass to obtain stained-glass window effects. Contemporary reviews reveal that *La Tentation de saint Antoine* was based on a combination of Flaubert and contemporary detail: 'the devil appears in frock-coat, and the temptations begin in modern Paris: gourmandise (les Halles), greed (the Bourse), political power (the saint may choose between the powers of President Sadi Carnot and those of General Boulanger)'.[55] The musical accompaniment to this story relied on the audience's familiarity with hackneyed tunes. Steven Moore Whiting writes that 'The "Ride of the Valkyries", for example, accompanied a procession of Norse gods' and

> The political power of General Boulanger was offered (of course) to the strain of Paulus's march-song 'En revenant de la Revue'. Such musical allusion was commonplace in theatrical revues, the advertisements for which likewise refer to 'musique nouvelle et arrangée', and it recalls the chansonnier's habit of retexting familiar tunes. Whether he knew it or not, Satie was witnessing not only a spectacle that would inspire his own *Uspud* some five years later, but also a technique of allusion that would eventually become part and parcel of his compositional style.[56]

In fact, Satie's own shadow play *uspud* – the work's title and text are in lower-case letters throughout – was more than 'inspired' by *La tentation de saint Antoine*. Andrew Hugill, who published an edition of *uspud* in 1992, notes that

> In November [1892] Satie, in conjunction with the Spanish writer 'Patrice' Contamine (also known as 'Lord Cheminot' and, here, J. P. Contamine de Latour), prepared first a text and then music for a shadow play which bore a startling and parodistic resemblance to *The Temptation of St. Antony*. Nicolas Bataille [...] has confirmed that the second act of *uspud* is lifted wholesale from *The Temptation* ... and that the other two acts are satirical in tone. He has also observed that the preparation of the puppets would require at least four months' labour, all of which leads one to suppose that the

---

[54] Oberthür, *Le Cabaret du Chat noir*, p. 81. The shadow play was first performed on 28 December 1887.

[55] Whiting, *Satie the Bohemian*, pp. 71–2 cites information from a review by Jules Lemaître published in *Impressions de théâtre*, ii, pp. 331–43.

[56] Whiting, *Satie the Bohemian*, p. 72.

'run-through' which took place at the Auberge du Clou, witnessed by Debussy, must have comprised the music on harmonium, a recitation of the text, and, perhaps, the sketchiest of shadow-plays using the puppets from *The Temptation* ..., or, indeed, no shadow-play at all. In any case, the run-through was not a success and all present were harsh in their criticism of Satie's intensely minimal score.[57]

For instance, the opening of Act III – where 'uspud, dressed in a cowl, lies prostrate before the crucifix; for a long time he prays and weeps' – features a single sustained first inversion chord of G major played on the harmonium for seven bars marked 'très lent' (very slow). Individual lines may be doubled by another instrument, but contrapuntal writing is almost completely absent. Satie's experience of shadow plays may have inspired another of his works. In January 1893, a shadow play entitled *Sainte Geneviève de Paris* by Claudius Blanc (1854–1900) and Léopold Dauphin (1848–1925) was premiered at the Chat Noir, and only a few years later, in 1900, Satie composed his own work based on the legend of the patron saint of Paris, *Geneviève de Brabant*.

An advertisement published in *Chat noir* on 17 May 1890 promotes the in-house shadow plays:

> The CHAT NOIR THEATRE offers every evening (apart from Sundays and holidays) a spectacle that cannot be found elsewhere.
>
> Neo-Chinese shadows, designed by Caran d'Ache, Willette, H. Rivière, Robida, Henri Pille, Sabattier, Bombled, Moynet, etc.
>
> Interludes filled with songs and poems performed by their authors.[58]

This publicity material is not only interesting because it provides information about the entertainment; it is also noteworthy that the plays are broken up by interludes (*intermèdes*). It is remarkable how many compositions by Satie have titles which suggest that they are an interlude, entr'acte or some other term connoting 'in-betweenness', as though they are not the main artistic event but a sideshow. Performance practice in the café-concert strongly suggests that this is the origin of Satie's fondness for these titles. It is also likely that Satie's concept of 'furniture music' (*musique d'ameublement*) – music designed to be heard in the

---

[57] Andrew Hugill, preface to *uspud* (Satie, arr. Hugill). Paris: Salabert, 1992, p. 2. I am very grateful to Hugill for giving me a copy of this score.

[58] p. 1542: 'Le THEATRE DU CHAT NOIR offre tous les soirs (hormis les jours de fête et dimanches) un spectacles qu'on chercherait vainement ailleurs. Ombres néo-chinoises, dessinées par Caran d'Ache, Willette, H. Rivière, Robida, Henri Pille, Sabattier, Bombled, Moynet, etc. Intermèdes remplis par des chansons et des vers que disent les auteurs.'

background – harks back to his time spent and misspent in Montmartre cafés.

Ornella Volta believes that 'It was probably Satie who accompanied the shadow plays at the [Auberge du] Clou on the keyboard. This job title "second pianist" which he was given could have been linked to his use of the "second" piano of this establishment, precisely the one installed in the basement. A piano, or more likely a harmonium, since it is the latter instrument which accompanied the shadow plays at the Chat Noir.' This does not sound like a prestigious job. In December 1892 Satie composed music for *Noël*, a shadow play by Vincent Hyspa; the music is now lost and Robert Orledge believes it may have been compiled from existing piano pieces such as the *Gnossiennes*.[59] It was premiered on 24 December 1892, the first shadow play to be performed in the Auberge du Clou. The scenery was created by Miguel Utrillo, the father of Suzanne Valadon's son, the painter Maurice. Montmartre was a small world: Satie's only known love affair was with Suzanne Valadon and lasted from 14 January to 20 June 1893. The affair is commemorated in Santiago Rusiñol's painting *Una romanza*, which shows Valadon posing at the piano, as if she were a bourgeois young lady, with Satie admiring her as if he were a bourgeois young man (see Fig. 4.1 on p. 140 below).

The café-concert proposed a new form of multimedia entertainment which prefigures Satie's collaborations of the late 1910s and 1920s, culminating in his cinema interlude, *Entr'acte*, to René Clair's film screened between the two acts of the Ballets Suédois production *Relâche* (1924). Cinema was an emergent art form in the Belle Epoque and was rarely a stand-alone entertainment. Rather, it was usually part of a variety bill; 'in 1900, when the cinema was still just a fairground attraction, short films, preferably comic, were shown during music hall revues'.[60] Chris Townsend also draws attention to connections with the Italian futurist Filippo Marinetti's *The Variety Theatre* (1913):

> Marinetti called for a combination of the arts that would destroy the serenity of the theatre. Included in that call is 'all the new significations of lights.' I take this to mean not only abstract, coloured projections in the manner proposed by Kandinsky, but film, for Marinetti is pursuing a performance very much like that of the café-concert or the music hall, where films were screened

---

[59] Robert Orledge, 'Chronological Catalogue of Satie's Compositions and Research Guide to the Manuscripts', in Caroline Potter (ed.), *Erik Satie: Music, Art and Literature*. Farnham: Ashgate, 2013, p. 257.

[60] Ornella Volta, 'Le rideau se lève sur un os: Quelques investigations autour d'Erik Satie', in 'Erik Satie – L'os à moelle.' *Revue internationale de musique française*, 23 (June 1987), p. 11; 'en 1900, lorsque le cinématographe n'était encore qu'une attraction foraine, on montrait de petits films, comiques de préférence, au cours des revues de music-hall?'

between other acts. This is, of course, exactly the kind of proto-cinematic environment that Clair said Picabia wanted to achieve with *Entr'acte*.[61]

The close connection between the nineteenth- and early twentieth-century variety theatre on the one hand, and the twentieth-century multimedia collaboration on the other, could not be clearer. Francis Picabia was obsessed in both solo and collaborative works with merging the human and the machine, and his Satie collaborations reflecting this obsession will be discussed in Chapter 6.

Rusiñol's *Portrait of Eric Satie at the Harmonium* (1891) shows Satie at work at the Auberge du Clou, and in the artist's charcoal sketch for this portrait, Satie, smoking a cigarette, appears to be in less good shape than in the painting. Volta located a programme which shows that 'For one of the shows at this cabaret, *La Marche à l'Etoile* [1890], Satie shared the role of organist with [the composer of the work] Georges Fragerolle.'[62] However, in the published score, there is a list of performers involved in the premiere on 6 January 1890; here, Fragerolle is listed as 'first reciter' (out of three). Charles de Sivry conducted the ensemble, which besides the reciters comprised a solo cellist, oboist and a cymbal player (Jean de Sivry).[63] One can assume that a keyboard player was also involved, as much of the score is unplayable by the small group listed on the score. The premiere date of *La marche à l'étoile* was Twelfth Night, and appropriately the story is drawn from the Bible. Various characters follow a star, including shepherds (whose music is marked 'Andantino pastoral' and features an oboe solo), soldiers whose melody is 'très martial', lepers and women; the Three Kings emerge late in the story. The climax of the work is the only four-part imitative choral passage, 'L'Adoration', which is unaccompanied. The story then moves swiftly through history to 'Le Golgotha' and finally an instrumental 'Apothéose', both accompanying imagery of Christ on the cross. The music is unimaginative, often using block chords and simple arpeggiated melodies, and the published score

---

[61] Christopher Townsend, 'The Last Hope of Intuition: Francis Picabia, Erik Satie and René Clair's Intermedial Project *Relâche*.' *Nottingham French Studies*, vol. 50 no. 3 (2011): pp. 43–66, at p. 63.

[62] Volta, 'Le rideau se lève sur un os', pp. 63–5; 'C'est sans doute Satie qui accompagnait au clavier les spectacles d'ombres du Clou. Ce titre de « deuxième pianiste » dont on l'affublait pourrait être lié à l'utilisation de sa part du « deuxième » piano de cet établissement, celui précisément qui avait été installé au sous-sol. Un piano, ou plus probablement un harmonium, puisque c'est avec ce dernier type d'instrument que l'on accompagnait les ombres du Chat Noir. Pour l'un des spectacles de ce cabaret, *La Marche à l'Etoile*, Satie avait partagé le rôle d'organiste avec Georges Fragerolle.'

[63] The score was published by Enoch (no date given) as a 'mystère en 10 tableaux' including reproductions of Henri Rivière's images.

gives no indication of the reciters' roles. No doubt the score was a starting point for improvisation.

Satie got to know the composer and writer Charles de Sivry in the Montmartre café scene. The brother of the cymbal player mentioned above, Sivry was a Hydropathe who was also a friend of Debussy. Roy Howat writes that Debussy's

> first childhood encounter, at about the age of nine, with the artistic avant-garde [was] brought about through the eccentric figure of Charles de Sivry, brother-in-law of Paul Verlaine and, according to Emile Goudeau 'musician too, but more particularly a cabbalist passionately embroiled in occult science.' Sivry encountered the young Debussy through knowing Debussy's father during the 1871 Paris Commune, after which de Sivry's mother, by then Mme Mauté de Fleurville, took charge of the young Debussy's musical education.[64]

Sivry was interested in mysticism and joined Charles Cros in experiments in alchemy.[65]

Like Satie, Sivry accompanied singers at the Chat Noir, and both men also provided musical illustration to shadow plays. But according to Whiting, 'Sivry's particular talent was his ability to improvise, during the shadow shows, music that uncannily suited [Rodolphe] Salis's improvised narrations. [...] Improvisation was not a skill of Satie's, and this deficiency must have become glaringly apparent whenever he stood in for Sivry.'[66] Sivry's compositions include *Ailleurs*, a 'revue symbolique en 20 tableaux' for the Chat Noir, which premiered on 11 November 1891. Set mostly in the august academic institution the Institut de France but featuring other, very different, locations including a suburban factory, its characters include Voltaire. Sivry later became music director at the rival cabaret Les Quat'z'Arts, which opened in 1893.

Another person Satie met in the Montmartre café scene was Jules Dépaquit (1869–1924). At the cabaret Le Lapin Agile, Dépaquit 'became notorious by reciting Racine's "Le Songe d'Athalie" to the [popular] tune "la Mère Michel"'.[67] Poking fun at the classics was standard fare in the cabarets, but Dépaquit was ultimately better known as a cartoonist. He was a regular contributor to satirical newspapers such as *Le Rire* and the *Chat noir* journal, and also provided illustrations for published sets of

---

[64] Roy Howat, *Debussy in Proportion*. Cambridge: Cambridge University Press, 1983, pp. 163–4.

[65] Whiting, *Satie the Bohemian*, p. 74 note 33.

[66] Ibid., p. 89.

[67] Jean-Emile Bayard, *Montmartre hier et aujourd'hui*. Paris: 1924; 'Jules Dépaquit s'y fait une réputation en récitant Le Songe d'Athalie de Racine sur l'air de "la Mère Michel".'

cabaret songs including *Chansons immobiles* by Jacques Ferny. Dépaquit was politically active, being the inaugural mayor of the Commune libre de Montmartre in 1921, standing on an 'antigrattecieliste' ticket (anti-skyscraper). In the last year of the nineteenth century he collaborated with Satie on a pantomime, *Jack in the Box*: although this work does not survive in complete form, it is an intriguing case study of Satie as collaborator and composer in this period.

Jack in the Box

Satie was struggling with composition and his artistic direction in the last years of the nineteenth century. In 1899 he wrote a series of despairing letters to his brother Conrad, revealing in one of them that he was only able to do some accompanying work for Vincent Hyspa because Conrad had given him some of his old clothes.[68] On 15 May, Satie wrote to 'mon bon Pouillot' (his nickname for his brother):

> All this isn't much fun: for my part, I'm starting to feel overburdened: being starving hungry and dry gusseted gives me no pleasure. Tired and anaemic, I can see misery, that old bat, growing as I look, even with an ox or veal eye; while childish calculations, like most of my calculations are, happily make me realise with exquisite precision that things are going fatally badly for me, perhaps for everyone.[69]

Continuing in this vein for a couple more paragraphs, Satie shows no respite from this mood until the postscript: 'Note to the addressee: I am working with Dépaquit on a pantomime which should be performed at the Comédie parisienne next October. Details to follow.' This project, which raised his spirits, temporarily at least, was *Jack in the Box*, a collaboration with Jules Dépaquit. Ornella Volta believes that Satie wrote a first, five-act version of his play *Le piège de Méduse* around 1898 in collaboration with Dépaquit, though this play did not surface (in one-act form with Satie credited as sole author) until 1913. Although the complete text of *Jack in the Box* is now lost, the work was performed

---

[68] Letter of 14 March 1899, cited in Ornella Volta (ed.), *Erik Satie: Correspondance presque complète*. Paris: Fayard/IMEC, 2/2003, p. 89.

[69] Ibid., p. 83; 'tout cela n'est pas drôle; pour ma part, je commence à en avoir le dos rempli outre mesure: crevaison de faim, gousset desséché, ne me font aucun plaisir. Fatigué et anémié, je vois la misère, cette vieille garce, augmenter à vue d'œil, même de bœuf ou de veau; tandis qu'un calcul enfantin, comme la plupart des calculs, du reste, me fait agréablement apercevoir avec une exquise précision, que toutes ces choses tourneront fatalement pour moi, peut-être pour tout le monde. [...] Avis au destinataire: Je travaille avec Dépaquit à une pantomime qui doit passer à la Comédie parisienne en octobre prochain. Détails suivent.'

on 29 November 1937 in its original version with Dépaquit's play at the Salle d'Iéna, Paris, as part of an evening entitled 'L'Humour d'Erik Satie'. Enough survives of Dépaquit's text to suggest that there are indeed some connections between *Jack in the Box* and *Le piège de Méduse*.

It is worth pausing to reflect on the English title. Satie's mother, who died when he was six years old, was Scottish, and a very small number of documents show that the composer understood English reasonably well. When the Satie family moved from Honfleur to Paris after the 1870 Franco-Prussian War, Alfred Satie found work as a translator, first for the Foreign Ministry and later for an insurance company.[70] A letter from Erik to Conrad Satie dated 22 January 1899, written shortly after the composer's move to Arcueil and around the time he composed *Jack in the Box*, starts by commenting on his new neighbour in an entertaining mixture of English and French: 'Mon Home me convient suffisamment, la place y est grande. En face, je vois un cottage appartenant à un lord de la contrée faisant profession de maître maçon. Ce travailleur modeste, qui a su économiser quelques pences et un plus grand nombre de shillings sans qu'on le lui apprît, est père d'une jeune miss, digne et jolie comme un lady.' (Satie's Arcueil home was far from 'large' – it was a single room without private facilities – and his stonemason neighbour is most unlikely to have been a 'country lord'!)

Man Ray, who met Satie in the early 1920s, confirmed that Satie spoke some English. He described the composer in this period as 'A strange voluble little man in his fifties' who approached the artist in a gallery where his work was being exhibited. Man Ray continued: 'I was tired with the preparations of the opening, the gallery had no heat, I shivered and said in English that I was cold. He replied in English, took my arm, and led me out of the gallery to a corner café, where he ordered hot grogs. Introducing himself as Erik Satie, he relapsed into French, which I informed him I did not understand. With a twinkle in his eye he said it did not matter. We had a couple of additional grogs; I began to feel warm and lightheaded.' The connection between Man Ray and Satie led to a set of charming photographs of the composer – one with a wonderfully cheeky expression – and their drinking session in the corner café was followed, according to Man Ray, by a chance visit to 'a shop where various household utensils were spread out in front. I picked up a flatiron, the kind used on coal stoves, asked Satie to come inside with me, where, with his help, I acquired a box of tacks and a tube of glue. Back at the gallery I glued a row of tacks to the smooth surface of the iron, titled it The Gift, and added it to the exhibition. This was my first Dada object in France.'[71]

Satie described *Jack in the Box* as a 'suite anglaise', a 'pantomime' or a

---

[70] Orledge, 'The Musical Activities of Alfred Satie and Eugénie Satie-Barnetche', p. 272.

[71] Man Ray, *Self Portrait*. Boston: Little, Brown & Company, 1963, pp. 96–9.

'cloonerie' (reflecting the French attempt to pronounce 'clown'). His hope that this collaboration with Dépaquit would be performed at the Comédie-Parisienne in October 1899 was sadly not to come to fruition. This theatre, originally the foyer of the enormous Eden-Théâtre, existed under the name Comédie-Parisienne only from 1894 to 1899; its most famous premiere performance was Oscar Wilde's *Salomé* in 1896. By 1899, the theatre was in a physically precarious state, not least because demolition work was being carried out around it, and the building was completely renovated that year and reopened as the larger Théâtre de l'Athénée. It is likely, therefore, that plans to perform *Jack in the Box* at the Comédie-Parisienne were scuppered because of the renovation work.

Jules Dépaquit is one of few people with whom Satie stayed in touch, on and off, for almost all of his working life. Satie's song *Un dîner à l'Elysée* was published in a volume of *Chansons d'humour* in 1903, illustrated by Dépaquit;[72] on 24 October 1909, Satie's friends Vincent Hyspa, Paulette Darty and Dépaquit participated in a festival in Arcueil;[73] and Dépaquit published (with Hyspa) an 'ouvrage fantaisiste' *L'éponge en porcelaine* with Editions de La Sirène in 1921. (Its title, *The Porcelain Sponge*, has a paradoxical flavour shared with many of Satie's titles.) In the same year, Dépaquit also illustrated an edition of Max Jacob's play *Matorel en province*: Satie was acquainted with Jacob and composed *musique d'ameublement* for a play by him in the same period.[74] Satie and Dépaquit must have been in very regular contact during the gestation of *Jack in the Box*. Volta mentions that Satie's 'working method required almost daily, and exclusive, contact with the author who was working with him'[75] and Whiting notes that, as Dépaquit habitually worked while drinking in bistros, it is probable that Satie joined him.[76]

La Sirène published a number of works by Satie and associates of his including Cocteau and members of Les Six, and, indeed, Pascal Fouché states that 'the catalogue advertised a long series of works which would never come out: among others [...] *Motifs lumineux*, piano pieces by Erik Satie illustrated by Jules Dépaquit which could have included the three gigues written by Satie for *Jack in the Box*, a "cloonerie" by Dépaquit which Cocteau thought about publishing'.[77] Ornella Volta reproduces

---

[72] Volta (ed.), *Correspondance*, p. 107.

[73] Ibid., p. 130.

[74] The play is *Ruffian toujours, truand jamais* (1920): see Chapter 4 for details of this collaboration.

[75] Volta, 'Erik Satie: l'os à moelle', p. 18: 'sa méthode de travail exigeait une collaboration presque quotidienne, et exclusive, avec l'auteur qui travaillait avec lui'.

[76] Whiting, *Satie the Bohemian*, p. 173.

[77] Pascal Fouché, *La Sirène*. Paris: Bibliothèque de littérature française contemporaine de l'Université Paris 7, 1984, pp. 100–2; 'le catalogue

the proposed front cover of this score[78] and states that 'A sketch, drawn by Cocteau, seems to prove that Satie thought about publishing *Jack in the Box* (from his sketches?) around 1918–19. In this sketch, made for «l'Edition musicale de La Sirène, 12 bis rue de La Boétie», this title is supposed to designate an "English suite for piano duet".'[79] The simple front cover gives *Jack in the Box* the subtitle 'croquemitaine', denoting a bogeyman, an evil personage whose role is to scare children into behaving better.

The publication history of *Jack in the Box* is unusually complex. It is strange that Satie did not register the music with the French copyright society SACEM until 1905 and then lost track of the manuscript, believing he had left it on a bus. The score was only rediscovered after Satie's death (which is why Volta assumes that the projected 1918–19 publication would have drawn on his sketches): he had put it in the pocket of one of his velvet suits. The year 1905 marks the beginning of Satie's study at the Schola Cantorum and his change of image from bohemian corduroy suits to the 'uniform' of a civil servant. Satie apparently stated in the early twentieth century that he could no longer look at velvet, even in a painting ('ne pouvant plus voir le velours même en peinture') and, while he kept his old corduroy suits, he did not use them.[80] The resulting published score has three movements, each described as a 'gigue': a Prelude, an Entr'acte and a Final. This score is for solo piano rather than piano duet, although it would be easier to play if arranged for two performers. After Satie's death, it was orchestrated by Milhaud in 1926 for a ballet by George Balanchine, with sets and costumes by André Derain, which was produced for the Ballets Russes season, and the orchestrated version was published by Universal three years later.

Satie's beautifully calligraphed title page (Fig. 1.3) describes it as a 'pièce en deux actes', which explains why the published score has three movements including an Entr'acte. The title page features his name and address in the bottom left-hand corner.

prévoit toute une série d'ouvrages qui ne verront jamais le jour: entre autres [...] *Motifs lumineux*, pièces pour piano d'Erik Satie illustrées par Jules Dépaquit qui aurait peut-être inclus les trois gigues écrites par Satie pour *Jack in the Box* «cloonerie» de Dépaquit que Cocteau envisagea d'éditer'.

[78] In *L'ymagier d'Erik Satie*. Paris: Van de Velde, 1979, p. 43.

[79] Volta (ed.), *Correspondance*, p. 1111; 'Une maquette, dessinée par Cocteau, prouverait cependant que Satie avait songé à publier *Jack in the Box* (à partir de ses brouillons?) dès les années 1918–19. Dans cette maquette, établie pour «l'Edition musicale de La Sirène, 12 bis rue de La Boétie», ce titre est censé désigner une «suite anglaise pour piano à quatre mains».'

[80] Volta (ed.), *L'ymagier*, p. 43.

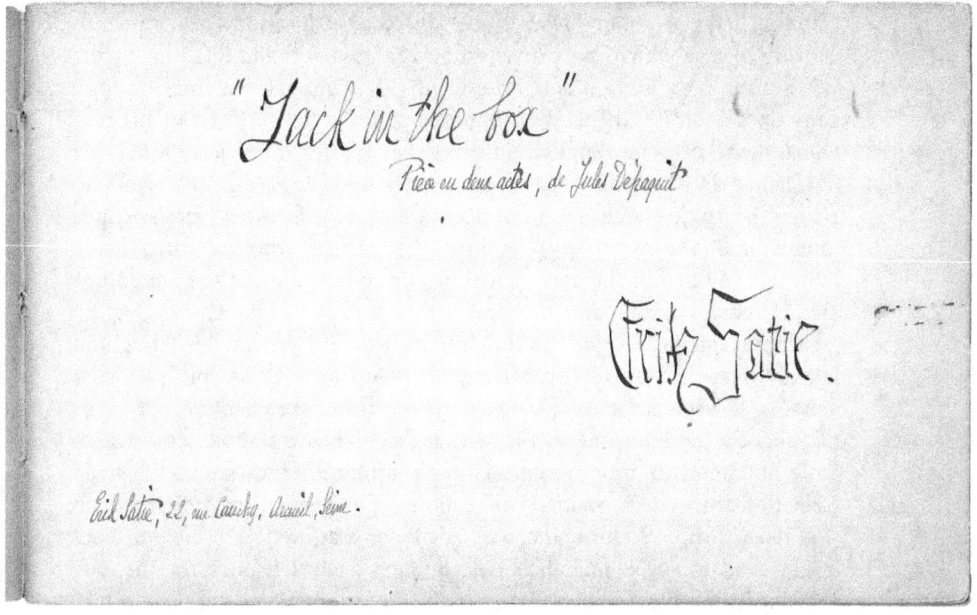

Fig. 1.3 Satie's title page for *Jack in the Box* (Erik Satie papers, bMS Mus 193 (28), Houghton Library, Harvard University)

The plot of *Jack in the Box*, if one might dignify it with that title, is summarised by Steven Moore Whiting after a description by Francis Jourdain, who knew Satie in this period:

> the curtain was to rise on a character who bites his fingernails, rummages fruitlessly amongst his files, closes the file drawer, and then counts to 100,000! Thereupon a second character was supposed to enter and, in a stunning display of clairvoyance, assert, 'Monsieur, you have just bitten your fingernails, rummaged amongst your files, and after having closed this drawer, counted to 100,000.' 'But Monsieur, how could you have guessed ...?' 'Monsieur, I was behind this door and watched you through the keyhole.' Jourdain goes on to relate the following subplot: 'During the five acts [sic] of the drama, a strange, mysterious fellow went back and forth across the back of the stage, his arms loaded with clocks. Why? The key to the enigma was presented only at the end of the last scene: the man so burdened was a clock-maker.[81]

Incidentally, while Jourdain's stated duration of *Jack in the Box* might suggest that this is a very long work, play texts published in the *Chat noir* journal in the 1890s strongly hint that it may in fact have been very short. For instance, a tribute to Charles Cros published on 4 July 1891 features

---

[81] Whiting, *Satie the Bohemian*, pp. 247–8. Whiting cites Francis Jourdain, *Né en 76*. Paris: Les Editions du Pavillon, 1951, p. 248 note 5.

unpublished poems and *Les surprises du cocuage*, a parody of eighteenth-century theatre which is a very short 'drama in 4 acts and one line' by the late author.[82] Its longest act – the third – has only eleven lines, though Cros does indicate different sumptuous settings for each act of his play, whose location is the English embassy. For his revival of *Jack in the Box* performed by the troupe Rideau de Paris at Salle d'Iéna, Paris on 29 November 1937, Marcel Herrand notes that six performers were engaged (one woman and five men) plus 'little "Gribisches" who saw furniture in half, put goldfish in the stew, put shoes on to roast, sit on the pendulum, etc.'.[83] Slapstick and magic tricks were thus also part of the show.

Many sketches for *Jack in the Box* are now housed in the Houghton Library, Harvard University, almost all using both the treble and bass stave as if written for the piano. However, these sketches are not easily playable on the instrument, suggesting that they are a short score which Satie intended to orchestrate. A small number of these sketches do indeed feature instrumental indications, for instance material which was used in the 'Prélude' includes 'Violons, Clar[inette] en la' and 'Petit bugle' next to some melodic lines. Some sketches feature fragmentary texts in Satie's hand which were surely connected to Dépaquit's odd tale; it is not clear whether Satie may have been the co-author of these texts. (None of these texts feature reference to a man counting, another looking through a keyhole, or to a clockmaker burdened with his wares!) One of these texts, which appears below sketches for the second movement, is 'Marche sourde des Repasseurs de couteaux, des Tireurs de chenilles, et des Casseurs de briques' (Deaf march of the Knife ironers, the Silk spinners, and the Brick breakers)[84] – a Satiean trio of occupations whose title recalls Alphonse Allais' entirely silent *Marche Funèbre composée pour les Funérailles d'un grand homme sourd* (Funereal March composed for the Funeral of a great deaf man; 1897). A second 'Marche sourde' text, this time devoted to more violent occupations, appears next to another sketch and is followed by blank staves; this may have happened purely by chance, or could the blank space signify the 'deaf march'?:

> Marche sourde de hordes de Coupe-Jarrets, d'Ecorcheurs, de Fanatiques, d'Incendiaires, d'Eventreurs, de Vagabonds et de Pillards.

---

[82] *Chat noir*, p. 1775.

[83] Marcel Herrand, 'L'humour d'Erik Satie', *Le Figaro*, 23 November 1937, p. 5: 'les petits «gribiches» qui scieront les meubles, mettront les poissons rouges dans le pot-au-feu, feront rôtir les souliers, s'assiéront sur la pendule, etc.'. 'Gribische' is a Norman dialect word meaning 'wicked woman', though the word also has several other meanings: it can signify a graphical or numerical representation of an object, or an original manuscript.

[84] Erik Satie papers (MS Mus 193, 59). Houghton Library, Harvard University.

Assassins – Coupe-Jarrets
Ecorcheurs
Eventreurs
Incendiaires
Pillards
Spadassins

[Deaf march of hordes of Leg-Breakers, Swindlers, Fanatics, Fire-raisers, Gutters, Vagabonds and Looters. Assassins – Leg-Breakers/ Swindlers/ Gutters/ Fire-raisers/ Looters/ Swordsmen]

It is unclear whether these texts are linked to *Jack in the Box*. Satie was keen to save paper and used his notebooks for different purposes, and in the absence of Dépaquit's complete text it is impossible to know for sure whether the gory goings-on are related to the play. But another fragment of text, 'L'orgue de barbarie du compère Wegg le fou', is more obviously linked to the collaboration because it appears next to a music extract which is the first draft of the opening of the Entr'acte (Ex. 1.2). The dotted rhythms evoke a wheezy squeezebox being pulled and pushed, and even the heavy block chords in the bass would be easy to realise on an accordion, where one finger pressed on a left-hand button can produce a triad or seventh chord. The sketch (Ex. 1.2a) suggests that Satie knew at an early stage that he wanted to introduce an irregular rhythmic grouping into the otherwise four-square repetitive structure, but he was initially unsure how to notate this. Ex. 1.2b shows that his solution was to introduce a 3/4 bar as the irregular element, suggesting a faulty mechanism.

Who is 'the boss, the madman Wegg' who owns a barrel organ? I believe this is a reference to the character Silas Wegg in Charles Dickens' last novel *Our Mutual Friend* (1864–5). Silas Wegg is a ballad seller who has a wooden leg, which for many other characters renders him only part human.[85] In the novel, the socially ambitious Podsnap family seek 'a well-conducted automaton to come and play quadrilles for a carpet dance' for a party in their home (shades of Napoleon's parties at Compiègne): perhaps a reference to a barrel organ, though the novel keeps us in suspense as to whether the performer is a mechanism or a human being, as Dickens refers to the player on three occasions as 'the discreet automaton'. Katherine Inglis highlights, in terms which resonate with Satie's former employment as a café pianist: 'The musician is effectively a commodity. He has been purchased at the music shop just as an automaton would have been purchased, and is fixed in a single position just as an automaton is fixed to a box within which its mechanism is concealed. Constraint characterises Dickens's musician, who like even the most sophisticated automata-musicians, can only perform the sequence

---

[85] Chapter 3 will expand on the importance of the wooden head to Satie.

Ex. 1.2 (a) Satie, *Jack in the Box*: sketch 'L'orgue de barbarie du compère Wegg le fou'; (b) Satie, *Jack in the Box*: opening of 'Entr'acte'

he has been hired/programmed to play.'[86] This deliberate mystification of the 'real' identity of the performer is commonplace with mechanical instruments: Carolyn Abbate points out that 'In the eighteenth century, music machines were often given android form, whether or not the puppet actually played an instrument (true automata) or mimed performing while music was played by a hidden mechanism (false automata).'[87]

---

[86] Katherine Inglis, 'Becoming Automatous: Automata in *The Old Curiosity Shop* and *Our Mutual Friend*.' *Interdisciplinary Studies in the Long Nineteenth Century*, 6 (2008), www.19.bbk.ac.uk.

[87] Abbate, 'Outside Ravel's Tomb', p. 488.

The few instrumental indications in Satie's sketches for *Jack in the Box* leave open the question whether the music was to be performed by mechanical means. Although the short score is not easily playable by a human pianist, it would pose no difficulties to a player piano – an instrument in its infancy when Satie composed his music – or a barrel organ. Much of the sinister quality of Dickens' musician in *Our Mutual Friend* lies in the slippery uncertainty of his identity: is he human, a machine, or (queasiest of all) something in between? Inglis notes that a well-known illustration for *Our Mutual Friend*, Marcus Stone's 'Podsnappery', shows 'the musician is literally fading into the background and melting into his piano. It is difficult to discern where his hands end and his piano begins, as if he is not distinct from the instrument. He is starting to disappear.' Music which is based on repeated mechanistic blocks can be perceived as sinister because it exists on the border between human and machine – a border which we think should be solid, but which can be uncomfortably porous.

If this single reference to 'L'orgue de barbarie du compère Wegg le fou' does indeed refer to Dickens' character, it is not difficult to understand why the novel appealed to Satie, who had extensive experience as a musician for hire and whose music is often repetitive and yet always written for humans to perform. And Satie's close friend Debussy was also interested in Dickens: he made his own reference to a Dickens character in the ninth piece in his second book of piano *Préludes* (1912–13), 'Hommage à S. Pickwick Esq. P.P.M.P.C.'. This piece, which cites *God save the King*, references the name character of Dickens' *The Pickwick Papers* (1836).

Another reference to a barrel organ appears on the same page as sketches for *Jack in the Box*:

> For a moment, everyone thinks he's going to play the game with the cork, using the one from the carafe.
>
> The door opens: the Gentleman and Lady enter without noticing the bear. They seem to think that people are playing a party game – not an amusing one, either.
>
> They are surprised to see everyone climbing everything that is climbable. They have come to ask the young lady's hand in marriage for their son – and they move towards the Lady, greet her and compliment her.
>
> He has come to flirt with the young lady, because he intends to marry her himself.
>
> Completely overwhelmed, the Lady tries to explain the situation to everyone.
>
> As soon as they see the bear, the poor people, deeply scared, immediately clamber on all the furniture and stick themselves on the ceiling. The panic is at its height. When will this all end?

But the Bear Tamer has moved towards the window and opened it. He reappears with a barrel organ.

This animal doesn't recognise his master any more.

Straight away, the bear dances, even having the cheek to smile.[88]

I proposed elsewhere that this text may have been an early draft of some ideas used in *Le piège de Méduse*: a bourgeois domestic setting where people behave oddly, a marriage proposal and a dancing animal are all features of Satie's play.[89] This also backs up Volta's belief that Dépaquit and Satie may have written an initial version of *Le piège de Méduse* together. And Jules Dépaquit was sufficiently interested in the barrel organ to dedicate a poem to the instrument; 'L'orgue de barbarie' was published in 1911.[90]

While there is an English connection through the title of *Jack in the Box* and its probable Dickens connection, the rhythmic language of Satie's surviving music suggests a more specifically Scottish link. The jig is, of course, a Scottish dance form and all three movements are jigs featuring a characteristic dotted rhythm. I have already mentioned that Satie's mother, née Jane Leslie Anton, was Scottish, though it is Satie's friend Debussy who offered the composer a musical rather than familial Scottish connection. Debussy received one of his strangest commissions in 1890 from an American general of Scottish heritage, Meredith Read, who asked for a work based on an ancestral theme. Debussy initially gave

---

[88] Sketch located in the Satie collection of Houghton Library, Harvard University and reprinted in Volta (ed.), *Satie Ecrits*, p. 151: 'Pendant un instant, tous s'imaginent qu'il va jouer au bouchon avec celui de la carafe. ¶ La porte s'ouvre: le Gentleman et la Lady pénètrent sans remarquer l'ours. Ils ont l'air de croire que l'on joue à un jeu de société – peu amusant, du reste. ¶ Ils sont surpris de voir toute la compagnie grimpée sur tout ce qui est grimpable. Ils viennent demander la main de la jeune fille pour leur fils – et se dirigent vers la Dame, la saluent et lui font des compliments. ¶ Il est venu flirter avec la jeune fille – car il a l'intention de l'épouser lui-même. ¶ Complètement ahurie, la Dame essaie de leur expliquer la situation. ¶ Dès qu'ils voient l'ours, les pauvres gens, pris d'une frousse intense, escaladent aussitôt tous les meubles et vont s'accrocher au plafond. La panique est à son comble. Quand tout cela finira-t-il? ¶ Mais le Montreur d'Ours a pu gagner la fenêtre et l'ouvrir. Il réapparaît avec un orgue de Barberie [sic]. ¶ Cet animal ne reconnaît plus son bon Maître. ¶ L'ours danse immédiatement, ayant même le culot de sourire.'

[89] Potter, 'Satie as Poet, Playwright and Composer', in Potter (ed.), *Erik Satie*, pp. 67–84.

[90] Published in *Les veillées du Lapin Agile, Scènes de la vie de Montmartre*, preface by Francis Carco. Paris: L'Edition Française Illustrée, 1919, p. 34. The poem begins as a Verlaine parody: 'C'est la musique incomprise/ Qui fait vomir et qui grise/ Et qui tue ...'

the resulting piece the imposing title *Marche des Anciens Comtes de Ross, Dédiée à leur Descendant le Général Meredith Read, Grand-Croix de l'Ordre Royal du Rédempteur*, though it is better known as *Marche écossaise*. The work was published in versions for piano solo and piano duet in 1891 and orchestrated in 1908.[91] Marie Rolf speculates that Read may have covered the costs of production as well as a commission fee, not least because there is an unusually elaborate preface to the score:

> L'origine des Comtes de Ross, Chef du Clan de Ross/ en Rossshire, Ecosse, remonte aux temps les plus reculés./ Le chef était entouré par une bande des 'Bagpipers' qui/ jouaient cette Marche devant leur 'Lord' avant et pendant/ la bataille et aussi aux jours de gala. La Marche primitive/ est le choeur de la Marche actuelle.
>
> [The origin of the Earls of Ross, chief[s] of the Ross clan in Rossshire, Scotland, goes back to the most remote times. The earl was surrounded by a band of 'bagpipers' who used to play this march in front of their 'Lord' before and during battle, and also on festival days. The original march [melody] is the refrain of the current march.][92]

Robert Orledge points out that 'In 1924, Erik Satie echoed this phrase when he wrote "L'origine des Satie remonte, peut-être, aux temps les plus reculés" ("The origin of the Saties goes back, perhaps, to the most remote times") in "Recoins de ma vie: L'origine des Satie".'[93] We know that Debussy and Satie met on the Montmartre scene around 1889 and remained friends until the success of Satie's ballet *Parade* troubled their relationship in 1917. There is compelling evidence for a Satie link to *Marche écossaise*: Debussy offered the manuscript of the theme to Satie, surely in honour of his friend's part-Scottish origins.[94] Debussy's heading of this manuscript, including his signature, is copied by Satie on the reverse side of the score.

Satie, as we have seen, tends to introduce flaws into otherwise mechanical structures and passages. In *Jack in the Box*, two different types of 'flaw' are present. Steven Moore Whiting notes that 'In composing the score to *Jack in the Box*, Satie set for himself a task much like those given him by Hyspa. He harmonized tunes of decidedly popular character

---

[91] See Marie Rolf's informative and entertaining article 'General Meredith Read and Claude Debussy's *Marche écossaise*.' *Musical Quarterly*, vol. 95 nos. 2–3 (Summer–Fall 2012): pp. 252–98.

[92] Ibid., p. 272; translation by Marie Rolf.

[93] Ibid., p. 295 note 117. Satie's ironic biographical note was first published as 'Mémoires d'un amnésique' in *Les Feuilles libres*, vol. 6 no. 35 (January–February 1924), p. 329.

[94] The manuscript is now owned by the Musée des Lettres et des Manuscrits, 222 boulevard Saint-Germain, 75007 Paris.

Ex. 1.3 Satie, *Jack in the Box*, Final: bars 23–34

as if they were *objets trouvés,* but in a manner far more extravagant than Hyspa (or probably he himself) would have found appropriate for cabaret chansons.'[95] More precisely, Satie's tunes in *Jack in the Box* are simple – in the sense that they are four-square and based around repetitive rhythmic figures and a small number of notes – but his harmonisation introduces deliberate dissonance, registral dislocation and other complications. Ex. 1.3, from the final movement, also shows Satie varying his simple material by introducing classic variation techniques such as increased rhythmic elaboration.

The second type of 'flaw' is the disruption of a regular rhythm. This happens in all three movements: all of the music is in 2/4, but in every movement Satie introduces a 3/4 bar. It is as if he wants dancers to get used to a regular rhythm and then trip over their feet at the unexpected change of metre. This surprise element could explain something which otherwise is a mystery – the title *Jack in the Box*. In the absence of Dépaquit's complete text, there is nothing to explain why this title was chosen, but the unexpected introduction of triple metre bars in a 2/4 context provides the surprise element which is essential to the children's toy: the music proceeds mechanically and therefore predictably, when suddenly a surprise pops out to the ear (Ex. 1.4):

[95] Whiting, *Satie the Bohemian*, p. 250.

Ex. 1.4 Satie, *Jack in the Box*: Prélude, bars 17–24

The circus

Another popular form of entertainment which had an impact on Satie was the circus. Perhaps the best-known circus in Paris in his time was the Cirque Médrano, which was located on the southern fringe of Montmartre at 63 boulevard Rochechouart, on the corner of rue des Martyrs. Founded in 1872, it was originally known as Cirque Fernando; its jugglers, riders and acrobats were immortalised by artists including Degas, Toulouse-Lautrec and Renoir. The original owner was bought out in 1897 by the clown known as 'Boum-Boum', whose real name was Geronimo Médrano, hence the change of name. The best-known clowns of the age, the Fratellini brothers, were engaged at the Cirque Médrano from 1915 to 1923, and today the name Médrano is still used by a touring circus.

Circus performers, like street or café performers, were figures at the margins of society whose livelihood was precarious. Humans and animals would perform together, just as barrel organ performers were often accompanied by a dancing bear or monkey. Music associated with circuses was popular, loud, repetitive and mechanical: as a roundabout whirls round and round, the music accompanying it is similar, rotating constantly through a set playlist until the machine comes to a standstill. Satie's *Jack in the Box* could be seen as circus music in this sense: its three sections are virtually identical in character and tempo, all being in perpetual motion and with unvarying dynamic levels and rhythmic figures. As in many of his works in three parts from the *Gymnopédies* until the end of his career, Satie here shows himself to be unconcerned with variety in a multi-movement structure.

Picasso was obsessed with the theme of travelling circus performers during his so-called 'rose' period around 1904–6 – well before he met Satie and collaborated with him on *Parade* in 1916–17 – and he was a regular attender of the Cirque Médrano. Paintings inspired by this theme include *The Hurdy-Gurdy Man* (1905): an old circus performer in a worn Harlequin outfit is seated with a barrel organ on his lap, and a younger Harlequin sits by him. *Parade*, Satie's collaboration with Picasso, the Ballets Russes and Jean Cocteau, shows Satie engaging directly with the circus theme, as does a proposed Cocteau collaboration *Cinq grimaces* (for which only Satie produced anything). Deborah Menaker Rothschild writes: 'Even before he met Picasso, who also subscribed to these beliefs, Cocteau had adopted his fellow-poet, Apollinaire's point of view. Apollinaire believed Western culture's most cherished forms were born in the street and that the basis of Western "high" culture derived from the soul of the common people. In line with this view, Apollinaire often conflated in his poetry the elevated, classical and erudite with the base, sleazy and vulgar.'[96] Although Satie and Apollinaire were never close personally and did not work together on a project, their artistic identities are strikingly similar, as will be explored in more depth in Chapter 2.

Cocteau showed a great deal of interest in the concepts of the circus and music hall, though he was less enthusiastic about actually visiting them. He did, however, attend local popular entertainment including the Foire de Montmartre and Cirque Médrano with friends from Les Six. In his polemical tract *Le coq et l'arlequin* (1918; dedicated to Auric, who was then still a teenager) he raised up Satie as an ideal musical role model for young composers and promoted the circus and music hall as ideal sources of inspiration. Indeed, the fourteen-year-old Auric was the author of one of the first extensive published articles on Satie's music, 'Erik Satie: musicien humoriste', which appeared in *Revue française de musique* on 10 December 1913. Cocteau was attracted to popular entertainment as a 'real', unpolished and unmediated source: 'Music hall, circus, American black orchestras, these enrich an artist just as life does. Using the emotions provoked by this form of entertainment does not amount to making art after other art [one of Cocteau's bugbears]. These spectacles are not art. They excite us in the same way as machines, animals, landscapes, danger.'[97]

Cocteau would therefore not have agreed with Roland-Manuel's appraisal of the impact of the circus on Satie. Roland-Manuel was a composer who was sometimes referred to as the seventh member of Les Six, as their music often appeared on the same concert programmes; he was close to both Ravel and Satie, and wrote a biographical sketch

---

[96] Deborah Menaker Rothschild, *Picasso's 'Parade.'* New York: Sotheby's Publications/The Drawing Center, 1991, p. 44.

[97] Jean Cocteau, *Le coq et l'arlequin*. Paris: Editions de La Sirène, 1918, p. 34; 'Le music-hall, le cirque, les orchestres américains de nègres, tout cela féconde un artiste au même titre que la vie. Se servir des émotions que de tels spectacles éveillent ne revient pas à faire de l'art d'après art. Ces spectacles ne sont pas de l'art. Ils excitent comme les machines, les animaux, les paysages, le danger.'

of Satie as early as 1916. Here, Roland-Manuel uses his contemporary Henri Bergson's definition of the comic formula of laughter in a sophisticated analysis of humour in Satie: 'This rupture of equilibrium, this *mechanical encrusted on the living* – as Henri Bergson excellently said – these grimaces, these disarticulations precisely constitute the everyday practices of the circus, that must be considered as superior aesthetic entertainment.'[98] Roland-Manuel understood that circus humour is often rooted in the performance of everyday actions which are disrupted: the man walking who is hit by a plank, slips on a banana skin or drops a heavy load. While Bergson would not have agreed that popular entertainment was 'superior', his reference to the mechanical as a key element of humour is central to an understanding of Satie's music.[99] In many pieces – *Jack in the Box* is only one example – Satie sets up a regularly repeating rhythm which, with no preparation, is altered and put out of joint, like a musical slip on a banana skin. Ann-Marie Hanlon highlights that 'Bergson describes how comedy is created through the "mechanical inelasticity" or "rigidity of momentum" of repetition.'[100] Bergson mentions the jack in the box toy as an example of comic repetition, and repetition is indeed a prominent feature of the three movements of Satie's *Jack in the Box*.

Darius Milhaud's splendidly evocative memoir of the period post-World War I describes outings with Cocteau and his fellow members of Les Six in Montmartre: they regularly dined together at his flat on Saturday nights. He wrote:

> After dinner, attracted by the steam-driven roundabouts, mysterious shops, the Girl from Mars, shooting galleries, lottery wheels, the animals, the racket of the mechanical organs with perforated card rolls which seemed to implacably and simultaneously grind together all the music hall and revue refrains, we went to the Foire de Montmartre, and sometimes to the Médrano circus to attend the

---

[98] [Alexis] Roland-Manuel, *Erik Satie. Causerie faite à la Société Lyre et Palette, le 18 Avril 1916*. Paris: Roberge, 1916, p. 6: 'Cette rupture d'équilibre, ce *Mécanique plaqué sur du vivant* – comme l'a dit excellemment Henri Bergson – ces grimaces, ces désarticulations constituent justement les procédés ordinaires du Cirque, qu'il faut considérer comme le divertissement esthétique supérieur.'

[99] See Ann-Marie Hanlon's chapter for a penetrating analysis of this topic: 'Erik Satie and the Meaning of the Comic', in Caroline Potter (ed.), *Erik Satie: Music, Art and Literature*. Farnham: Ashgate, 2013, pp. 19–48.

[100] Bergson, *Laughter*, pp. 12–13; cited in Ann-Marie Hanlon, 'Satie and the French Musical Canon: A Reception Study' (2 vols). Unpublished PhD thesis, University of Newcastle, 2013, vol. 1 p. 179.

Fratellini shows which demonstrated so much imagination and poetry that they were worthy of commedia dell'arte performers.[101]

(The 'Girl from Mars' had a fabulously extended neck.)

The *fête foraine* was an annual event in most French towns, though Milhaud mentions a weekly fair in Montmartre. The entertainment in Montmartre included a shooting gallery, where 'one tried to hit targets adorning a series of little cupboards. When the player succeeded, the doors of the cupboard opened and out popped tiny dolls that danced or performed a simple scene to the accompaniment of a music box. Such a game may have inspired the title of Satie's *Jack in the Box*, written for a pantomime by Jules Dépaquit.'[102]

The circus tent at the *fête foraine* was, judging by Nancy Perloff's description, even closer to a work composed by Satie, in this case *Parade*, his collaboration with Picasso, Cocteau and Massine:

> Each afternoon several clowns, some dancers and acrobats, and a group of small animals including ponies and monkeys advertised the evening programme at the circus by executing a few brief scenes on a small platform called the *parade*. The performance, also known as the *parade*, was accompanied by a brassy orchestra [...] Then the orchestra struck up a boisterous march and some of the spectators approached the ticket counter while others wandered off to another fair booth which may also have featured a *parade*.[103]

---

[101] Darius Milhaud, *Ma vie heureuse*. Paris: René Julliard, 1949, p. 112: 'Après le dîner, attirés par les manèges à vapeur, les boutiques mystérieuses, la Fille de mars, les tirs, les loteries, les ménageries, le vacarme des orgues mécaniques à rouleaux perforés qui semblaient moudre implacablement et simultanément tous les flonflons de music-hall et de revues, nous allions à la Foire de Montmartre, et quelquefois au Cirque Médrano pour assister aux sketchs des Fratellini qui dénotaient tant d'imagination et de poésie qu'ils étaient dignes de la commedia dell'arte.' The 'Martian girl' or 'Girl from the Moon' was a regular attraction at fairs: '"La Femme Lunaire" appelée aussi "La Fille de Mars" eut un succès considérable, on se pressait en d'interminables files d'attente devant sa baraque. On voyait à l'intérieur dans un joli cabinet très éclairé, une jeune femme assise ayant des ailes et un cou extensible de plusieurs mètres de longueur au bout duquel "sa tête remue, parle, chante et mange". Cette "fille de Mars" était présentée par un bonisseur habile, il débitait un texte scientifique à la blague qui corsait adroitement l'attraction. Il faut dire que l'effet était saisissant, cette femme prenait des allures effrayantes de dinosaurien, elle paraissait être avec son cou démesuré un spécimen attardé de brontosaure ou de quelques autres reptiles monstrueux de la préhistoire, tant l'illusion était parfaite.' (Excerpted from Jacques Garnier, *Forains d'hier et d'aujourd'hui*. Orléans: Jacques Garnier (chez l'auteur), 1968, pp. 68–9.)

[102] Perloff, *Art and the Everyday*, p. 30.

[103] Ibid., pp. 31–2.

In fact, the *parade* itself was an anachronism by the early twentieth century (Jeffrey Weiss points out that legal restrictions on parade entertainment were brought in as early as the 1840s) and 'the true *parade* seems to have been reduced to vestigial examples at the itinerant *fête foraine*. The *parade* sensibility, however, thrived as a form of commercial advertising, and the word itself enjoyed great currency as a figure of speech.'[104] The concept of music as promotional material for a main event which is happening elsewhere is oddly commonplace in Satie and shared by the café-concert, with its musical interludes between the acts of shadow plays, as well as the *fête foraine*. Music for the circus, or for its promotion, is popular in character (perhaps a dance form such as a march), simple in structure and repetitive – all of which is readily recognisable in Satie. And there are genuine links between this type of popular entertainment and *blague*, as 'the *fête foraine* was widely associated in the public imagination with promotionalism and hoax'.[105]

Deborah Menaker Rothschild encapsulates the connection between Satie's musical style, the cabaret and the wider artistic context of his time:

> Simple, unadorned, almost monotonous sound is the hallmark of [Satie's] style. [...] Satie's score for *Parade* has been dubbed 'Cubist' on the basis of the abrupt shifts in the music from one 'act' to another. While these disjunctions may be thought of as Cubist, they are also standard for music-hall evenings where one act follows rapidly on the heels of another, without any attempt at continuity. The quick shifts, discontinuity, coarse jokes and puns, and especially the violation of expectations that are part and parcel of the Cubist aesthetic were also characteristic of the cabarets where Satie entertained and where Picasso, Jacob, and Apollinaire often sat in the audience or participated. [...] At the Lapin Agile and the Closerie de Lilas, for example, it was not unusual for serious poetry readings to be interrupted by a boisterous song or joke.[106]

■ ■ ■

STREET music in Paris in the Belle Epoque had resonances that went far beyond a single performance at a specific moment. The individual performer was not celebrated or indeed known by name: this is a musical genre for which conventional performance qualities such as virtuosity, or a distinctive voice or style, were simply irrelevant. Many writers draw attention to the impersonal and yet affecting qualities of Satie's music, and I would say this is yet another factor his music has in common with barrel organ performance. Mechanical performance is inherently repetitive, measuring out time in short tunes which can be repeated as

---

[104] Weiss, *The Popular Culture of Modern Art*, p. 181.
[105] Ibid., pp. 180–1.
[106] Rothschild, *Picasso's 'Parade'*, p. 87.

often as desired, and this very repetition causes the music to retreat from the forefront of the listener's attention. While slight tempo fluctuation is inevitable in music controlled by a human turning a handle, a barrel organ performance should keep to a constant pulse as much as possible. Tempo fluctuations for expressive purposes indicated on the text are extremely rare in Satie and, in his earlier pieces especially, he is more likely to give a similar or identical tempo marking to each of a set of three pieces. His is a musical style where variety of texture, mood or tempo from one movement to another is not the most important factor.

While the barrel organ was a common sight on the streets of Paris in the late nineteenth century, this was also a period of great technological change which was reflected in the work of composers, poets and artists, as we will see in the next chapter. Mechanistic effects in contemporary music – including relentlessly repeated rhythms, the increased use of percussion and the employment of noise effects not previously associated with music – had a substantial impact on Satie and his musical and poetic contemporaries.

CHAPTER 2

Futurism, the New Avant-Garde and Mechanical Music

SATIE went through a crisis of creative confidence in the early twentieth century which prompted him to enrol in the Schola Cantorum in 1905 as a mature student. His friend Debussy strongly opposed the decision: 'At your age', he said, 'a leopard doesn't change his spots.'[1] While the first decade of the twentieth century is creatively a lean period for Satie, the techniques he learned at the Schola fed into his later music – and, unexpectedly, performances of his early works promoted by Ravel and others from 1911 made him more notorious than he had ever been. His music from his Schola period to the end of his life is multimedia, often collaborative, and marked both by his studies and by contemporary innovations. Satie contributed to many of the small-circulation art magazines of the period and was closely connected to the most innovative writers, composers and artists of his age. The knowingly modern turn of the new century, with its shiny new technology and inventions, resonated with Satie. The Italian futurist movement also had a high profile in Paris in the early twentieth century, communicating its ideas through multiple manifestos.

Innovation affected the creative world of Satie and his contemporaries, not least by giving rise to a consciously modernist movement which prized new, distinctly urban, sounds. In the first two decades of the twentieth century in Paris, cutting-edge music was indivisible from the other arts, especially literature and visual art. We encounter poets and musicians responding both to older mechanical instruments such as the barrel organ and to electricity, shiny newness and factories. However, the poetic themes of banality and the everyday – the relationship between the human being and the machine – remained constant, whether the machine were a barrel organ, a typewriter, an engine or a siren.

Satie's music should also be considered in the context of the many interart ideas and movements in Paris in the 1910s, many of which centred on Montparnasse. When, in this period, slum-clearance projects in Montmartre changed the character of the area, Montparnasse became more attractive as a meeting place. The café La Rotonde opened in 1911 and quickly became a favourite haunt of artists of all types. Round the corner from La Rotonde, an artists' studio at 6 rue Huyghens was reinvented during World War I as a venue for music, poetry and exhibitions of sculpture and painting, in the absence of more

[1] Cited in Ornella Volta (ed.), *Erik Satie: Correspondance presque complète*. Paris: Fayard/IMEC, 2/2003, p. 116.

conventional venues which had closed or curtailed their activities during the war. Some of the rue Huyghens events were promoted under the explicitly interart banner 'Lyre et Palette'.

Concepts relating to the simultaneous production of two or more different media or texts were also promoted by the Italian futurists, notably Filippo Tommaso Marinetti, and there was much polemical debate about different interpretations of the term 'simultanism' by authors including Apollinaire, the Italian futurists, and authors associated with the magazine *Poème et drame*.[2] The term could refer to a 'polyphony' of words (voices speaking different things together); this could incorporate other art forms, as in Blaise Cendrars' and Sonia Delaunay's poem/art work *La prose du transsibérien et de la petite Jehanne de France* (1913). These are works that can only truly exist as performance.[3] Simultanism could also relate to the typographical distribution of words on a page, pioneered by Mallarmé's *Un coup de dés* (1892) and theorised by Apollinaire in an article, 'Simultanéisme – librettisme' (1914), written for another short-lived art magazine, *Les Soirées de Paris*. In Apollinaire's own poems *Calligrammes* (1913–16), the shape of the text corresponds to its poetic theme.

Most significantly where Satie is concerned, Apollinaire's novella *Le roi lune* (1916) features multiple conversations and sounds. Marc Battier explains that 'He [Apollinaire] did not hide the fact that this idea came to him while listening to groups of friends engaged in lively discussions at the back of a Paris bistro, and that the crossing of voices created layers which were simultaneous but whose content was distinct.'[4] This ties

---

[2] In 1912 Henri-Martin Barzun (1881–1974), with Sébastien Voirol and Fernand Divoire, founded the magazine *Poème et drame*: simultanism is a prime focus, particularly in three essays: 'L'ère du drame' (1912), 'Du symbole au drame' (1913) and 'Voix, rythmes et chants simultanés' (1913). The last of these was considered by Apollinaire to be a manifesto for simultanism (see Apollinaire's article 'Simultanéisme – librettisme)'. Sébastien Voirol's multicoloured poetic response to Stravinsky's *Rite of Spring* (*Le sacre du printemps*, 1913) was published in *Poème et drame* no. 6 (September 1913).

[3] See Katherine Shingler, 'Visual and Verbal Encounters in Cendrars' and Delaunay's *La Prose du Transsibérien*.' *e-France: an on-line Journal of French Studies*, vol. 3 (2012), pp. 1–28, http://www.reading.ac.uk/web/FILES/modern-languages-and-european-studies/Katherine_Shingler_Visual_Encounters_in_Cendrars_and_Delaunays.pdf.

[4] Marc Battier, 'De la symphonie du monde à la symphonie de bruits.' *Filigrane*, 7 (2008), special number 'Musique et bruits' edited by Makis Solomos, full text available at http://revues.mshparisnord.org/filigrane/pdf/228.pdf; 'Il [Apollinaire] n'a pas caché que cette idée lui vint en écoutant les discussions animées de groupes d'amis au fond d'un bistrot parisien, et que le croisement des voix créait des couches simultanées mais au contenu différencié.'

in with Satie's concept of *musique d'ameublement* (furniture music), suggesting the concept may be linked to his past experience as a café pianist. However, Apollinaire and Satie did not meet until the *Parade* collaboration in 1917 and their personal relationship was never as close as their shared aesthetic concerns might suggest.

Music and noise: the Italian futurists

The Futurist Manifesto, written by the Italian poet Filippo Tommaso Marinetti (1876–1944), was published in the *Gazzetta dell'Emilia* in Bologna on 5 February 1909, then in French as 'Manifeste du futurisme' in *Le Figaro* on 20 February 1909.[5] The futurist movement was urban and dynamic, rejected the past and was a youth cult. Its antipathy to nineteenth-century Romanticism is clear:

> Literature having, until now, praised pensive immobility, ecstasy and sleep, we want to praise aggressive movement, feverish insomnia, gymnastic movements, daring jumps, the slap and the punch. We declare that the splendour of the world has been enriched by a new beauty: the beauty of speed. A racing car with a boot decorated with big pipes like snakes with explosive breath ... A roaring car, which looks like it's running on a hail of bullets, is more beautiful than the Winged Victory of Samothrace.[6]

Action, speed and aggression were, at least in theory, essential futurist characteristics. The later futurist synthetic theatre manifesto (18 February 1915), written by Marinetti in collaboration with Emilio Settimelli and Bruno Corra, used more explicitly bellicose language:

> As we await our much prayed-for great war, we Futurists carry our violent antineutralist action from city square to university and back again, using our art to prepare the Italian sensibility for the great hour of maximum danger. Italy must be fearless, eager, as swift and elastic as a fencer, as indifferent to blows as a boxer, as impassive at the news of a victory that may have cost fifty-thousand dead as at the news of a defeat. [...] We are convinced that mechanically, by force

---

[5] The French version of the manifesto can be seen at http://www.italianfuturism.org/manifestos/fondation-et-manifeste-du-futurisme/ (accessed 5 April 2015).

[6] 'La littérature ayant jusqu'ici magnifié l'immobilité pensive, l'extase et le sommeil, nous voulons exalter le mouvement agressif, l'insomnie fiévreuse, le pas gymnastique, le saut périlleux, la gifle et le coup de poing. Nous déclarons que la splendeur du monde s'est enrichie d'une beauté nouvelle la beauté de la vitesse. Une automobile de course avec son coffre orné de gros tuyaux tels des serpents à l'haleine explosive ... Une automobile rugissante, qui a l'air de courir sur de la mitraille, est plus belle que la Victoire de Samothrace.'

of brevity, we can achieve an entirely new theatre perfectly in tune with our swift and laconic Futurist sensibility. Our acts can also be moments only a few seconds long. With this essential and synthetic brevity the theatre can bear and even overcome competition from the cinema.[7]

The proto-fascism in this document was as far politically from the left-wing and anti-militarist Satie as can be imagined. And while brevity is a characteristic of almost all Satie's works, there is also a paradox at the heart of Satie which distances him from the futurist movement. Daniel Albright sums up the repetitive, mechanical aspects of Satie: 'What is the chief property of music? – to Satie, the answer was inertia.'[8] Mechanistic repetition, for Satie, is nothing to do with aggression or even dynamism, quite the opposite: the lulling regular rhythm of the three *Gymnopédies* is a long way from the brutality and gymnastic physical jerks praised by Marinetti. The essential reserve of Satie's musical aesthetic can also be linked to the advice Satie gave Debussy in 1891 about getting away from Wagner's influence. Cocteau recalled in 1920 that Satie had told Debussy: 'The orchestra should not grimace when characters enter on stage. Look. Do the trees on stage grimace? We should provide musical scenery, create a musical climate where characters can move and speak.'[9] Albright comments: 'Behind that remark lies a whole philosophy of music theatre: the music ought to be a rigid, immiscible background for the stage action, simply a sonorous equivalent to the cutout trees and two-dimensional houses. Theatre music should exercise discretion and tact, like any good piece of furniture.'

About the only thing Satie and Marinetti had in common was a willingness to draw on popular theatre, though Satie's long practical experience performing in café-concerts contrasts with Marinetti's essentially theoretical interest. Marinetti wrote yet another manifesto on 29 September 1913, this time on 'Variety Theatre': he praises the energy and dynamism of the brief 'turns' of the variety stage which draw on contemporary events, are often satirical and use new technology such as film. Of course, this is several years before Satie's ballet collaborations *Parade* (1917) and *Relâche* (1924), the latter featuring a film interlude.

---

[7] http://www.391.org/manifestos/19150218marinetti.htm (accessed 5 April 2015).

[8] Daniel Albright, *Untwisting the Serpent*. Chicago: University of Chicago Press, 2000, p. 192.

[9] Cocteau's 'Fragments d'une conférence sur Eric [sic] Satie' was written in 1920 but not published until 1924; *Revue musicale*, vol. 5 no. 5 (1 March 1924), pp. 217–23, at p. 221: 'Il faudrait, dit-il ... que l'orchestre ne grimace pas quand un personnage entre en scène. Regardez. Est-ce que les arbres du décor grimacent? Il faudrait faire un décor musical, créer un climat musical où les personnages bougent et causent.'

And in January 1924, Marinetti published a tract, *Le futurisme mondial*, in which Satie is mentioned as one of 'the creators of modernities, futurists without knowing it'.[10] This is a commonplace critical trope of the period, painting Satie as an amateur precursor.

While the Futurist Manifesto was not specifically related to music, the composer Francesco Balilla Pratella (1880–1955) joined the futurist movement in 1910 and wrote a *Manifesto of Futurist Musicians* in which he appealed to the young (as had Marinetti), because only they could understand what he had to say.[11] Pratella's musical theories are, to say the least, confused: he lumps Elgar, Sibelius, Richard Strauss, Debussy and the late Mussorgsky together as contemporary musical innovators (he writes 'In England, Edward Elgar is cooperating with our efforts to destroy the past by pitting his will to amplify classical symphonic forms, seeking richer ways of thematic development and multiform variations on a single theme'!). Pratella's main aim is, however, to attack the 'vegetating schools, conservatories and academies' of Italy. He calls on the public to reject the music, stage sets and costumes of the past and to embrace modernity, though he is curiously unspecific about the manner in which this should happen.

Moving beyond manifestos, the music of Italian futurist composers was becoming known in Paris in the 1910s. Critics drew parallels between Satie and the futurist movement, particularly Gaston Picard, who claimed in 1919 that Satie is a 'disciple of Socrates, and also a follower of Marinetti'.[12] Satie was always a composer willing to draw on anything which took his fancy, whether from the avant-garde or from the distant past. But while Satie was acquainted with Marinetti through the soirées of his future collaborator Valentine de Saint-Point, to term the composer 'a follower of Marinetti' is taking things too far.

The experimental theatre Art et Liberté devoted an evening of theatrical and musical performance to futurism on 17 February 1918, including a short play by Marinetti and music by Tommasini, Francesco Malipiero, Mario Castelnuovo-Tedesco, Ildebrando Pizzetti da Parma and Alfredo Casella.[13] As soon as these composers are viewed outside the context of an evening of experimental entertainment, it is hard to understand why any of them could have been considered revolutionary innovators. Casella

---

[10] Cited in Volta (ed.), *Correspondance*, p. 579; 'les créateurs de modernités, futuristes sans le savoir'.

[11] This document can be accessed in English translation at http://www.unknown.nu/futurism/musicians.html (accessed 5 April 2015); translator not credited.

[12] Gaston Picard, 'Une enquête sociale', *La Renaissance: Politique, littéraire, économique*, 30 August 1919, p. 8: 'Disciple de Socrate, il est aussi un adepte de M. Marinetti.'

[13] Michel Corvin, *Le théâtre de recherche entre les deux guerres: Le laboratoire art et action*. Lausanne: La Cité – L'Age d'Homme, 1976, p. 83.

is perhaps the best known of this group and is usually described as a neoclassical composer. Satie made a very rare analytical statement about another composer when he described Casella's music in 1918: 'the form is generally lacking in sincerity and he switches too easily from the style of Fauré to the style of Stravinsky'.[14]

Although less highly trained as a composer than Pratella (who composed a work entitled *Musica futurista* in 1913), Luigi Russolo (1883–1947) was ultimately a far more influential figure in the futurist musical debate. His manifesto *L'arte dei rumori* (*The Art of Noises*) (1913) rejected traditional musical values such as melody and exalted sounds more appropriate to the modern age, such as machine noises, and sounds produced by human beings which are not traditionally classified as music. He classified sounds into six groups based on their mode of production:

1. rumbles, roars, explosions, crashes, splashes, booms
2. whistles, hisses, snorts
3. whispers, murmurs, mumbles, grumbles, gurgles
4. screeches, creaks, rumbles, buzzes, crackles, scrapes
5. percussive noises obtained by striking metal, wood, skin, stone, terracotta etc.
6. voices of animals and people: shouts, screams, groans, shrieks, howls, laughs, wheezes, sobs[15]

Russolo and Ugo Piatti designed their own instruments, known as Intonarumori, and presented concerts of Russolo's works played on these instruments.[16] Russolo was based in Paris at the time he wrote his manifesto, which was summarised in *Paris Journal* on 1 April 1913, and he attracted a good deal of press attention that year, though as Hugh Davies points out, 'the first French translation (by Maurice Lemaître) of Russolo's manifesto *The Art of Noises* only appeared in 1954'.[17] While interest in Russolo has focused on his status as a precursor of electronic music and *musique concrète*, Davies mentions that he was inspired by the principles

---

[14] Cited in Robert Orledge, 'Satie's Musical and Personal Logic' in Caroline Potter (ed.), *Erik Satie: Music, Art and Literature*. Farnham: Ashgate, 2003, pp. 1–17, at p. 12.

[15] Translation of Russolo, *The Art of Noises*, http://www.unknown.nu/futurism/noises.html (accessed 5 April 2015); spelling corrected.

[16] See Valerio Saggini, http://www.thereminvox.com/article/articleview/116/1/31/ (accessed 5 April 2015).

[17] Hugh Davies, 'The Sound World, Instruments and Music of Luigi Russolo.' The Expanding Medium. *Lmc*, vol. 2 no. 2 (1994); http://creativegames.org.uk/modules/Art_Technology/theory/authors/hugh_davies.htm (accessed 5 April 2015).

of the ancient mechanical instrument, the hurdy-gurdy (vielle). Perhaps it is significant that Russolo's father was a clockmaker.[18] While Russolo's ideas were in the Parisian air in the early 1910s, Satie collaborated with a less-known creative artist associated with the futurist movement: Valentine de Saint-Point.

Valentine de Saint-Point and *Les Pantins dansent*

The Italian futurist movement was driven by men and promoted an aggressively masculine aesthetic. Indeed, several of its published manifestos are explicitly anti-woman; in the Second Futurist Proclamation, *Let's Kill off the Moonlight*, we read: 'Yes, our very sinews insist on war and scorn for women, for we fear their supplicating arms being wrapped around our legs, the morning of our setting forth!'[19] This provoked a reaction from the eccentric dancer and writer Valentine de Saint-Point, who responded with her own *Manifesto of the Futurist Woman* in 1912. Her manifesto proclaimed that 'Women are Furies, Amazons, Semiramis, Joans of Arc, Jeanne Hachettes, Judith and Charlotte Cordays, Cleopatras, and Messalinas,' and claimed that a 'complete being' is comprised of both (stereotypically) masculine and feminine elements.[20] Saint-Point is now little known, but she deserves to be remembered as a creative artist and as a supporter of contemporary music and art. She was connected to the rise in interest in Satie's music which was triggered by Ravel's promotion of early works including the *Sarabandes*: she and her partner, the poet and film enthusiast Ricciotto Canudo, hosted a salon, and on 11 June 1912, Florent Schmitt and Maurice Ravel played Satie's piano duet piece based largely on cabaret songs he had composed in Montmartre, *Trois morceaux en forme de poire* (1903), at their home.[21]

---

[18] Ibid.

[19] Cited in Vera Castiglione (2011), 'Dehistoricising the AvantGarde: An "outoftime" Reading of the AntiLove Polemic in the Writings of Tommaso Marinetti and Valentine de Saint-Point' [online article], *452°F: Electronic Journal of Theory of Literature and Comparative Literature*, no. 5, pp. 99–114. http://www.452f.com/en/vera-castiglione.html (accessed 5 April 2015).

[20] The manifesto can be accessed in English translation at http://www.wired.com/2008/11/the-manifesto-1/ (accessed 5 April 2015); translator not credited.

[21] Ravel's connection with Canudo – his *Frontispice* for piano duet (1918), composed as a prelude to a poem by Canudo – is outlined on pp. 93–4 below. Canudo initially referred to cinema as the 'sixth art' in his manifesto *The Birth of the Sixth Art* (1911), though he later named this medium the seventh art – the sixth being, instead, dance. See Richard Abel (ed.), *French Film Theory and Criticism: A History/Anthology, 1907–1939*. Princeton, NJ: Princeton University Press, 1993.

In February that year, Satie had attended her salon with other guests, including Canudo and the painters Albert Gleizes and Léon Bakst.[22]

Canudo was founder and editor of *Montjoie!*, one of many short-lived artistic journals of the period. This 'organe de l'impérialisme artistique français', as he described it, was published from 1913 to 1914. He was active across the arts and his 'organe' reflects his eclectic interests. He is remembered today as a pioneering film critic and he also wrote the scenario of Honegger's ballet *Skating Rink*, premiered by the Ballets Suédois in 1922. In the 1 June 1913 number of *Montjoie!*, he named Satie as one of the 'best young musicians' of the day, alongside Casella, Stravinsky, Ravel, Manuel de Falla and Florent Schmitt. Satie, who celebrated his forty-seventh birthday a few days before the issue was published, always aligned himself with 'young' composers. But, as with Marinetti, Satie would not have sympathised with the political views of Canudo. Richard Taruskin has aptly described *Montjoie!* as 'Ricciotto Canudo's riotous protofascist rag',[23] and indeed when Canudo died in 1923, 'Mussolini sent his widow a telegram in which he stated that he "appreciated madly the great spiritual and human qualities of your late lamented husband".'[24]

Valentine de Saint-Point's multiple artistic interests included experimental dance, though she was never as successful in this medium as contemporaries such as Isadora Duncan, Loïe Fuller[25] and Ida Rubinstein. Her only French public performance took place on 18 and 20 December 1913 at the Salle Léon-Poirier (part of the Théâtre des Champs-Elysées complex), though this 'Metachoric Festival', as she described it, was given again in New York in 1917.[26] The critic Carl van Vechten described the New York performance, conducted by Pierre Monteux at the Metropolitan Opera House, as a 'somewhat extraordinary evening'.[27] Satie's short piece *Les Pantins dansent* was written for the Paris event, and the complete piano version of the work was first published in the January–February 1914 number of *Montjoie!* alongside articles on contemporary

---

[22] Volta (ed.), *Correspondance*, p. 162.

[23] Richard Taruskin, 'Back to Whom? Neoclassicism as Ideology', review article in *19th-Century Music*, vol. 16 no. 3 (Spring 1993), pp. 286–302, at p. 297. Also see Jane F. Fulcher, *French Cultural Politics and Music: From the Dreyfus Affair to the First World War*. New York: Oxford University Press, 1999.

[24] Francesco Parrino, 'Alfredo Casella and "The *Montjoie!* Affair".' *repercussions*, vol. 10 no. 1 (Spring 2007), pp. 96–123, at p. 121 n. 116.

[25] Florent Schmitt's ballet *La tragédie de Salomé* (1907) was written for Loïe Fuller and later performed by the Ballets Russes.

[26] Volta (ed.), *Correspondance*, p. 1173.

[27] Carl van Vechten, 'Erik Satie: Master of the Rigolo.' *Vanity Fair* (March 1918).

dance and Satie's friend Valentine Gross' illustrations of dancers in the *Rite of Spring*.

The concept of 'métachorie' is one that Saint-Point felt the need to explain at length. Her principal article on the topic, which was first delivered as a lecture by Georges Saillard of the Théâtre Antoine on 29 December 1913, appears in the same number of *Montjoie!* as Satie's score. Here, she explains that the term derives from the Greek and means 'beyond the [Greek] chorus' (*au-delà du chœur*). She contends that music has always depended on ideas and that dance should as well. Her overarching aim is 'a fusion of all the arts: uniting music, poetry, dance and geometry, because geometry is the synthesis of architecture and its derivatives, painting and sculpture'.[28] Various numbers of *La Revue musicale S.I.M.* from 1913 feature correspondence from her, arguing with a M. Paulo Litta about the aims and objectives of her art form. In one of these responses (which refers to yet another newspaper debate of hers), she explains that 'In my Metachorie, music and dance are equal partners, both depending uniquely and in parallel on the Idea, that is the idea evoked in the poem or drama. And as I wrote in my letter to *Le Figaro*: the contribution of my metachorie is dance based on an idea [*idéiste*], dance which is not merely the sensually human rhythm in motion of music, but dance created and directed by the brain, dance which expresses an idea, placed in strict boundaries akin to contrapuntal music.'[29] Canudo classified dance alongside music and poetry as rhythmic arts: whether this was his idea alone or Saint-Point's is unclear, but this belief reinforces Saint-Point's desire to unify these arts in *métachorie*.

The title of Satie's collaboration with her ('The Puppets are Dancing') immediately places the work in the context of the composer's mechanical enthusiasms. Robert Orledge writes: 'It is easy to see why the whole concept attracted Satie with its modern spirit of participation and intellectual aims. Both the composer and the dancer were to be separately inspired by a common poem with their creations combined on

---

[28] Valentine de Saint-Point, 'La métachorie.' *Montjoie!* (January–February 1914), pp. 5-7, at p. 6: 'Je tente donc, dans la *Métachorie*, la fusion de tous les arts: en unissant la musique, la poésie, la danse et la géométrie, car la géométrie est la synthèse de l'art architectural et de ses dérivés, la peinture et la sculpture.'

[29] Valentine de Saint-Point, letter to *Revue musicale S.I.M.*, 1 January 1914, p. 71; 'Dans ma Métachorie musique et danse sont égales et dépendent toutes deux uniquement et pareillement de l'Idée, c'est-à-dire de l'idée évoquée dans le poème ou la drame. Et ma lettre au *Figaro* dit: Ma métachorie apporte les danses idéistes, la danse qui n'est pas seulement le rythme plastique sensuellement humain de la musique, mais la danse créée, dirigée cérébralement, la danse *qui exprime une idée*, arrêtée dans des lignes strictes comme la musique l'est dans le nombre du contrepoint.'

stage.'[30] *Les Pantins dansent* was composed at a time when Satie was particularly active in interart works: it follows his play with musical interludes *Le piège de Méduse*, and most of his texted piano works were written between 1912 and 1916. However, *Les Pantins dansent* is Satie's first collaborative work with another artist since his ventures with Contamine de Latour and Jules Dépaquit in the last decade of the nineteenth century.

Les Pantins dansent was completed on 16 November 1913 and survives in two distinct versions: the first, which is eighty-two bars long and scored for two flutes, clarinet in B♭, bassoon, horn, two trumpets, harp and strings, was reconstructed by Robert Orledge from sketches now housed in the Bibliothèque Nationale de France. The second version is slightly shorter, seventy-six bars long, and scored for piano or a small orchestra of flute, oboe, clarinet in B♭, bassoon, horn, trumpet, and strings. Although the elaborate tempo marking is 'Lentement (sans trop) presque modéré: une sorte de lent avec mouvement' ('Slowly (not too much) almost moderately; a kind of flowing slowness'), this is a tiny work which lasts no more than ninety seconds in performance.

The two pieces entitled *Les Pantins dansent* are somewhat different. Robert Orledge considers why this might be:

> Satie's first version may well have been a joke at Valentine's expense. After all, she was diverging somewhat from her Metachoric ideals in writing the poem as well as dancing its interpretation. What resulted in November 1913 was a strikingly dissonant introduction followed by a jaunty little piece somewhat reminiscent of 'Cherry Ripe'. And it was far too short for the poem, which was to be read by the portentous actor Edouard de Max at the premiere [...]. However, Satie even drafted the orchestration of this version, featuring his only known harp solo, and either he thought better of making a travesty of the festival, or Valentine cheated again [not being spontaneously inspired by the music], looked at it, and told him it would have to be rewritten. Whatever the reason, Satie (probably to keep his commission) then composed the strange, disembodied piece we know as *Les Pantins dansent*.[31]

The definitive piano version of the score was published in the January–February 1914 number of *Montjoie!* in a facsimile edition of the composer's manuscript, and an extract of the orchestral score had appeared in the previous number. In the second, piano, version, four bars (37–40) have been interpolated; whether this was due to a copying error by

---

[30] Robert Orledge, *Satie the Composer*. Cambridge: Cambridge University Press, 1990, p. 121.

[31] Robert Orledge, preface to his edition of the two versions of *Les Pantins dansent*; SOUNDkiosk SKPE10.

Satie or whether they were a last-minute addition cannot be determined. The differences between the two versions are clearly shown by comparing a section from the beginning of each (bars 1–4 of the first version are repeated at bars 5–8; Ex. 2.1).

The texture is considerably chunkier in the first version; Satie strips back the chords and reduces the volume in the second version. Bar 9 onwards of the first version are far closer to the definitive *Les Pantins dansent*, as the light staccato texture and characteristic stuttering rhythm are already present here. The concept was for the music to be inspired by

Ex. 2.1 (a) Satie, *Les Pantins dansent*: first version, piano, bars 5–16; (b) Satie, *Les Pantins dansent*: second version, piano, bars 1–12

a poem written by Saint-Point, who in turn would improvise movement to the music. There is no obvious correspondence between poem and music: in Orledge's words, 'Satie cannot have intended the regular 4-bar phrases of his final version to each fit one line of Saint-Point's poem, for the music would then finish at the first line of stanza 5. So the poem and music *must* have been performed independently.'[32] The poem was published as part of Saint-Point's collection *Poèmes ironiques* in 1917, before the New York performance; its first verse (which is identical to the last one) is shown below:

> Je mourrai, un jour de fête
> Alors que les pantins dansent.
> Je n'entre pas dans leur danse,
> Je ne fête pas leurs fêtes.
> Je mourrai, un jour de fête
> Alors que les pantins dansent.

[I will die on a feast day while the puppets dance. I won't dance with them, I won't celebrate with them. I will die on a feast day while the puppets dance.]

It appears that the talent and poetic renown of Saint-Point's great-uncle Alphonse de Lamartine were not passed down to her. The poem is of interest purely because it reflects the themes of dualism and human/puppet interaction which were so popular in the nineteenth and early twentieth centuries. And Satie was a great enthusiast of Hans Christian Andersen's tales, many of which explore the feelings of puppets or the relationship between people and inanimate beings. The numerous contemporary works featuring puppets on stage with humans include Stravinsky's *Petruskha* as well as works by Satie including *Le piège de Méduse*, whose dancing monkey Jonas is accompanied by interludes for prepared piano.

Albert Bazaillas wrote a detailed review of the Paris performance for *La Renaissance politique, littéraire et artistique* on 3 January 1914. The author initially seems more interested that Valentine de Saint-Point is the great-niece of Lamartine, though he then presents her theory about the role of dance at some length. Bazaillas mentions Satie towards the end of his review, a critique which is worth quoting in full:

> As for M. Erik Satie, already well known for his *Préludes flasques*, his *Aperçus désagréables* and his *Descriptions automatiques*, he surrounds the *Poèmes d'atmosphère* with disturbing humour. One is unsure who he is mocking here. In his *Pantins qui dansent* [sic] his art is precious and sardonic. Here, we recognise the tender irony which a talented young critic, M. Georges Auric, has shown us releasing

---

[32] Orledge, *Satie the Composer*, p. 122.

'little boats on a fast-flowing stream which flows between rushes and creepers, murmuring soft and discreet songs under the late-rising sun.' But, on that topic, what is this amusing music mocking, while puppets wander through our imagination, and which ideist dance makes omnipresent on stage? Who is being mocked? Us, or metachorie? I would not be comfortable to have such a collaborator, were I in the shoes of Madame de Saint-Point.[33]

It is interesting that the 'talented young critic' Georges Auric was already known to Bazaillas; Auric was only fourteen years old and had already met Satie after publishing an article on his music, 'Erik Satie, musicien humoriste'.[34] The notion that Satie's work could be anything other than ironic or humorous does not appear to have occurred to Bazaillas, who like many of his contemporaries is more interested in Satie's unusual titles than anything else. Satie's imaginatively titled flabby preludes, disagreeable glances and automatic descriptions evidently drew attention, though this was largely confined to the titles. But as always with Satie, multiple interpretations of this phenomenon are possible. Did Satie mind that his music was relegated to second place behind his words? No evidence exists to support this idea. I believe that he conceived his work as a totality, as a complete artistic experience of which music was but one element. Satie's collaborations, in this case with Valentine de Saint-Point's words and dance, add extra layers of meaning to an already complex artwork, further ensuring his music is perceived as only one part of the

---

[33] Albert Bazaillas, 'La musique: Réflexions sur la danse et la féerie. – A propos des danses idéistes et des contes de Perrault.' *La Renaissance politique, littéraire et artistique*, 3 January 1914, pp. 22–4, at pp. 23–4: 'Quant à M. Erik Satie, très connu déjà pour ses *Préludes flasques*, ses *Aperçus désagréables* et ses *Descriptions automatiques*, il entoure les *Poèmes d'atmosphère* d'un humour inquiétant. On ne sait vraiment de qui il se moque. Dans les *Pantins qui dansent* il pratique un art précieux et narquois. Et je reconnais bien là l'ironiste, pourtant attendri, qu'un jeune critique de talent, M. Georges Auric, nous a montré lançant «de petits bateaux sur le ruisseau vif qui court entre les joncs et les lianes, murmurant, sous le soleil enfin levé, les chansons les plus douces et les plus discrètes.» Mais, à propos, de qui se moque-t-elle donc cette plaisante musique, pendant que les «pantins» déambulent dans notre imagination, et que la danse idéiste sévit sur la scène? De qui enfin? De nous, ou de la métachorie? A la place de Mme de Saint-Point, je ne serais pas rassurée d'avoir un tel partenaire.'

[34] Auric's article, 'Erik Satie: Musicien humoriste', was originally published in *Revue française de musique*, 4 (10 December 1913), pp. 138–42. Carl B. Schmidt notes that Satie and Auric first met in 1913 in the office of the music critic Emile Vuillermoz. See Carl B. Schmidt (ed.), *Ecrits sur la musique de Georges Auric*, vol. 1. Lewiston: Edwin Mellen, 2009, p. 30. Schmidt reproduces Auric's article on Satie in volume 4 of this publication (pp. 1415–19).

conception. But if *Les Pantins dansent* is performed today, it is as a concert work or a sound recording, though this presentation ignores the other elements of Satie and Saint-Point's novel conception.

■ ■ ■

RUSSOLO had an impact on Cocteau when the writer devised the scenario of *Parade*, his collaboration with Satie, Picasso and Massine. Cocteau and Picasso travelled to Rome with Diaghilev from February to April 1917 to work on the ballet, though Satie, never a keen traveller, stayed in Arcueil to work on the music. In Rome, the collaborators encountered the futurist movement and were prompted by Russolo's notion of an orchestra of noises to incorporate non-musical noises in *Parade*, including a lottery wheel, typewriter and revolver.[35] Cocteau was particularly keen to include these noises, even describing the piano duet version of Satie's score as 'the musical backdrop which throws into relief the foreground of percussion and stage noises'.[36] However, the precise connection between Russolo and Satie is otherwise fuzzy, and I would suggest that the little-known figure Louis Carol-Bérard (1888–1942), Edgard Varèse and Apollinaire are the missing links between Satie and the futurist movement.

Carol-Bérard

Carol-Bérard (he always signed articles and compositions with his surname only) was born in Marseille and was active as a composer and music critic. He composed songs to his own texts and piano music, some on non-European themes (such as the songs *Haï-Kaï* (1912) and piano suites *Extrême-Asie* and *Egypte*). He also knew the pianist Ricardo Viñes well, and was closely linked to Spanish composers including Isaac Albéniz and French composers such as Albert Roussel and Paul Dukas. Satie wrote in a postscript to Ricardo Viñes on Monday 5 March 1917: 'Do you have Bérard's address? I'd like to have it.'[37] As a music critic, Carol-Bérard wrote regularly for *La Semaine à Paris* in the early 1920s. Like Satie, Carol-Bérard also composed light music: his 'valse tzigane' *Obsession* was a hit in 1910 and described on a postcard issued by the publisher

---

[35] See Malou Haine, 'Jean Cocteau, impresario musical à la croisée des arts', in Sylvain Caron, François de Médicis and Michel Duchesneau (eds), *Musique et modernité en France*. Montréal: Presses Universitaires de Montréal, 2006, pp. 69–134.

[36] Deborah Menaker Rothschild, *Picasso's 'Parade'*. New York: Sotheby's Publications/The Drawing Center, 1991, p. 88; 'le fond musical destiné à mettre en relief un premier plan de batterie et de bruits scéniques'.

[37] Volta (ed.), *Correspondance*, p. 281: 'Avez-vous l'adresse de Bérard? J'aimerais bien l'avoir.' Volta mentions on p. 1165 that 'Une photo de Satie par Carol-Bérard est conservée à l'IMEC/Archives Erik Satie.'

Parmentier as 'l'une des plus jolies valse [sic] de la saison'.[38] As a critic, he was a long-term supporter of Satie; he favourably reviewed *Socrate*,[39] and later became well known as a writer on topics including dance and Czech music.

Most interestingly in the context of musical futurism, he composed a *Symphonie des forces mécaniques* in 1908 which sadly is now lost. In an article published in *Revue musicale* in 1922, Carol-Bérard describes this work: 'in a Symphony written in 1908, where I sought to express the synthesis of mechanical forces – locomotive, steamboat, aeroplane – the conquerors of the elements of Earth, Water and Air – I used motors, electric bells, whistles and sirens with chorus and orchestra. Since then, [other] composers have done better.'[40] This symphony predates George Antheil's notorious *Ballet mécanique* by some fifteen years; we will see that Satie was involved in the raucous premiere of Antheil's work.

Carol-Bérard predicted in an article titled 'Recorded Noises: Tomorrow's Instrumentation'[41] that recorded sounds could be the basis of a new musical language, though rather like Ferruccio Busoni's *Sketch of a New Aesthetic of Music* (1907), Carol-Bérard's theoretical writings were never tested by him in practice. Marc Battier sums up Carol-Bérard's article: 'Just as Apollinaire predicted for poetry, Carol-Bérard imagined that a new notation method should be developed for recorded sounds. This would be a taxonomy of sounds, in order that the composer might have access to a palette of ordered and classified sounds, just like the instruments of the orchestra.'[42] Apollinaire's poetic and theoretical innovations will be discussed later, but at this point it is interesting to note that Carol-Bérard was to collaborate with Apollinaire in *Couleur du temps* (1918), written for the experimental theatre Art et Liberté.

---

[38] Card in the author's collection.

[39] In *La Semaine à Paris*, 23 January 1923, pp. 8–9.

[40] Carol-Bérard, 'La couleur en mouvement, décor rationnel de la musique.' *Revue musicale*, 10 (1 August 1922): pp. 147–61, at p. 150; 'dans une Symphonie écrite en 1908, symphonie où je cherchais à exprimer la synthèse des forces mécaniques, – locomotive, navire à vapeur, aéroplane, – conquérantes des éléments: la Terre, l'Eau et l'Air, j'ai utilisé des moteurs, des sonneries électriques, des sifflets et des sirènes en adjonction aux chœurs et à l'orchestre. Depuis on a fait mieux.'

[41] Published in *Modern Music*, 6 (January–February 1929): pp. 26–9.

[42] Marc Battier, 'De la symphonie du monde à la symphonie de bruits.' *Filigrane*, 7 (2008), special number 'Musique et bruits' edited by Makis Solomos; full text available at http://revues.mshparisnord.org/filigrane/pdf/228.pdf: 'Comme l'avait prédit Apollinaire pour la poésie, Carol-Bérard imagine qu'il faudra instituer une méthode d'écriture pour les bruits ainsi captés. Elle serait fondée sur une taxinomie des bruits, de sorte que le musicien dispose d'une palette de sons ordonnés et classés, comme le sont les instruments de l'orchestre.'

Apollinaire's death that year meant that he did not finish the project, and for that reason many of his friends opposed the production which was staged on 24 November 1918. In this play, an aeroplane transports the characters from place to place in a vain search for peace.[43]

Satie and Varèse

At the Schola Cantorum, Satie studied counterpoint under Roussel for four years from October 1905, and attended parts of Vincent d'Indy's composition, analysis and orchestration courses from the same date until 1911 or 1912.[44] Neither the institution nor their teachers are at all associated with modernism or technological innovation – quite the opposite. In fact, d'Indy's minor aristocratic background and conservative politics could not be further from Satie's origins and political stance, though their teacher–pupil relationship was successful. Edgard Varèse was another unexpected student at this institution, which was primarily a training ground for organists and choir directors; he studied there in the academic year 1904–5.

There are several odd connections between Satie and Varèse, though while their paths frequently crossed, there is little evidence that they were more than acquaintances. Ornella Volta believes they met around 1914 either at the home of the Godebskis (who were close friends of Ravel) or at Debussy's home,[45] but they may have known of each other's existence earlier than this, not least because both attended Canudo and Saint-Point's gatherings. Varèse planned to write an opera on Sâr Péladan's text *Le fils des étoiles*, a text for which Satie had already composed incidental music in 1891–2 (indeed, Péladan approached other composers to write music on this text when he broke with Satie).[46] Péladan, founder of the Rose+Croix movement, described Varèse's early orchestral work *Rapsodie*

---

[43] Corvin, *Le théâtre de recherche*, p. 88.

[44] Orledge, *Satie the Composer*, p. xxvii. Orledge's chapter on Satie's studies at the Schola Cantorum (pp. 81–104) is based on extensive study of Satie's many surviving notebooks.

[45] Volta (ed.), *Correspondance*, p. 1146. Mimi Godebska is 'M. God', the author of the text of Satie's song 'Daphénéo' (1917). As a child, she and her brother Cipa (Cyprien) were the dedicatees of Ravel's piano duet suite *Ma mère l'oye* (Mother Goose) (1907).

[46] Heidy Zimmermann, 'The Lost Early Works: Facts and Suppositions', in Felix Meyer and Heidy Zimmermann (eds), *Edgard Varèse: Composer, Sound Sculptor, Visionary*. Woodbridge: The Boydell Press, 2006, p. 45. Zimmermann here references Fernand Ouellette, *Edgard Varèse*, trans. Derek Coltman. New York: Orion, 1968, p. 39. Satie and Péladan's friendship ended when Satie published an open letter in *Gil Blas* expressing his independence of thought (Volta (ed.), *Correspondance*, p. 1019).

romane (1905) as 'a profane Gregorian chant',[47] a description which could apply to much of Satie's early piano music and which suggests why Varèse appealed to Péladan. Indeed, Varèse's amanuensis Chou Wen-Chung wrote of Varèse that 'only his studies of the music of medieval, Renaissance, and early Baroque masters with Charles Bordes at the Schola made an impact on him'.[48]

Evidence suggests that Varèse appreciated Satie's music more than vice versa. The younger composer particularly admired Satie's *Messe des pauvres*, which he considered to be 'a sort of pre-electronic music',[49] a striking view of a work composed in 1893–5. Perhaps the scoring of the work, largely for solo organ with short choral interjections in the Kyrie, evoked parallels in Varèse's mind with the performance of recorded music, as there is no obviously visible performer in both cases. The mystic value of the invisible sound source, as evoked by Carolyn Abbate in the context of Debussy, is also relevant here: 'invisible speech is equivalent to divine speech, and [...] God's authority is predicated on the presence of his voice in the absence of his body'.[50] More specifically, *Messe des pauvres* is unusual because it is almost entirely homophonic in texture and features very little rhythmic variety; most of its movements are entirely composed of crotchet chords, and the few sections which are more varied rhythmically feature almost random arrangements of crotchets and quavers, as if the rhythms were added at the last minute.

After the two composers met in 1914, Varèse had the idea for a collaboration, conceived as a 'homage to Satie', in which they would contribute incidental music alongside Florent Schmitt, Stravinsky and Maurice Ravel for a Cocteau reworking of *A Midsummer Night's Dream*. Only Satie completed music for this project, now known as *Cinq grimaces pour 'Le Songe d'une nuit d'été'*. This music is the only surviving element of an ambitious creative collaboration which was to have involved many of the leading Parisian musicians and artists of his time. Around 1915, Cocteau had the idea for a production of Shakespeare's *A Midsummer Night's Dream* to be performed in the Cirque Médrano, with the leading clowns of the day, the three Fratellini brothers, performing the 'rude mechanicals'. The impresario Gabriel Astruc, who is best known for his association with the Ballets Russes performances at the Théâtre de Champs-Elysées, was also involved. Steven Moore Whiting writes: 'The idea of using the Cirque Médrano pleased Astruc because, as the Chat Noir poet Surtac, he had written his first revues for that circus in 1888

---

[47] Ouellette, *Edgard Varèse*, p. 19.

[48] Chou Wen-Chung, 'Varèse: A Sketch of the Man and his Music.' *Musical Quarterly*, vol. 52 no. 2 (April 1966): pp. 151–70, at p. 152.

[49] Volta (ed.), *Correspondance*, p. 1146 (citing Gunther Schuller).

[50] Carolyn Abbate, 'Debussy's Phantom Sounds.' *Cambridge Opera Journal*, vol. 10 no. 1 (1998): pp. 67–96, at p. 70.

(incidentally, the very year he would have met Satie at the cabaret).' He goes on to say, 'Much of the set was to be projected, as coloured shadows, upon the backdrops – an obvious variant of the shadow theatre made famous by the Chat Noir.'[51] Among other composers involved in the collaboration was Varèse, who was back in Paris after several years in Berlin. He reminisced about the *Midsummer Night's Dream* project in a 1961 interview: 'We did not want Mendelssohn at that time [during World War I], so consequently it was: Satie, and then Florent Schmitt, Satie, and then Ravel, Satie, and then Stravinsky, and then Satie, myself, and then ending by Satie. Five things by Satie, and four people to put the whole thing together. Just an *Hommage à Satie.*'[52]

The painters Albert Gleizes and André Lhote were to be in charge of sets and costumes. Olivia Mattis cites Gleizes' unpublished memoirs, written after World War II: 'The sets would be schematically represented on a backdrop. Projected on it, through the use of magic lanterns, would be different colors and images. André Lhote was to be in charge of making the projection gels [...]. The accompanying music was to be entrusted to Edgar Varèse and Georges Auric.'[53] No mention of Satie or Cocteau here! Milorad claims that Cocteau was always referred to as the author of the text, although he did not know English.[54] However, Mattis tells us that Henri-Pierre Roché 'was fully bilingual and left us a French adaptation of Shakespeare's play from this very period [1914]'. Mattis believes this could have been an operatic collaboration, perhaps a completely separate project to be set by Auric. Roché was close to both Satie and Auric in this period, and a charming letter from the fifteen-year-old Auric to Roché in poetic form alludes to their various Shakespearian ideas:

> *Dream* of Georges Auric who in Issoire
> *Dreams*
> About H.P. Roché who *dreams* about the Americas
> – About the sweet Americas that only *dream*
> about Us. – And Erik? –
> Oh! may New York some day hear us
> both
> Discussing a whimsical *ballet mécanique.*[55]

---

[51] Steven Moore Whiting, *Satie the Bohemian*. Oxford: Clarendon Press, 1999, p. 463.

[52] Olivia Mattis, 'Theater as Circus: 'A Midsummer Night's Dream.' *The Library Chronicle of the University of Texas at Austin*, vol. 23 no. 4 (1993): pp. 43–77, at p. 59.

[53] Ibid., p. 63.

[54] Milorad, 'Jean Cocteau avec les musiciens.' *Cahiers Jean Cocteau*, 7 (1978), pp. 13–106, at p. 65.

[55] Letter of 22 November 1914, cited in Mattis, 'Theater as Circus', p. 71.

No text survives for this collaboration, however. Mattis believes that

> Cocteau's production seems to have been a spoken drama, coupled with circus acrobatics. Rather than 'setting scenes to music', Varèse chose incidental music that would be played during the scene changes. In calling the project a 'Hommage à Satie' in his 1961 reminiscence, Varèse revealed that he considered the music to be an independent element from the text, rather than a setting of it. This view corresponded with that of Cocteau, who saw the music as a 'potpourri of favorites', independent of text. Satie concurred with them both: his *Cinq Grimaces*, the only surviving music from this venture, is a trivial, fanciful, purely instrumental piece, all five movements lasting only three-and-a-half minutes.[56]

Again, we see Satie composing music 'between' the stage action rather than directly being part of it.

Whiting notes that

> there is evidence, starting with the title, that Satie was put off by the entire project. Why refer to a set of incidental numbers as facial contortions, as expressions of discontent? At one point Satie contemplated a longer title, *Grimaces, Pataquès & Interstices ('Songe d'une Nuit d'Eté')*, which might be (somewhat freely) translated as Grimaces, Bad Joins, and Time-Fillers. [...] Even less engaging is the overall plan drafted in another notebook. Unless Varèse used such language in dictating Satie's assignment, which seems unlikely, the descriptions may tell us how Satie really felt about the project.[57]

These titles are:

1. Préambule – Fanfare de cirque burlesque: 20 mesures ignoblement bêtes. [Preamble – Burlesque circus fanfare. 20 ignobly stupid bars. This 'grimace' is, in fact, 42 bars long]
2. Coquecigrue[58] – Chants de coqs & cocasseries diverses: 16 mesures [Tale about nothing – Cockerel sounds and various stupidities: 16 bars. Actually 26 bars long]
3. Chasse – Stupide fanfare de chasse. Cuivres, puis bois: deux reprises de 8 mesures. [Hunt – Stupid hunt fanfare. Brass, then woodwind: two repeated sections, 8 bars each. Actually 22 bars long]
4. Fanfaronnade – Sonnerie abjecte jouée par tout l'orchestre: Polka militaire & grossière, fortement idiote: 16 mesures.

---

[56] Ibid., pp. 69–70.
[57] Whiting, *Satie the Bohemian*, p. 465.
[58] The term 'coquecigrue' was first used by Rabelais to mean 'tell a story about nothing'. Jules Renard used the word as the title of a novel in 1893.

[Bombast – Abject trumpet call played by the whole orchestra. Military vulgar polka, greatly idiotic: 16 bars long]

5. Pour sortir [incomplete, expanded by Milhaud to fifty-two bars] – Retraite ridicule & saugrenue rendue par tout l'orchestre: 12 mesures, répétées 200 fois. [Leavetaking – Ridiculous retreat played by the whole orchestra: 12 bars, repeated 200 times.]

Perhaps Satie's language, and no doubt his reference to a short idea 'repeated 200 times', does indeed reflect his frustration about the project. Or perhaps this is another example of his love of wordplay, or simply Satie showing a desire to distract attention from his music by creating a ridiculous façade. As often with Satie, a combination of these three suppositions is likely to be nearest the truth. Again, we see him describing his music as entr'actes, though in this case Satie found several synonyms for the term.

Apollinaire

Guillaume Apollinaire was a key contributor to art magazines (some of which he founded), a prolific author of manifestos and a central figure across the arts in Paris at the start of the twentieth century. His poetry, like Satie's music, addresses themes connected with the mechanical, encompassing both new and older technologies. He drew inspiration from the everyday and he evokes the life of ordinary Parisian inhabitants rather than some idealised world of the ancient past. With his fellow poet Max Jacob, and Picasso and other artists on the Montmartre scene, he was a regular attender at Paris cabarets and circuses in the first decade of the 1900s. Apollinaire had an encyclopedic knowledge of contemporary art and, like Satie, knew many of the prominent artistic figures of his time well. He was born in Rome, the illegitimate son of a Polish noblewoman, and settled in Paris at the age of eighteen. Unlike many of his artist contemporaries, he fought in World War I, having volunteered to serve in the French army in 1914. Two years later, a serious head wound meant he was sent back to Paris; he never fully recovered from this injury and died during the influenza epidemic in 1918.

He was also one of the first French artistic figures to be in close contact with the Italian futurists. Apollinaire and a group of friends founded the art magazine *Les Soirées de Paris* in 1912, and in the following year he published an essay, *L'antitradition futuriste*, which the poet terms a 'manifeste-synthèse'. It is typographically adventurous and whimsically dated 'PARIS, 29 June 1913, day of the Grand Prix [horse race], 65 metres above Boulevard St-Germain'. After an image of music notation which appears to be a random selection of notes rather than a quotation of anything in particular, Apollinaire's tract ends by dividing his hates and loves under two headings, 'MERDE' and 'ROSE'. He modestly includes himself under the 'rose' heading, together with Picasso, Stravinsky,

Picabia, Valentine de Saint-Point and many other contemporary Paris-based artistic figures – though not Satie.

This text shows Apollinaire was very much in tune with contemporary trends: he rejects 'poetic sadness, snobby exoticism, [...] the orchestra' among much else, preferring instead '*Onomatopoeic Description/* Total Music and *Art of Noises* .../*Machinism* Eiffel Tower Brooklyn and skyscrapers ... Direct quivering at great free spectacles circuses music halls etc.' He evokes Russolo's manifesto written in the same year; more importantly, Deborah Menaker Rothschild notes that 'Apollinaire's stream-of-consciousness formula is too close to Cocteau's character descriptions for *Parade* to be mere coincidence.'[59] Cocteau devised the scenario for *Parade*, his collaboration with Picasso, Satie and Massine, three years later and Apollinaire's only contribution to the ballet would be a programme note. Rothschild translates the descriptions for the third dance of *Parade* (for two Acrobats) as: 'Médrano – Orion – two biplanes in the morning ... the archangel Gabriel balancing himself on the edge of the window ... the diver's lantern ... Sodom and Gomorrah at the bottom of the sea ... the meteorologist – the telescope ... the parachutist who killed himself on the Eiffel Tower – the sadness of gravity – soles of lead – the sun – man slave of the sun'.[60] Apollinaire's and Cocteau's descriptions cited here have much in common with Satie's obsessions as a writer: topics such as religion, contemporary events, extreme dislike of the sun and popular entertainment are omnipresent. It is well nigh impossible to disentangle influence from borrowing from ideas in the air, such are the close artistic connections between Apollinaire, Cocteau and Satie at this time.

Apollinaire's poem *Un fantôme de nuées* (1913) was inspired by Picasso's saltimbanque paintings of the first decade of the twentieth century. These works from Picasso's 'rose' period portray circus performers of different ages in tatty Harlequin, dance or acrobat outfits. In *La famille de saltimbanques* (1905), an overweight elderly man with a straggly beard wearing a red jester hat and carrying a heavy bag is surrounded by younger performers in different costumes, though the group are not interacting or even looking at each other. *Un fantôme de nuées* has a prose-like quality, and one of the street performers described resembles the older bearded man in Picasso's painting *The Hurdy-Gurdy Man* (1905):

> Vois-tu le personnage maigre et sauvage
> La cendre de ses pères lui sortait en barbe grisonnante
> Il portait ainsi toute son hérédité au visage
> Il semblait rêver à l'avenir
> En tournant machinalement un orgue de Barbarie
> Dont la lente voix se lamentait merveilleusement
> Les glouglous les couacs et les sourds gémissements

---

[59] Rothschild, *Picasso's 'Parade'*, p. 51 n. 16.
[60] Ibid., pp. 83 and 85.

[See that thin savage one
The ashes of his ancestors are coming out in his grey beard
He carries all his heredity in his face
And seems to dream of the future
While mechanically turning a barrel organ
Whose sweet voice wails marvellously
Gurgling false notes and muffled groans][61]

As Apollinaire had such a strong interest in the concrete and the everyday, it is perhaps odd that, while many of his poems mention music, actual musical works (as opposed to an imaginary, idealised music) were of little interest to him. Peter Dayan writes of Apollinaire and music: 'Alberto Savinio smashing pianos, like the child destroying the music of the mechanical "orgue de Barbarie" in "Un fantôme de nuées", seems to symbolise, for Apollinaire, the sheer poverty of all music that can be heard, and the superiority of imagined music over real music. His ears could hear no music worthy of contemporary art.'[62]

Readers of Apollinaire's poetry will also immediately notice the complete absence of punctuation. Apollinaire's friend Louise Faure-Favier 'tells how he was so exasperated by the number of mistakes in the proofs of this volume [*Alcools*, 1913] that he inscribed on them one magnificent *delete* for all the punctuation'.[63] Punctuation was also on the list of things mentioned in *L'antitradition futuriste* that Apollinaire wanted to ban. It is tempting to parallel this with the absence of bar lines in many of Satie's piano works: pieces as early as the first three *Gnossiennes* (1890–3) have no bar lines, and they are also absent from his texted piano works, which are contemporaneous with Apollinaire's major poems. Apollinaire could use line breaks to convey the pauses that punctuation would otherwise provide; for Satie, phrase marks could have the same function. Satie's rhythmic structures tend to be regular, though the lack of bar lines in many of his piano pieces might suggest otherwise. He surely omitted bar lines primarily to create a visually striking image. Indeed, Satie wrote in a short article on publishing in 1922: 'I fear that Music could never have the same "publication" qualities as Literature. Typographically, it would need

---

[61] Translated by Roger Shattuck in *Selected Writings of Guillaume Apollinaire*. New York: New Directions, 1971, p. 161. Also see John Richardson, *A Life of Picasso: 1881–1906*. London: Pimlico, 1992, p. 349.

[62] Peter Dayan, 'Apollinaire's Music.' *Forum for Modern Language Studies*, vol. 47 no. 1 (2011): pp. 36–48, at p. 45. In footnote 29 on the same page, Dayan adds 'as Auric noted, [Apollinaire] was fond of popular tunes; but for him as for Savinio, they could not constitute a "musique nouvelle", an art for modern times'.

[63] Shattuck (ed. and trans.), *Selected Writings of Guillaume Apollinaire*, p. 26.

to have a completely different look. It is certain that "engraving" gives it a heavy look. The future will decide. Yes.'[64]

Apollinaire, like Satie, had a strong visual sense and experimented with the presentation of his work. His *Calligrammes* (1913–16) are tiny poems, like a snapshot in time, whose typographical design echoes their subject. His and Satie's art could embrace quotation of or allusion to popular material; as Deborah Menaker Rothschild puts it, 'Many of Apollinaire's poems in *Alcools* allude to philosophy, religion and history, while at the same time rendering matter-of-fact details of Parisian life. Like Cubist canvases, his poems introduce street cries, signs, and contemporary urban intrusions within a format distinguished by formal austerity.'[65] Similarly, Satie's music draws on everything from pseudo-Gregorian chant to contemporary popular song. His texted piano works are multilayered artistic experiences which combine calligraphy, text and music which can incorporate quotation of other sources. While Satie's texted piano works are the central topic of Chapter 3, here it is worth considering one of his twenty *Sports et divertissements* (1914) as an interesting parallel to Apollinaire's blending of the visual and verbal.

'Le Golf' (Fig. 2.1) is a truly interart work whose text, image and music support each other. Written to appear alongside pochoir prints by Charles Martin, Satie composed twenty tiny pieces and an introductory chorale in 1914, though the war put paid to plans for publication. The project was revived in 1922 and new cubist-inspired illustrations were drawn which fit less well with Satie's music and words. Satie naturally responds to the sporting elements in the 'Golf' drawing, with a golfer practising his swing and followed by his caddie, but the sophisticated lady and gentleman in the foreground of the 1922 drawings are completely ignored. The part-Scottish Satie draws special attention to the Scotch tweed clothing of the golfer (which, not surprisingly for a practitioner of this sport, is a lively shade of green – 'vert violent' in Satie's words).

His text points up the clothing, and his music responds in a Scottish-style dotted rhythm which is shared with his earlier *Jack in the Box* (1899).[66] The dotted rhythm returns at 'Les nuages sont étonnés' (The clouds are astonished), highlighting the changeability of Scottish weather no doubt, and at 'Le voici qui assure le coup' (Here he is making a fine swing), when attention turns back to the individual golfer. Noteworthy too is Satie's use of the English language (Scotch tweed, caddie, bags, holes,

---

[64] Ornella Volta (ed.), *Erik Satie: Ecrits*. Paris: Editions Champ Libre, 1979, pp. 44–5, at p. 45; original in *Catalogue*, no. 3 (30 May 1922), p. 3): 'Je crains que la Musique ne puisse avoir jamais les mêmes qualités «d'édition» que la Littérature. Typographiquement, elle aurait, peut-être, une toute autre représentation. Il est certain que la «gravure» l'alourdit physiquement. L'avenir en décidera. Oui.'

[65] Rothschild, *Picasso's 'Parade'*, p. 45.

[66] Chapter 1 argued that this work may have a Scottish connection.

Fig. 2.1 Erik Satie, 'Le Golf' (*Sports et divertissements*). Satie's score. Typ. 915.14.7700, Houghton Library, Harvard University

club) to evoke the scene of the game. This is combined in macaronic fashion with French, as in a peculiar letter he sent to his brother Conrad on 30 August 1897 which is probably connected with the sale of a bicycle. This letter includes the marvellous phrase 'cette vénérable Dame ayant amené avec elle une sorte de maquereau, lequel se disait marchand de cycles (mackerel cycle manufacturer) [this venerable Lady having brought with her a sort of pimp, who said he was a cycle salesman].'[67] Satie, ever the food lover and pun enthusiast, enjoys the double meaning of 'maquereau' – a mackerel, or a pimp.

Two gestures in 'Le Golf' could be described as musical onomatopoeia: the chromatically winding and descending figure at 'Les «holes» sont tout

---

[67] This incomplete and unsigned letter is now housed in Houghton Library, Harvard University, and reproduced in Volta (ed.), *Correspondance*, pp. 80–1.

Ex. 2.2 Satie, *Avant-dernières pensées*, 'Idylle': 'Mais mon cœur est tout petit'

tremblants' gives life to the inanimate holes which, to the player at least, seem to shift unpredictably. This 'trembling' gesture is almost identical to a passage in 'Idylle', the first of Satie's *Avant-dernières pensées* (1916), at 'Mais mon cœur est tout petit' (But my heart is very small; Ex. 2.2). While it is not always easy to draw specific parallels between music and in-score text in Satie, this suggests that emotional unease, even if attributed to a hole, can be associated with chromaticism. The virtuosic gesture of rapid ascending fourths at 'son «club» vole en éclats!' points up the surprise felt at the club suddenly shattering into pieces.

It is odd, and unfortunate, that Apollinaire and Satie never really got on. Satie was approached by Apollinaire to compose incidental music for his play *Les mamelles de Tirésias* (which was set by Poulenc as an opera in 1939–44) and Georges Auric tells the story of this collaboration that never happened:

> Apollinaire met Satie rather late in his career and these two men, who seemed to have so much in common, did not get each other. I will never forget a rather difficult late afternoon (in 1916 or 1917?) when Apollinaire had invited us to a workshop close to Montparnasse station. He wanted to introduce us to *Les mamelles de Tirésias* and wanted incidental music for it. Evidently, he wasn't the best reader ever, but I had always considered him to be a fine poet. Yet, I was disappointed when I listened to this play, a fact I found difficult to hide. Satie, for his part, remained silent and we left, hugely embarrassed.[68]

---

[68] Auric, 'Apollinaire et la musique', *La revue musicale*, 210 (January 1952), pp. 147–9: 'Apollinaire ne rencontra Satie que fort tard et ces deux hommes que tant de choses semblait rapprocher se comprirent assez mal. Etait-ce en 1916 ou en 1917? Je n'oublierai jamais une fin d'après-midi assez sinistre où Apollinaire nous avait réunis, dans un atelier tout proche de la gare Montparnasse. Il voulait nous faire connaître *Les Mamelles de Tirésias* pour lesquelles il souhaitait une musique de scène. Evidemment, il n'était pas un admirable lecteur. Mais, depuis toujours, je savais qu'il était un poète admirable. Et pourtant, j'écoutais sa pièce avec une déception que j'avais grand'peine à dissimuler. Satie, lui, demeurait silencieux et nous partîmes atrocement embarrassés.'

Although Satie did not write the music for this play, there is evidence that he was to have contributed unspecified 'noises' (*bruits*) to its first performances. Robert Orledge writes: 'A publicity flyer of mid-May 1917 for the premiere of Apollinaire's "moralité en deux actes" *Les Mamelles de Tirésias* (on 10 June) states that the music will be by Germaine Albert-Birot, with "bruits réglés par Eric [*sic*] Satie. Satie [...] may have been persuaded to improvise some sort of *musique concrète* on the night."'[69] Germaine Albert-Birot was the wife of the publisher of *Sic*, one of many avant-garde magazines published in this period. Pierre Albert-Birot's magazine – the three letters of the title stand for 'Sons, Idées, Couleurs', showing the multimedia aims of the publication – was a strong supporter of Apollinaire; indeed, the magazine financed the premiere performances of *Les mamelles de Tirésias*. The eighteenth number of *Sic* (June 1917) was devoted to *Les mamelles*, and Sic Editions published the play and its score by Germaine Albert-Birot, who was described by Poulenc in an interview in 1954 as an amateur composer, 'une musicienne de dimanche'.[70] Her incidental music comprised an overture; a funeral march accompanying the duel of Presto and Lacouf (Act 1 scene 4); a song preceding the second act, sung by three choirs in front of the lowered curtain to the left, right and at the back of the room; an entr'acte at the start of Act 2, and a song which is the final number, sung by all characters. The use of popular song, an entr'acte and the spatial distribution of the three choirs suggest that while Satie was not the composer of this music, he was perhaps its model.

There is one further intriguing link between Satie and Apollinaire's play. Peter Read notes that in an early version of *Les mamelles de Tirésias*, a reference to 'the paintbrush of the friend Picasso', is followed by 'the affectionate evocation of another major cultural figure':

> *Son*: The well-known South American maestro
> Señor Erik Satie
> Is finishing an opera which has four bars in duple time
> *Husband*: 4 bars We'll talk of it again it's not finished

Read believes this must be 'an ironic reference to the ballet *Parade*',[71]

---

[69] Orledge, *Satie the Composer*, p. 362 note 56. This information was communicated to Orledge by David Mateer, who located the document in the Harry Ransom Center, Austin, Texas.

[70] Cited in Peter Read, *Apollinaire et Les mamelles de Tirésias: La revanche d'Eros*. Rennes: Presses Universitaires de Rennes, 2000, p. 97. Extracts of Germaine Albert-Birot's score are cited on pp. 99–103 of Read's book.

[71] Ibid., pp. 127–8: 'Après la référence au pinceau de «l'ami Picasso», vient dans le manuscrit l'évocation affectueuse d'une autre grande figure de la vie culturelle: ¶ *Le Fils* – Le maestro sud-américain bien connu ¶ Senior Erik Satie ¶ Termine un opéra qui a quatre mesures à deux temps ¶ *Le Mari* – 4 mesures On en reparlera c'est pas fini ¶ S'agit-il d'une référence ironique au ballet *Parade* [?]' Read notes that many versions of

for which Apollinaire wrote a preface where he famously coined a new word, 'sur-réalisme'. It is certainly surreal to see Satie being described as South American[72] and *Parade* being alluded to as an opera. Happily, the composer did complete the ballet in time for its premiere in May 1917.

Parade and its 'bruits'

The story of the collaboration of Cocteau, Satie, Picasso and Massine for *Parade*, a Ballets Russes commission, has been told many times.[73] Here, I will focus on the mechanical aspects of *Parade* and Satie's use of 'noises' ('bruits') which are not conventionally part of an orchestra. The trained monkey on Picasso's magnificent curtain is typical of 'fête forain' troupes[74] and is also associated with the barrel organ. Another dancing monkey, Jonas, appears in Satie's play *Le piège de Méduse* and starts moving when the barrel organ-like repetitive dances are played on a prepared piano.

The structure of *Parade* can be traced back to *Trois morceaux en forme de poire*. Indeed, Cocteau's wish to collaborate with Satie was triggered by a performance of the *Trois morceaux* at a Festival Satie-Ravel at 6 rue Huyghens on 18 April 1916. Satie performed the duet with Ricardo Viñes, and according to Ornella Volta, 'Jean Cocteau wanted to see [Satie] again to propose a ballet for Diaghilev which would use this score.' She continues:

> they met on 26 April at Valentine [Gross's flat]. Cocteau brought along three sheets of onion skin paper on which, in picturesque language of lyrical/futurist inspiration, he proposed to illustrate the *Morceaux en forme de poire* by three fairground turns: a Chinese conjuror (then a familiar figure in the music hall); a Little American Girl (inspired by fashionable short films featuring Pearl White or Mary Pickford); and an Acrobat, well-trained in the dangerous arts of the circus. Satie was hostile to the use of one of his 'old pieces'

---

the play exist, including a collage-like manuscript which is now housed in the Bibliothèque littéraire Jacques Doucet. Its first page is signed: 'Guillaume Apollinaire *Les Mamelles de Tirésias* en 2 actes et un prologue 1903–1915–1917.'

[72] Though his sister Olga emigrated to Buenos Aires in 1902 following the breakdown of her relationship with her late husband's family.

[73] Most notably by Deborah Menaker Rothschild in a splendidly detailed documentary account (*Picasso's 'Parade'*), and in Christine Reynolds' chapter, based on manuscript sources, which convincingly outlines connections between Satie's musical structure, geometrical shapes and scientific discoveries ('Parade, ballet réaliste', in Caroline Potter (ed.), *Erik Satie: Music, Art and Literature*. Farnham: Ashgate, 2013, pp. 137–60).

[74] Rothschild, *Picasso's 'Parade'*, p. 220.

(the *Morceaux* were composed thirteen years earlier) and would only accept to work with the poet on condition they did something completely new.[75]

Satie's score for *Parade* was certainly not the same as his earlier work, but *Parade* and the *Trois morceaux* do have an odd sevenfold structure in common: three dances in the centre of the work are framed by two introductory sections and two concluding ones. *Trois morceaux en forme de poire* starts with a 'Manière de commencement' and 'Prolongation du même' ('Way of beginning' and 'Prolonging of the same'), and the three dances are followed by 'En plus' and 'Redite' ('More' and 'Restatement'). *Parade* begins with a 'Choral' and 'Prélude au Rideau rouge', and its last two sections framing the three dances are 'Final' and 'Suite au Prélude au Rideau rouge'. Although *Parade* was originally conceived as a stage production, its piano duet concert version was, like *Trois morceaux en forme de poire*, frequently performed in 6 rue Huyghens and other contemporary venues, often with the composer as one of the pianists.

While the origins of *Parade* in the circus and street entertainment are clear, it also has a number of possible French stage ancestors. A great admirer of Chabrier, Satie perhaps knew that the composer had collaborated with Paul Verlaine and Lucien Viotti in two unfinished opéra-bouffes, *Fisch-Ton-Kan* (1863) and *Vaucochard et fils 1er* (1864). The former one-act work was premiered in a voice and piano version on 31 March 1875, with Chabrier playing the piano, and some of its plot and material were recycled in his opera *L'étoile* (1877). The title of *Fisch-Ton-Kan* (which looks like an exotic name but sounds like 'Fiche ton camp', or 'fuck off') reflected the contemporary vogue for all things Oriental, and the work is also of interest in this context because the characters include Poussah, a tumbling mechanical toy. David Drew refers to *Fisch-Ton-Kan* as a 'circus operetta' and specifically mentions 'Chabrier's tender lament for a fallen acrobat and his *bâton poli*'. Drew also draws attention to Louis Ganne's

---

[75] Volta (ed.), *Correspondance*, pp. 727–8: 'Jean Cocteau a souhaité revoir notre compositeur pour lui proposer un ballet pour Diaghilev qui utiliserait cette partition [...] ils se retrouvent, le 26 avril, chez Valentine [Gross]. Cocteau apporte trois feuillets de papier-pelure où, dans un langage imagé d'inspiration lyrico-futuriste, il propose d'illustrer les *Morceaux en forme de poire* par trois attractions foraines: un Prestidigitateur chinois, vedette habituelle des music-halls de l'époque, une Petite fille américaine, issue des feuilletons cinématographiques alors en vogue, interprétés par Pearl White ou Mary Pickford, et un Acrobate, bien entraîné aux jeux périlleux du cirque. ¶ Satie se montrera hostile à l'utilisation d'une de ses «vieilles œuvres» (les Morceaux ont été composés treize ans plus tôt), et n'acceptera de collaborer avec le poète qu'à condition de faire quelque chose de complètement nouveau.'

then-popular operetta *Les saltimbanques* (1899) as another possible source for the plot of *Parade*.[76]

Cocteau's scenario for *Parade* was printed in the programme book for the premiere performances. It is, in full:

> The stage set represents Paris houses on a Sunday. Fairground theatre. Three music hall numbers serve as a promotional act (*parade*).
> Chinese conjuror
> American girl
> Acrobats
> Three managers organise the publicity. They communicate with each other in such terrifying language that the crowd takes the promotional act to be the spectacle inside; the managers try vulgarly to make the crowd understand.
> Nobody is convinced.
> After the final music hall turn, the managers make a supreme effort.
> The Chinese man, acrobats and girl leave the empty theatre.
> Seeing the managers' failure, they try one last time to demonstrate their virtues.
> But it is too late.[77]

The 'spectacle inside' has a dual meaning: both the 'real' show happening in the circus tent which the promotional acts and managers are plugging, and one's personal perception of the show. Small wonder that such a plot, full of ambiguity and double meaning, suited Satie so well. He often styles his music as an entr'acte, a sideshow rather than the real spectacle, and popular entertainment is central to his musical language. The poignancy of the ultimate failure of the managers' and performers' efforts, even after what are described in the score as

---

[76] David Drew, 'The Savage Parade – from Satie, Cocteau and Picasso to the Britten of Les Illuminations and Beyond.' *Tempo*, 207 (2001): pp. 7–21, at pp. 10–11. Francis Poulenc, in his book *Emmanuel Chabrier*, recalls the second performance of the two operettas 'à la Salle du Conservatoire, le 22 April 1941. J'ai eu l'honneur de tenir la partie du piano dans *Fisch-Ton-Kan* et Roger Désormière, chabriériste ému, dirigeait *Vaucochard*.' (Geneva and Paris: La Palatine, 1961, p. 37).

[77] 'Le décor représente les maisons à Paris un dimanche. Théâtre forain. Trois numéros de music-hall servent de parade. ¶ Prestidigitateur chinois ¶ Petite fille américaine ¶ Acrobates ¶ Trois managers organisent la réclame. Ils se communiquent dans leur langage terrible que la foule prend la parade pour le spectacle intérieur et cherchent grossièrement à le lui faire comprendre. ¶ Personne ne se laisse convaincre. ¶ Après le numéro final, suprême effort des managers. ¶ Chinois, acrobates et petite fille sortent du théâtre vide. ¶ Voyant le crach des managers, ils essayent une dernière fois la vertu de leurs belles grâces. ¶ Mais il est trop tard.'

'supreme efforts', surely resonated strongly with Satie, who was not afraid to confront the ultimate meaninglessness of art or life. His music for *Parade* is a repetitive backdrop, its tunes constantly rotating around a small number of notes. And when it appears to be going somewhere in traditional musical terms, as in the introductory fugue, he cuts it off abruptly and moves on to a new, trivial idea (see Ex. 2.4 below).

Most accounts of the *Parade* collaborative process mention that Satie was reluctant to go along with Cocteau's wish that everyday sounds be included in his score. John Richardson notes that

> Satie was not prepared to have his music serve as a background to Cocteau's secondhand bruitism: mechanical noises that mimicked the din of modern life and, the poet felt, would serve the same purpose as bits of papier collé and trompe l'œil in a cubist composition. [...] As a seemingly conciliatory gesture, Satie agreed to incorporate some of 'Jean's noises' – trains, sirens, airplanes, revolver shots and the like – into his score, but he did not conceal his distaste and, with Picasso and Diaghilev's connivance, had the noises suppressed at the first performance.[78]

But Satie's attitude to the inclusion of the noises was more ambiguous than this suggests, judging by the score: the unconventional sounds are unequivocally the centre of attention because they always appear against a lightly scored ostinato backdrop. Once again, we see Satie composing music intended to be heard in the background, here taking second place to a foreground of non-musical noises.

The unconventional sounds used in this 'ballet réaliste sur un thème de Jean Cocteau', as the score is described on the title page, are, in order of appearance (and somewhat at odds with Richardson's description), a high-pitched siren, lottery wheel, squishy puddles (*flaques sonores*), typewriter, revolver, and a low-pitched siren. The first three of these 'instruments' appear in the first of the three dances, for a Chinese conjurer, and the typewriter, revolver and low-pitched siren accompany the American girl's dance (Satie's Trinitarian obsession extends as far as the number of 'noises' used). The low-pitched siren heralds the orchestral wave which depicts the sinking of the *Titanic*; Robert Orledge has shown that Satie drafted this passage eight times before he was satisfied with it.[79]

On Satie's manuscript, which is now housed in the Frederick R. Koch Foundation, Yale University, Cocteau wrote: 'The Little American Girl's entire number is accompanied by the uninterrupted chime of an electronic cinema bell.' What Satie would have made of this sonic invasion of his score can only be imagined. In similarly impractical terms, Cocteau noted later on the score, 'here the orchestra accompanies a solo

---

[78] John Richardson, *A Life of Picasso*, vol. 2. London: Pimlico, 1996, p. 420.

[79] Orledge, *Satie the Composer*, pp. 128–31 and 313–14.

Ex. 2.3 Ranges of bouteillophone and xylophone in 'Acrobates' (*Parade*, third dance)

of 20 typewriters', and the gunshot is cued with 'revolver shots from Westerns'.[80] The noises used in the final version of the ballet are therefore a scaling back, which would surely have earned the composer's approval, of Cocteau's concepts as noted on this manuscript. It is hardly surprising that the ballet proved highly controversial at its first performances in May 1917: the wartime audience would not have been used to perceiving siren sounds and gunshots as sources of entertainment. The American Girl's dance 'Ragtime du paquebot' (Liner Ragtime), which is rhythmically modelled on Irving Berlin's 'That Mysterious Rag', reminds us that the Americans had entered the war on 6 April 1917, only a month before the premiere of the ballet – though Satie could hardly be credited with this foresight.

The third dance, for two acrobats, does not feature sounds which audiences would immediately associate with everyday activities, but it has a prominent part for 'bouteillophone'. The wide range of this bottle-based instrument is indicated at the start of the acrobats' dance, together with that of the xylophone (Ex. 2.3). In this dance, the range of the bouteillophone is therefore as extensive as that of the xylophone and there is no duplication of notes in their ranges. Perhaps Satie is here making a sly connection with another Ballets Russes commission, Stravinsky's *Petrushka* (1910–11), which was performed on the same programme as the *Parade* premiere. Its eponymous puppet is constantly associated with a piano figuration which juxtaposes white and black notes, symbolising his two sides. Petrushka is a puppet, though he has human feelings, resulting in an uncomfortable juxtaposition of two distinct worlds. (The *Titanic* wave mentioned above is similarly bitonal, perhaps symbolising the human/nature clash.)

While performers of the ballet and Satie scholars have assumed that the bouteillophone is a homemade contraption based on bottles filled with different amounts of water, played by striking the bottles with a hard beater, the origins of this instrument are rather more interesting. An instrument called the bouteillophone has been known in France since the

---

[80] Cited in Rothschild, *Picasso's 'Parade'*, p. 89: 'Tout le numéro de la petite fille américaine est accompagné par un timbre électronique cinéma ininterrompu [...] ici l'orchestre accompagne le solo de 20 machines à écrire [...] coups de revolver des films du Far West.'

Fig. 2.2 Bouteillophone

nineteenth century: Gavioli, the celebrated manufacturer of mechanical instruments, built an elaborately housed bouteillophone in 1900–8 which is illustrated in Fig. 2.2. An anonymous author writing for the newspaper *Le Parisien* describes this instrument as being like an organ, but 'its pipes have been replaced by bottles which are more or less filled with wine. It has a position of honour on a rostrum at the back of a huge Art Deco reception hall and right on cue, when you sit down at your table in front of your carved gargoyle, at the very moment when you are going to raise your glass of Morgon, the "bottlephone" starts working!'[81] The article goes on to state that only two examples of the instrument are known to survive in France today, including the example illustrated above which is now owned by the Dubœuf winemaking family and housed in 'Le Hameau du Vin', their museum on the outskirts of Lyon. A mechanical instrument based on wine bottles would surely have been an irresistible concept for Satie, who died of cirrhosis of the liver in 1925, though it is

---

[81] *Le Parisien*, 3 June 2012; 'ses tuyaux ont été remplacés par des bouteilles plus ou moins remplies de vin. Il trône sur une estrade au fond d'une vaste salle de réception Art déco et pile, lorsque vous vous attablez devant votre guéridon, au moment où vous allez lever votre verre de morgon, le «bouteillophone» se met en route!'

likely that the *Parade* instrument was a simpler contraption of filled bottles which were struck by a percussionist.

Honegger used the bouteillophone in *Le dit des jeux du monde* in 1918,[82] commissioned by Jane Bathori for the Théâtre du Vieux-Colombier and based on a creation myth-themed text by the Belgian poet Paul Méral. Given his connections with Satie, it is inconceivable that he was not inspired by Satie's use of the instrument. Like *Parade*, *Le dit des jeux du monde* was an ambitious fusion of the arts, this time including movement and a spoken chorus. Michel Corvin writes that the director Louise Lara 'collaborated with talented artists and conceived a daring production in which the concept of simultanism was not expressed in the combination of voices, but in the convergence of the arts of dance, mime, music and words, producing what we would now term "total theatre"'.[83] While *Le dit des jeux du monde* was critically a failure, largely because of its weak text, it did create a minor scandal thanks to its eighth number, 'L'Homme et la Femme', with shrieking cellos representing a woman in the throes of erotic ecstasy, responded to by a male-representing trumpet.

The piano duet score of *Parade* was published by Rouart-Lerolle in 1917 with a preface by Georges Auric. The young composer writes:

> The terrible mysteries of China, the sadness of a bar at night of the little American girl, the astonishing gymnastics of the acrobats: all the poignancy of the trestle tables is there – nostalgia for the barrel organ which will never play Bach fugues.
>
> Satie's score is conceived as a musical background to a foreground of percussion and stage noises.
>
> Thus it submits, humbly, to reality which muffles the nightingale's song beneath the wheels of a tram.[84]

Auric's rich text is both suggestive and is such a close echo of Cocteau's *Le coq et l'arlequin* that the two authors must have been working together.

---

[82] Douglas Kahn, *Noise, Water, Meat: A History of Sound in the Arts.* Cambridge, MA: MIT Press, 1999, p. 416 note 12.

[83] Corvin. *Le théâtre de recherche*, p. 76: 'Louise Lara s'était assuré le concours d'artistes de talent et elle avait conçu une mise en scène audacieuse où le simultanéisme ne résidait plus dans la combinaison des voix, mais dans la convergence des arts de la danse, de la mime, de la musique et de la parole, selon une formule que nous qualifierons aujourd'hui de «théâtre total».'

[84] Score, p. 3: 'Les mystères terribles de la Chine, la tristesse de bar nocturne de la petite américaine, les gymnastiques étonnantes des acrobates: c'est là toute la douleur des trétaux, – la nostalgie de l'orgue de barbarie qui jamais ne jouera de fugues de Bach. ¶ La partition de Satie est conçue pour servir de fond musical à un premier plan de batterie et de bruits scéniques. ¶ Ainsi elle se soumet très humblement à la réalité qui étouffe le chant du rossignol sous le roulement des tramways.'

Cocteau's famous statement that 'The piano duet score of *Parade* does not represent the exact work, but the musical backdrop which throws into relief the foreground of percussion and stage noises'[85] is almost identical to Auric's words. And the 'Prélude au rideau rouge' starts as a four-voice fugue, with instruments entering in turn from the bass upwards, but rather than following classic fugal development processes, it falls apart and is followed by two unrelated repetitive figures. The barrel organ takes over from the Bach fugue (Ex. 2.4).

The eclectic range of material in the music, staging and choreography shows the Ballets Russes had, after eight years of Paris performances, moved well beyond their origins as a Russian ballet company. And, *pace* Cocteau, *Parade* is not specifically French either, but a work reflecting both the borderless world of the circus and newer popular forms of American entertainment. Did Satie agree with Auric that his music is potentially a nightingale which is squashed by modernity? Whether or not Satie concurred with this symbolic interpretation, it is true that his music has an unusually humble quality: witness also *Socrate*, whose simple melody lines support the text without providing superfluous decoration. Satie is content for his music to act as an unobtrusive background and as part of a broader multimedia concept.

Not everyone noticed this humility. The critic Jean Poueigh took an interest in 'cubism in music', writing an article on that topic for the weekly *La Rampe* on 24 May 1917. Here, he noted that simultanism is a key concept in contemporary music: 'For a long time, notes, themes, counterpoints have been used to expressing themselves together. Simultanism of tonalities is therefore not something which surprises us, even though its use is currently limited to simple discords whose systematic repetition blunts them and makes them uniform.' Carol-Bérard and the Italian futurists are both cited here, though Poueigh stresses he considers Carol-Bérard to be a composer 'of no originality'. Finally, he criticises Satie for adding irrelevant texts to his piano music and presenting his work eccentrically, with no bar lines and odd enharmonic notations: Poueigh believes 'this lack of humour must be deliberate and must be a result of M. Erik Satie's superior irony'.[86]

---

[85] Cited in Rothschild, *Picasso's 'Parade'*, p. 88; 'Le piano à quatre mains de Parade ne présente pas l'œuvre exacte mais le fond musical destiné à mettre en relief un premier plan de batterie et de bruits scéniques.'

[86] Octave Séré [Jean Poueigh], 'Le cubisme et la musique.' *La Rampe: Revue Hebdomadaire des spectacles* (24 May 1917): p. 1; 'Notes, thèmes, contre-points, sont depuis longtemps habitués à s'exprimer ensemble. Le simultanéisme des tonalités n'est donc point pour nous surprendre, encore qu'il se borne actuellement à nous offrir de simples discordances que leur répétition systématique a tôt fait d'émousser et d'uniformiser. [...] cette absence d'humour doit être voulue et provenir de l'ironie supérieure de M. Erik Satie.'

Ex. 2.4 *Parade*, 'Prélude au rideau rouge': piano duet version

Continued overleaf

But Poueigh's review of *Parade* offended Satie far more. The critic had complimented Satie on the work on 18 May but then, hypocritically in Satie's view, published a hostile review on 27 May in *Les Carnets de la Semaine*, though this barely mentions the music.[87] The composer was

[87] See Orledge, *Satie the Composer*, p. xxxii.

Ex. 2.4 continued

moved to send him a postcard three days after this review appeared, accusing him of being 'an arsehole – I daresay an unmusical arsehole'.[88] This missive, together with two other postcards using similar language and sentiments (and written in similar florid calligraphy), prompted Poueigh to sue Satie for libel: after all, anyone could have read these insults written on open postcards. June and early July 1917 saw Satie growing increasingly worried by this legal action, writing to Ricardo Viñes early in July 'I've "had it." Everything's against me.'[89] Several artists spoke in Satie's defence as character witnesses at his trial – Cocteau, Gino Severini, André Lhote and Juan Gris all appeared – but he was convicted, sentenced to a week in prison and required to pay damages of 1000 francs to Poueigh. An appeal that November was unsuccessful. Two leading music patrons in Paris came to Satie's aid: Misia Edwards (later Sert) and the Princesse de Polignac lobbied their legal contacts on Satie's behalf and

---

[88] Postcard to Jean Poueigh, 30 May 1917, cited in Volta (ed.), *Correspondance*, p. 289: 'vous êtes un cul – si j'ose dire, un «cul» sans musique'.

[89] Ibid., p. 291 (undated, Volta suggests 9 July 1917): 'Je suis «frit». Tout est contre moi.'

the Princesse loaned him the money to pay the fine. As Mary Davis wrote, 'thanks no doubt to their influence, the affair came to a close, as the court suspended Satie's sentence' on 18 March 1918. He never did pay Poueigh the damages.[90]

Satie, Cocteau and Les Six

Cocteau's musical manifesto *Le coq et l'arlequin* proclaimed Satie, after their *Parade* collaboration, as a truly French composer who should be the model for young musicians. Although not a musician himself, Cocteau knew what he liked and was happy to give detailed advice to composers about what sounds were to be preferred. He wrote in his manifesto:

> Soon we can hope for an orchestra without caressing strings. A rich wind band with woodwind, brass and percussion.
> It would not be disagreeable to us to replace the cult of Saint Cecilia with that of Saint Polycarp.
> It would be fine if a composer wrote for a mechanical organ, a true factory of sounds. We would hear, if well used, the riches which this device accidentally provides us among those old chestnuts.[91]

While it is unclear to what extent Cocteau was explicitly referring to Satie in this passage, it is striking that he mentions 'Saint Polycarp' as Polycarpe is one of the characters in Satie's play *Le piège de Méduse* and the music Satie wrote for his play is essentially barrel organ music, to be repeated as often as required, but played by a human performer. In his manifesto, Cocteau opposes the patron saint of music, Saint Cecilia, with Saint Polycarp, the patron saint of noise (and earaches). And as Cocteau, according to Auric at least, wrote *Le coq et l'arlequin* 'after "all kinds of conversations with Satie and Auric"',[92] it is impossible to distinguish with confidence Cocteau's view from Satie's and/or Auric's.

The first encounters between the future members of Les Six and Satie happened around 1915 in Montparnasse. While Cocteau was part

---

[90] Mary E. Davis, *Erik Satie*. London: Reaktion, 2007, p. 120.

[91] Jean Cocteau, *Le coq et l'arlequin*. Paris: Editions de la Sirène ('Collection des Tracts no 1'), 1918, p. 35. New edition, Paris: Stock, 1979, p. 65: 'On peut espérer bientôt un orchestre sans la caresse des cordes. Un riche orphéon de bois, de cuivres et de batterie. ¶ Il ne nous déplairait pas de substituer au culte de sainte Cécile celui de saint Polycarpe. ¶ Il serait beau qu'un compositeur composât pour un orgue mécanique, véritable usine à sons. On entendrait, bien employées, les richesses que cet appareil prodigue accidentellement autour des rengaines.'

[92] Cited in Jann Pasler, 'New Music as Confrontation: The Musical Sources of Jean Cocteau's Identity.' *Musical Quarterly*, vol. 75 no. 3 (1991): pp. 255–78, at p. 271; see also Auric, 'Témoignages' (*Cahiers Jean Cocteau* 7, 'Avec les musiciens'), p. 62.

Fig. 2.3 Photo of Satie by Henri Manuel (April 1917) dedicated 'à Jean Cocteau, son gros vieil ami' (Archives de la Fondation Erik Satie)

of this circle, he did not meet Satie until 18 October 1915 at the home of their friend Valentine Gross,[93] when their proposed collaboration on *A Midsummer Night's Dream* was already losing momentum. Most of these composers were involved in concerts which took place in unconventional venues, many traditional concert halls being closed because of the war. One of these venues was 6 rue Huyghens, a Montparnasse artists' workshop off boulevard Raspail, round the corner from grand brasseries

---

[93] See Volta (ed.), *Correspondance*, p. 726.

such as La Coupole and Le Dôme. This space was owned by the Swiss painter Emile Lejeune, who suggested to a friend, the concert impresario Arthur Dandelot, that his studio be used as a concert venue; Dandelot took up this suggestion but soon passed the role of organiser to the Swedish composer Henrik Melchers.[94] Many of these concerts were given in conjunction with poetry readings and exhibitions. Lejeune published his memoirs of Montparnasse in a series of articles in a Geneva newspaper in 1964. He described the venue in an article illustrated with a drawing of Satie by Picasso:

> To the right of the entrance, a fairly low platform was a suitable stage for musicians. On the opposite side, a much higher platform allowed listeners in this part of the room to follow the musicians and singers above the audience seated in the central space. This area with a stone floor was the only part with a skylight, but the blinds I had installed with a view to running evening classes had a dual purpose as they filtered the light, all artificial light being forbidden in wartime Paris. The precarious light of a lantern near the entrance door indicated the path towards the courtyard. For the seating, I rented a hundred seats from the Jardin de Luxembourg for our Saturday evenings and had to return them the following morning. [...] This modest and basic space saw the birth of the famous 'Group of Six' under the patronage of Erik Satie, allowed Modigliani relief from his miserable existence, and housed exhibitions where works by Matisse, Picasso, Kisling, Vlaminck, Juan Gris, Waroquier and many others who are less well known were shown, not to mention the mornings when Max Jacob, Apollinaire, Jean Cocteau and Blaise Cendrars read their poems.[95]

---

[94] Emile Lejeune, 'Montparnasse à l'époque héroïque, 6.' *Tribune de Genève*, no. 31, 6 février 1964, p. 1.

[95] Emile Lejeune, 'Montparnasse à l'époque héroïque, 5.' *Tribune de Genève*, no. 30, 5 février 1964, p. 1: 'A droite en entrant, un plancher assez bas était d'ores et déjà destiné à recevoir les exécutants. Dans le fond opposé, un plancher beaucoup plus élevé allait permettre aux auditeurs de cette partie de suivre musiciens et chanteurs par-dessus le public de la partie centrale. Celle-ci, macadamisée, était la seule surmontée d'une verrière mais les vélums que j'avais fait installer en vue d'hypothétiques cours du soir avaient eux aussi trouvé leur destination en ne laissant filtrer qu'une vague lueur, tout foyer de lumière étant interdit à Paris en temps de guerre. L'éclairage précaire d'une lanterne, près de la porte d'entrée indiquait le chemin à suivre dès l'abord de la cour. Quant aux sièges, j'en avais loué une centaine à la chaisière du Jardin de Luxembourg pour nos samedis soirs et on devait les lui rapporter le lendemain. [...] Ce modeste et rudimentaire local vit naître le fameux « Groupe des Six » sous l'égide d'Erik Satie, permit à Modigliani de sortir de la misère et d'abriter des expositions où les œuvres de Matisse, Picasso, Kisling, Vlaminck, Juan

One of the first musical events in this space was a Satie-Ravel festival promoted by Lyre et Palette which took place on 18 April 1916,[96] introduced by the composer Roland-Manuel. His talk was published with a bibliography by Henri Roberge in the same year. Artists were also involved in designing the programmes. The attractive folded programme for the Satie-Ravel concert features a black, red and blue woodcut design by Henri Hayden on the front, with motifs including a tricolour flag, bread and wine glass, musical score, stave with treble clef and notes, cello and a cockerel – in other words, a celebration of things musical and French.

A group of young composers supported Satie when *Parade* was attacked by critics such as Jean Poueigh. These composers put on a concert at 6 rue Huyghens on 6 June 1917 featuring the piano duet version of *Parade* (played by the composer and Juliette Méerovitch, one of his favourite pianists who died suddenly in 1920), Georges Auric's *Pièces en trio*, Louis Durey's *Carillons* for two pianos[97] and three poems by Apollinaire set by Arthur Honegger. The group became known as the Nouveaux Jeunes, though the three younger composers, together with Germaine Tailleferre, Francis Poulenc and Darius Milhaud, would become more notorious under the banner Les Six.

The journey from the Nouveaux Jeunes to Les Six and the involvement of Satie and Cocteau in these groups is complex. Robert Orledge claims that Satie came up with the slogan 'Nouveaux Jeunes' and this 'referred back to the pre-war support he had received from the Jeunes Ravêlites who [...] he preferred to call simply "Jeunes"'. The 'Nouveaux' prefix makes sense in this context, not least because Satie's friendship with Ravel cooled during the war years. Satie used the term 'le groupe des musiciens "Nouveaux Jeunes"' on a publicity document he wrote for a projected 'musique d'ameublement' concert at the Jove gallery in March 1918 (quoted in Chapter 4), and drafted an introductory text for a concert at the Théâtre du Vieux-Colombier which Orledge believes is the concert held on 5 February 1918.[98] This concert included works by Honegger, Durey, Tailleferre and Auric as well as Satie himself. Satie's text begins: 'The four first ones are young – very young ... My youth is

Gris, Waroquier et de bien d'autres non moins connus garnissaient les cimaises, sans compter les matinées où Max Jacob, Apollinaire, Jean Cocteau et Blaise Cendrars disaient leurs poèmes.'

[96] A copy of the programme is housed in IMEC, SAT 25.11.

[97] Durey's brother René was a painter acquainted with Moïse Kisling; Harry Halbreich notes that the painter introduced his brother to the venue (Arthur Honegger, *Lettres à ses parents, 1914–1922*, preface and annotations by Harry Halbreich. Geneva: Editions Papillon, 2005, p. 130 note 10).

[98] Robert Orledge, 'Satie & Les Six', in Richard Langham Smith and Caroline Potter (eds), *French Music since Berlioz*. Aldershot: Ashgate, 2006, pp. 223–48, at p. 233.

in my character. We got together because we like each other ... We rub along very well together ... We have neither President nor Treasurer nor Archivist nor Bursar ... Besides, we don't have any treasure. That suits us fine.'[99]

Later in 1918, Satie invited Charles Koechlin to be part of the Nouveaux Jeunes: Satie was then aged fifty-two and Koechlin was fifty-one. His letter to Koechlin, dated 28 September 1918, was to have 'No subscription; No rules; No Committee; Just – Us' and Koechlin claims that the forty-nine-year-old Albert Roussel, Satie's former teacher at the Schola Cantorum, was also invited to join this group.[100] Being young in spirit was, for Satie, obviously more important than chronological age. Cocteau's name does not appear in any discussions about this group, though as he read his poetry at Lyre et Palette events at the rue Huyghens studio and was invited to programme a 'Séance Music-Hall' at the Théâtre du Vieux-Colombier, including works by young composers and Satie, he moved in the same circles as the Nouveaux Jeunes. Satie's next move was perhaps unexpected: he wrote to Durey on 1 November 1918: 'Would you please be so kind as to consider me no longer part of the "Nouveaux Jeunes" group?'[101] Orledge believes his reasons for this resignation 'lay in Durey's growing friendship with (and admiration for) Ravel, to the extent of wanting to include him in the group's concerts'.[102] Indeed, Durey's *Carillons* for two pianos, a staple of rue Huyghens and Vieux-Colombier concerts, is far more reminiscent of Ravel than of Satie. It is also true that Satie was never temperamentally a group-joiner (nor was Koechlin), always preferring to assert his artistic and personal independence.

Later rue Huyghens concerts including all six members of Les Six (plus Roland-Manuel) include one which took place on 5 April 1919: Honegger is represented by *Entrée, Nocturne et Berceuse* (his furniture music pieces, discussed in more detail in Chapter 4), Tailleferre by *Image* for piano, string quartet, clarinet and celesta, and Durey by his song cycle *Images à Crusoé*. Poulenc's Sonata for two clarinets is also programmed, as is Milhaud's Fourth String Quartet and Auric's setting of three poems by Cocteau, sung by the singer-actor Pierre Bertin with accompaniment of

---

[99] Undated text, reproduced in Volta (ed.), *Satie Ecrits*, p. 80: 'Les quatre premiers sont jeunes – tout jeunes ... Ma jeunesse à moi est dans le caractère. Nous nous sommes réunis par sympathie ... Nous faisons très bon ménage ... Nous n'avons ni Président ni Trésorier ni Archiviste ni Econome ... Nous n'avons pas de trésor, du reste. Cela nous est très commode.'

[100] Orledge, 'Satie & Les Six', p. 233.

[101] Volta (ed.), *Correspondance*, p. 343: 'Voulez-vous être assez aimable pour me considérer comme ne faisant plus partie du groupe « Nouveaux Jeunes »?'

[102] Orledge, 'Satie & Les Six', p. 234.

string quartet, flute, clarinet and celesta.[103] The Auric work is a part of his collection of eight Cocteau settings which were completed in 1919. While the programme does not list which songs were performed, the first of Auric's collection is a setting of Cocteau's 'Hommage à Erik Satie', which references the Douanier Rousseau's paintings more than it does Satie's music. Only the last line 'Un morceau en forme de poire' specifically evokes the composer, the fruit's shape presumably also echoing that of the balloon lifting the painter's wife off the ground which is mentioned in other verses.

Les Six were baptised by the journalist Henri Collet, who had a regular column in the arts newspaper *Comœdia*. The group's official formation

> dates from one evening in December 1919, when Honegger and [his future wife] Andrée Vaurabourg played the Andante from Honegger's Second Sonata for violin and piano, at Milhaud's flat. Present were Auric, Poulenc, Durey and Tailleferre, and Henri Collet, who wanted to meet some of the younger members of the avant-garde. [...] On January 16, 1920, he headed his article 'Les Cinq Russes, les Six Français et M. Erik Satie', following it up with another on the same lines on the 23rd.

In this second article, Collet wrote that the six composers (whom he refers to as 'les Nouveaux Jeunes') had 'by a magnificent and voluntary return to simplicity, brought about a renaissance of French music, because they understood the lesson of Erik Satie and followed the clear precepts of Jean Cocteau'.[104] The group's existence was short-lived: they produced only one joint publication, a set of six short piano pieces titled *L'album des Six* (1920), and this was a compilation of pieces which had been composed earlier and not a unified set. While they were all scheduled to collaborate in Cocteau's ballet *Les mariés de la Tour Eiffel* (1921), Durey left the group before composing his contribution, and in one of the more unusual career moves by a composer, he left Paris for St Tropez to devote himself to Communist activity as well as music. Auric's overture for the ballet is an orchestration of his piano piece for *L'album des Six* – only the introductory section is new – and the industrious Tailleferre and Milhaud replaced Durey at the last minute.

Satie was again drawn into Les Six activity during his first trip abroad as an adult, when he visited Brussels for a performance of his work and that of other contemporary French composers. Cocteau was to have introduced the Les Six concert on 11 April 1921 and a Satie programme which was performed on the following day, but as his lover, the writer

---

[103] These programmes are housed in the Fonds Erik Satie at IMEC, SAT 25.11, SAT 25.15 and SAT 25.25.

[104] Martin Howe, 'Erik Satie and his Ballets, I.' *Ballet*, vol. 5 no. 8 (August–September 1948): pp. 25–32, 37, 39, 53–4, at p. 39.

Raymond Radiguet, was ill, Satie replaced Cocteau at the last minute. Satie's introduction features the highly individual punctuation style he used for spoken texts, indicating the place and length of pauses, and has a strangely mixed tone for a publicity talk. He starts by evoking his pleasure at introducing these composers, even saying 'I have shared great joy with them ... Yes ... I am very proud to find myself with Les Six. They know I love them very much. So ... they keep me near them. They keep me as a fetish object – which is pretty odd.'[105]

When he starts talking about the composers individually, his views are more nuanced. Discussing Apollinaire's concept of the 'Esprit Nouveau', which he used in his programme note for *Parade*, Satie said:

> For me ... the Esprit Nouveau is mainly a return to classical form – with a modern sensibility ...
>
> You'll find this modern sensibility in some members of Les Six ...
>
> Georges Auric ...
>
> Francis Poulenc ...
>
> Darius Milhaud ...
>
> ...
>
> ... As for the three other members of Les Six ...
>
> Louis Durey ...
>
> Arthur Honegger ...
>
> Germaine Tailleferre ...
>
> they are pure 'impressionists' ...

He clarified these remarks, up to a point, later in his talk:

> Back to my original subject ...
>
> Spontaneity ... Fantasy ... Daring ... this is what you see, ... at first sight, ... in Auric, ... Milhaud, ... Poulenc; ... concern for academic conventions, ... tried and tested harmonic formulae, ... these are the choice of Durey, ... Honegger, ... Tailleferre ...
>
> They are free to do that ...[106]

---

[105] Satie, 'Conférence sur les Six', dated 'Bruxelles, le 11 avril 1921', reprinted in Volta (ed.), *Satie Ecrits*, pp. 87–91, at p. 87: 'Avec eux, j'ai partagé de grandes joies ... [...] / Oui ... Je suis très fier de me trouver avec les «Six». / Ils savent que je les aime beaucoup. / Aussi ... me gardent-ils près d'eux. / Ils me conservent comme fétiche – ce qui est assez curieux.'

[106] Ibid., pp. 89–90: 'Pour moi ... l'Esprit Nouveau est surtout un retour vers la forme classique – avec sensibilité moderne ... ¶ C'est cette sensibilité moderne que vous rencontrez chez certains des «Six» ... ¶ Georges Auric ... ¶ Francis Poulenc ... ¶ Darius Milhaud ... ¶ ...¶ Quant aux trois autres «Six». ¶ Louis Durey ... ¶ Arthur Honegger ...¶ Germaine Tailleferre ...¶ ce sont de purs «impressionnistes» ...' [...] 'Je reviens à

It appears that 'impressionism' had become the new academicism.

Satie was not considered to be a good influence on Les Six. Writing in *Le Ménestrel* on the state of contemporary music, Paul Bertrand expressed anxiety about the future of French music, partly because he believed that the natural inclination of southern European composers (he calls it 'le génie gréco-latin') is for dramatic rather than symphonic music. He starts by considering that a reaction against impressionism (by which he means Debussy) was to be expected; Bertrand believed that 'Just as Claude Monet called to Picasso, Debussy's impressionism prepared the polytonal darings of the latest Stravinsky, continued with great clamour by Les Six, who praise as a symbolic rallying figure the facetious insignificance of Erik Satie. Besides, they have already been succeeded in the fashion stakes (doesn't it always happen?) by the teams of Italian "noisemakers".'[107]

It is therefore clear that Satie and Les Six were personally and professionally connected for a few years in the late 1910s and early 1920s: their music often appeared on the same programmes, and many of them were commissioned to compose for Rolf de Maré's Ballets Suédois, which was active in Paris from 1920 to 1925.[108] But did Satie exert any musical influence on Les Six? Although Honegger's mature musical language is distant from Satie's, he was the only member to be stimulated by the more experimental side of Satie, such as furniture music and the use of the bouteillophone. Towards the end of his life, in a letter to Poulenc dated 10 May 1954, Honegger wrote: 'I consider Satie an exceptionally honest spirit, but devoid of all creative ability – "Do what I say, never what I do".'[109] He had evidently forgotten his youthful enthusiasm for doing what Satie did. Tailleferre, whom Satie described on a score of *Parade* as

> mon sujet ... ¶ La Spontanéité ... la Fantaisie ... l'Audace, ... voilà ce qui se voit, ... en premier lieu, ... chez Auric, ... Milhaud, ... Poulenc; ... le souci des conventions d'Ecole, ... des formules harmoniques éprouvées, ... tel est le lot que choisissent Durey, ... Honegger, ... Tailleferre ... ¶ Ils sont libres d'agir ainsi ...'

[107] Paul Bertrand, 'Musique pure et musique dramatique', *Le Ménestrel*, 17 June 1921, pp. 249–51, at p. 250: 'De même que Claude Monet appelait Picasso, l'impressionnisme de Claude Debussy préparait les outrances polytoniques de Stravinsky dernière manière, continuées à grand tapage par les musiciens du groupe des «Six», qui exaltent, comme un signe de ralliement symbolique, l'insignifiance facétieuse de M. Erick Satie [sic]. Ils se trouvent d'ailleurs déjà dépassés (comme il arrive toujours), dans la voie des surenchères, par les équipes de «bruiteurs» italiens. [...]'

[108] Examples include Tailleferre's *Le marchand d'oiseaux* (1923), Honegger's *Skating Rink* (1921–2) and the collective *Les mariés de la Tour Eiffel* (1921), as well as Satie's *Relâche* (1924).

[109] See Harry Halbreich, *Arthur Honegger: Un musicien dans la cité des hommes*. Paris: Fayard, 1992. Translated by Roger Nichols, Portland, OR: Amadeus Press, 1999, p. 41.

his 'fille musicale', shows audible connections to Satie in the deliberately banal, nursery rhyme-like melodic lines of movements such as 'Cache-cache mitoula', from her two-piano work *Jeux de plein air* (1917). Similarly, the simple melodic outlines, stripped-down texture and mechanical quality of Poulenc's *Mouvements perpétuels* for piano (1918) nod to Satie's style. More generally, what Cocteau described as Satie's orchestra 'without sauce' is echoed in many chamber works dominated by brass and woodwind. Punchy, brief pieces such as Poulenc's Sonata for two clarinets (1918) are obviously indebted to Satie, and it could be argued that the brevity of Milhaud's six *Symphonies de chambre* (1917–23) and three *opéras-minutes* (1927) is very much in the spirit of the older composer. Durey is the member of Les Six who is least obviously inspired by Satie: his *Carillons* and *Neige* for two pianos (1916), which were often played in the late 1910s, are far closer to Ravel in their harmonic language and texture.

Satie and Stravinsky ... and Ravel

Although Satie never composed for a mechanical musical instrument, Stravinsky, who was acquainted with Satie, wrote a Study for pianola in 1917 which was first performed in 1921. Here Stravinsky, unlike Satie in any of his works, is deliberately writing music for a superhuman with multiple hands, music which is unplayable by a pianist with the usual number of limbs. He is of interest in this context because Satie wrote two articles on Stravinsky for *Vanity Fair* and *Feuilles libres* which are very rare examples of him exploring another composer in detail in writing that was painstakingly researched. Indeed, Satie wrote to Stravinsky on 17 October 1922: 'I'm writing another article on you, for *Feuilles libres* this time. [Marcel] RAVAL (not Ravel) asks me if you might have a scrap of paper which could be reproduced. I would like to talk to you about your "mechanical" works. A few bars of your choice on this matter would be tremendously useful to me.'[110]

In his 1922 article for *Feuilles libres*, Satie chooses to focus on some lesser-known works by Stravinsky, notably his Study for pianola, dedicated to Eugenia Errazuriz who was also a patron of Picasso. Satie writes on this work:

> Hearing a mechanical instrument is a revolt against tradition, appals common practice; and such novel sound production produces all sorts of difficulties (the material ones being the most

---

[110] Volta (ed.), *Correspondance*, p. 497: 'J'écris un autre article sur vous, pour les « Feuilles Libres », cette fois. [Marcel] RAVAL (pas Ravel) me demande si vous n'auriez pas un bout de page à envoyer pour être reproduit là. Je voudrais parler de vous au sujet de vos travaux « mécaniques ». Quelques mesures, à votre choix, sur ce cas feraient richement mon affaire.' Marcel Raval was the editor of *Feuilles libres*.

welcome and most amusing of them all). How fruitless it is to go back on well-trodden ground in the name of supposed traditions, whose only attractive feature is decrepitude. Yes. One might be surprised to hear talented virtuosi tell us they think mechanical instruments are possible competitors. It appears to me that it is an insult to oneself to even think such a thought, to have such a fear.

After all, the pianola is not the same instrument as its friend the piano, with whom it has only brotherly relations. Igor Stravinsky, before anyone else, has written a work in which certain capabilities peculiar to this instrument are genuinely used. Keyboard virtuosi should know very well that they could never do what an ordinary pianola is capable of; and on the other hand, a machine could never be substituted for them.[111]

As always with Satie, it is perilous to try to untangle what is merely a humorous remark from what might be a serious aesthetic point. His charming description of the pianola and piano being friends and brothers subtly undermines the reader's assumption that the mechanical instrument is an alien creation which might put human pianists out of work. What is clear, though, is that Satie enjoys the provocative aspects of this new instrument. He alludes to typical arguments against mechanical instruments – that 'this is not the way things have been done in the past', that they are new and probably expensive – and counteracts these arguments by undermining the value of 'supposed traditions'. Most importantly, Satie appreciates Stravinsky's use of the pianola as an independent instrument which has capabilities (even if the pianola is an 'ordinary' one) which virtuoso pianists do not possess. I am unsure, however, whether this important passage should be read in the light of Satie's own music; would a machine not be the 'best' performer of

---

[111] Published in *Feuilles libres*, 29 (October–November 1922), reproduced in Volta (ed.), *Satie Ecrits*, pp. 38–41 (this extract at p. 40): 'L'audition d'un instrument automate révulse les coutumes, indigne les usages; et une réalisation sonore aussi neuve offre des difficultés de toutes sortes (celles matérielles sont les plus clémentes, les plus souriantes). Combien est-il aride de remonter des courants créés au nom de prétendues traditions, et dont l'unique agrément est la vétusté. Oui. ¶ Il y a lieu d'être surpris lorsque nous entendons des virtuoses de talent nous dire qu'ils jugent les *instruments enregistreurs* comme de possibles concurrents. C'est, il me semble, se faire injure à soi-même que de concevoir une telle pensée, que d'avoir une telle crainte. ¶ Avant tout, le *pianola* est un autre instrument que son camarade le piano, dont il n'a que de fraternelle attaches. Igor Strawinsky, avant tout autre, a réellement écrit un morceau où certaines ressources propres à cet instrument se trouvent employées. Que les virtuoses du clavier sachent bien que jamais ils ne pourront faire ce que fait un ordinaire pianola; mais que, par contre, jamais un moyen mécanique ne pourra leur être substitué.'

Vexations (1893), which according to Satie's note on the score could be played 840 times? And although Satie's piano music was championed by celebrated soloists of his time, including Ricardo Viñes and Marcelle Meyer, his music is not designed for performance by 'keyboard virtuosi'.

Stravinsky planned to compose again for player piano. *Les noces* went through several iterations for different ensembles, including a second version sketched in Switzerland in 1918 for harmonium, two cimbaloms, pianola and percussion,[112] before the definitive version for four pianos and percussion was completed. Robert Craft described *Les noces* as 'Stravinsky's most mechanized creation, inspired in this sense by the orchestrion of Beethoven's time'.[113] Craft also claims that 'Stravinsky once commissioned Pleyel to build a mechanical cimbalom for him, but nothing came of the request.' But even before this flurry of interest in the pianola, Stravinsky showed an interest in music based on mechanical instruments. In *Petrushka* we see him using the orchestra to imitate a hurdy-gurdy – and, of course, the tale of a puppet who springs to life and demonstrates human feelings is a traditional theme which at the same time betrays contemporary anxieties about the links between the human and the mechanical. This is a ballet in which the puppets act like human beings, and the human characters act like automata. In the first scene of the ballet, the orchestra mimics a barrel organ which, typically, plays not a newly created melody but a well-known song, in this case the French popular song *Une jambe de bois* (A wooden leg). There is a dancing bear in the final scene, led by a peasant – though it is not dancing to the traditional accompaniment of a barrel organ. In fact, Stravinsky wrote to Andrei Rimsky-Korsakov, son of his former teacher, in 1910 urgently requesting him to send transcriptions of music box and barrel organ tunes: he was already thinking about *Petrushka*.[114]

Stravinsky's Etude for pianola was one of a series of works commissioned for the new instrument by Aeolian in 1917–18. Other composers commissioned included the Italians Gian Francesco Malipiero and Alfredo Casella, and Rex Lawson persuasively argues that Ravel may have also been asked to compose for the instrument.[115] Ravel's tiny *Frontispice* for piano duet (1918) was composed 'as a frontispiece for Ricciotto Canudo's *S.P.503: le poème du Vardar*'; Lawson notes that 'the

---

[112] Robert Craft, 'Stravinsky Pre-Centenary.' *Perspectives of New Music*, vol. 19 nos. 1–2 (1980–1), pp. 464–77, at p. 464. This version was premiered on 10 June 1981, conducted by Pierre Boulez.

[113] Ibid.

[114] Richard Taruskin, 'Stravinsky's *Petrushka*', in Andrew Baruch Wachtel (ed.), *Petrushka: Sources and Contexts*. Evanston, IL: Northwestern University Press, pp. 67–114, at p. 93.

[115] Rex Lawson, 'Maurice Ravel: *Frontispice* for Pianola.' *The Pianola Journal*, no. 2 (1989). Reproduced at http://www.maurice-ravel.net/frontisp.htm (accessed 5 April 2015).

musical staves are allocated in such a way that the first piano handles all the treble and the second piano all the bass. [...] Multiple staves in descending order of pitch is the standard way of writing music for the pianola.' He also points out that 'a simple start in one part leads to a greatly increasing complexity in five parts, and at the end a series of five chords is repeated with ever greater octave doublings', which again effectively uses the resources of the pianola.[116] Ravel, a master of orchestration, would have relished the challenge of writing idiomatically for this new instrument, and it must be said that the published score of *Frontispice*, for five hands on one piano, is far from being a practical performance option. Satie, of course, had his own connections with Canudo and his partner, the writer and dancer Valentine de Saint-Point.

Ravel's interest in the mechanical is often ascribed to his engineer father. He recalled that 'in my childhood I was much interested in mechanisms. These machines fascinated me. I visited factories often, very often, as a small boy with my father. It was these machines, their clicking and roaring, which, with the Spanish folk songs sung to me at night-time as a *berceuse* by my mother, formed my first instruction in music!'[117] Ravel even published an article, 'Finding Tunes in Factories', in *New Britain* on 9 August 1933 in which he claims 'My own *Bolero* owed its inception to a factory. Some day I should like to play it with a vast industrial works in the background.'[118]

Vladimir Jankélévitch provides the most subtle and penetrating analysis of Ravel as a composer with roots in the mechanical, significantly linking this characteristic of Ravel to Satie. Jankélévitch notes that Ravel 'enjoyed broken mechanisms and like Satie, he must have had a special liking for detuned pianos or slithering old phonographs'.[119] This raises the interesting question that, for these composers, mechanisms would be creatively interesting only if they were imperfect. After all, their music is written for human beings, not for machines. And as Jankélévitch is quick to point out: 'Even where there are no machines, pianolas or musical snuffboxes, Ravel's writing bears a trace of cogs [...]. Already, an

---

[116] Ibid.

[117] 'Maurice Ravel, Man and Musician', interview by Olin Downes for *New York Times* (7 August 1927); reprinted in Arbie Orenstein, *A Ravel Reader: Correspondence, Articles and Interviews*. Minneola, NY: Dover, 2003, pp. 448–53, at p. 450.

[118] Reprinted in Orenstein (ed.), *A Ravel Reader*, pp. 398–400; translator unknown. See also Deborah Mawer, 'Musical Objects and Machines', in Mawer (ed.), *Cambridge Companion to Ravel*. Cambridge: Cambridge University Press, 2000, pp. 47–70.

[119] Vladimir Jankélévitch, *Ravel*. Paris: Seuil, 1959, p. 77: 'Il [Ravel] aimait la mécanique détraquée et il devait avoir comme Satie, une prédilection particulière pour les piano désaccordés ou les vieux phonographes chevrotants.'

automatic flavour is present in [the early song] *Sainte* where the rather sleepy ritual procession of parallel chords evokes Debussy's dreamy chord progressions and Satie's stiff liturgies.'[120] Indeed, *Sainte* has the highly Satiean tempo marking 'Liturgiquement'.

Satie and Antheil

Satie's support of machine-driven or machine-inspired music can also be seen in his vociferous enthusiasm for the young George Antheil, who performed his violently provocative piano pieces *Sonata Sauvage*, *Airplane Sonata* and *Mechanisms* as a prelude to a Ballets Suédois performance at the Théâtre des Champs-Elysées on 4 October 1923. Satie and Milhaud were in the audience, most of which was raucous in its disapproval; Antheil recalled hearing 'Satie's shrill voice saying "Quelle précision! Quelle précision! Bravo! Bravo!" and he kept clapping his little gloved hands'; he added: 'The endorsement of Satie made it fairly certain that my career in Paris was a settled matter, at least for the next three or four years.'[121] The composer recalled the critical reception of his performance: 'The next morning the Parisian newspapers caricatured me on the front page. One caricature showed me dressed in overalls, standing before a piano that had a small steam engine attached to it. I was controlling a system of indicators, gauges, levers substituting for a keyboard. Its caption read: "Last Night's Music of the Future at the Ballets Suédois".'[122]

What Antheil does not say here is that this riot was staged. The performance on 4 October 1923 was an invitation-only event which was filmed by Marcel L'Herbier and became part of his *L'inhumaine* (Fig. 2.4).[123] This aimed to demonstrate that film was the perfect medium for a synthesis of all the arts, an idea which recalls Ricciotto Canudo's

---

[120] Ibid., p. 78: 'Là même où il n'y a ni machinerie, ni pianolas, ni tabatières à musique, l'écriture de Ravel conserve la trace des roues dentées [...]. Déjà l'automatisme se fait jour dans *Sainte* où la raideur rituelle et un peu somnambulique des accords parallèles évoque les rêveuses processions d'accords de Debussy et les liturgies compassées de Satie.' Ravel's *Sainte*, composed in 1896, is a setting of Mallarmé's poem which is dedicated to the poet's daughter Geneviève. In 1901, Geneviève Mallarmé married Edmond Bonniot, the Ravel family doctor.

[121] Antheil, *Bad Boy of Music* (1945); cited in Robert Orledge (ed.), *Satie Remembered*. London: Faber, 1995, pp. 190–1.

[122] George Antheil, *Bad Boy of Music*. New York: Da Capo Press, 1981 (original 1945), p. 134.

[123] Note, however, that Antheil's piano performance was not filmed. While the audience reaction to the 'inhuman' figure in L'Herbier's work was captured on film, Satie and Milhaud do not appear in the surviving footage. (Information communicated by Ornella Volta; email to the author, 22 April 2015.)

Fig. 2.4 Photo taken on 4 October 1923 at Théâtre des Champs-Elysées on the occasion of the filming of *L'inhumaine*. Left to right: Darius Milhaud, Erik Satie, Georgette Leblanc, Fernand Léger, Marcel L'Herbier (Archives de la Fondation Erik Satie)

conception of film. Lynn Garafola notes that 'the audience included Picasso, Satie, Man Ray, Ezra Pound, Constantin Brancusi, Milhaud (who wrote the film score), and various surrealists'.[124] Antheil claims that he announced the composition of his *Ballet mécanique* after this notorious concert, and that he 'sought a motion-picture accompaniment to this piece. [...] Erik Satie immediately announced that he too would write a mechanical ballet, to be called "Relâche". It was to be accompanied (in part) by a surrealist film by René Clair and Man Ray. This, of course, was the compliment supreme.'[125] Antheil is not to be trusted as an accurate source: elsewhere in his autobiography he recalled Satie as 'a most peculiar little old man, working in the daytime as a clerk in a post office, selling stamps, and in the late afternoon and at night becoming a high and mighty potentate in the decisions of musical France'![126] But his and Satie's common interest in mechanical music cannot be disputed.

[124] Lynn Garafola, *Legacies of Twentieth-Century Dance*. Middletown, CT: Wesleyan University Press, 2005, p. 114.
[125] Antheil, *Bad Boy of Music*, pp. 134–5.
[126] Ibid., p. 131.

Satie's *Relâche* will be explored in Chapter 6, but Antheil's *Ballet mécanique* is a curiosity worth mentioning here. Whether it influenced Satie or vice versa is a question impossible to answer, given the vagaries of both composers' recollections. What is certain is that Antheil's score exists in a number of versions. His first version, written in 1924, calls for sixteen player pianos playing four separate parts, for four bass drums, three xylophones, a tam-tam, seven electric bells, a siren and three different-sized airplane propellors (high wood, low wood and metal), as well as two human-played pianos.[127] Unsurprisingly, this instrumentation proved impractical. Antheil revised the score and *Ballet mécanique* was first performed publicly on 19 June 1926 in a reduced version for one pianola with amplifier, two pianos, three xylophones, electric bells, small wood propeller, large wood propeller, metal propeller, tam-tam, four bass drums and siren. Linda Whitesitt, writing in the *New Grove*, notes that the work was modelled on Stravinsky's *Les noces* for four pianos and percussion.[128]

■ ■ ■

SATIE'S music was the perfect vehicle to embody the contemporary vogue for the mechanical, the blending of 'high' and 'low' culture and cross-art collaboration. By the end of Satie's life, the pre-eminence of Paris as an artistic centre was attracting newcomers from the rest of Europe and, increasingly, the United States. The sensational impact of the Ballets Russes' arrival in Paris in 1909 was followed by the equally innovative Ballets Suédois. The Swedish troupe's ethos of collaboration, modernity and (often) shock value ensured their prominent place in the avant-garde in the first half of the 1920s, and Satie was part of their most notorious production, *Relâche*, a ballet which incorporated film, provocative costumes, a literally dazzling stage set and a car driven on stage. But Satie did not need collaborators to create artworks which were a true fusion of different media: his texted piano works are amongst his most original and most misunderstood creations, as we will see in the next chapter.

---

[127] Paul D. Lehrman, 'About the Ballet Mécanique', http://www.antheil.org/balletmec.html (accessed 5 April 2015).

[128] Linda Whitesitt, Charles Amirkhanian and Susan C. Cook. 'Antheil, George [Georg Carl Johann]. *Grove Music Online. Oxford Music Online*. Oxford University Press, accessed 4 April 2015, http://www.oxfordmusiconline.com/subscriber/article/grove/music/00997.

CHAPTER 3

Satie's Texted Piano Works

IF Satie is known to the general music-loving public for one thing, it is for his oddly titled piano works: the three *Gymnopédies* (1888) are among the earliest of these. And from the early 1890s, Satie further extended his imaginative approach to words in connection with piano pieces where he introduced unusual performance directions, the meaning of which continues to intrigue and baffle performers and listeners alike. His *Gnossiennes* feature the first eccentric performance instructions. The first, unbarred, *Gnossienne* (1890), dedicated to Roland-Manuel, features such directions as 'Très luisant' (Very shiny), 'Questionnez', 'Du bout de la pensée' (On the tip of the thought), 'Postulez en vous-même' (Wonder in yourself), 'Pas à pas' (Step by step) and over the final phrase, 'Sur la langue' (On the tip of the tongue). All these directions appear above phrases which have already been heard earlier in the piece and there is therefore no simple connection to be made between music and text as, at the first appearance, no words were present. Perhaps, by including verbal stimuli, Satie is prompting the pianist to consider repeated material differently on each occasion of its appearance. The performance indications for *Prélude à la Porte héroïque du ciel* (1894) – a work the composer dedicated to himself – include 'Superstitieusement', 'Avec déférence' and 'Très sincèrement silencieux', the latter appearing not over a pause, but over a notated section.

However, there is a difference between these short, quirky performance directions (italicised) and the more substantial, prose poem-like texts (in roman) which appear from 1912, when he started to compose what are commonly, if misleadingly, known as his humoristic piano works (I prefer the neutral term 'texted piano works'). Satie's enthusiasm for short piano works, which are almost invariably grouped in threes, is evidenced by his composing no fewer than sixty pieces of this type in 1912–15. The year 1912 also marked the beginning of the explosion of Satie's creativity in other art forms, which was eventually to include playwriting (*Le piège de Méduse*, 1913) and in 1914, the *Trois poèmes d'amour*, for which he wrote both poems and music. Steven Moore Whiting has convincingly argued that Satie's increasingly public profile, following the promotion of his early piano works by Ravel and Debussy, enhanced his confidence and stimulated this burst of creativity in different media.[1]

The years of the texted piano pieces were creatively a rich period for

---

[1] Steven Moore Whiting, *Satie the Bohemian*. Oxford: Clarendon Press, 1999, p. 442.

Satie, and they also mark a turning point in his critical reception. In 1911, Satie was described by the anonymous reviewer of a Salle Gaveau concert on 14 January, which included Ravel's performance of Satie's second *Sarabande*, as a composer who

> has a truly exceptional place in the history of contemporary art. A marginal figure, this isolated composer wrote some short pieces which reveal him as a precursor of genius. These works, which sadly are few in number, surprise the listener with their anticipation of modernist vocabulary and by their almost prophetic character of their harmonic novelties. This disturbing inventor of neologisms seems, though, to be oddly uninterested in his discoveries and has not pursued this path.[2]

This is one of the first assessments of Satie to use the term 'precursor of genius', which would become a critical commonplace in Satie reception in this period. The 'neologisms' described by this reviewer were not therefore the unique titles and texts which ornament his piano works, but the harmonic innovations which Ravel so admired, such as unresolved sevenths and ninths and modally flattened cadences. The reviewer was almost certainly Michel-Dimitri Calvocoressi, a friend of Ravel and fellow Apache.

In an article written later in 1911, Calvocoressi admits that Satie's titles can be a distraction for him. Surely drawing on information supplied by the composer, he writes that 'the names of his past or future works, together with some performance instructions, are noteworthy; for instance, the (unpublished) set of piano pieces *Pièces froides*, which comprises *Airs à faire fuir* and *Danses de travers*; and ballets which are "in preparation", *Onotrotance*, *Irnebizolle*, *Corcleru*. Really, one could be forgiven for not taking too seriously a man who does not take seriously some of his artistic functions.'[3] The ballets exist only in the form of

---

[2] Anon, 'Salle Gaveau', *Le Guide du Concert*, 14 January 1911, pp. 156–7: 'Erik Satie occupe dans l'histoire de l'art contemporain une place véritablement exceptionnelle. En marge de son époque, cet isolé a écrit jadis quelques courtes pages qui sont d'un génial précurseur. Ces œuvres, malheureusement peu nombreuses, surprennent par une prescience du vocabulaire moderniste et par le caractère quasi-prophétique de certaines trouvailles harmoniques. Ce troublant inventeur de néologismes semble d'ailleurs, s'être assez étrangement désintéressé de ses découvertes et n'a pas persévéré dans ses explorations.' An almost identical assessment of Satie was published under the name of Michel-Dimitri Calvocoressi, 'Société musicale indépendante', *Musica*, February 1911, pp. 33–4.

[3] M. D. Calvocoressi, 'M. Erik Satie', *Musica*, 103, April 1911, pp. 65–6: 'les dénominations de ses œuvres parues ou à paraître, certaines indications de nuances aussi, sont suffisamment révélatrices; par exemple, le recueil (inédit) pour piano *Pièces froides*, comprenant, après les *Airs à faire fuir*,

titles; indeed, Orledge notes that these titles, plus the equally fantastical *Tumisrudebude*, were 'planned with Contamine de Latour as offshoots to *uspud* featuring members of the *uspud* clan' and first mentioned as far back as 1893 in publicity material for *uspud*.[4] And the composer and writer Roland-Manuel – a close friend of Ravel as well as Satie – echoes Calvocoressi's judgement of these piano works: 'the *Pièces froides*, *Airs à faire fuir* and *Danses de travers* are superbly written for the piano, and deeply moving in spite of their extravagant titles'.[5] Calvocoressi's critique predates the more extravagant titles Satie gave to his texted piano works.

The 'precursor of genius' trope is echoed in 1912 by Albert Bertelin, who wrote that Satie 'deserves to be considered as the father of impressionism; he was, in fact, the first to use the procedures which characterise the genre, he was one of the first to delete bar lines'.[6] Most contemporary critics would question the validity of the term 'impressionism', which tends to be a catch-all term used to reference a style supposedly linked to Debussy which privileges drifting chords, shifting orchestral colours and the absence of conventional formal structures. Debussy's music is no more vague and blurry than Satie's, and he never omitted bar lines from his scores,[7] even though late Debussy works such as the Sonata for flute, viola and harp (1915) feature flexible, quasi-improvisatory solo lines.

The critical response to Satie at this stage focused primarily on his innovative harmonic and rhythmic language; the titles of his piano works were certainly considered striking and perhaps even a distraction for the listener, but Satie's music was central to the discussion. Following the

---

les *Danses de Travers*; et les ballets annoncés un beau jour comme «en préparation», *Onotrotance, Irnebizolle, Corcleru*. Vraiment, on fut assez excusable de ne pas prendre trop au sérieux cet homme qui prenait si peu au sérieux tout un aspect de ses fonctions artistiques.'

[4] Robert Orledge, 'Chronological Catalogue of Satie's Compositions and Research Guide to the Manuscripts', in Caroline Potter (ed.), *Erik Satie: Music, Art and Literature*. Farnham: Ashgate, 2013, pp. 243–324, at p. 259.

[5] Alexis Roland-Manuel, 'Silhouettes d'artistes: Erik Satie', *L'Echo musical (Revue mensuelle illustré)*, 5 April 1913, pp. 1–3: 'les *Pièces Froides* avec les *Airs à faire fuir* et les *Danses de travers*, d'une délicieuse écriture pianistique, et fort émouvantes en dépit de leur titre extravagant'.

[6] Albert Bertelin, 'L'évolution de la musique contemporaine (III)', *Le Courrier musical*, 15 October 1912, pp. 529–37: 'C'est lui, en somme, qui mériterait d'être considéré comme le père de l'impressionnisme; il a été en effet le premier à se servir des procédés qui caractérisent le genre, il fut l'un des premiers adeptes de la suppression des barres de mesures.'

[7] The only exception I know of is the tiny flute piece *Syrinx* (1913) which was originally incidental music written for Gabriel Mourey's 'dramatic poem' *Psyché*. An early manuscript (not in Debussy's hand but formerly owned by Louis Fleury, who premiered the work) is unbarred.

critically acclaimed performances of Satie's piano works by Ravel and the great pianist Ricardo Viñes in Parisian concert halls, Satie attracted the attention of publishers: Eugène Demets (1858–1923) was especially eager to publish more piano pieces by the composer. Having been turned down by Debussy and Ravel's prestigious publisher, Durand, Satie had been advised by Roland-Manuel to approach Demets. On 13 September 1913, Demets, whom Satie described as a 'decent fellow', accepted the *Véritables Préludes flasques (pour un chien)*: the composer 'immediately obtained a contract for this work and 50 francs in exchange for his rights'.[8]

The publication and performance of these new works, all of which had extravagant titles and in-score texts, led to a step change in the public view of Satie. The first author to draw attention to Satie as a humorist was Georges Auric, who published an article, 'Erik Satie: Musicien humoriste' in the *Revue française de musique* in December 1913; astonishingly, Auric was only fourteen years old and already emerging as a composer as well as a critic whose judgements were respected by his elders.[9] Auric's article is a sophisticated assessment which recognises the multiple sources of Satie's texts and links Satie's and Debussy's use of musical quotation. He starts by noting the text/music relationship in part of 'd'Holothurie', the first of Satie's *Embryons desséchés* whose title alludes to a sea cucumber:

> Next to some deliciously spirited arpeggios, he writes: 'Don't make me laugh, foamy spatter, you're tickling me! ...' It's fashionable to criticise this 'sweet-talking clown'. But whatever one's views of him, one can recognise, in a passage dealing with boats, a well-known popular song which the most straightforward association of ideas calls to mind. Or he can recall an operetta aria on the subject of quarrelsome fish who glide quickly in the water: 'Ah! don't run like that ...' which is enveloped in the least predictable manner by subtle harmonies. All that is no less musical than evoking, on the subject of Mélisande, the main theme of someone else's score, or citing *God save the Queen*, in homage to S. Pickwick, or hinting at the supple line of a Weber theme as a 'souvenir' of something.[10]

---

[8] Ornella Volta (ed.), *Erik Satie: Correspondance presque complète*. Paris: Fayard/IMEC, 2/2003, p. 793: 'Satie [...] a apporté à ce «brave homme» ses *Véritables Préludes flasques (pour un chien)* le 13 septembre 1912, et obtenu sur-le-champ un contrat pour cette œuvre, ainsi que cinquante francs, pour prix de cette «cession».' Demets was bought out by Max Eschig in 1923.

[9] Georges Auric, 'Erik Satie: Musicien humoriste', *Revue française de musique*, 4–10 December 1913, pp. 138–42.

[10] Auric's article is reproduced in Carl B. Schmidt (ed.), *Ecrits sur la musique de Georges Auric*, vol. 4. Lewiston: Edwin Mellen, 2009, pp. 1415–19, at p. 1418: 'sur des arpèges délicieusement spirituels, note-t-il ces mots: «Ne me faites pas rire, brin de mousse, vous me châtouillez! ...» Il est de bon ton de châtier ce «boniment de clown». Et pourtant, si l'on y songe bien,

Ex. 3.1 Satie, *Embryons desséchés*, 1 ('d'Holothurie'): 'Ne me faîtes pas rire, brin de mousse'

In the extract above, Auric first refers to a passage in 'd'Holothurie' cited in Ex. 3.1 (Satie's texted piano works are all unbarred and only feature clefs at the start of each piece). Auric convincingly suggests that this could be interpreted as a witty version of word painting, where the foamy spatter (*brin de mousse*) could be evoked by the rising arpeggios, and the sensation of tickling (*vous me châtouillez*) by the reiterated D♯/E gesture. (Note that this is a polite sea cucumber that uses the formal 'vous' mode of address to the water.) But the text–music relationship in Satie's music is far more complex and thought-provoking than simple word painting. Ex. 3.1 is followed by a passage which cites the well-known French folk tune 'J'ai du bon tabac', though Satie's humour by inversion is apparent in the text which appears alongside this tune: 'Je n'ai pas de tabac/ Heureusement je ne fume pas' (I don't have any tobacco/ Just as well I don't smoke).

Satie's humour is often expressed in words or phrases with a double meaning, literal and figurative: Léon Guichard, paraphrasing Henri Bergson, notes that 'A comic effect is obtained when one pretends to hear an expression at face value when it was in fact employed figuratively.'[11] In Satie's letters, prefaces and prose works, this shift from literal to figurative or vice versa is commonplace. While the text–music link may be obvious in 'd'Holothurie', what it ultimately means is open to speculation. Is a sea cucumber (holothuria) connected with the citation of a folk tune

faire deviner, à propos de bateaux, une chansonnette célèbre que la plus simple des associations d'idées impose aussitôt à l'esprit, ou rappeler, au sujet de poissons batailleurs, qui glissent rapidement entre les eaux, un air d'opérette. «Ah! ne courez donc pas comme ça ...» que de subtiles harmonies enveloppent de la façon la moins prévue, tout cela n'est pas moins musical que d'évoquer, à propos de Mélisande, le thème essentiel d'une partition étrangère, de citer, en hommage à S. Pickwick le *God save the Queen*, et d'insinuer la souple ligne sonore d'un thème de Weber en manière de «souvenir.»'

[11] Léon Guichard, 'A propos d'Erik Satie: Notules incohérentes.' *Université de Grenoble, U.E.R. de Lettres, Recherches et travaux Bulletin no. 7*, pp. 63–80, at p. 79: 'On obtient un effet comique quand on affecte d'entendre une expression au propre alors qu'elle était employé au figuré.'

about smoking because of its fat cigar-like shape? What, if anything, does the creature have to do with the reiterated G major triads, marked 'Grandiose', which conclude 'd'Holothurie'? All the *Embryons desséchés* parody the standard classical repertoire, whether through this ludicrously extended conclusion which takes the end of Beethoven's Fifth Symphony to absurd heights, or the mangled quotation of Chopin's funeral march in 'd'Edriophthalma' which is marked 'Citation de la célèbre mazurka de SCHUBERT'. Satie's work could most fruitfully be viewed in the context of the avant-garde poetry of contemporaries such as Blaise Cendrars and Guillaume Apollinaire, whose collections of seemingly unrelated images emerge from a stream of consciousness which is strikingly similar to Satie's *modus operandi*.

Auric picks up that Satie shares a fondness for quotation of music of all types with his friend Debussy, though Alan Gillmor considers Satie's use of other sources is distinctive: 'Not unlike the majority of his French contemporaries Satie seemed to have had a strong need for extramusical stimuli in order to set his musical imagination in motion. And although both Debussy and Ravel occasionally made use of preexisting material for particular expressive purposes, Satie's "found objects" seem to have been the actual stimuli that sparked a chain of events leading to the finished musico-poetic products.'[12] It is also likely that Satie's in-score texts, which are uniquely used by him, acted as an additional trigger for extramusical associations. While it is not always clear whether music or text was composed first, the existence of titles and texts without music in Satie's notebooks suggests that the text came first for some pieces. Satie, like a magpie, alights on a variety of sources and uses them as the basis for many of his piano works.

Vladimir Jankélévitch is more provocative in his assertion that Debussy is a key influence on Satie's texted piano works of 1912–16. Benefiting from a longer perspective than the fourteen-year-old Auric, the philosopher wrote in 1936: 'Doesn't the acidulous scale in minor seconds in "Españaña" mock the second tableau of [Debussy's] *La Boîte à joujoux*? [...] even the groaning Edriophthalmas, those neurasthenic crustaceans, recall in sacrilegious fashion Debussy's homage to S. Pickwick Esq. Satie always layers irony on top of Debussy's irony; it's second-degree irony, which apes the second book of Preludes. It's true that here again, Debussy blazed a trail [which Satie followed].'[13] We saw in Chapter 1 that

---

[12] Alan Gillmor, *Erik Satie*. London: Macmillan, 1988, p. 151.

[13] Vladimir Jankélévitch, 'Le symbolisme et la musique: Satie le simulateur', *Europe*, 15 June 1936, pp. 249–56, at p. 255: 'Cette gamme acide de secondes majeures qui est dans *Españaña*, ne raille-t-elle pas le second tableau de la *Boîte à joujoux*? [...] et de même les gémissements de Edriophthalmas, les crustacés neurasthéniques, rappellent de façon sacrilège l'hommage à S. Pickwick Esq. Car Satie ne cesse d'ironiser sur l'ironie debussyste; c'est de l'ironie à la seconde puissance, et qui singe à

there is a likely Dickensian connection to Satie's *Jack in the Box*, written over a decade before Debussy composed his second book of Preludes; the notion of 'second-degree irony' could therefore apply to Debussy aping Satie as well as the other way round. Debussy's and Satie's shared playful and allusive approach to titles and texts incorporates references to each other's works (whether these are 'sacrilegious' is a matter of opinion), and both composers quote the folk songs 'Nous n'irons plus aux bois' and 'Dodo, l'enfant do'. There is also a striking similarity between the tempo indication of Satie's *Prélude de la Porte héroïque du ciel* – 'calme et profondément doux' – and Debussy's tempo indication for 'La cathédrale engloutie' (composed fifteen years after Satie's work), 'Doux et profondément calme'. Roger Nichols cites *Le coq et l'arlequin*, writing that 'Cocteau was probably right on all counts when he wrote that the bizarre titles Satie gave some of his piano pieces, "apart from protecting his music from persons in thrall to the 'sublime' and authorising the laughter of those who do not understand his music's value, are explicable in terms of Debussy's abuse of precious titles." But the relationship between the music and the passing verbal comments Satie makes on it is less easily explained.'[14]

Beyond questions about the meaning of Satie's in-score texts and their interaction with the music, we also need to consider whether these texts are private messages from composer to performer, whether they should be shared with the listener, or even whether they should be part of a performance. By including texts in a piano score, Satie is inviting his performer to see links between music and words, to consider the work as a totality. Alan Gillmor thinks that the audience should be let in to the secret: he believes that 'the ideal performance of his music would be in semi-private, with the audience able to see the score and appreciate every dimension of the work'.[15] None of Satie's texts are given rhythmic notation, none of his piano works are 'for piano and reciter', and the performance or non-performance of the texts is generally not addressed. There is one exception to this: Satie prefaced his set of three piano pieces *Heures séculaires et instantanées* (1914) with an 'Avertissement' ('Warning') to the performer stating that the extensive and complex texts for these works should not be read out loud, though surely this was a tongue-in-cheek statement. And there is one tantalising hint that a performer who knew Satie well may have experimented with verbal and piano performance of his texted pieces. The Paris newspaper *Le Matin* publicised a tribute concert to Satie held at the Sorbonne and broadcast

son tour l'emphase humoristique du deuxième cahier des *Préludes*. Il est vrai qu'ici encore Debussy montrait le chemin.'

[14] Roger Nichols, *The Harlequin Years*. London: Thames and Hudson, 2002, p. 217.

[15] Gillmor, *Erik Satie*, p. 149.

on 7 December 1925 which featured performances by Jane Mortier of unspecified Satie works for 'piano parlé' ('talking piano').[16] Perhaps it is significant that Mortier waited until Satie had died before carrying out this experiment.

Some Satie commentators, notably Jankélévitch, insist that Satie's titles and in-score texts should be considered as separate and distinct entities. In his essay *Satie et le matin*, Jankélévitch is persuasive when he writes 'his [Satie's] aim is not only not to express himself, but to express something else, something insignificant or which is an alibi for his true message'. He goes on to describe the texts accompanying his piano works: 'These soliloquies, with no relationship to the music, seem to tell us: let's speak, if we may, of something else ...'[17] As early as 1936, Jankélévitch was wondering 'whether joking, in [Satie's] music, is hiding a secret'.[18] The notion that Satie is concealing meaning behind a distracting veil of words rings true for the composer who put on a show every day, leaving his grubby room in Arcueil immaculately dressed to face the public. Humour was one of Satie's weapons in his mystification of the public, as was his concealment of his left-wing political engagement in Arcueil which was almost completely unknown to the Parisian artistic social circles in which he also moved. And Satie's delight in words as a form of publicity can be seen from his earliest years, in his half-joking advertisements for his own works published in the *Chat noir* journal and the imaginary advertisements with more than a grain of truth which he wrote for his own amusement. My analyses will show that there are very often specific connections between words and music in Satie's texted piano pieces. Far from having 'no relationship' to the music, the text can act as a stimulus or trigger for a musical gesture.

One of the first critiques of Satie published outside France anticipated Jankélévitch; Carl van Vechten wrote an article on the composer in the American magazine *Vanity Fair* in 1918, showing that Satie's reputation had extended over the Atlantic in his lifetime. He believed that 'His [Satie's] titles ordinarily seem to have nothing to do with the music, which is frequently exquisite, and never programmatic. True ironist that he is, he conceals his diffidence under these fantastic titles. He ridicules his

---

[16] *Le Matin* (7 December 1925), p. 4; radio programme announcement for that day, Station de l'Ecole supérieure des P.T.T.: 'Album (piano parlé), Erik Satie, Jane Mortier'.

[17] Vladimir Jankélévitch, 'Satie et le matin', in *La musique et les heures*. Paris: Seuil, 1988, pp. 141–2: 'son propos est non seulement de ne pas s'exprimer, mais d'exprimer autre chose, quelque chose d'insignifiant ou de saugrenu qui sert d'alibi à son vrai message. [...] Ces soliloques sans aucun rapport avec la musique semblent nous dire: parlons, si vous le voulez bien, d'autre chose ...'

[18] Jankélévitch, 'Le symbolisme et la musique: Satie le simulateur', p. 250: 'si la plaisanterie, dans sa musique, ne dissimule pas quelque secret'.

own emotion at just the point at which the auditor is about to discover it. He also protects himself against the pedants and the philistines by raising these titular and descriptive barriers.'[19] On the other hand, the pianist Jean-Joël Barbier believes that Satie's in-score texts, for all their apparent eccentricity, are for the most part expressive, serving to communicate to the pianist an idea relating to the way in which the music should be played.[20]

Recent Satie scholars, such as Mary Davis and Helen Julia Minors,[21] have used interart methodologies to investigate *Sports et divertissements*, the most multimedia of the piano works as the music is presented alongside Charles Martin's pochoir prints as well as Satie's own texts. Early twentieth-century anxieties about 'programme music', expressed above by Carl van Vechten, are here rejected in favour of a more sophisticated approach to narrative through interrelated arts. Mary Davis explains how Satie links music, words and image in 'Le Golf':

> Satie's musical score [...] evokes these images explicitly, particularly through the use of a vacillating chromatic descent to represent the 'trembling holes' and an ascending flourish based on quartal harmonies, marked fortissimo, to represent the breaking [golf] club. Satie meticulously coordinates these musical gestures and textual events in his score; moreover, the musical notation provides a visual metaphor for both the shaking holes and the club breaking in the air. With [Charles] Martin's graphic representation, Satie's music and texts create a tripartite and interrelated rendition of the story.[22]

Satie's titles and texts eventually became an easy way of pigeonholing him as a creative artist. The artist Amédée Ozenfant's memoirs recall his encounters with Satie from the Great War years, and he is enlightening about Satie's contemporary reputation as a composer:

> Having lived the Montmartre cabaret lifestyle for a long time, he retained the habit of making witty remarks about everything and nothing. He was funny but more than anything else, he was a creature of the Belle Epoque. He was bitter, and for good reason: the

---

[19] Carl van Vechten, 'Erik Satie: Master of the Rigolo', *Vanity Fair*, March 1918.

[20] Jean-Joël Barbier, *Au piano avec Erik Satie*. Paris: Garamont-Archimbaud, 1986, p. 47.

[21] Mary E. Davis, *Erik Satie*. London: Reaktion, 2007; Helen Julia Minors, 'Exploring Interart Dialogue in Erik Satie's *Sports et divertissements* (1914/1922)', in Caroline Potter (ed.), *Erik Satie: Music, Art and Literature*. Farnham: Ashgate, 2013, pp. 115–35.

[22] Mary E. Davis, 'Modernity à la mode: Popular Culture and Avant-Gardism in Erik Satie's "Sports et divertissements".' *Musical Quarterly*, vol. 83 no. 3 (Autumn 1999): pp. 430–73, at pp. 447–8.

snobs were then making a fuss of him, but when they invited him it was mainly so he could be the clown. His compositions are jewels, though with absurd titles: *Airs à faire fuir, Musique à faire peur, Embryons desséchés, Trépied à deux pieds*, etc. People would burst out laughing when they read the programme and their laughter covered the music.[23]

Ozenfant is not the only contemporary to point out that Satie's imaginative way with words distracted attention from his music and, from the mid-1910s, ensured he was seen by many as a buffoon. The artist does not help his broadly pro-Satie case when he makes up titles which Satie did not in fact use: there are no pieces or collections by this composer entitled *Musique à faire peur*. His mention of *Trépied à deux pieds*, however, is intriguing, as this is a title Satie included in a list of possible furniture music works in a sketchbook but never used.[24] Perhaps Satie was willing to share his ideas for future projects with Ozenfant, with whom he discussed selling his furniture music scores as works of visual art.

Parody was the house style of the *Chat noir* journal, a style Satie employed in the texts and music of many of his humorous piano pieces. Steven Moore Whiting wrote 'at some point in the summer of 1912, he [Satie] decided to transfer the principles of parodic distortion to piano music – specifically, to miniatures arranged, like his now famous *Gymnopédies*, in suites of three, usually with the slowest piece in the middle'. Whiting compares him to Vincent Hyspa, the cabaret singer Satie accompanied at the piano, who was known for 'retext[ing] a series of well-known tunes, excerpting a refrain or key phrase from each, to create a composite parody'.[25] Whiting's book outlines the very many instances where Satie bases a piece on a popular song of his time, convincingly demonstrating the central role of parody in his music, and Ann-Marie Hanlon explores in detail the notions of parody and irony in Satie in her thesis and book chapter.[26]

---

[23] Amédée Ozenfant, *Mémoires, 1886–1962*. Paris: Seghers, 1968, p. 91: 'Ayant longtemps vécu la vie des cabarets montmartrois, il en avait gardé la travers de faire de l'esprit à propos de tout et de rien, il était drôle mais à tout prix, c'était un héritier de la Belle Epoque. Aigri, son amertume avait bien des excuses: un tout petit milieu snob lui faisait maintenant fête, main quand on invitait le musicien c'était surtout pour que vienne l'humoriste; ses musiques, purs bijoux, étaient il est vrai, absurdement titrées: *Airs à faire fuir, Musique à faire peur, Embryons desséchées, Trépied à deux pieds*, etc. Les gens s'esclaffaient en lisant le programme et leurs rires couvraient la musique.'

[24] The sketchbook is now housed in the Bibliothèque Nationale de France, Département de la Musique, Ms 9623(2).

[25] Whiting, *Satie the Bohemian*, pp. 354–5.

[26] Ann-Marie Hanlon, 'Satie and the French Musical Canon: A Reception Study.' Unpublished PhD thesis, Newcastle University, 2013; and 'Satie

Satie's parodies could also focus on more serious musical genres, such as his song *Le chapelier* (1916), a parody marked 'genre Gounod' whose melodic line is partly borrowed from that composer's *Mireille* (the 'Chanson de Magali') and whose throbbing accompaniment conjures up an image of a well-upholstered singer leaning on a grand piano. The vocal line begins in the style of a nineteenth-century operatic number, though the descending quaver pattern at the end of the first verse brings in a humorous note when it goes on far longer than it should (Ex. 3.2). The song lampoons the conventions of an established genre and further pokes fun at these conventions by using a semi-nonsense text (written by his friend René Chalupt) based on Lewis Carroll's character the Mad Hatter.

It is therefore not surprising to see Satie parodying other writers in the texts of his humorous piano works. Although Satie left formal education at a young age, he was exceptionally curious and well read. Alan Gillmor rightly emphasises that 'We know that he [Satie] was an inveterate reader, with a special fondness for anything that struck him as strange and exotic.' Gillmor specifically mentions that the *Nouveau Larousse illustré* encyclopedia (in the 1898–1904 edition, edited by Claude Augé) was Satie's principal source of background research for his texted piano works, from which he gleaned popular melodies as well as odd or amusing facts.[27] The child Satie and his father attended talks at the Collège de France, a Paris educational institution which is open to all and free of charge, and Jane Fulcher states that Satie's father 'engag[ed] a tutor to instruct him privately in Latin and Greek'.[28] Fulcher also suggests that Satie's interest in the classics could have had an impact on his work:

> an analogy is illuminating – an analogy with a genre that was used in the culture to which Satie had been introduced as a child – that of ancient Greece. The ancient Greeks developed a literary genre referred to as 'Meneppian discourse', which employs a series of citations from texts that are intended to avoid any unequivocal of 'fixed' meaning: as distinct from the postmodern play with styles, originality, and citation, the expressive goal is to suggest the distance of the author from these sources and, consequently, from his own text; this indicates a profound cultural alienation.[29]

---

and the Meaning of the Comic', in Caroline Potter (ed.), *Erik Satie: Music, Art and Literature*. Farnham: Ashgate, 2013, pp. 19–48.

[27] Alan Gillmor, 'Musico-poetic Form in Satie's 'Humoristic' Piano Suites (1913–1914).' *Canadian University Music Review*, vol. 8 (1987): pp. 1–44, at p. 9.

[28] Jane F. Fulcher, *French Cultural Politics and Music: From the Dreyfus Affair to the First World War*. New York: Oxford University Press, 1999, p. 195.

[29] Ibid., p. 198.

Satie's Texted Piano Works 109

This may suggest Satie's enthusiasm for ancient Greece went beyond his setting of Plato's dialogues in translation for *Socrate* and the title *Gymnopédies*.

Léon Guichard's enlightening article on Satie's language focuses on the role of humour in the piano works and its relationship to contemporary French authors. Guichard believes that Satie's verbal style is 'very close to [Jules] Renard in its poetic concision, deliberate limitations, the extreme economy of musical and literary means, and the density of

Ex. 3.2 Satie, 'Le chapelier' (*Trois mélodies*, no. 3): bars 1–6

(The mad hatter is astonished/ to realise that his watch/ is late – three days late.)

his "delicately lyrical" short phrases'.[30] But while Satie's textual style has provoked commentary, the topics he addresses in his texted piano works have received surprisingly little attention. A small number of overarching topics recur again and again in Satie's texts: body parts and bodily functions; social life and human behaviour; the natural world; music; time. The topics of Satie's texts are categorised in Table 3.1 under these headings. Most works mentioned in the list are texted piano works composed in 1912–17, but I have included other works whose texts or performance directions are particularly extensive; these are *Choses vues à droite et à gauche* (1914) for violin and piano, and the tiny piece for two trumpets with a long title, *Sonnerie pour réveiller le bon gros Roi des Singes (lequel ne dort toujours que d'un œil)* (1921). Two other topics appear only twice: one is money or gold, which appears in 'Chez le marchand d'or' (*Vieux sequins*) and *Sonatine bureaucratique* (hopes for a pay rise and promotion). The devil surfaces in 'Le tango perpétuel' (*Sports et divertissements*) and in 'Méditation' (*Avant-dernières pensées*).

Why might Satie have been obsessed with these topics? It is understandable that a composer would have an interest in music and instruments, and his multiple references to time will be investigated later in this chapter, but some other recurring topics merit further exploration. First, Satie was, if not exactly a bon viveur, a man with a reputation for eating and drinking copiously when he had the opportunity; his prose works also show a deep interest in food, drink and the body. Satie's brother Conrad claimed the composer 'with whom he dined on Sundays [...] could demolish 150 oysters or an omelette made of 30 eggs at a single sitting!'[31] Robert Orledge reports that 'No one ever saw him drunk, though his capacity for alcohol of all types and for mixing his drinks was legendary. His one lament was that "the bars are full of people quite happy to offer you a drink. But none of them ever thinks of lining your stomach with a sandwich"'.[32] It is curious to note the number of advertisements for digestion aids and purgative medicines in contemporary journals such as *Chat noir* and *Comœdia*: the standard

---

[30] Guichard, 'A propos d'Erik Satie', at p. 77: 'je le vois aussi très proche de Renard, par la concision poétique, la limitation volontaire, l'extrême économie des moyens musicaux ou littéraires, et la densité de ses courtes phrases, « délicatement lyriques. »' [...] 'Il est évident que Satie savourait les mots, comme il savourait les sons.'

[31] Cited in Robert Orledge, *Satie the Composer*. Cambridge: Cambridge University Press, 1990, p. 14.

[32] Robert Orledge, 'Satie's Personal and Musical Logic', in Caroline Potter (ed.), *Erik Satie: Music, Art and Literature*. Farnham: Ashgate, 2013, pp. 1–16, at p. 6. Orledge here cites an interview in *Matin d'Anvers* given by René Lanser on 9 July 1925, a few days after Satie's death: 'On trouve dans tous les bars des gens disposés à vous offrir un verre. Aucun ne songera à vous lester d'un sandwich.'

Table 3.1 Satie texted works: topics

1. Body parts and bodily functions	
Heart	La Balançoire (*Sports et divertissements*); Colin-Maillard (*Sports*); Le Water-chute (*Sports*); Idylle (*Avant-dernières pensées*); Méditation (*Avant-dernières pensées* – weeping like a willow)
Body parts	Le Tennis (*Sports* – legs, nose); Son binocle (*Les Trois Valses distingués du précieux dégoûté*) – face, stomach etc. in piano directions); Ses jambes (*Les Trois Valses* – legs); Obstacles venimeux (*Heures séculaires et instantanées* – brain, hands); Le chant guerrier du roi des haricots (*Menus propos enfantines* – stomach, hairy nose); Fugue à tâtons (*Choses vues à droite et à gauche* – many references, including eyes, head); *Sonnerie pour réveiller le bon gros Roi des Singes (lequel ne dort toujours que d'un œil)* – eyes; Danse cuirassée (*Vieux sequins* – 'Les danseurs reçoivent chacun un coup de sabre qui leur fend la tête'); Etre jaloux de son camarade qui a une tête (*Peccadilles importunes* – head); Lui manger sa tartine (*Peccadilles importunes* – 'faire gonfler la tête', swollen head); Tyrolienne turque (*Croquis et agaceries d'un gros bonhomme en bois* – throat (dans le gosier) and eyes (du bout des yeux)); Danse maigre (*Croquis et agaceries d'un gros bonhomme en bois* – 'sans rougir du doigt', without blushing on the finger); *Sonatine bureaucratique* ('Content, il hoche la tête', satisfied, he shakes his head; mounting staircase 'sur son dos', on his back)
Bones	Valse du chocolat aux amandes (*Menus propos enfantines* – child thinks the sweet contains a bone, and it's actually an almond); Fugue à tâtons (*Choses vues* – 'les os secs et lointains', dry and distant bones); Celle qui parle trop (*Chapitres tournés* – 'Madame Chose a un parapluie en os', Mrs Thingy has a bone umbrella)
Food/eating	La pieuvre (*Sports*) – an octopus which eats a crab sideways and swallows a glass of salt water; Le Picnic (*Sports*); *Pièces froides* (Ne pas trop mangez – twice); Le chant guerrier du roi des haricots (*Menus propos enfantines*); Ce que dit la petite princesse des tulipes (*Menus propos enfantines* – cabbage soup); Valse du chocolat aux amandes (*Menus propos enfantines*); Sévère réprimande (*Véritables préludes flasques* – Imbibus/Corpulentus – allusion to overeating); Lui manger sa tartine (*Peccadilles importunes*)

continues overleaf ...

Table 3.1 *continued*

Illness (often connected with food or eating)	Ce que dit la petite princesse des tulipes (*Menus propos enfantines* – headache); Crépuscule matinal (du midi) (*Heures séculaires et instantanées* – cow eating itself sick); Valse du chocolat aux amandes (*Menus propos enfantines* – indigestion); Celle qui parle trop (*Chapitres tournés en tous sens* – concierge 'a mal dans les côtes', husband dies 'en un pauvre souffle'); Lui manger sa tartine (*Peccadilles importunes* – smoking dog with stomach ache); Profiter de ce qu'il a des cors au pieds pour lui prendre son cerceau [= toy hoop] (*Peccadilles importunes* – corns); Méditation (*Avant-dernières pensées* – indigestion); Le Feu d'Artifice (*Sports* — madness); d'Holothurie (*Embryons desséchés*, 'Comme un rossignol qui aurait mal aux dents', 'like a nightingale with toothache')
Carrying a heavy load	Fantaisie musculaire (*Choses vues* – 'le dos vouté'); Le porteur de grosses pierres (*Chapitres tournés*)

2. Social life and human behaviour

Conversation	Le Bain de mer (*Sports*); Le Yachting (*Sports*); La Pêche (*Sports*); Le Water-chute (*Sports*); Le Flirt (*Sports*); Aubade (*Avant-dernières pensées*); Celle qui parle trop (*Chapitres tournés* – wife/husband relationship)
Military	La Comédie Italienne (*Sports*); Le Golf (*Sports* – colonel); Sur un casque (*Descriptions automatiques* 3 – 'C'est le colonel' preceded by tritone military drum); La Défaite des Cimbres (*Vieux sequins*)
Aristocracy and royalty	Sa taille (*Les Trois Valses*); Le chant guerrier du roi des haricots (*Menus propos enfantines* – king); Chez le marchand d'or (*Vieux sequins* – king); Danse cuirassé (*Vieux sequins* – 'Pas noble et militaire'); La Défaite des Cimbres (*Vieux sequins*)
Social occasion	Sur un casque (*Descriptions automatiques* – people arriving, 'Ils arrivent. Que de monde!'); d'Edriophthalma (*Embryons desséchés* – funeral)
Playing sport	Le Golf (*Sports*); Le Tennis (*Sports*)
Carnival/masks	Le Carnaval (*Sports*)
Chasing/hide-and-seek	Colin-Maillard (*Sports*); Les Quatre Coins (*Sports* – cat and mouse); de Podophthalma (*Embryons desséchés* – hunt)
Dancing	Le Tango (*Sports*); Ses jambes (*Les Trois valses*); Le chant guerrier du roi des haricots (*Menus propos enfantines* – king and his horse); Tyrolienne turque, Danse maigre, Españaña (*Croquis et agaceries d'un gros bonhomme en bois*); Sonatine bureaucratique (3rd movement – 'Il ose valser! (Lui, pas le piano)' (He dares to waltz! (Him, not the piano))
Poet	Aubade (*Avant-dernières pensées*); Méditation (*Avant-dernières pensées*)

Table 3.1 *continued*

3. The natural world	
Trees	Aubade (*Avant-dernières pensées*); Obstacles venimeux (*Heures séculaires*); Affolements granitiques (*Heures séculaires*)
Animals	La Chasse (*Sports* – rabbit, wild boar); Le Réveil de la Mariée (*Sports* – dog); Les Courses (*Sports* – horse racing); Les Quatre Coins (*Sports* – cat and mouse); Obstacles venimeux (*Heures séculaires* – toads, snakes); Crépuscule matinal (*Heures séculaires* – cow); Le chant guerrier du roi des haricots (*Menus propos enfantines* – horse); Sur un casque (*Descriptions automatiques* – sow ('lourd comme une truie, léger comme un œuf'); Sonnerie pour réveiller le bon gros Roi des Singes (*lequel ne dort toujours que d'un œil*) (monkey); Lui manger sa tartine (*Peccadilles importunes* – dog)
Birds	La Chasse (*Sports* – nightingale, owl); Etre jaloux de son camarade qui a une tête (*Peccadilles importunes* – parrot); Danse maigre (*Croquis et agaceries d'un gros bonhomme en bois* – 'dry as a cuckoo'); Celle qui parle trop (*Chapitres tournés en tous sens*: 'un homme qui est sec comme un coucou', again 'dry as a cuckoo'); d'Holothurie (*Embryons desséchés*, 'Comme un rossignol qui aurait mal aux dents', 'like a nightingale with toothache')
Fish	La Pêche (*Sports*)
Moon/Sun	Le Flirt (*Sports* – wishing to be on the moon); Idylle (*Avant-dernières pensées* – moon and sun); Crépuscule matinal (de midi) (*Heures séculaires*); Regrets des enfermés (*Chapitres tournés en tous sens* – sun)
Water	La Pêche (*Sports*); Le Yachting (*Sports* – sea); Sur un vaisseau (*Descriptions automatiques* – 'Au gré des flots', 'mélancolie maritime' and 'Le vaisseau ricane'); Le Bain de Mer (*Sports* – sea); La Pieuvre (*Sports*); Le Water-chute (*Sports*); Idylle (*Avant-dernières pensées* – brook); d'Holothurie (*Embryons desséchés*, 'Ne me faites pas rire, brin de mousse: vous me châtouillez', 'Don't make me laugh, foamy spatter: you're tickling me')
Weather	Le Yachting (*Sports* – wind); Le Golf (*Sports* – clouds); Méditation (*Avant-dernières pensées* – wind, goose bumps); Crépuscule matinal (*Heures séculaires* – hot, prehistoric, burning, storm); Affolements granitiques (*Heures séculaires* – rain, dust); Sur un vaisseau (*Descriptions automatiques* – 'Petite brise', wind); Sonatine bureaucratique (wind – 'Quel coup de vent!'); Le Picnic (*Sports* – aeroplane which is actually a storm); d'Holothurie (*Embryons desséchés*, 'Il pleut' and many other weather references)
Coldness	Le Tango (*Sports*); Le Traîneau (*Sports*)
Darkness/ night	Le Feu d'Artifice (*Sports*); Sur une lanterne (*Descriptions automatiques* – 'Nocturnement'); Regrets des enfermés (*Chapitres tournés* – shadow, 'ils sont assis dans l'ombre', reference to Jonah; Seul à la maison (*Véritables préludes flasques* – 'Nocturnus')

continues overleaf...

Table 3.1 *continued*

4. Music	
Musical instruments	Le Réveil de la Mariée (*Sports* – guitar); *Sonatine bureaucratique* (piano)
Allusion to other music	Sa taille (*Les Trois Valses* – fifteenth-century tune); Aubade (*Avant-dernières pensées* – rigaudon); Chez le marchand d'or (*Vieux sequins* – leads to Gounod 'Golden Calf' quotation); La Défaite des Cimbres (*Vieux sequins* – refers to Le Sacre de Charles X (267bis)); Españaña (*Croquis et agaceries d'un gros bonhomme en bois* – Carmen); *Sonatine bureaucratique* (Clementi, and in third movement humming an old Peruvian air collected from a deaf-mute in Lower Brittany); 'd'Edriophthalma' (*Embryons desséchés* – Chopin's Funeral March distorted and marked 'Citation de la célèbre mazurka de SCHUBERT'); 'de Podophthalma (*Embryons desséchés* – 'Cadence obligée (de l'Auteur), 'Obligatory cadenza (by the Author)')

5. Time	
	Obstacles venimeux (*Heures séculaires*); Affolements granitiques (*Heures séculaires*); Regrets des enfermés (*Chapitres tournés* – 'Plusieurs siècles les séparent'); Sévère réprimande (*Véritables préludes flasques* – 'Très "neuf heures du matin"' – after overeating)

Parisian diet must have been poor if there were a genuine regular need for these products. In his *Mémoires d'un amnésique*, when outlining his alleged daily routine, Satie riffs on food: 'I only eat white foodstuffs: eggs, sugar, grated bones; the fat of dead animals; veal, salt, coconut, chicken cooked in white water; mould growing on fruit, rice, turnips; camphorated sausage, pastry, cheese (white), cotton salad and selected fish (skinless).'[33] Writers including Christopher Dawson have explored the symbolism of whiteness in Satie;[34] here it is interesting to note Satie's love of lists and vivid culinary imagination triggered only by a colour. And surely Satie's 'white food' riff is also a comic inversion of the 'black dinner' scene in Joris-Karl Huysmans' novel *A rebours* (1884).

---

[33] Cited in Ornella Volta (ed.), *Erik Satie: Ecrits*. Paris: Editions Champ Libre, 1979, p. 23: 'Je ne mange que des aliments blancs: des œufs, du sucre, des os râpés; de la graisse d'animaux morts; du veau, du sel, des noix de coco, du poulet cuit dans de l'eau blanche; des moisissures de fruits, du riz, des navets; du boudin camphré, des pates, du fromage (blanc), de la salade de coton et de certains poissons (sans la peau).'

[34] Christopher Dawson, 'Menus propos modernistes: Absurdity in Erik Satie's "La Journée du musicien".' *Nottingham French Studies*, vol. 44 no. 2 (2005): pp. 55–62, especially pp. 58–60.

Satie's social situation was unusual. From 1898 he lived in a single room without private facilities in Arcueil, accommodation usually occupied by unskilled labourers. His friends and acquaintances in Arcueil were either from the working class, or middle-class professionals such as the architect Alexandre Templier who shared his strong left-wing political allegiance. Satie also mixed with artists of all types, professional musicians and high-society patrons of the arts on his almost daily trips into Paris. He was in sporadic contact with his brother Conrad, whose job as an industrial chemist and marriage situate him as bourgeois, though his political views were well to the left of most people of his social class. Satie's access to people from all sectors of society gave him a vantage point on human behaviour across the social spectrum. He remained an amused and probably bemused onlooker rather than a participant in most of the situations he observed, almost always concealing his thoughts and feelings behind witty, ironic or sarcastic remarks. One of very few exceptions to this is the heartfelt note he sent to Francis Poulenc on 16 July 1917. Satie had just heard via Poulenc's piano teacher Ricardo Viñes that Poulenc's father had died, and he would have known that the young composer had lost his mother two years earlier. The eighteen-year-old Poulenc was an orphan, and Satie wrote to him: 'My poor friend, Yesterday evening Viñes told me the terrible news. I'm with you with all my heart, dear friend; and beg you to consider me your devoted Erik Satie.'[35]

Satie's interests in nature and natural phenomena are more difficult to pin down. His two homes as an adult, Montmartre and Arcueil, were both working-class areas on the outskirts of Paris whose main topological features are hills: Montmartre is criss-crossed with steep streets accessed by long flights of steps and the only public funicular in Paris (which opened in 1900 and leads to Sacré-Cœur), and Arcueil is bordered by a viaduct. Walking to and from central Paris from either of his homes, Satie must sometimes have felt like Sisyphus carrying a burden up a hill. He had no personal ties to the French countryside, though he must have thought that fresh air and access to Nature were important as he took groups of children from Arcueil on country walks as part of his civic activity. As a child in Honfleur, he would have seen boats coming and going in the busy central harbour which is still the heart of the small town. He would have known that the sea was a source of business and pleasure, but also danger as his grandmother drowned on a visit to the tiny beach on the outskirts of Honfleur. Satie's paternal uncle Adrien, nicknamed 'Sea Bird', was a sailor who was considered to be the family's eccentric member: it is hardly surprising to learn that the young Erik was fond of him. Unlike contemporary composers including dog owners Debussy

---

[35] Volta (ed.), *Correspondance*, p. 291: 'Mon pauvre Ami. Hier au soir Viñes m'a annoncé le terrible malheur qui vous frappe. Je suis avec vous de tout cœur, Cher ami; et vous prie de voir en moi votre tout dévoué Erik Satie.'

and Lili Boulanger and the cat-loving Ravel, Satie did not own pets, but we know that dogs were the only creatures allowed to enter Satie's filthy room in Arcueil because calcified dog excrement was found in the room after his death.

It is possible that Satie's obsession with body parts, particularly heads, dates back to his Honfleur youth. He was born in what is now boulevard Charles V (when Satie was born in 1866, it was rue Gambetta), a road which is linked by an alley with a flight of stone stairs to rue de l'Homme de Bois. The latter street – Wooden Man Street – takes its name from a well-known landmark in the town, a gargoyle-like figure which seems to be poking his head out of the wall of number 23 (Fig. 3.1). The face and especially the figure's goatee beard even look not unlike Satie. Could this figure have inspired the following anonymous description of Satie, published in the *Chat noir* journal on 9 February 1889?:

Fig. 3.1 Head looking out of 23 rue de l'Homme de Bois, Honfleur

> Finally! Lovers of cheerful music will be able to enjoy it with great pleasure.
>
> The indefatigable Erik Satie, the sphinx man, the composer with the wooden head, announces the appearance of a new musical work of which he has been saying, up until now, the most flattering things.
>
> It's a set of songs conceived in the mystical-liturgical vein favoured by the author, with this suggestive title: Les Ogives.
>
> We wish Erik Satie the success he obtained recently with his 3rd Gymnopédie, a work currently underneath all pianos.
>
> On sale at 66, boulevard Magenta.[36]

---

[36] *Chat noir*, 9 February 1889, p. 1276 (anonymous): 'Enfin! les amateurs de musique gaie vont pouvoir s'en donner à cœur joie. ¶ L'infatigable *Erik-Satie*, l'homme-sphinx, le compositeur à la tête de bois, nous annonce l'apparition d'une nouvelle œuvre musicale dont il dit, dès à présent, le plus grand bien. ¶ C'est une suite de mélodies conçues dans le genre mystico-liturgique que l'auteur idolâtre, avec ce titre suggestif: *Les Ogives*. ¶ Nous souhaitons à Erik-Satie un succès semblable à celui qu'il obtint jadis avec sa Troisième Gymnopédie, actuellement sous tous les pianos. ¶ En vente, 66, boulevard Magenta.'

Satie is surely the author of this witty promotional text. Certainly, Robert Orledge says that references to 'Satie as the "composer with the wooden head" recurs on various occasions from the *Ogives* (1888) onwards. It became a standing joke between Satie and Debussy.'[37] In his texts, Satie tends to view the human body not as a total person but as isolated fragments, just like the mysterious gargoyle in rue de l'Homme de Bois: a disembodied head with a very human expression, but no body. Similarly, Satie's epigrammatic texts have no space for character development or for showing a fully rounded personality. Instead, ever the ironist or comedian, he points to one particular feature – and there is never any sense that this feature, be it a head, pair of eyes or stomach, represents the whole person. Sometimes a head is, literally, just a head.

Sketchbook evidence shows that Satie often came up with texts and titles which were not ultimately used in a piece. The text for 'Regard', the proposed first piece of *Les Globules ennuyeux* which was sketched in 1913 but has no music associated with it, is worth quoting in full as it shows Satie incorporating almost all his textual obsessions in one short prose poem:

> Son regard est une tiède parure. Vous le voyez lorsqu'elle ouvre les yeux. Que cherche-t-il?
> La beauté des navires qui se balancent?
> L'endroit où se tient le vieux rossignol?
> La maison où est né le poète?
> Non:
> Elle va sortir et ne trouve pas son ombrelle de soie,
> Celle qui a l'air d'une tomate.[38]
>
> [Her gaze is lukewarm finery. You can see when she opens her eyes. What is her gaze looking for?
> The beauty of ships at sea?
> The place where the old nightingale lives?
> The house where the poet was born?
> No:
> She's going to go out and can't find her silk umbrella.
> The one that looks like a tomato.]

Orledge notes that this text 'begins with a Verlaine parody ('Son regard est une tiède parure')',[39] perhaps of Verlaine's 'Mon rêve familier', the final tercet of which begins 'Son regard est pareil au regard des statues' ('Her gaze is like a statue's gaze'). The imagined woman's eyes

---

[37] Robert Orledge, 'Chronological Catalogue', p. 286. Orledge's comment appears in an entry for *Croquis et agaceries d'un gros bonhomme en bois* (1913).

[38] The text was first published in the special number of *Revue musicale* devoted to Satie in 1952; p. 64.

[39] Orledge, *Satie the Composer*, p. 217.

are the isolated part of the body on which Satie alights. It is suggested that they might be gazing on one of a trio of Satiean obsessions: a boat, a nightingale and a house (though the poet rather than the house is the recurring Satie motif). However, in a shift back to reality which is absolutely typical of Satie, she is in fact performing a banal activity, looking for her umbrella. But this umbrella is not of the everyday type amassed by the composer; this woman is more like a fictional character who shared Satie's Normandy origins, the clothes-loving Madame Bovary. The reference to the umbrella sharing its colour with a food is yet another characteristic Satie twist.

Another text that Satie did not ultimately use in a piano piece is unusual and particularly charming:

> La vieille maison qui se tient accroupie au cœur des bois, est mal peinte, mal dessinée &, surtout, très inconfortable. On y remise des râteaux, quelques bêches, des arrosoires & un vieux jardinier. Nos peintres de paysage se refusent à reproduire les traits de la vieille maison, de ses râteaux, de ses bêches, de son arrosoire & du vieux jardinier. Tout cela n'est que barbouillage.[40]

> [The old house crouched in the heart of the wood is badly painted, badly drawn and, above all, very uncomfortable. Some rakes, a few logs, watering cans and an old gardener have been put back there. Our landscape painters refuse to reproduce the features of the old house, of its rakes, of its logs, of its watering can and of the old gardener. All that is simply daubing.]

No other Satie text deals explicitly with the visual arts, and we can speculate that the composer did not provide it with a musical counterpart because he did not have two other texts with which it could form a triptych. Here, Satie is taking traditional landscape painters to task for not dealing with the reality of a rural scene, inhabited as it is by an unattractive dwelling which is surrounded by logs which will provide essential heating in cold weather, standard gardening equipment and an old gardener. Satie's left-wing views are coming to the surface: this is no rural idyll, but life as it is really lived in the countryside by people scraping a living in circumstances which are far from picturesque.

■ ■ ■

I WILL now present a series of case studies to demonstrate some of the ways Satie combines music and text. 'Celle qui parle trop' (*Chapitres tournés en tous sens* no. 1) shows the development of a work from sketch to publication, and exemplifies how Satie tells a story through text and music; the three *Avant-dernières pensées* reveal several of Satie's obsessions;

---

[40] Text included in a sketchbook which is now in the Département de Musique, Bibliothèque Nationale de France, Ms 9615(3).

and the texts of *Heures séculaires et instantanées* are unusually extensive and rich in allusions.

'Celle qui parle trop'

Extensive sketches for 'Celle qui parle trop' ('She who talks too much') are housed in the Bibliothèque Nationale de France. As there are several significant differences between these sketches and the finished product, it is an interesting case study of Satie at work. While the published version of the piece has no bar lines, in common with Satie's other texted piano works, the sketch is barred: for this piece, the metre is 6/8. At this stage, Satie appears to be most concerned about the notes and text, as few dynamic markings are present and there are almost no expressive indications for the pianist. The published version of the piece features texts in roman in the middle of the piano stave; indications above the stave, sometimes denoting which character is 'talking' or being represented in the music; and another layer of text in italics.

The published version of the text is: 'Laissez moi parler [in italics: *Marques d'impatience du pauvre mari*]/ Ecoute-moi/ J'ai envie d'un chapeau en acajou massif/ [above stave] Madame Chose a un parapluie en os/ Mademoiselle Machin épouse un homme qui est sec comme un coucou/ [middle of stave] Ecoute-moi donc!/ La concierge a mal dans les côtes/ Arrêt [above stave] Le mari meurt d'épuisement.' (Let me talk [*The poor husband shows signs of impatience*]/ Listen to me/ I want a hat in solid mahogany/ Mrs Thingy has a bone umbrella/ Miss Whatsit is marrying a man who is as dry as a cuckoo/ But listen to me!/ The concierge's sides are hurting/ Stop. The husband dies, exhausted.)

Some texts are not included in the final version of the piece, for instance a prefatory note describing the domestic bourgeois scene: 'Intérieur de braves gens ... les beautés de l'existence & des Grands Magasins/ La femme explique à son mari comment son cerveau a le sens de la bénédiction' (Interior of decent people ... the beauties of life and of Department Stores/ The wife explains to her husband how her brain is blessed). Other textual differences between the sketch and final version are listed below:

- Over the first two bars, Satie writes 'Laisse-moi parler' in the sketch, replacing this with 'Laissez-moi parler' in the final version. Rather than being a peculiar inconsistency between the informal and formal pronouns, this is more likely to show in the latter case that the female character is speaking to more than one person, not just her husband.
- There is no tempo marking in the sketch.
- The italicised indication '*Marques d'impatience du pauvre mari*' is not included in the sketch; Satie added most of these 'stage directions' later in the compositional process. Another example of this appears

at 'J'ai envie d'un chapeau en acajou massif', which features the indication 'Le pauvre mari (son thème)' in the score but not in the manuscript sketch.

- 'Madame Chose a un parapluie en os': the original is in the past tense – 'avait un parapluie tout en os' – and the text begins in the manuscript at the point when there are staccato interjections in the left hand of the piano (Ex. 3.3). The repeated Gs after this passage feature a 'Laisse-moi parler' indication in the manuscript, a verbal repetition which is not preserved in the published score.
- 'Mademoiselle Machin va épouser un homme qui est ~~grand~~ sec comme un coucou' in the sketch; 'épouse un homme' in the score.
- The sketch has an additional 'laisse-moi parler' before the interjection 'Ecoute-moi donc!'
- The text 'Le concierge a mal dans les côtes' is not in the manuscript; presumably this refers to a man struggling under the weight of the lady's purchases.
- The final bars are particularly rich in textual indications (see Ex. 3.4). 'Il meurt épuisé', noted above the stave, and the piano performance direction 'pp Lentement', are both included in the sketch; 'Le mari se meurt d'épuisement' and 'Lent (très)', plus 'pp en un pauvre souffle' are given in the score.

The perpetual quaver motion (as shown in Ex. 3.3) evokes the female character's bustling activity, flitting from one thought to another and one consumer product to another. Here and elsewhere, Satie employs classic rhythmic and melodic hunting topoi – the 6/8 metre, 'horn call' fifths from G to C in the bass, and staccato gestures from a weak to a strong beat – placing them in the contemporary context of a bourgeois room, where the hunter is the lady and her quarry is the perfect product for her home. This lady consumer would like a hat in solid mahogany, a variation of the Satiean wooden head. She has a concierge to help her deal with her purchases, a servant figure who is a regular character in Satie's non-musical texts such as *Mémoires d'un amnésique*, though a rare sight in his texted piano pieces. While Satie's wealthy or high-born acquaintances would have employed staff, the notion that someone living in a labourer's room in Arcueil would have done so is an extreme example of humour by inversion.

The lady's combination of gossip, consumerism and prattling eventually kills her husband, prompting the ultimate 'this is the end' closing gesture (Ex. 3.4). Here, the horn call is slowed down and deformed both internally and externally, with a dissonant tritone C–F♯ replacing the open fifth C–G *in extremis* and the melody line becoming a chromatic deformation of its former self. The perpetual motion grinds to a halt and 'in a feeble breath', the husband drops dead, exhausted. In this last line of the piece, we find out that he was the quarry.

Ex. 3.3 *Chapitres tournés en tous sens*, 1 ('Celle qui parle trop'): top of p. 2, printed score

Ex. 3.4 *Chapitres tournés en tous sens*, 1 ('Celle qui parle trop'): end

Avant-dernières pensées

Each of these three pieces is dedicated to a composer. 'Idylle' is dedicated to Debussy and the manuscript is dated '23 Août 1915' (the day after Debussy's fifty-third birthday). The text reads:

> Que vois-je?
> Le Ruisseau est tout mouillé;
> & les Bois sont inflammables & secs comme des triques.
> Mais mon cœur est tout petit.
> Les Arbres ressemblent à de grands peignes mal faits;
> & le Soleil a, tel une ruche, de beaux rayons dorés.
> Mais mon cœur a froid dans le dos.
> La Lune s'est brouillé avecque ses Voisins;
> et le Ruisseau est trempé jusqu'aux os.

[What do I see?
The Brook is all wet;
and the wood is inflammable and dry like a rod of iron.
But my heart is very small.
The Trees look like big odd-shaped combs;
and the Sun has, like a beehive, lovely golden rays.
But my heart has shivers of fright.
The Moon is scrambled with its Neighbours;
and the Brook is soaked to its bones.]

The title 'Idylle' immediately recalls the sixth of Chabrier's *Pièces pittoresques* (1880). This was a pivotal work for Poulenc, who first heard it in 1914 in a jukebox and wanted to listen to it again and again; he wrote in his biography of Chabrier, 'a universe of harmony suddenly opened up for me and my music has never forgotten this first kiss of love'.[41] Chabrier's idyll has a mechanical, though not precisely repetitive, bass line, while Satie's high-pitched left hand repeats the same four notes over and over. This ostinato (which Satie marks 'smooth, isn't it?') is wave-shaped, no doubt representing the brook and alluding to the dedicatee of Satie's work, the composer of the most celebrated musical seascape of the twentieth century.

The text and music of 'Idylle' combine in hackneyed fashion. 'What do I see?' partners an ascending 'questioning' piano gesture, while 'but my heart is very small' is coupled with a descending chromatic passage. The heart makes a second appearance, when it 'shivers with fright', and here the chromaticism is unfolded in an ascending sequence. An ABA structure is created by the repetition of material and the near-repetition of the text about the brook, suggesting we have classical 'balance' but in far from classical language. Satie's trees which 'look like big odd-shaped combs' are paired with a wide-ranging descending arpeggio, suggesting height (Ex. 3.5).

Ex. 3.5 Satie, *Avant-dernières pensées*, I ('Idylle'): 'The trees look like big odd-shaped combs'

Les Arbres ressemblent à de grands peignes mal faits;

[41] Francis Poulenc, *Emmanuel Chabrier*. Paris and Geneva: La Palatine, 1961, p. 62: 'un univers harmonique s'ouvrit soudain devant moi et ma musique n'a jamais oublié ce premier baiser d'amour'.

Roger Nichols sees other Debussy connections in 'Idylle':

> Both tempo and performing indications are couched in the language of the piano teacher. How does this marry with the title of 'Idylle'? Surely idylls are by nature spontaneous and effortless? [...] Finally, the banality of 'Le Ruisseau est tout mouillé' is explained, as Cocteau says, by the water fixation of Debussy and his followers. We may then note that the piece is dedicated to Debussy, and that in that same year of 1915 Debussy was writing his Etudes for piano, beginning with the teacherly 'Pour les cinq doigts', marked as being 'in the tradition of Czerny' and to be played 'sagement' – 'sensibly', 'in a well-behaved manner', itself a decidedly Satiean instruction.[42]

Nichols' persuasive interpretation suggests that Satie's title is ironic: what could be less idyllic than a piano exercise? Satie and Debussy's friendship foundered from 1917, the penultimate year of Debussy's life, because Satie did not appreciate Debussy's comments on *Parade*. However, uniquely, Satie did apologise before Debussy's death on 25 March 1918.

'Aubade' is dedicated to Paul Dukas and dated '3 Octobre 1915' – two days after Dukas' birthday. Dukas helped Satie financially during the war years, sometimes by recommending him for charitable assistance, and this piece is perhaps a small tribute of thanks to Dukas. The ostinato this time is in the treble register and right hand, and is arpeggiated like a strummed guitar, suggesting a Spanish alba (dawn song). The text is an odd love story featuring a beauty and poet (rather than la Belle et la Bête, we have la Belle et le Poète). But this is hardly a classic fairy story, as the poet goes down with flu and there are a couple of references to a rigaudon.

'Méditation' is dedicated to Satie's Schola Cantorum teacher Albert Roussel and dated '6 Octobre 1915' (as he was born on 5 April, the notion that these three pieces may have been birthday gifts to their dedicatees does not hold up); this ostinato, in the treble register, features alternating fourths. Again, we encounter a poet, who this time is chained in a tower; we hear the wind, the poet shivers and has goose bumps – because the devil is present (in a very low register). The text then suggests that the wind is the wind of inspiration which has passed by. The wind, genius and inspiration are all characterised by rapid arpeggiated material. The poet 'smiles maliciously, though his heart weeps like a willow': at the mention of his heart, we read a hackneyed poetic image similar to the one in 'Idylle'. At the end, the poet is humble and blushes. The left hand of the piano outlines fourth- and semitone-based material, and open fifth chords when the text mentions the poet has indigestion, caused by a mixture of blank verse (or perhaps white worms – 'vers blancs' could signify both) and bitter disillusion. The clichéd rhyme vers/amères tells us again that the poet is perhaps not very inspired. The fourth-based material evokes

---

[42] Nichols, *The Harlequin Years*, pp. 217–18.

Roussel's style, or is it a deliberate attempt by Satie to create harmonies not approved by the Schola Cantorum?

Heures séculaires et instantanées[43]

The most extensive texts written for a set of piano pieces are those for *Heures séculaires et instantanées*, a triptych composed in late June–July 1914. Satie's preface explicitly forbids performers to read them out loud: 'A quiconque./ Je défends de lire, à haute voix, le texte, durant le temps de l'exécution musicale. Tout manquement à cette observation entraînerait ma juste indignation contre l'outrecuidant. Il ne sera accordé aucun passe-droit.' (To whomever it may concern./ I forbid the reading out loud of the text during the performance of the music. All infractions of this matter would entail my righteous indignation against the offender. No exceptions to this rule will be permitted.) Whether this admonition should be taken seriously is, as often with Satie, moot, though this is the general opinion of Satie scholars and performers. One could just as convincingly read this statement as a parody: Victor Hugo's statement 'Défense de déposer de la musique le long de mes vers' ('It is forbidden to place music alongside my poetry') springs to mind, and, as we will see, the final piece of *Heures séculaires et instantanées* features a Hugo parody. I am also reminded of those officious French announcements which implore people to leave the bathroom in the clean condition in which they would wish to find it. Finally, of course, Satie's statement could simply be interpreted as a joke – though, as often with this composer, a combination of these three readings is likely to be the most convincing interpretation of all.

The work is 'pleasantly' dedicated to the mysterious 'sir William Grant-Plumot'. Satie continues this florid dedication: 'Up to now, two characters have surprised me: Louis XI and Sir William; the first by the oddness of his good nature; the second, by his continuous immobility. It is an honour for me to say the names of Louis XI and Sir William Grant-Plumot.'[44] These two figures, one historical and one fictional, have bizarrely obscure connections to Satie's own origins and they may well be the dedicatees of the piece because the composer identified with them both and considered this to be a recondite way of dedicating a work to himself. Sir William's identity, if indeed he has connections to the real world, has never been discovered, and I wonder whether his half-Anglo-Saxon, half-French name is a pointed reference to Satie's own Franco-Scottish origins. Louis XI

---

[43] Parts of this section, particularly material related to the first piece 'Obstacles venimeux', were published in my article 'Erik Satie's "Obstacles venimeux"', *Ars Lyrica*, 20 (2011), pp. 99–114.

[44] 'Jusqu'ici, deux figures m'ont surpris: Louis XI et sir William; le premier, par l'étrangeté de sa bonhomie; le second, par sa continuelle immobilité. Ce m'est un honneur de prononcer, ici, les noms de Louis XI et sir William Grant-Plumot.'

(1423–83), for his part, was known as a shrewd, scheming monarch who at the age of thirteen married Margaret, the eleven-year-old daughter of James I of Scotland. Like Satie's Scottish mother, she died young and her husband later remarried. Towards the end of his life, Louis XI drove the English out of France and the English renounced their claim to Normandy, the future home region of our composer.

Heures séculaires et instantanées originate partly in a set of three *Obstacles venimeux* for piano, sketched late in June 1914. Orledge believes that these pieces were 'probably replaced by the first of the *Heures*...' with which they share a title. Sketches for all three pieces are housed in the Bibliothèque Nationale, and the extant texts are as follows: 'No. 1: Le Résident Général sommeille doucement, étendu sur un paquet de hamac. 1er obstacle: un scorpion. 2me obstacle: un boa. 3me obstacle: son concierge.' The second piece is untitled, and the third is marked: 'La chaleur est diluvienne'.[45] (No. 1: The resident general gently rests, stretched out immobile on a hammock. 1st obstacle: a scorpion. 2nd obstacle: a boa. 3rd obstacle: his concierge ... no. 3: The heat is stormlike.) This suggests an exotic setting – a country where a nap could be interrupted by a Satiean trio of venomous creatures – reminiscent of contemporary paintings by the Douanier Rousseau such as *La charmeuse de serpents* (1907) or *Le rêve* (1910), where a figure is depicted against a jungle backdrop.[46] The notion that a concierge could be an 'obstacle' echoes the upside-down master–servant relationship depicted in *Le piège de Méduse* (1913), where the servant Polycarpe calls his master 'tu' and informs him that he cannot serve him because he is going out to a billiard match. Satie's fondness for wordplay is shown by his unconventional use of 'diluvienne' rather than 'antédiluvienne', and his harking back to the word's original connection with a storm. Perhaps the lack of a title for the second piece in this proposed series shows Satie's dissatisfaction with the project at this stage, and he later adapted some of the ideas in *Heures séculaires et instantanées*.

The multiple origins of the half-serious, half-joking texts of *Heures séculaires et instantanées* have remained unnoticed until now. The consensus view on the texts which appear on the score is that they are proto-surreal or Dadaesque: Alan Gillmor points out that these texts were written 'five years before the Romanian-born Tristan Tzara brought his Zurich-born Dada movement to Paris';[47] Whiting draws attention to the 'contrasting, even contradictory images' in a single phrase, which 'resemble the language of Satie's absurdist farce *Le piège de Méduse*'.[48] The

---

[45] Orledge, *Satie the Composer*, pp. 306–7.
[46] Satie could well have seen *La charmeuse de serpents* at the fifth Salon d'Automne at the Grand Palais in October 1907.
[47] Gillmor, *Erik Satie*, p. 173.
[48] Whiting, *Satie the Bohemian*, p. 409.

pianist and author Jean-Pierre Armengaud, for his part, writes of Satie's texts in general: 'try to say Satie's words as if they were pronounced by a drunkard, and things become much clearer'.[49] In fact, the most obvious interpretation of these texts has not yet been considered: that they could, at least in part, be taken literally. Without a basis in reality, the surreal could not exist.

Whiting remarks that the overall title of the work 'connotes three different ways of dividing time – into hours, centuries, or instants – and implies that they are all, from some perspective, equivalent'.[50] There are several ambiguities at the heart of this title. Here, Satie refers both to time which is very rare and/or durable ('séculaire' meaning something happening once in a century, or which has existed for a century) or very brief ('instantané' meaning a snapshot in time). The plays on time in the title echo Psalm 90, verse 4 – 'For a thousand years in thy sight are but as yesterday when it is past, and as a watch in the night' – which is perhaps a rather conventional religious reference from a composer who founded his own church in the 1890s.

I will focus on Satie's texts for *Heures séculaires et instantanées* in ascending order of interest: discussion of the second of these pieces will be followed by the third and finally the first piece in the set. The combination of parody of a well-known poet with absurd imagery is characteristic of Satie's style, and is apparent in the second of the *Heures séculaires et instantanées*, as can be seen below.

2. Crépuscule matinal (de midi)

Le soleil s'est levé de bon matin et de bonne humeur[.] La chaleur sera au dessus de la normale, car le temps est préhistorique et à l'orage. Le soleil est tout en haut du ciel; il a l'air d'un bon type. Mais ne nous y fions pas. Peut-être va-t-il brûler les récoltes ou frapper un grand coup: un coup de soleil. Derrière le hangar, un bœuf mange à se rendre malade.

[Morning twilight (at midday). The sun rose early in the morning and in a good mood. It will be warmer than usual, because the weather is prehistoric and storm-ridden. The sun is at the very top of the sky: he seems like a decent sort. But let's not worry about it. Perhaps it will burn the harvest or deliver a mighty stroke: a sunstroke. Behind the shed, a cow is eating itself sick.]

The second and third texts of *Heures séculaires et instantanées* feature a phrase ending with a colon on the topic of 'striking a blow', followed by Satie twisting the meaning of the expression:

---

[49] Jean-Pierre Armengaud, *Erik Satie*. Paris: Fayard, 2009, p. 20: 'essayez de scander les phrases de Satie comme si elles étaient dites par un ivrogne, beaucoup de choses s'éclairent'.

[50] Whiting, *Satie the Bohemian*, p. 409.

Peut-être va-t-il brûler les récoltes ou frapper un grand coup: un coup de soleil. (2)

L'horloge du vieux village abandonné va, elle aussi, frapper un grand coup: le coup de treize heures. (3)

This may suggest that the second and third pieces were conceived together. The second of the *Heures séculaires et instantanées* has few obvious sources, and it is curious to note that the second of the sketched ideas for 'Obstacles venimeux' did not have a specific title or concept, which suggests that Satie had no particular plan for this piece. Nevertheless, the completed 'Crépuscule matinal (de midi)' is a good illustration of the multiple temporal perspectives suggested by the overall title of the work and by the verse of Psalm 90 I have already cited; it also evokes Debussy's *La mer*. The title refers to three different time periods (twilight, morning and midday), and the 'prehistoric' behaviour of the weather is noted. Incidentally, Satie's brother Conrad reported in 1914 that his brother hated sunshine and saw the sun as 'his personal enemy' who is 'brutal' and 'says nasty things about him'.[51]

Satie's verbal humour takes many forms: humour by inversion, by undermining a clichéd expression, or by being excessively pedantic. These are all commonplace and all present in the text of 'Crépuscule matinal (du midi)'. The title itself exhibits these features, as we do not expect to experience twilight in the morning, and the bracketed insistence that this phenomenon is occurring at midday adds to the impression that the world is not operating according to normal rules. The language of a weather report ('La chaleur sera au dessus de la normale') is followed by a play on the word 'temps', which can signify weather, time or a grammatical tense. 'Le temps est historique' – a pedantic grammatical observation – is twisted on its axis by Satie making 'le temps' refer to the weather and adding an intensifying prefix to form 'préhistorique'. This is no ordinary weather forecast, not least because the sun is personified. Going beyond clichés about the sun rising and being at the very top of the sky, Satie adds that it is 'in a good mood' and 'seems like a decent sort'. But the rest of his text shows the sun as a destroyer of crops, a cause of sunstroke, and possibly something which provokes a cow to eat too much (though the causation is equivocal).

Verlaine's poems often feature nature and weather imagery, one well-known example being 'Le ciel est, par-dessus le toit/ Si bleu, si calme' (The sky above the roof is so blue, so peaceful). Satie does the same in the text of 'Crépuscule matinal (de midi)', giving a factual statement about the weather which is then given a strange twist with a comment suggesting the sun is actually a person, a decent fellow. The closest Verlaine poem

---

[51] Quoted by Robert Orledge in *Satie Remembered*, trans. Roger Nichols. London: Faber, 1995, p. 161.

to this Satie text is *L'échelonnement des haies* (which was memorably set by Debussy in 1891), a portrait of a landscape with farm animals. But while Verlaine paints a rural scene featuring sheep in a field, Satie's evocation of the countryside is a good deal less idyllic, with images of burning and a cow eating itself sick.

3. 'Affolements granitiques'

L'horloge du vieux village abandonné va, elle aussi, frapper un grand coup: le coup de treize heures. Une pluie antédiluvienne sort des nuages de poussière; les grands bois ricaneurs se tirent par des branches; tandis que les rudes granits se bousculent mutuellement et ne savent où se mettre pour être encombrants. Treize heures vont sonner, sous les traits représentatifs de: Une heure de l'après-midi. Hélas! ce n'est point l'heure légale.

[Granitic panic: The clock of the old abandoned village will, also, strike a great blow: the hour of 13 o'clock. Rain preceding a storm falls from dust clouds; the great laughing wood runs off through the branches; while the rough granite rocks snuggle up to each other and don't know where to put themselves to get in the way. The clock will strike thirteen, under the representative traits of: One o'clock in the afternoon. Alas! It isn't the legal hour.]

The text of 'Affolements granitiques' features several direct and oblique references to poetry. The final line echoes the last line of 'Obstacles venimeux', 'Ce n'est pas l'heure du berger' (which negatively evokes Verlaine's poem 'L'heure du berger'). This and 'Hélas! ce n'est point l'heure légale' are both negative clauses which focus on time. There are also a number of textual indications in italics which should no doubt be interpreted as performance directions; while these indications exist in the first two pieces of *Heures séculaires et instantanées*, the only marking of this type which is out of the ordinary appears in 'Affolements granitiques'. At the start of this piece, Satie gives the queasy performance direction *(Les mauvais miasmes s'amusent dans l'herbe)*, combining the odours of decay (*miasmes*) playing with fresh grass (*l'herbe*); a direction which seems to apply more to the mood of the poem, with its Verlaine-like nature imagery,[52] than to the performance of the piano piece.

There are also close references in Satie's text to Victor Hugo's unfinished epic poem *Dieu*, which the poet started in 1855 but had not completed by the time of his death in 1885. Specifically, Satie echoes the second volume of this poem, 'L'Océan d'en haut'; the relevant extract is as follows:

---

[52] For instance, in 'Dans les bois', where 'le vent ... s'éparpille, ainsi qu'un miasme, dans l'espace' (*Poèmes saturniens*, 1866).

> dans une clarté de vision, je vois
> Ce livide univers, vaste danse macabre,
> Où l'astre tourbillonne, où la vague se cabre,
> Où tout s'enfuit! Je vois les sépulcres, les nids,
> Le hallier, la montagne, et les rudes granits,
> Du vieux squelette monde informes ankyloses,
> La plaine vague ouvrant ses pâles fleurs écloses,
> Les flots démesurés poussant de longs abois,
> Et les gestes hideux des arbres dans les bois.

[Clearly, I see/ This livid universe, vast macabre dance/ Where the star whirls, where the wave bends/ Where everything flees! I see the tombs, the nests/ The thicket, the mountain, and the rough granite/ Of the old shapeless stiff skeleton world/ The distant plain opening its pale blooming flowers/ The overwhelming floods howling like a dog/ And the hideous gestures of trees in the woods.]

The reference to 'rudes granits' appears in a section about the creation of the world, and just before this, the line 'Ce livide univers, vaste danse macabre' is another evocation, at least to readers of Satie's generation and beyond, of Saint-Saëns' famous tone poem in which the clock also strikes thirteen. Hugo's use of unexpected adjectives before the noun ('livide univers', 'rudes granits'), which give human emotions to inanimate objects, is mocked by Satie's even more peculiar imagery: Hugo's trees making 'hideous gestures' and floods 'howling' have parallels in Satie's laughing wood running off, panicking granite and rocks snuggling up to each other. Satie also seems amused by the literal meaning of 'antediluvian' ('before a storm'), and this phrase recalls the idea for the third piece of the sketched 'Obstacles venimeux'. In Satie's peculiar literary universe, events happen in the wrong order, the rain coming before the storm, perhaps because the clock has unexpectedly struck thirteen.

We know that Satie would have found Hugo-style descriptions of Nature absurd, as Cocteau reported the famous views he expressed to Debussy about music on stage: 'Here', said Cocteau, 'I wish to cite a phrase of Satie's which Debussy told me and which determined the aesthetic of *Pelléas*: "The orchestra should not grimace when a character enters on stage. Do the property trees grimace? We should create musical décor, a musical atmosphere where the characters move and converse with each other. No couplets, no leitmotifs, using the sort of atmosphere one finds in Puvis de Chavannes!"' [53] Perhaps unsurprisingly for a piece

---

[53] Jean Cocteau, 'Fragments d'une conférence sur Eric [sic] Satie', written in 1920 and published in *Revue musicale* in March 1924, p. 221: 'Ici, déclare Cocteau, je vais citer une phrase de Satie qui m'a été dite par Debussy et qui décida l'esthétique de *Pelléas*: « Il faudrait que l'orchestre ne *grimace* pas quand un personnage entre en scène. Est-ce que les arbres du décor

in 'granitic' mood, Jean-Pierre Armengaud considers that 'a certain "cubisation" of the line and rhythm can be seen, in the sense that the melodic line is deformed, syncopation is omnipresent, varied melodic elements are juxtaposed, as are dissonances which twist the meaning and destabilise the auditory "perspective"'.[54]

The other main topic of Satie's text is time, a topic shared by all three *Heures séculaires et instantanées*. It is salutary to remember that Paris mean time was introduced as the standard time in France only in 1891, at the beginning of Satie's career. (The relevant law required clocks inside railway stations and train schedules to be set five minutes late to allow travellers to arrive late without missing their trains.)[55] Perhaps, therefore, it is not surprising that Satie shows an obsession with time in many of his writings, whether they be stand-alone texts written for publication in magazines or the in-score texts which are omnipresent in his piano works from 1912 to 1917. Whiting remarks that 'Satie was evidently fascinated by the phenomenon of the government changing the designation of hours through simple imposition of the 24-hour clock. [...] In 1952, René Chalupt recalled that Satie, "whenever he fixed the time of a meeting ... would use both the new and the old designation: 'I'll be there at 1800 hrs (6 o'clock old style)'".'[56]

The benefits and drawbacks of the twenty-four-hour clock were a topic of debate in early twentieth-century France. The guidebook of the Paris Exposition in 1900 states: 'Let's remember that Belgium is the only country to have officially adopted the 24-hour clock, just as the Observatory of Paris has done since 10 January 1900.'[57] In 1914, the year Satie composed *Heures séculaires et instantanées*, an article denouncing the

---

grimacent? Il faudrait faire un *décor musical*, créer un *climat musical* où les personnages bougent et causent. Pas de couplets, pas de *leitmotive*, se servir d'une certaine atmosphère de Puvis de Chavannes!»'

[54] Armengaud, *Erik Satie*, p. 577; 'on observe une certaine "cubisation" des lignes et des rythmes, au sens d'une déformation mélodique, d'une généralisation de la syncope, de la juxtaposition des éléments mélodiques hétérogènes, de l'introduction de dissonances qui pervertissent le sens et déstabilisent la "perspective" auditive'.

[55] See Vanessa France, 'A Brief History of French Time', http://vanessafrance.wordpress.com/2012/03/25/a-brief-history-of-french-time/ (accessed 6 April 2015).

[56] Whiting, *Satie the Bohemian*, p. 410.

[57] Anonymous author, *Paris Exposition, 1900: Guide pratique du visiteur de Paris et de l'exposition* (Paris: Hachette, 1900), p. xiv: 'Rappelons que la Belgique est le seul pays qui ait adopté officiellement le cadran de 24 heures, comme l'a fait l'Observatoire de Paris depuis le 10 janvier 1900.'

recent adoption of the twenty-four-hour clock in France was published in a science magazine.⁵⁸

The text of 'Affolements granitiques' can only be understood in the light of this new way of telling the time. 'Thirteen o'clock' can mean both 1 p.m. in the twenty-four-hour clock, and the sinister clock striking thirteen heard, for instance, in Saint-Saëns' *Danse macabre*. Referring to 13.00 hours as 'one o'clock in the afternoon' was, in 1914, no longer 'the legal hour'. The thirteen strokes are played by the piano in 'Affolements granitiques', an idea which was present in a sketch which otherwise barely resembled the final version (Ex. 3.6). And (surely not coincidentally) Debussy's proposed opera *Le diable dans le beffroi* (The Devil in the Belfry), based on Edgar Allan Poe, also focuses on this horologically unexpected moment. Debussy tinkered with this project over many years, and he and Satie must have discussed it, probably as late as 1912, after which there is no further evidence that Debussy worked on this opera. The central plot event of *Le diable dans le beffroi* is the clock striking thirteen in the Dutch village of Vonderwotteimittis⁵⁹ (a name which has to be read aloud to make sense).

Satie's fondness for humour involving time is also shown in his response to Debussy's *La mer*; he allegedly said of the first movement, 'De l'aube à midi sur la mer', 'Ah, my dear friend, there's one particular moment between half past ten and a quarter to eleven that I found stunning!'⁶⁰

The text of the first piece of *Heures séculaires et instantanées* is the most intriguing of them all:

1. 'Obstacles venimeux'

Cette vaste partie du monde n'est habitée que par un seul homme: un nègre. Il s'ennuie à mourir de rire. L'ombre des arbres millénaires marque 9h.17. Les crapauds s'appellent par leur nom propre[.] Pour mieux penser, le nègre tient son cervelet de la main droite, les doigts de celle-ci écartés. De loin, il semble figurer un physiologiste distingué. Quatre serpents anonymes le captivent, suspendus aux basques de son uniforme que déforment le chagrin et la solitude réunis. Sur le bord du fleuve, un vieux palétuvier lave lentement ses racines, répugnantes de saleté. Ce n'est pas l'heure du berger.

---

⁵⁸ Charles Lallemand, 'Contre le cadran de 24 heures.' *La nature: Revue des sciences et de leurs applications aux arts et à l'industrie*, vol. 42 no. 2131 (28 March 1914): p. 291.

⁵⁹ See Robert Orledge, *Debussy and the Theatre*. Cambridge: Cambridge University Press, 1982, pp. 102–9 and Linda Cummins, *Debussy and the Fragment*. Amsterdam and New York: Rodopi, 2006, pp. 131–2.

⁶⁰ Cited in Orledge (ed.), *Satie Remembered*, p. 97, quoting Hélène Jourdan-Morhange; trans. Roger Nichols.

Ex. 3.6 (a) Satie, *Heures séculaires et instantanées*, 3 ('Affolements granitiques'): opening of sketch (BNF 9593); (b) Satie, *Heures séculaires et instantanées*, 3 ('Affolements granitiques'): opening of final version

[Venomous obstacles. This vast part of the world is inhabited by only one man: a black man. He is bored to dying of laughter. The shadow of the millennial trees indicates 9.17 a.m. The toads call themselves by their real name. To think better, the black man holds his brain in his right hand, with fingers spread. From a distance, he seems to resemble a distinguished physiologist. Four anonymous snakes captivate him, clinging to the lapels of his uniform, deformed by a combination of unhappiness and solitude. On the bank of the river, an old mangrove tree slowly washes its roots, which are disgustingly filthy. It's not the lovers' hour.]

No commentators have yet considered that the text could, in fact, be interpreted literally for the most part. Whiting notes that Satie 'had recourse to the devices of authors like Verlaine, who emphasised the musical resonances of words so as to distract from their conceptual content'[61] though he does not specifically identify the two near-quotations from Verlaine in this text. First, Satie borrows the first words of a poem sent by Debussy in 1885 as the third of his *Ariettes oubliées*, 'L'ombre des arbres', imagining that these shadows are casting on an unusually precise sundial. The last line refers to Verlaine's poem 'L'heure du berger' (1866), though as it is 'not the lovers' hour' (literally 'not the shepherd's hour'), there is none of the red sunset, mist or croaking frogs evoked by Verlaine. Nevertheless, there are some toads which unashamedly call themselves by their real name, defying the Symbolist dictum that suggestion is superior to statement.

The tempo given is crotchet (quarter-note) = 104, and Satie plays on the French word for 'crotchet' – 'un noir' – by giving the tempo marking 'noirâtre' ('blackish'). There are a number of references to blackness in the text, not least the ethnicity of the solitary character.[62] While, on the surface, the reference to 'four anonymous snakes' appears to be an example of Satie's fondness for the animal kingdom, the precise number of snakes provides the key to understanding the text. The old flag of the French colonies of Martinique and St Lucia features four white coiled snakes on a sky blue background; this flag was imposed on the inhabitants of the islands from 4 August 1766 by the French colonial administration, and it flew on ships transporting slaves across the

---

[61] Whiting, *Satie the Bohemian*, p. 409.

[62] The setting could also suggest a Robinson Crusoe connection: see Robert Orledge, 'Satie at Sea, and the Mysteries of "La Belle Cubaine".' *Music & Letters*, vol. 71 no. 3 (1990), pp. 361–73. Orledge states on p. 368 that in the mid-1920s, Satie was considering a work based on this story, together with a *Paul & Virginie* collaboration with Cocteau and Radiguet and a work on *Don Quichotte*. The sketchbook BNF Ms 9576 includes some simple musical and textual material for the *Robinson Crusoe* and *Paul & Virginie* projects.

Atlantic.[63] Therefore, the uniform of the black man surely has the flag – a symbol of the enslaved condition of his ancestors – stitched to his lapels. Small wonder the uniform is 'deformed by a combination of unhappiness and solitude'. What seems on the surface to be a bizarrely surreal image of dangling beasts is, viewed another way, a perfectly conventional picture of a man in uniform. These poisonous snakes, which some sources say are only found on Martinique and are now rare, are one of the 'venomous obstacles' encountered on the island, as they are around one metre long and can kill a human being as their venom makes human blood coagulate.[64] Satie would have loved (and was surely aware of) the Greek-derived French name of the snake, 'trigonocéphale', a name which refers to its triangular head. (In English the creature is known as the fer-de-lance snake.)

The colonial and snake themes link 'Obstacles venimeux' to the sketched set of three pieces mentioned earlier, and the Martinique connection makes sense of most of the rest of Satie's text. Its coastal town of Saint-Pierre, once the most populous town on the island, was destroyed on 8 May 1902 at 7.50 a.m. by a volcanic eruption of Mount Pelée.[65] Fifty people and around 200 animals died of snakebites after the eruption, the snakes having been driven from their territory in the volcano by ash fall,[66] and the eventual death toll was over 30,000: it was the most deadly volcanic eruption of the twentieth century. It is these 'venomous obstacles' that Satie must have had in mind, and one imagines the roots of the tropical trees being washed by filthy, ashy water, and the solitary black inhabitant being the only survivor of the tragedy. Indeed, contemporary newspapers featured many stories about a certain Louis-Auguste Cyparis (known as Samson), a convict held in Saint-Pierre who claimed (falsely) to be the only survivor of the eruption; 'after he recovered, he received a pardon and eventually joined the Barnum & Bailey Circus, where he toured the world billed as the "Lone Survivor of St. Pierre"'.[67] Most certainly, 'ce n'est pas l'heure du berger'.

There are a number of clear connections between the music and text.

---

[63] For the history of the flag, see Claudette Duhamel, http://www.alterpresse.org/spip.php?article5862#.VLftnFqRPFI (accessed 15 January 2015). Duhamel, a Martinique lawyer, ran a campaign in 2007 to ban the flag from these islands.

[64] http://www.guidemartinique.com/conseils/serpents.php (accessed 15 January 2015). The *Petit Larousse* (1910) claims that the snake is native to Asia and Africa (p. 1014).

[65] *Petit Larousse illustré*, 56th edition (1910), ed. Claude Augé, p. 1576.

[66] http://www.geology.sdsu.edu/how_volcanoes_work/Pelee.html (accessed 15 January 2015).

[67] See http://www.geology.sdsu.edu/how_volcanoes_work/Pelee.html (accessed 15 January 2015). Most reports claim that at least two other inhabitants of Saint-Pierre survived the eruption.

While there are no bar lines in 'Obstacles venimeux', the piece follows a regular 4/4 metre for the most part. Exceptions to this are striking: at ('l'heure') we lose the sense of a regular pulse, surely an example of Satie's twisted sense of humour. The overall structure of the piece can be described with reference to the number of crotchet beats in each section; the sections are clearly delineated by repetition of material and each, apart from the fourth, concludes with a break in the texture (a rest of at least a quaver). There are 32 beats in each section, apart from the last, which has 31½ – a deliberate flaw also present in the other two pieces of the set.

The five-section structure is articulated by the repetition or near-repetition of textual and musical themes as follows:

1. Cette vaste partie du monde n'est habitée que par un seul homme: un nègre. Il s'ennuie à mourir de rire. (section A)
2. L'ombre des arbres millénaires marque 9h.17. Les crapauds s'appellent par leur nom propre[.] ('Counting' section with unclear pulse; chromaticism; odd notation; amphibian in text)
3. Pour mieux penser, le nègre tient son cervelet de la main droite, les doigts de celle-ci écartés. De loin, il semble figurer un physiologiste distingué. (A transposed, this time with an arpeggiated accompaniment; text focuses on 'le nègre')
4. Quatre serpents anonymes le captivent, suspendus aux basques de son uniforme que déforment le chagrin et la solitude réunis. ('Counting' section; chromaticism; odd notation; reptile in text)
5. Sur le bord du fleuve, un vieux palétuvier lave lentement ses racines, répugnantes de saleté. Ce n'est pas l'heure du berger. (A repeated, an octave lower compared to its first appearance; negative emotions, but the man is no longer present)

The pianist is asked to 'breathe' before the final cadence. This is a traditional 'this is the end' gesture familiar from romantic piano music: the dynamic level is loud and getting louder, the texture is thick, the gesture expansive ('Large au possible' is the instruction) and the right-hand part features spread chords: as we have seen, the text 'it's not the lovers' hour' is a reversal of Verlaine's poetic title, and Satie's conclusion is likewise a parody of nineteenth-century piano music, a parody which unexpectedly ends in conventional fashion on a B♭ major triad.

The most obvious mimesis in this piece is the ticking of a clock, which ties in with the overall title of the work and is a mechanistic gesture which also appears in the second and third of the *Heures séculaires et instantanées*. At the top of the second page of the printed text, Satie chimes the hour (×9) and then, at a higher pitch and lower dynamic level, the seventeen minutes. Satie also counts out the number of snakes ('Quatre serpents anonymes' are heralded by four C♭s), and his peculiar chromatic notation, also used in works such as *Vexations* (1893), provides an extra layer of discomfort for the performer. While the musical material here is unremarkable, the notation is deliberately complex. This odd notation is confined to the second and fourth sections and text associations with darkness and discomfort: double flats for 'L'ombre des arbres', double sharps for 'que déforment le chagrin et la solitude réunis' (the latter made even more treacherous for the performer with the addition of flats in the left hand).

At the words 'un nègre', Satie channels popular music of his time: an added 9th and chromatic inflections evoke American-style black music, specifically the fashionable ragtime and cakewalk style which is also evoked by Satie's friend Debussy in a number of piano works, and was exploited by Satie himself in several popular songs he composed in the early years of the twentieth century.

Conclusion

Ann-Marie Hanlon rightly emphasises that 'Only a handful of contemporary commentators noted that Satie had indeed created a new genre of piano music with these works and only one of these recognised it as an inter-art genre: however none of them took his innovations seriously.'[68] Hanlon specifically cites Gabrielle Buffet (who later married Francis Picabia), who identified 'Satie's "new genre" following the premiere of *Chapitres tournés en tous sens*. Buffet wrote that these texted piano works are 'no longer essays in pure music, but of semi-dramatic, semi-musical forms, that is to say that the ideal architecture of the old forms, sonatas, symphonies, etc., etc., is replaced by a literary motive to which the music is rigorously subjugated and which is the foundation itself of the work.'[69] In 'Obstacles venimeux', we see the text outlining a rough ABABA form which is reflected in the music, though we see thematic connections rather than precise repetition. Elsewhere, Satie clearly associates particular words with particular musical devices; it is especially interesting to see him using these associations across more than one piece, for instance his use of chromaticism at mentions of 'mon cœur' (my heart) in different *Avant-dernières pensées*. While Jankélévitch believed that text and music are two separate entities in Satie's texted piano works, there is plenty of evidence suggesting the opposite is true. Whiting states, 'Sketch and manuscript evidence shows that Satie usually

---

[68] Ann-Marie Hanlon, 'Satie and the French Musical Canon: A Reception Study.' Unpublished PhD thesis, University of Newcastle, 2013, p. 195.

[69] Gabrielle Buffet, 'Musique d'aujourd'hui', *Soirées de Paris*, III (15 March 1914), pp. 181–3, at pp. 181–2: 'Les œuvres ultra-modernes nous en sont une preuve. Plus d'essais de musique pure, mais des formes mi-dramatiques, mi-musicales, c'est-à-dire que l'architecture idéale des formes anciennes, sonates, symphonies, etc., etc., est remplacée par un motif littéraire auquel la musique s'assujettit rigoureusement et qui est la carcasse même de l'œuvre [...].'

wrote his in-score texts after the music,'[70] though the existence of texts which were not ultimately used in a piano work shows that there are exceptions to this.

Whiting writes of Satie's musical parodies: 'Beginning with stylistic allusion (*Véritables préludes flasques*), Satie moved on to the quotation of single phrases, then to the reworking of entire tunes, and finally to something like Hyspa's composite parodies, in which he juggled quotations from more than one source.'[71] The example of 'Obstacles venimeux' demonstrates that Satie practised this juggling and parodying of quoted material in textual as well as musical form. His considerable literary knowledge is apparent from his use of quotation, near-quotation and parody of a wide variety of sources.

This raises the question of the roles of foreground and background in relation to Satie's texted piano works: should the media of music and text have equal status? As live and commercially recorded performances of these pieces invariably omit Satie's words, we can safely assume that the music is considered to be the primary, indeed sole, concern of performers. But Satie's concept of 'musique d'ameublement' shows the composer questioning traditional assumptions about the audience's attention. The care Satie took with his words, and the myriad connections between words and music, suggests that we should pay attention to both media and their interrelations and that we should question traditional performance practices for Satie's texted piano works.

---

[70] Whiting, *Satie the Bohemian*, p. 356.
[71] Ibid., p. 355.

CHAPTER 4

Repetition and Furniture Music

SATIE liked to organise his music in groups of three, and variety within a triptych was of little or no interest to the composer. The series of contrasting movements typical of the Austro-German sonata tradition is completely foreign to Satie: pieces such as *Gymnopédies* and *Jack in the Box* may be threefold, but all three are based on a small amount of similar musical material which is constantly reiterated and hardly varied at all. Pushed to extremes, music of this type could simply be a repeating loop, with no variation or contrast whatsoever. This chapter deals with Satie's works for which repetition, usually of indeterminate duration, is their *raison d'être* – works which are therefore closer to the mechanical aesthetic than any others in Satie.

Ornella Volta stresses that the concept of background music was present in Satie's work almost from the beginning: initially his conception was music as decoration, almost as wallpaper. She writes:

> Fascinated by the serene harmony of Puvis de Chavannes' frescos, he aspired from the 1890s to compose 'decorative' music, not in the sense of ornamental music but rather as part of a sonic environment uniting, in an ideal symbiosis, composer, interpreter and listener. With his three preludes for [Péladan's play] *Fils des Etoiles*, he made this clear when he specified the 'decorative themes' that inspired them, which corresponded simply to the décor and ambience in each act of the play: the Night of Kaldea, the Low Room of the Grand Temple and the Terrace of the Goudéa Palace.[1]

Le Fils des étoiles was composed for the salon of the Rose-Croix du Temple and rehearsed in public on 22 March 1892, the play having been turned down by two more prestigious Parisian theatres, the

---

[1] Ornella Volta, preface to Salabert score *Erik Satie: Musiques d'ameublement pour petit ensemble* (EAS 17141X, 1998), p. iv; 'Fasciné par le sérénité harmonieuse des fresques de Puvis de Chavannes, il a aspiré, dès le début des années quatre-vingt-dix, à composer une musique «décorative», cet adjectif n'était pas pris au sens d'ornement mais renvoyant plutôt à la notion d'un environnement sonore qui réunirait, en une symbiose idéale, le compositeur, l'interprète et l'auditeur. ¶ C'est pour rendre cette notion plus évidente qu'il a tenu à préciser, à propos de ses trois préludes du *Fils des Etoiles*, les «thèmes décoratifs» qui les avaient inspirés, et qui correspondaient tout simplement aux décors et aux ambiances qui se seraient succédés dans la pièce, à savoir La Nuit de Kaldée, La Salle basse du Grand Temple et La Terrasse du Palais Goudéa pour chacun des trois actes, respectivement.'

august Comédie-Française and the more experimental Odéon. Satie's contribution to 'Sâr' Joséphin Péladan's play was three preludes, one for each act of the play, and three *Sonneries de la Rose+Croix* for trumpets and harps. The acts, titled 'La Vocation', 'L'Initiation' and 'L'Incantation', show the intended devotional flavour of this multimedia work. The preludes are described by the composer as 'for flutes and harps of an admirably oriental character', instrumentation which was no doubt suggested by the principal character Œnohil, a 'shepherd-poet' who plays the lyre. Satie's passing reference to 'oriental' should be considered in the context of his own time and place, without addressing the considerable colonial baggage that 'oriental' carries today. Rather than relating the term to any real East European or East Asian music, Satie surely used it as a commonplace expression to denote music which is repetitive, non-developmental, lacking the goal direction characteristic of the sonata and symphonic traditions. As with the *Gymnopédies*, we see Satie composing music which is repetitive and slow, even if it cannot literally live up to the tempo marking of the first prelude, 'En blanc et immobile' (In white and immobile). And whiteness and immobility are descriptions Satie often applies to music whose principal characteristic is repetition.

Vexations: to be repeated?

Satie's creative output in the 1890s focused on the two types of repertoire associated with the barrel organ: private religious or quasi-religious works (his Rose+Croix piano pieces and *Messe des pauvres*) and popular song, including music for the cabaret. In this period – precisely in April 1893 – Satie composed his notorious *Vexations* during his only documented romantic relationship, with Suzanne Valadon (see Fig. 4.1 for a painting of Satie and Valadon by Santiago Rusiñol, a staged image suggesting they are a typical bourgeois young couple). This most infamous of Satie's works was published well after his death, first in facsimile in *Contrepoints* (1949) and in more accessible form in 1969, as the second of three pieces edited by Robert Caby as *Pages mystiques*.

Vexations is best known for the composer's note at the head of the manuscript: 'Pour se jouer 840 fois de suite ce motif, il sera bon de se préparer au préalable, et dans le plus grand silence, par des immobilités sérieuses.' (To play oneself this motif 840 times in a row, it would be good to prepare oneself in advance, in the most profound silence, by serious immobilities.) The performance history of the piece has focused on this marathon duration, anything between eighteen and twenty-four hours depending on the tempo chosen.[2] But the literary scholar Christopher Dawson was the first to draw attention to the reflexive verb in Satie's note.

[2] Matthew Mendez's chapter is the most comprehensive overview of the performance history; see Mendez, 'History, Homeopathy and the Spiritual Impulse in the Post-war Reception of Satie: Cage, Higgins, Beuys', in

Fig. 4.1 Santiago Rusiñol (1861–1931), *Una romanza* (1893). Museu de Arte Moderno, Barcelona (Archives de la Fondation Erik Satie, Paris)

Satie does not write 'Pour jouer 840 fois de suite ce motif' (To play this motif 840 times in a row) but 'Pour se jouer': in other words, to play this motif *to oneself* 840 times in a row.[3]

Vexations is a work without bar lines which is notated in a peculiarly unfriendly manner, with myriad double sharps and flats which have no tonal logic. There is a conscious dissociation between the experiences of the performer reading the score and of the listener, a technique Satie used in later piano works including all three of his *Heures séculaires et instantanées*. About the only predictable feature of the score is that every other chord incorporates the interval of a tritone, a pattern employed by Satie in other Rose-Croix piano works. Its 'unappetising chorale' qualities – to borrow the title of the introduction to Satie's *Sports et divertissements* (1914) – cannot be linked to his studies at the Schola Cantorum from 1905 to 1909 as it predates them; perhaps *Vexations* and the other pieces in the *Pages mystiques* triptych hark back to his far less successful studies at the Paris Conservatoire, an establishment from which he was dismissed in 1886.

Caroline Potter (ed.), *Erik Satie: Music, Art and Literature*. Farnham: Ashgate, 2013, pp. 183–228.

[3] Christopher Dawson, 'Erik Satie's *Vexations* – an Exercise in Immobility.' *Canadian Music Review*, vol. 21 no. 2 (2001): pp. 29–40. I am very grateful to Dawson for sending me a copy of this article.

The stoic, prayer-like attitude required of the performer of *Vexations*, if indeed it was intended to be performed, only enhances its status as a grotesque hymn. Surely the ideal mechanism for playing it 840 times would have been the barrel organ or player piano, though the deliberately awkward notation and constant dissonances of *Vexations* are very distant from the popular and fashionable tunes which formed the barrel organ repertoire. Rather, it is a deformed chorale, a broken-down hymn tune. Some people who knew Satie well do not believe that *Vexations* was intended for performance: Henri Sauguet 'considered *Vexations* a joke and claimed that Satie himself did not take it seriously, while Darius Milhaud felt that the composer would not have approved of a literal interpretation of his score, that his essential *pudeur*, or modesty, would not have allowed it'.[4]

Instead of dwelling further on the performance or non-performance of *Vexations*, it is more fruitful to think about the meaning of repetition for Satie. I have already noted that Satie's fixation on a particular outfit was an aspect of obsessive repetition in his daily life: as an adult, he consciously chose an image to present to the world and wore this outfit every day without exception. He seemed to have a desire to control his life, his feelings, through repetition. Contemporary psychologists have used Satie as a case study, and both Catherine Fung and Ioan James conclude he may have had Asperger's syndrome. Fung writes that individuals with this condition 'tend to be absorbed with a particular interest, which is enthusiastically pursued. Their "special interests" are self-selected leisure activities that are narrow in nature, and are pursued without regard to social implications. They often involve repetition, such as routines and collecting, or the more elaborate production of stereotyped drawings.'[5] Satie's creative activity could not be better described: repetition, whether literal or varied, is central to his musical style and he is the first composer to employ extended repetitive structures. He often incorporates 'found objects' such as musical or textual quotations in his music, and one of his non-musical interests was drawing: after his death, Darius Milhaud discovered hundreds of index cards on which Satie had created an ink drawing or calligraphy. Fung also notes Satie's 'perfectionism and [...] desire for order and structure', traits which can be related to his painstaking calligraphy as well as his musical style, and she considers his

---

[4] Cited in Alan Gillmor, *Erik Satie*. Boston: Twayne, 1988, p. 273 note 49.

[5] Catherine H. M. Fung, 'Asperger's and Musical Creativity: The Case of Erik Satie.' *Personality and Individual Differences*, vol. 46 no. 8 (2009): pp. 775–83, at p. 776. See also Ioan Mackenzie James, *Asperger's Syndrome and High Achievement: Some Very Remarkable People*. London: Jessica Kingsley, 2006 (James' case study of Satie is on pp. 89–96) and the psychiatrist Michael Fitzgerald's book *The Genesis of Artistic Creativity: Asperger's Syndrome and the Arts*. London: Jessica Kingsley, 2005.

'music reflects the ideal of renunciation, in that he strived to create austere simplicity, bareness, and sparseness'.[6]

The expression 'immobilités sérieuses' in Satie's preface to *Vexations* is odd, especially in a plural form. While with Satie one can never rule out the possibility that the expression is simply a provocation or a joke, one can also wonder whether the plural form is connected to the extreme multiple in the performance direction. Immobility is a state which is frequently encountered in Satie's writings and performance directions. In his article on Satie's 'La Journée du musicien', Christopher Dawson notes that Satie says 'immobility' is one of his 'occupations diverses'. Immobility is surely synonymous with meditation, but Satie first pokes fun at musical biographers by drawing up a precise timetable for his activities which reads like a parody of a diary of a creative genius:

> The artist must regulate his life.
>
> Here is the precise timetable of my daily routine:
>
> I wake at 7.18; inspiration: 10.23 to 11.45. I have lunch at 12.11 and leave the table at 12.14.[7]

Dawson believes that

> the absurd timetable points towards a more fundamental aspect of Satie's musical aesthetic, the nature of temporality in modern music and the effect of this on thematic development. [...] Given the expressive nature of much of the eccentric imagery in his writings, it is arguable that the conflicts underlying the absurd temporality in 'La Journée du musicien' are reflective of the temporal conflicts within his compositional style. [...] In the light of this, the idea of immobility being one of his 'occupations diverses' could be said by itself to take on a figurative charge; for in endeavouring to break away from normal conceptions of temporality in his music, he effectively wrote music that went nowhere, that is to say, was 'immobile.'[8]

Satie's move away from conventional musical notions of duration can be contrasted with Morton Feldman's later works, in which the composer said he was investigating scale. In conversation with John Rockwell in 1985, Feldman said, 'Form is easy – just the division of things into parts.

---

[6] Fung, 'Asperger's and Musical Creativity', p. 777.

[7] Originally published in *La Revue musicale S.I.M.*, 15 January 1913, p. 71 and reproduced in Ornella Volta (ed.), *Erik Satie: Ecrits*. Paris: Editions Champ Libre, 1979, pp. 22–3: 'L'artiste doit régler sa vie. ¶ Voici l'horaire précis de mes actes journaliers: ¶ Mon lever: à 7h18; inspiré: de 10h23 à 11h47. Je déjeune à 12h11 et quitte la table à 12h14.'

[8] Christopher Dawson, 'Menus propos modernistes: Absurdity in Erik Satie's "La Journée du Musicien".' *Nottingham French Studies*, vol. 44 no. 2 (2005), pp. 55–62, at p. 57.

But scale is another matter. You have to have control of the piece – it requires a heightened kind of concentration. Before, my pieces were like objects; now, they're like evolving things.'[9]

For Satie, musical works could be objects, as if they were frozen in time. And his use of extreme repetition, whether a work is to be performed publicly or privately, could well have been a ritualistic action to rid the music of whatever expressive content it may have had: the more music is repeated, the less we notice its salient details and the more it fades into the background. Manufacturers of muzak are well aware of this, as muzak takes popular songs and flattens them, removing lyrics, dynamic contrast, the original instrumentation and tempo contrast, stringing songs together to create an environment conducive to shopping.[10] As Daniel Albright puts it, 'For Satie, music was not expression, but a barrier against expression.'[11] A classic example of this type of flattening in Satie is his deformed quotation of Chopin's Funeral March trio theme in the second of his *Embryons desséchés* (1913), 'de Podophthalma'. Here, Chopin's tune is recognisable, though its dynamics and phrasing have been simplified, lessening the emotional charge of the original.

Satie employs the term 'immobility' in other textual contexts, for instance in his commentary to the piano piece 'Danse cuirassée' (Armourplated dance), the second of the *Vieux sequins et vieilles cuirasses*: 'Se danse sur deux rangs. Le premier rang ne bouge pas. Le second rang reste immobile. Les danseurs reçoivent chacun un coup de sabre qui leur fend la tête.' (Is danced in two rows. The first row does not move. The second row remains immobile. The dancers each receive a sabre blow which cleaves their head.) Immobility is a most unusual occupation for dancers, and Satie's text shows it can be a perilous one – unless the dancers are, perhaps, made of wood, like table football players stuck to a bar. One of the many paradoxes of repetitive works such as *Vexations* is that the overriding characteristic of the work is stasis – just as the last piece of the first book of Debussy's *Images* for piano (1905) is entitled 'Mouvement', though musically it is essentially static (an image, indeed), surface animation over long pedal points. Debussy's 'Mouvement' is like a mechanism which has been wound up and allowed to run for a set duration. With the text of 'Danse cuirassée', again we have a paradox: not, this time, music which aims to be static, but another art form which takes

---

[9] http://www.cnvill.net/mfrockwl.htm (accessed 7 April 2015).

[10] See Joseph Lanza, *Elevator Music: A Surreal History of Muzak, Easy-Listening, and Other Moodsong* (revised edition). Ann Arbor: University of Michigan Press, 2004, and Hervé Vanel, *Triple Entendre: Furniture Music, Muzak, Muzak-Plus*. Urbana, Chicago and Springfield: University of Illinois Press, 2013.

[11] Daniel Albright. *Untwisting the Serpent*. Chicago: University of Chicago Press, 2000, p. 191.

place in time (dance) which is frozen in time because the dancers are model replicas.

Dawson makes an interesting parallel between Satie's twin textual and musical obsessions with *blancheur* (whiteness) and silence: 'The similarity with musical *blancheur* and *silence* is clear, constituting for painting and music respectively the canvas upon which artistic elements are presented. But silence is also linked to his more fundamental aesthetic objective, to undermine established notions of thematic development and produce a "static sound-object".'[12] Surely the sculptures of Satie's friend Constantin Brancusi, which are often white and smooth-textured and inevitably immobile, are another pertinent artistic comparison. This stasis, whiteness and (figurative) silence culminated in Satie's furniture music (*musique d'ameublement*): music which is designed not to be the focus of attention.

Musique d'ameublement

Music as mechanism, music as a backdrop to other activity reaches an apogee in Satie's furniture music. The origins of Satie's furniture music are usually ascribed to an experience Satie had during a lunch with the painter Fernand Léger (1881–1955) and some other friends:

> Obliged to put up with unbearable vulgar music, we left the room and Satie said to us: 'Furniture music is something that should be created – that is, music which would be part of the ambience, which would take account of it. I imagine it being melodic in nature: it would soften the noise of knives and forks without dominating them, without imposing itself. It would furnish those silences which sometimes hang heavy between diners. It would save them from everyday banalities. At the same time, it would neutralise those street sounds which impinge on us indiscreetly.' It would, he said, respond to a need.[13]

---

[12] Dawson, 'Menus propos modernistes', p. 59; Dawson here is citing Robert Orledge, *Satie the Composer*. Cambridge: Cambridge University Press, 1990, p. 142.

[13] Fernand Léger, 'Satie inconnu'. *Erik Satie: son temps et ses amis*, special number of *La Revue musicale* (June 1952), p. 137: 'Obligés de subir une musique tapageuse, insupportable, nous quittons la salle et Satie nous dit: « Il y a tout de même à réaliser une musique d'ameublement, c'est-à-dire une musique qui ferait partie des bruits ambiants, qui en tiendrait compte. Je la suppose mélodieuse, elle adoucirait le bruit des couteaux, des fourchettes sans les dominer, sans s'imposer. Elle meublerait les silences pesant parfois entre les convives. Elle leur épargnerait les banalités courantes. Elle neutraliserait, en même temps, les bruits de la rue qui entrent dans le jeu sans discrétion. » Ce serait, disait-il, répondre à un besoin.'

This conversation was published in the *Revue musicale* 1952 tribute to Satie edited by Rollo Myers; Léger knew Satie slightly in the last years of the composer's life, and it is unwise to assume that the painter was recalling Satie's exact words more than thirty years after their lunch.

Léger's recollection can be compared with an undated note from Satie to Jean Cocteau which is reproduced in Ornella Volta's edition of Satie's writings. As Satie's first experiments in *musique d'ameublement* were made in 1917, also the year of *Parade*, his collaboration with Cocteau, Picasso and Massine, it is reasonable to assume that his note to Cocteau was written around this date. It begins:

> 'Furniture Music' is something which is manufactured. What usually happens is that people make music on occasions when music has *no purpose*. People play waltzes, 'fantasies' based on operas, & similar things, written for another reason.
>
> We, however, want to establish a musical genre made to satisfy 'needs.' Art doesn't come into it. 'Furniture Music' creates vibrations; it has no other aims; it fulfils the same role as light, heat and *comfort* in all its forms.[14]

Again, Satie is poking fun at pretension and posturing in music. This note resembles Satie's fake advertisements for musical services, the 'we' suggesting that a company is behind this idea. As a former café pianist, Satie had first-hand experience performing popular tunes of the day as background to everyday activity: perhaps his café repertoire included arrangements of 'waltzes, "fantasies" based on opera, & similar things'. The idea was clearly an obsession of Satie's at this time and it resurfaces in unexpected contexts. For instance, another reference to furniture music appears on Satie's hand copy of Victor Cousin's translation of Plato, made in 1917:

Le banquet. – Musique d'ameublement.	Encadrement (danse).
– Pour une salle.	Tapisserie (le Banquet, sujet).
	Encadrement (danse, reprise).
Phèdre. – Musique d'ameublement.	Colonnade (danse).
– Pour un vestibule.	Bas-relief (marbre, sujet).
	Colonnade (danse, reprise).

---

[14] Volta (ed.), *Satie Ecrits*, p. 190: 'La «Musique d'Ameublement» est foncièrement industrielle. L'habitude – l'usage – est de faire de la musique dans des occasions où la musique n'a rien à faire. Là, on joue des «Valses», des «Fantaisies» d'Opéras, & autres choses semblables, écrites pour un autre objet. ¶ Nous, nous voulons établir une musique faite pour satisfaire les besoins «utiles». L'Art n'entre pas dans ces besoins. La «Musique d'Ameublement» crée de la vibration; elle n'a pas d'autre but; elle remplit le même rôle que la lumière, la chaleur & *le confort* dans toutes ses formes.'

Phédon. Musique d'ameublement. – Pour une vitrine.	Ecrin (duvet de porc, danse). Camée (Agate d'Asie-Phédon, sujet). Ecrin (danse, reprise).[15]
The Banquet. – Furniture music. – For a drawing room.	Frame (dance). Tapestry (the Banquet, subject). Frame (dance, repeat).
Phaedrus. – Furniture music. – For an entrance hall.	Colonnade (dance). Bas-relief (marble, subject). Colonnade (dance, repeat).
Phaedo. – Furniture music. – For a glass display case.	Casket (hog's hair, dance). Cameo (agate of Asia – Phaedo, subject). Casket (dance, repeat).

This description features the odd combination of Plato (including various characters who appear in Satie's *Socrate*), furniture music composed for particular spaces, and the tripartite division omnipresent in Satie's work. The three sections are themselves divided into ABA sections combining dances of various sorts with a central solo turn or 'sujet'. All three dances sound more like poses than anything involving movement (more 'serious immobility') and the Phaedo dance sounds like it was created for a wind-up ballerina in a music box. Marble and so-called Greek agate are also typically pale (Greek agate ranges in colour from white to pale tan); the finest ancient cameos are carved from a single agate block, often a carved relief portrait against a background, revealing the contrasting colours of the naturally striped rock. There had been links in Satie's mind between ancient Greek settings, static poses and musical repetition or near-repetition since his *Gymnopédies* and *Gnossiennes*, and here we see the concept of whiteness used figuratively to indicate a blank canvas or plain backdrop. Satie also uses the term 'tapisserie' in one of his furniture music titles in 1917, as if this music had essentially visual rather than sonic qualities.

Satie's music for *Socrate* is often described as 'white', the suggestion being that it was intended as a simple, unobtrusive background. Might *Socrate* originally have been conceived as furniture music, as an inherently multimedia project which incorporated Grecian dancers against various antique-themed backdrops in imagined spaces? Roger Shattuck notes that 'Alfred Cortot classified it [*Socrate*] as "furniture music"'[16] – making one wonder whether Cortot had insider information – and Shattuck himself draws attention to 'figures that are endlessly repeated and scarcely varied at all' in *Socrate*.[17] Perhaps the complexity of this plan, especially if Plato's

---

[15] Reproduced in Pierre-Daniel Templier, *Erik Satie*. Paris: Editions Rieder, 1932, p. 44; the document is housed in the Bibliothèque Nationale de France, MS 9623 (2), pp. 26–7.

[16] Roger Shattuck, *The Banquet Years*. London: Jonathan Cape, 1969, p. 160.

[17] Ibid.

Ex. 4.1 Satie, *Carrelage phonique*

text were part of the mix, prompted Satie to divide these ideas between *Socrate* and his 1917 furniture music.[18]

The two 1917 furniture pieces were written for specific imagined spaces: 'Carrelage phonique' (Sonic floor tiles) for flute, clarinet and strings 'peut se jouer à un lunch ou à un contrat de mariage. Mouvement: Ordinaire' (may be played at a lunch or when signing a marriage contract. Tempo: Ordinary; Ex. 4.1). The other, 'Tapisserie en fer forgé' (Wrought iron tapestry) for flute, clarinet, trumpet and strings, was composed 'pour l'arrivée des invités (grande réception). A jouer dans un vestibule. Mouvement: Très riche') (For the arrival of guests at a grand reception. To be played in an entrance hall. Tempo: Very rich; Ex. 4.2). The quite distinct social status of these occasions is reflected not so much in the musical content – both pieces are four bars long and repeated as often as required – but in the textual commentary. The 'mouvement' (conventionally translated as 'tempo') for this sonic 'wrought iron tapestry' is not a tempo at all, nor, I believe, does it denote the texture of the music. Rather, it surely refers to the fact that the people who would purchase this music for their homes are, indeed, very rich – unlike the designated users of his other furniture piece, who are 'ordinary' folk. The four-bar piece immediately sounds as though it is a two-bar consequent

---

[18] See Ornella Volta (ed.) *Erik Satie: Correspondance presque complète.* Paris: Fayard/IMEC, 2003, p. 1093. It is interesting to note that Satie was prepared to sanction performances of *Socrate* that were different from his original conception of a vocal work with chamber orchestra or piano. On 20 February 1919, the author André Gide acted as narrator for a performance at the home of the Godebski family, probably accompanied by Satie at the piano.

Ex. 4.2 Satie, *Tapisserie en fer forgé*

followed by a two-bar antecedent, though as the piece is to be repeated as often as wished, the consequent then succeeds the antecedent and the unusual structure is put out of the listener's mind. Like Satie's many movements titled Entr'acte, this is music written for a transitional space or a transitional moment. Marked with a single dynamic indication, this music has the same qualities as music played by a barrel organ: the more it is repeated, the less we notice it.

One of Satie's sketchbooks, which also features sketches for *Socrate* and for his talk 'Eloge des Critiques',[19] shows that he had other ideas for furniture music pieces for very specific spaces: *Carrelage pour cabinet noir de luxe* (Tiling for luxurious black office); *Tenture sonore*, 'ferait très bien dans un salon Louis XVI pendant une réception de parents de province (fin de soirée)' (Sonic wall hanging, 'would be very good in a Louis XVI salon when welcoming provincial relatives (end of an evening)'); *Trépied à deux pieds* 'soirée intime (trente personnes)' (Two-footed tripod, 'intimate evening (30 guests)'); *Papier phonique* 'pour chambre d'ivrogne très ordinaire, ameublement économique' (Sonic paper 'for a very ordinary drunk's room, cheap furniture').[20] The latter sounds as though it would have been suited to a space with which Satie was intimately familiar, though no music was composed under this title. It seems that Satie would not allow glimpses into his own lodgings in Arcueil, even in the form of furniture music. Other titles evoke the sumptuous lifestyle which Satie

[19] This talk was given on 5 February 1918.

[20] Now housed in the Bibliothèque Nationale de France, Département de la Musique, Ms 9623(2).

Ex. 4.3 Satie, *Carrelage pour cabinet noir de luxe*

suggests in his *Mémoires d'amnésique*: after being inspired and dining in specific timeframes, the composer claims he rides around his estate, or asks a servant to perform tasks for him. This sketchbook includes short scores of *Tapisserie en fer forgé* and *Carrelage phonique*, plus the unpublished short score of *Carrelage pour cabinet noir de luxe* (Ex. 4.3):

The title *Carrelage pour cabinet noir de luxe* has several potential meanings: a 'cabinet' could refer to an item of furniture, a box of curiosities or a lavatory cubicle as well as an office. Satie's friend Max Jacob, with whom he collaborated in *Ruffian toujours, truand jamais*, a play-plus-furniture-music interart extravaganza, published a collection of fictional letters entitled *Le cabinet noir* in 1922. The title refers to an administrative office charged with controlling mail after the monarchy was restored in 1815.[21] Both Satie and Jacob were prolific correspondents, and given the date of *Le cabinet noir* and their friendship and collaboration, it is likely that the title intrigued them both.

Satie conceived *Tapisserie en fer forgé* and *Carrelage phonique* partly as visual art. As Ornella Volta notes,

> He was soon going to make careful neat copies of these two scores on two large Bristol sheets, in order to exhibit them (just like his artist friends did with their paintings) and no doubt to put them

---

[21] I am very grateful to Gilles Christoph for this suggestion (email to the author, 22 November 2013). In his preface to *Le cabinet noir* in the edition of Jacob's *Œuvres complètes*, Antonio Rodriguez notes that Jacob used the expression in a poem he wrote in 1907: 'Ténèbres! une porte ouverte! les mares de sang ont la forme, la forme des nuages! les sept femmes de Barbe Bleue ne sont plus dans le cabinet noir!' (Paris: Quarto-Gallimard, 2012, p. 967). The first dedicatee of *Le cabinet noir* was the composer Roland-Manuel, a friend of both Satie and Jacob in this period.

up for sale at the Jove gallery, run by the painter and 'purist' theoretician Amédée Ozenfant, who had agreed to play these 'furniture entertainments' in a public demonstration. This event was planned for spring 1918. The bombing of Paris at this time meant that the Jove had moved, until the end of the war, to Bordeaux and that the launch of these 'furniture entertainments' was postponed until better times.[22]

While there is little evidence of Satie's business dealings with Ozenfant, the artist mentions Satie several times in his memoirs,[23] and the composer wrote enigmatically in *Cahiers d'un mammifère*:

> Crafty and inventive devils: Yes, Ozenfant is the more wicked of the two – though not too much;... but don't think that the 'Other One' is stupid – with his poor eyesight.
>
> In any event, ... they are each as 'purist' as the other – more, even.[24]

Furniture music in Montparnasse

Satie's first works in this new genre of furniture music were composed at an unusually exciting time for the arts in Paris: young composers were organising themselves in groups, sometimes aided and abetted by Cocteau, and in the absence of conventional concert performance opportunities during the war, their work was featured in new venues

---

[22] Ornella Volta, preface to 'Musiques d'ameublement', p. VI: 'Il allait bientôt mettre soigneusement au net ces deux partitions sur deux grandes feuilles de bristol afin de les exposer (comme ses amis artistes le faisaient avec leurs tableaux), et sans doute les proposer à la vente, dans la maison de couture et de décoration Jove, dont l'éminence grise était le peintre et théoricien «puriste», Amédée Ozenfant, qui avait accepté de faire exécuter ces «divertissements mobiliers» dans une séance publique de démonstration. ¶ Cette séance avait été prévue pour le printemps 1918. Les bombardements de Paris à cette date conseillèrent cependant la Maison Jove de se transporter, jusqu'à la fin de la guerre, à Bordeaux et de remettre donc le lancement des «divertissements mobiliers» à des temps meilleurs.'

[23] See Amédée Ozenfant, *Mémoires, 1886–1962*. Paris: Seghers, 1968.

[24] Reprinted in Volta (ed.), *Satie Ecrits*, p. 29; 'Roublards et inventifs: Oui, c'est Ozenfant le plus malin des deux – sans l'être trop; ... mais ne croyez pas que «l'Autre» soit bête – avec sa vue basse. ¶ En tous cas, ... ils sont aussi «puristes» l'Un que l'Autre – plus même.' The 'other purist' is certainly Ozenfant's collaborator Charles Edouard Jeanneret, known as Le Corbusier: earlier in *Cahiers d'un mammifère*, Satie writes 'Chez les "deux Puristes"... La prochaine fois, ce sera un tableau de Jeanneret qu'on lacérara ... Chacun son tour ... hein! ...' (At the 'two Purists' ... Next time, it'll be a painting by Jeanneret that's nicked ... Everyone takes his turn, eh?')

which were not previously associated with musical performance. One of these venues was an artists' studio at 6 rue Huyghens; the owner of this studio, Emile Lejeune, published his memoirs of Montparnasse in a series of articles in the *Tribune de Genève* in 1964. He tells an intriguing story about Satie:

> Poets also collaborated in these events [at 6 rue Huyghens]. For our catalogue, Jean Cocteau and Blaise Cendrars each wrote a poem dedicated to Satie. The latter, swearing me to secrecy, warned me that during the exhibition opening he would sit at the piano and discreetly improvise. He said 'It will be furniture music. I want the visitors to circulate: I'm counting on you and our friends, to whom I have also spoken, to set the tone.'[25]

Lejeune is probably referring here to the 'Instant musical' by Satie played at the vernissage (preview) on 17 November 1916 of the first exhibition organised at 6 rue Huyghens. This story – which, if true, would signal the birth of furniture music in an artistic context – is not corroborated in any other source and it is, of course, possible that Lejeune was confusing this with a performance on another date, but the story does underline the connection between 'art' furniture music and Satie's experience as a café pianist. The two poems were read as part of the performance: Cocteau's poem mentioned by Lejeune, 'Hommage à Erik Satie', echoes Satie's writings about being a 'phonometer', one who measures sounds,[26] while Cendrars' 'Le Musickissme' is a stream of consciousness which conjures up Satie's sound world.

The idea of combining music, words and art seems to have originated with Blaise Cendrars, who called on Satie to help with this multimedia project,[27] presumably by suggesting suitable composers and performers. Cendrars, the actor Pierre Bertin and the cellist and

---

[25] Emile Lejeune, 'Montparnasse à l'époque héroïque, 7: 1re exposition (du 19 Novembre au 5 Décembre 1916, Kisling, Matisse, Modigliani, Ortiz de Zarate, Picasso)', *Tribune de Genève* no. 33/6, 8–9 février 1964, p. 1: 'Les poètes aussi avaient collaboré. Pour notre catalogue, Jean Cocteau et Blaise Cendrars composèrent chacun un poème, dédiés l'un et l'autre à Erik Satie. Ce dernier, me mettant dans le secret des dieux, m'avait avisé qu'au cours du vernissage, discrètement, il s'installerait au piano et improviserait. « Ce sera, me disait-il, de la *Musique d'ameublement*. Aussi, je voudrais que les visiteurs continuent de circuler. Je compte sur vous et les copains, que j'ai du reste avertis, pour donner le ton. »'

[26] In an article 'Ce que je suis' ('What I am') in 'Mémoires d'un amnésique.' *Revue musicale S.I.M.*, 4 (1912), p. 69.

[27] Arthur Honegger, *Lettres à ses parents, 1914–1922*. Geneva: Editions Papillon, 2005 (preface, annotations by Harry Halbreich), p. 130 note 10. Cendrars also proposed that Editions de la Sirène, for which he was literary advisor, publish music scores as well as literary works.

impresario Félix Delgrange bankrolled the rue Huyghens concerts.[28] The rue Huyghens venue was significant for Satie, as 'Cocteau heard Satie's music for the first time at the soirée Satie-Ravel on 18 April 1916 at the Salle Huyghens.'[29] Artists including Braque and Picasso exhibited at the rue Huyghens studio, their works being co-presented with music, and the Picasso, Satie and Cocteau partnership moved to a larger stage in 1917 when their Ballets Russes collaboration *Parade* was premiered.

Satie's music became the rallying point for a loose association of young composers who were performed at 6 rue Huyghens and at the nearby Théâtre du Vieux-Colombier. Early in 1918, Satie introduced a Vieux-Colombier concert featuring music by Milhaud, Honegger, Tailleferre and Durey, as well as Satie himself. The four young composers were initially known as the 'Nouveaux Jeunes': as Satie put it, 'The first four are young – very young ... As for me, I am only young in spirit.'[30] Indeed, Satie and his near-contemporary Charles Koechlin were happy to ally themselves with their junior colleagues. The director of the Théâtre du Vieux-Colombier, Jacques Copeau, had left Paris for the United States in January 1917, and in his absence Jane Bathori and Pierre Bertin organised entertainment at the venue.[31] Satie, in his pre-concert talk, appreciated Bathori's efforts: 'By using the théâtre du Vieux-Colombier, Jane Bathori wanted to appeal to a public who wanted to hear both modern and classic works which other concert organisations did not feature in their programmes – either out of habit, or because of their conservative attitudes.'[32]

Cocteau was planning a 'séance de music-hall' featuring furniture music in the Théâtre du Vieux-Colombier in 1918, surely prompted by Satie's note quoted above and by the composition of *Carrelage phonique* and *Tapisserie en fer forgé*. Cocteau wrote to his mother: 'I decided, together with Mme Bathori and our friends (they asked me) to direct one or several spectacles focusing on young musicians. The first spectacle will be a

---

[28] Ibid., p. 151 note 12.

[29] Christine Reynolds, 'Parade, ballet réaliste', in Caroline Potter (ed.), *Erik Satie: Music, Art and Literature*. Farnham: Ashgate, 2013, p. 141.

[30] Reprinted in Volta (ed.), *Satie Ecrits*, p. 80; 'Les quatre premiers sont jeunes – tout jeunes ... Ma jeunesse à moi est dans le caractère.'

[31] In *Cahiers Jean Cocteau*, nouvelle série, 2 ('Cocteau, le cirque et le music-hall'), 2003, pp. 9–132, at p. 28: 'En effet, en l'absence de Jacques Copeau, parti pour les Etats-Unis en janvier 1917, la chanteuse Jeanne [sic] Bathori et l'acteur Pierre Bertin, gardiens des lieux, organisent diverses manifestations, spectacles et conférences.'

[32] Volta (ed.), *Satie Ecrits*, p. 80; 'En reprenant le théâtre du Vieux-Colombier, Jane Bathori a voulu satisfaire le goût d'un public désireux d'entendre des œuvres modernes et classiques que les autres concerts n'inscrivaient pas sur leurs programmes – soit par prudence, soit par habitude.'

music hall event for which I will choose the numbers, each accompanied by music and preceded by an introduction. During the interval a small orchestra will play in the foyer the famous "furniture music" by our Satie and the gang.'[33] He drew up a projected programme for this event: music by Les Six with 'Entracte, Musique d'ameublement' after the first half, and 'À bientôt (Retraite)' by Satie at the end. It is interesting to see Cocteau linking popular entertainment with furniture music, and interesting that Satie's furniture music was so notorious so soon after its composition that Cocteau's mother must have known about it. This enticing plan did not come to fruition: Malou Haine writes 'For reasons which are unclear – perhaps because he did not receive hoped-for financial support from the Princesse de Polignac – this music hall show did not take place, but soon Cocteau would reuse some of its ideas.'[34]

The member of the Nouveaux Jeunes who was, according to Cocteau, to write 'musique d'ameublement' for this spectacle in addition to Satie was Arthur Honegger. Though Honegger is not generally associated with the more experimental, farcical side of Les Six and not known for his admiration for Satie, this work is clearly an exception. It also shows an interest in musical mechanisms which he demonstrated at greater length in orchestral works including his 'mouvement symphonique' *Pacific 231* (1923). Honegger's *Trois Couleurs* was scheduled for the first half of the concert, to be sung by Pierre Bertin.[35] Cocteau claimed on 14 April 1919 in *Paris-Midi*, for which he then wrote a regular column,[36] that 'Honegger's little pieces were written as furniture music, as invented by Satie; he wanted the audience to talk and walk during the

---

[33] Cited in Malou Haine, 'Jean Cocteau, impresario musical à la croisée des arts', in Sylvain Caron, François de Médicis and Michel Duchesneau (eds), *Musique et modernité en France*. Montréal: Presses Universitaires de Montréal, 2006, pp. 69–134, at p. 80; 'J'ai décidé avec Mme Bathori et nos camarades (ils me l'ont demandé) de prendre la direction d'un ou des spectacles consacrés aux jeunes. Le premier spectacle sera une séance de music-hall dont je choisis les numéros, chacun accompagné de musique et précédé d'une introduction. Pendant l'entr'acte un petit orchestre jouera dans le vestibule les fameuses « musiques d'ameublement » de notre Satie et de la troupe.'

[34] Ibid., p. 82; 'Pour une raison non élucidée, sans doute parce qu'il ne reçoit pas le soutien financier escompté auprès de la princesse de Polignac, ce spectacle de music-hall n'aboutira pas, mais Cocteau réutilisera bientôt certains de ses éléments.'

[35] No work with this title exists in the catalogue compiled by Harry Halbreich. See his *Arthur Honegger: Un musicien dans la cité des hommes*. Paris: Fayard, 1992. Translated by Roger Nichols, Portland, OR: Amadeus Press, 1999.

[36] Cocteau's columns from 31 March to 11 August 1919 were published by La Sirène under the title *Carte blanche* in 1920.

performance'.[37] However, this review certainly refers to a concert given at Salle Huyghens on 5 April that year. In a letter to his parents written on 29 March 1919, Honegger wrote: 'On Saturday my little furniture pieces are being played at a "Painting and music" performance with string quartet, flute, clarinet and piano. I can't attend because I'm going to Paillard's for dinner with Gide and Méral.'[38]

In fact, Honegger's three unpublished pieces (a Satiean number, of course) of furniture music are not a vocal work entitled *Trois Couleurs* written for Pierre Bertin, but pieces for chamber ensemble which were composed in March 1919. The first is marked 'Vif' (Halbreich says 'Entrée') and composed for flute, clarinet in B♭, trumpet in C and piano; the next piece on the manuscript is marked as number 3 and is 'Modéré' ('Berceuse'), scored for flute, trumpet in C, violin, cello and piano; 'number 2' is 'Lent' ('Nocturne'), for flute, clarinet, string quartet and piano.[39] The Satie influence can already be seen in the non-sequential numbering 1, 3, 2 of these pieces, which mirrors Satie's original intentions for his *Trois poèmes d'amour* (1914). They are tiny works, the first being six bars long (though only bars 3–6 are marked with repeats), the third nine bars (with bars 2–9 to be repeated) and the third four bars long, to be repeated in its entirety. There is nothing on the manuscript to suggest that the pieces can be played as often as wished, though this is perhaps to be assumed given their 'furniture music' billing. According to a programme for a concert at 6 rue Huyghens, they were eventually premiered in that venue on 5 April 1919 under the title 'Entrée, Nocturne et Berceuse'.[40]

Piece number 3 is a collage of different cradle songs: a children's song 'Fais dodo, Colas mon p'tit frère' played by the flute, one by Benjamin Godard played by muted trumpet,[41] the principal theme of Fauré's 'Berceuse' played by the violin and cello and a Chopin 'Berceuse' extract on

---

[37] Cited in Haine, 'Jean Cocteau, impresario musical à la croisée des arts', p. 85; 'les petites pièces d'Honegger furent écrites pour la musique d'ameublement, inventée par Satie, et sur laquelle il voulait qu'on causât et promenât'.

[38] Honegger, *Lettres à ses parents*, pp. 193–4: 'Samedi on donne mes petites pièces d'ameublement à « Peinture et musique » avec quatuor, flûte, clarinette et piano. Je ne pourrais pas les écouter car je suis invité ce soir-là à dîner chez Paillard avec Gide et Méral.'

[39] The manuscript is now housed in the Paul Sacher Stiftung, Basel, Switzerland. I am very grateful to Johanna Blask, Robert Piencikowski and Michèle Noirjean for their assistance with my research on these pieces.

[40] A copy of this programme is housed in IMEC, SAT 25.25.

[41] As identified by Harry Halbreich; Haine, 'Jean Cocteau, impresario musical à la croisée des arts', p. 85.

the piano.[42] Honegger notes the authors of the Fauré, Godard and Chopin quotations on the manuscript. The instrumentation and use of extracts of popular and well-known classical repertoire are strikingly reminiscent of Satie's furniture music, as 'Carrelage phonique' and 'Tapisserie en fer forgé' are both composed for flute, clarinet, string quartet (and a trumpet is added for 'Tapisserie en fer forgé'), and Satie's 1920 *musique d'ameublement* pieces feature a piano duet as part of the ensemble and multiple citations.

1920 furniture music: Satie and Max Jacob

Three years after his first experiments in this genre, Satie composed a second *musique d'ameublement* set, this time to be played as entr'actes to a play by Max Jacob, *Ruffian toujours, truand jamais*. This play is unpublished and was thought lost, but the manuscript has resurfaced and is now housed in the Bibliothèque Nationale de France.[43] Jacob took some time to settle on a title for this play: the two manuscript copies show that he toyed with *L'enfant de la maison*, *La baronne* and *La tortue sentimentale et le buisson ardent* before deciding on *Ruffian toujours, truand jamais* (which can be roughly translated as 'Always a ruffian, never a crook') – a line spoken in the final scene of the play.

Max Jacob (1876–1944)[44] was, like Cocteau, an exceptionally multi-talented artist; he was active as a poet, novelist, critic, playwright, artist and astrologer. Unlike Cocteau, who was from a comfortably off Parisian family, he was from a modest Jewish background and brought up in Brittany. After experiencing an intense vision of Christ in 1909, Jacob became a practising Catholic and spent much of his later life in a monastery, though sadly this did not prevent him being transported to Drancy concentration camp where he died in 1944. It is not known precisely when Jacob met Satie, though as they had many artistic acquaintances in common it would have been surprising if their paths had not crossed frequently before their collaboration. Both were involved in 'Lyre et Palette' poetry and music wartime events at 6 rue Huyghens

---

[42] Ibid. The Honegger pieces were recorded on the compilation CD made for the Centre Pompidou, Paris, *DADA et la musique* (Muza MU/EN 2005-DD, 2006).

[43] It is part of the Max Jacob collection in the Département des Manuscrits and was formerly owned by Didier Gompel-Netter, editor of several volumes of Jacob's letters and of his *Œuvres complètes*. I am very grateful to the staff of the Département des Manuscrits, particularly Anne Mary, curator of the Fonds Max Jacob, for their assistance.

[44] He is not the same person as the composer Maxime Jacob (1906–77), a member of the group Ecole d'Arcueil. Like Max Jacob, he was born Jewish and converted to Catholicism, becoming a Benedictine monk: he was known from 1929 as Dom Clément Jacob.

organised by Blaise Cendrars. One of these events took place on 26 September 1916 and included readings of poems by Apollinaire, Cendrars, Cocteau, Jacob, Pierre Reverdy and André Salmon, and on 3 December, Paul Dermée gave a talk on Jacob's work in a *matinée littéraire* at the same venue.[45]

Many critics have remarked that Jacob and Satie broadly shared an artistic vision, combining satire with a pared-back, stripped-down aesthetic, though Jacob was less enthusiastic about the farcical side of Satie which was highlighted in his final ballets *Mercure* and *Relâche*. More specifically, the poet and composer both wrote while walking around Paris. Rosanna Warren notes that 'Jacob had initiated his walking discipline: in rambles throughout the city, he forced himself, in each interval between lamp posts, to come up with a new image or poetic idea or "relationship to a subject, whether a person, an object, a poster, a billboard, a postcard." If no idea appeared, he halted at the lamp post until something occurred to him and he jotted it down (sometimes on telegraph blanks filched from a post office).'[46] And according to the poet Louise Faure-Favier, 'Apollinaire liked Satie's fantasy – in his life as much as in his work. He liked to tell how Satie composed his music at night, walking from Montparnasse to Arcueil, where he lived, stopping at each street light to write it down.'[47] Max Jacob had sent poems to Satie in 1919,[48] and in the same year he was part of the select audience at a private premiere of Satie's *Socrate*.

Both Satie and Jacob were involved in performances at Paul Poiret's couture house on rue du Faubourg Saint-Honoré as part of 'a blockbuster series devoted to "Painting, Poetry, Music" known as the Salon d'Antin. Sponsored by the review *SIC* (Sons, Idées, Couleurs), the program for the salon included an exhibition of avant-garde art, two literary matinees, and two musical matinees.'[49] Jacob's close friendship with Poiret involved

---

[45] Billy Klüver, *A Day with Picasso*. Cambridge, MA: MIT Press, 1999, pp. 80–1.

[46] Rosanna Warren, *"Live Like a Poet!": At Home in the Bateau Lavoir*, http://littlestarjournal.com/wp-content/uploads/blog4.pdf (accessed 16 January 2015), p. 6; Warren is citing Robert Guiette, *La vie de Max Jacob*. Paris: Nizet, 1976, p. 77.

[47] Ornella Volta. *Satie et la danse*. Paris: Plume, 1992, p. 108, citing Faure-Favier, 'Apollinaire et la musique.' *Rimes et Raisons*, special Apollinaire number, Editions de la Tête Noire, 1948; 'Apollinaire aimait la fantaisie d'Erik Satie. Fantaisie dans sa vie autant que dans ses œuvres. Il se plaisait à conter comment Erik Satie composait sa musique, la nuit, en marchant de Montparnasse à Arcueil, où il habitait, et s'arrêtant à chaque réverbère pour la noter.'

[48] Orledge, *Satie the Composer*, p. 361 note 38.

[49] Mary E. Davis, *Classic Chic: Music, Fashion, and Modernism*. Berkeley: University of California Press, 2006, p. 115.

the multi-talented artist adopting his astrologer persona, as the couturier perhaps surprisingly 'consulted [Jacob] on the most auspicious colours of socks and ties to wear'.[50]

Ruffian toujours, truand jamais

This most unusual fusion of theatre and music was performed in an unconventional venue: an art gallery. Billy Klüver, in his fascinating short book about a set of photos taken by Cocteau in 1916, gives a detailed description of this space, which was part of various adjoining buildings in the 8th arrondissement of Paris owned by Paul Poiret including 107–9 rue du Faubourg Saint-Honoré and a mansion at 26 avenue d'Antin.[51] Klüver clarifies that

> No. 109 rue du Faubourg Saint-Honoré was a separate lot on the other side of the mansion. Around 1911 Poiret leased the space on the ground floor facing the street to Galerie Barbazanges. The gallery consisted of a front room behind which were several smaller rooms that led to a large 70-square-meter room 5½ meters high with no windows and a glass skylight roof. All in all there were approximately 250 square meters. Barbazanges agreed that Poiret could organize exhibitions of his own choosing in the gallery from time to time. Poiret also broke through the wall and made a door leading from the mansion to one of the rooms of the gallery.[52]

Klüver also states that 'There was a mezzanine level above the front room of the gallery, which might also have been used'[53] – a fact which is specifically relevant to the Jacob/Satie collaboration.

Max Jacob's first play, a 'pièce bouffe' entitled *Trois nouveaux figurants au théâtre de Nantes*, was premiered at Galerie Barbazanges on 24 June 1919.[54] On the same day, Satie wrote to his friends, the actor Pierre Bertin

---

[50] Klüver, *A Day with Picasso*, p. 88 note 16; the author is citing Pierre Andreu, *Vie et mort de Max Jacob*. Paris: La Table Ronde, 1982, p. 75.

[51] Klüver, *A Day with Picasso*, p. 62.

[52] Ibid., pp. 63–4. Billy Klüver interviewed several previous residents of this building complex, including François Heim, the owner of Galerie Heim which was located at 109 rue du Faubourg Saint-Honoré until the building was destroyed in 1970.

[53] Ibid., p. 65.

[54] Annie Marcoux and Didier Gompel-Netter (eds), *Max Jacob: Les propos et les jours. Lettres 1904–1944*. Paris: Zodiaque, 1989, p. 63. Jacob was clearly under a lot of pressure with his various commitments at the time: he wrote about this work to his friend Mme Henri (Emma) Hertz on 26 May 1919: 'P.S. On me demande une petite pièce en 1 acte pour un concert et elle n'est ni achevée, ni répétée, ni recopiée. Et la peinture!!!'

and his wife, the pianist Marcelle Meyer, that 'I would have liked to have heard the play by good Jacob. You know that Max and I are, now, friends. Besides, his talent had nothing to do with our quarrel.'[55] This was not the first argument Satie had had with Jacob, as they fell out badly during the Poueigh affair when Satie accused the poet of taking his legal troubles lightly.[56]

The two manuscript copies of *Ruffian toujours, truand jamais* are accompanied by an anonymous typewritten note which explains that 'a first sketch includes numerous corrections by the author in black and red inks, and the second features handwritten notes by Pierre Bertin concerning the staging of the play'.[57] The author of the note also mentions that Jacob wrote to Cocteau in 1919, probably in December, that '[Pierre] Bertin is rehearsing my play ...'[58] *Ruffian toujours, truand jamais* has three acts, the first of which is by far the shortest. Its characters are: Le baron Gimalac (Edouard); La baronne (Blanche); their daughter Germaine; her piano teacher, whose voice only is heard; Lucien (the baroness' lover, described at his first appearance in scene ii as being of 'very feminine appearance, wearing make-up and light colours');[59] his friend Arthur; Raoul, a police inspector referred to throughout as 'l'apache-policier'; Ferdinand le bistro, a café owner whose mysterious past is revealed in the final scene, and Joseph, a domestic servant. A preview of the play, published in *Comœdia* on 5 March 1920, reveals that 'The "piano teacher's voice" will be provided by the invisible organ of an artist who has chosen a strange pseudonym: Phanérogame.'[60] This name refers to a flower with exterior reproductive organs, and is also the title of a

---

[55] Letter of 24 June 1919 to Marcelle Meyer in Volta (ed.), *Correspondance*, p. 372: 'J'aurais voulu entendre la pièce du bon Jacob. Vous savez que Max & moi sommes, maintenant, amis. Son talent n'avait rien à voir dans notre brouille, *du reste.*'

[56] See a letter Jacob wrote to Jacques Doucet on 10 August 1917, published in English translation in Ornella Volta (ed.), Michael Bullock (trans.), *Satie Seen through his Letters*. London: Marion Boyars, 1989, pp. 135–6.

[57] Anonymous author, collection Max Jacob, BNF Département des Manuscrits: 'un premier bouillon portant de très nombreuses corrections de l'auteur à l'encre noire et rouge, le second des notes manuscrites au crayon de Pierre Bertin relatives à la mise en scène de la pièce'.

[58] 'En décembre (?) 1919 Max Jacob avait annoncé la pièce à Jean Cocteau dans une lettre: « Bertin fait répéter ma pièce ... »'

[59] 'très féminin, fardé, couleurs claires'.

[60] José de Berys, 'Chez Orphée: La Musique d'Ameublement. Une idée de M. Erik Satie. « Comme la tapisserie! » « Inutile d'écouter! »' *Comœdia*, 5 March 1920, p. 2: 'La « voix d'un professeur de piano » empruntera l'invisible organe d'un artiste qui a choisi un pseudonyme étrange: *Phanérogame.*'

Max Jacob 'humorous and philosophical novel' which he published at his own expense in 1918.[61] While this might suggest that Jacob was the mystery voice, he was unable to attend the performance of his play. Could Satie, the author of *Embryons desséchés* devoted to obscure creatures including the sea cucumber, have instead provided the voice of the piano teacher? Notes on the manuscript may clarify the identity of this mysterious figure, as we will see.

Music plays an essential role in the play. It acts sometimes as background to the stage action, in other words without the characters apparently being aware of it, and at other times it is the driving force of the action or something which is the prime focus of the characters' attention. Two characters are identified with specific instruments: the baron plays the trombone, and his daughter Germaine is a pianist. In the first scene, Germaine is heard 'à la cantonade' playing the piano and the baroness draws attention to this background music: 'A mes amours ... Ah! Ah! Ah! [she laughs and sings the tune played by the piano]'.[62] Here and elsewhere, there is a play between diegetic and non-diegetic musical functions, the music being a backdrop to the action to which the characters sometimes pay attention. Germaine's function in the play is almost exclusively as a piano student, either practising 'à la cantonade' or as the audience's sole focus during a piano lesson.

The expression 'à la cantonade', which appears frequently in the stage directions, is key to the meaning of the stage/music relationship in the play. It can signify 'in the box seats' or 'to no-one in particular', and can also refer to a character onstage talking to another character who is offstage or vice versa. The notion of characters conversing beyond the stage boundary, whether or not they are being listened to by other characters, blurs the stage/audience dividing line, and the concept of music played 'to no-one in particular' unifies the stage action and Satie's furniture music. This work was written for a specific space – we will see that Satie indicates a particular spatial distribution for the performers of his entr'acte music – and, as Klüver noted, the gallery had a mezzanine level: we can assume that this upper space was used for the 'à la cantonade' elements of the play.

The role of the baron is more varied than that of Germaine, but in the first act he is also presented as a musician, in his case an amateur trombonist. The second scene of Act I opens with the baroness wanting to spend time with her lover and nagging her husband: 'Go and amuse yourself with your trombone, idiot!' When he does not immediately obey, she insists a couple of times 'Your trombone, old

---

[61] See *Max Jacob: Œuvres complètes*, p. 64: 'roman humoristique et philosophique'.

[62] '[elle rit et chante l'air que joue le piano]'

chap!'[63] Having introduced both instruments, Jacob combines them in scene iii: Germaine plays the piano and the baron the trombone, again 'à la cantonade', and each line in the conversation between the baroness and Lucien ends with what is described in the manuscript as a 'gémissement du trombone' (groaning). In this broad comedy with sinister undertones, Jacob has the perfect opportunity to use an instrument with evident comedic potential. It is not clear what the piano is playing, or indeed whether it matters what music is used, though in the manuscript at the head of Act III there is a reference in Pierre Bertin's hand to Schumann. The curtain at the end of Act I falls while Lucien and the baroness kiss, and there is nothing in any of the manuscript material of the play acting as a cue to Satie's entr'acte music. Satie's title of the first entr'acte, 'Chez un bistrot', anticipates the location of the second act of Jacob's play: the music prolongs the action of the play, bringing the stage set to the interval venue, blurring the boundaries between the stage and public space and thus creating a total artistic experience.

For the second act, the stage set represents a liquor seller's front room, and in the first scene we see Lucien talking to his friend Arthur. Lucien is in far more colloquial mode when talking to Arthur, reflecting his friend's tone of voice rather than the stilted formal language, including the imperfect subjunctive, he used with the baroness: it appears that Lucien will be whatever others want him to be. We move from an upper-class household to a seedy criminal world: Lucien and his friend Arthur talk about forging post office documents, though they are soon joined by Raoul the policeman, who arrests Lucien and Arthur at the start of scene iii. Lucien wonders whether this is a joke and starts talking to Raoul about a girl called Mariette to distract him. The second act ends, a cue for Satie's second entr'acte, 'Un salon', to set the scene for the return of the stage setting in the baron and baroness' house.

The first scene of Act III is dedicated entirely to a piano lesson given to Germaine – a mixture of the teacher counting out beats, correcting her (she keeps missing a B♭), and asking after her family:

> The teacher (à la cantonade): (*spoken*) 'B flat, Germaine! (*sung*) and and two and and one and and three and four and one and two and three and … (*spoken*) and your mother's well? (*sung*) and-a four and and one and two and-a one and two and-a three and-a four … (*spoken*) she's so nice, so calm (*sung*) and one and and two and three and four … [*spoken*] Has your little brother been to work this week? No! He's away (*sung*) and one and two and three … [*spoken*] You must count, Germaine, otherwise you'll never get there (*sung*) and-a two and-a three and four and … [*spoken*] Daddy plays the trombone

---

[63] 'Nigaud! … Amuse-toi avec ton trombone, va t'amuser, va'. […] 'Ton trombone, pépère!'

(*sung*) and one and two and three and four and one and two and three ... (*spoken*) it's unusual, a good solo trombonist' [...]⁶⁴

Against the teacher's last words in this scene, Bertin has clearly written on the manuscript, then crossed out, the name 'Le Flem' – which must be a reference to the composer Paul Le Flem (1881–1984), assistant to Albert Roussel at the Schola Cantorum who had taught Satie.⁶⁵

In scene ii, Raoul takes Lucien, accompanied by Arthur, to the baroness' house. In the following scene, the animated discussion between Lucien, Arthur and Raoul is interspersed with the piano teacher 'à la cantonade', and again in the manuscript the name 'Le Flem' is clearly visible in pencil, this time not crossed out. The baroness mentions her family connections, such as a government minister, in an attempt to intimidate Raoul into dropping the charges against Lucien. She shows him a dagger when this does not work, and finally she tries to bribe Raoul to let her lover go. At the height of this drama, to puncture the tension, the piano teacher's words again come to the fore: 'One and two and three and four ... B flat, Germaine! There! Rinforzando ...' Raoul accepts a cheque as a bribe; he is also offered jewellery by the baroness but tells her that her rings are worthless because their stones are made of glass. In the seventh scene, the baron joins in the action, first accusing Lucien of stealing an objet d'art from his collection, then arguing with the baroness. She threatens her husband with a hatpin, and he responds by pulling out a gun. Naturally, Raoul reads out charges, in official style, against the couple for making threats. In the final scene, only Ferdinand le bistro speaks, summing up the scene, stating his motto is 'Ruffian toujours! Truand jamais', and revealing he is a former theatre claque leader, chef and grand inquisitor. He asks the baron not to 'forget that he owes his

---

⁶⁴ 'Le professeur (à la cantonade): (*parlé*) Si bémol, Germaine! (*chanté*) et et deux et et un et et trois z et quatre et un et deux et trois et ... (*parlé*) et la maman est bien (*chanté*) et de quatre et et un et deux z et z trois z et quatre ... (*parlé*) elle est si douce si paisible (*chanté*) et un et et deux et trois et quatre ... Le petit frère a travaillé cette semaine? Non! Il est en voyage (*chanté*) et un et deux et trois ... Il faut compter, Germaine, sans quoi vous n'arriverez pas (*chanté*) et deux z et trois z et quatre et ... Le papa fait du trombone (*chanté*) et un et deux et trois et quatre et un et deux et trois ... (*parlé*) c'est rare les bons trombones soli.'

⁶⁵ There is also a connection with Jacob here, because Le Flem was also Breton and set some of Jacob's poetry at different stages of his long career, including *Morvenn le Gaëlique* (1963), a title which also referenced a Breton pen name Jacob occasionally used. Jacob listed his nationality as 'Breton' in the catalogue of the Salon d'Antin in July 1916, an exhibition held at one of Poiret's venues. The exhibition catalogue is reproduced in Klüver, *A Day with Picasso*, p. 3.

freedom to his humble servant' and requests money – but the baron's pockets are empty.[66]

Pierre Bertin sketched two introductions for the performance, one for Jacob's play and one for the entr'acte music. On Jacob, he wrote:

> Innovation in art rarely happens with specialists – today, Max Jacob the poet presents to you Max Jacob the playwright. 'Ruffian toujours truand jamais' is Max Jacob's second play. We think it will reveal to you, as to us, a new spirit in theatre. [...] [B]road humour provides salvation for the worry and bitterness which turns the characters you will see into thieving puppets. It's new theatre which gives an odd relief to many current trends.[67]

Pierre Bertin also found it necessary to introduce the concept of furniture music before the performance, thus playing a triple role as singer, actor and compere:

> Also for the first time, thanks to Erik Satie and Darius Milhaud and conducted by M. [Félix] Delgrange, we present to you furniture music during the intervals of the play. We specifically wish to ask you not to give it any attention and to act during the interval as if it did not exist. This music, specially written for Max Jacob's play, claims to be part of life in the same sense as a private conversation, a painting in the gallery, or the chair on which one is sitting. Try it for yourself. Messrs Erik Satie and Darius Milhaud are available to answer any questions and discuss commissions.[68]

---

[66] 'Je pense que Mr la baron dans sa généreuse mansuétude n'oublie pas qu'il doit la liberté à son humble serviteur. Un beau geste, baron! Allons! Votre bourse, baron, votre bourse!'

[67] Bertin, document now housed in IMEC, SAT 40.7; 'L'innovation en art surgit rarement des spécialistes de cet art – Max Jacob poète vous présente Max Jacob auteur dramatique. « Ruffian toujours, truand jamais » est la seconde pièce de Max Jacob. Nous pensons qu'elle vous révélera comme à nous un esprit nouveau au théâtre. [...] la cocasserie sauve ce que l'inquiétude et l'amertume font des fauches fantins que vous allez voir. Théâtre nouveau qui donne un relief étrange à bien des tendances actuelles.'

[68] IMEC, SAT 15.8: 'Nous vous présenterons aussi pour la 1ère fois, par les soins de MM. Erik Satie et Darius Milhaud et sous la direction de M. Delgrange, la musique d'ameublement, pendant les entr'actes de la pièce. Nous vous prions instamment de ne pas lui attacher d'importance et d'agir pendant l'entr'acte comme si elle n'existait pas. Cette musique, spécialement écrite pour la pièce de Max Jacob, prétend à contribuer à la vie au même titre qu'une conversation particulière, qu'un tableau de la galerie, ou que le siège sur lequel on est assis. Vous en ferez l'essai. ¶ MM. Erik Satie et Darius Milhaud se tiennent à votre disposition pour tous renseignements et commandes.'

Satie gave his entr'acte music the overall title *Sons industriels*, a collective title he also used for his 1917 furniture music. The entr'acte music was written at the last minute, as a letter Satie addressed to Milhaud on 5 March 1920 reveals:

> Dear Milhe-Milhe,
> It's Tie-Tie writing to you: he's finished his two *'things.'* He's happy as a king. We'll *'have them.'* Have you read *Comœdia*? I'm very *'amazed'* by this article. Yes, very. They're talking about the *'mysterious collaborator'*, 'one of the most gifted young composers of the new school' – but shush! It's a surprise!
> Who is it?
> Thank you so much for coming to the 'Furniture Music.' Yes, old chap. See you on Sunday, won't I?[69]

Was Milhaud a 'mysterious collaborator' in the furniture music? The manuscript score and parts, which are now housed in IMEC, are exclusively in Satie's hand and there is no known manuscript material written by Milhaud, but does Satie's enigmatic statement 'we'll have them' mean that the composers wanted to trick the audience into believing that Satie was the sole composer? It is more likely that Milhaud's contribution to the event was a piano piece, *Printemps* (1919), written for the first-half concert: in his memoir *Notes sans musique*, he writes 'Satie and I wrote our scores [in the plural] for the instruments which were used in the play.'[70] The *Comœdia* preview article, by José de Berys, introduces the newspaper's readers to the concept of furniture music, asking them not to be alarmed: 'you will see that this novelty, despite its surprising name, is worthy of your attention. [...] Just like the decorative motifs of a tapestry or frieze are repeated uniformly to contribute to a bigger picture, the motifs of *furniture music* will be repeated incessantly *and it will be pointless to listen to them.*'[71] At the end of the article, de Berys wonders whether the authors

---

[69] Volta (ed.), *Correspondance*, pp. 397–8: [Vendredi 5 Mars 1920] 'Cher Milhe-Milhe. ¶ C'est Tie-Tie qui vous écrit: il a terminé ses deux «*trucs*». Il est heureux comme un roi. ¶ Nous les «*aurons*». Avez-vous lu *Comœdia*? Suis très «*épaté*» de cet article. Oui, très. ¶ On parle du «*mystérieux collaborateur*»:– «un des jeunes compositeurs les mieux doués de la nouvelle école – mais, chut! c'est une surprise!» ¶ Qui est-ce? ¶ Combien je vous remercie de votre venue à la «Musique d'Ameublement». Oui, mon vieux. ¶ A dimanche, n'est-ce pas?'

[70] Darius Milhaud, *Notes sans musique*. Paris: Julliard, 1949, p. 138: 'Satie et moi écrivîmes nos partitions pour les instruments qui étaient utilisés au cours du spectacle.'

[71] José de Berys, 'La musique d'ameublement.' *Comœdia*, 2636 (5 March 1920), p. 2 (emphasis in original); 'vous verrez que la trouvaille, malgré ce vocable surprenant, est digne d'attention. [...] de même que les motifs décoratifs, d'une tapisserie ou d'une frise se reproduisent uniformément

will be signing a publishing contract with a well-known Paris furniture retailer.

The instrumentation of Satie's furniture music entr'actes drew on the performers of the rest of the programme: the pianists Marcelle Meyer and Andrée Vaurabourg; three clarinettists, Linger, Duquès and Pigassou, who accompanied Pierre Bertin in Stravinsky's *Berceuse du chat*; and an unnamed trombonist contributed to Max Jacob's play.[72] Satie asked the clarinettists to position themselves in three corners of the room, the fourth corner being occupied by the piano, while the trombone was positioned in a box on the first floor of the gallery.[73] This surround sound effect was not calculated to make things easy for the conductor Félix Delgrange, though it does show that the spatial dimension of the music was crucial to Satie's conception.

Robert Orledge notes the origins of the material used by Satie in his 1920 furniture music set. In 'Chez un bistrot', Satie 'uses an as yet unidentified French popular song (which shows some similarities with the student song "Gaudeamus igitur"), and the second ["Un salon"] parodies first Mignon's romance "Connais-tu le pays, où fleurit l'oranger?" from Act I of Ambroise Thomas' opera *Mignon* (1866), and then Saint-Saëns' celebrated *Danse macabre* of 1874'.[74] Thomas was director of the Paris Conservatoire during Satie's unhappy student days at that institution; Georges Auric mentions that Thomas referred to Satie at the time he composed his *Sarabandes* (1886) as 'un élève bien insignifiant'.[75] Satie even wrote an article for *L'œil de veau* in 1912 which ostensibly is about Thomas, but which focuses more on his fruitless search for an umbrella than on the composer.

Satie's overall title for this music (*Sons industriels*) underlined its functional, anti-artistic intent, and he had given the same subtitle to his two published furniture music pieces composed in 1917. The reference to 'industrial sounds' suggests that the Thomas and Saint-Saëns extracts reference not so much the originals as their commercial dissemination in the form of household music for amateurs.

Saint-Saëns was never a favourite of Satie and his colleagues. The Chat Noir journal described him on 29 March 1890 as a 'musicien

pour donner une impression d'ensemble, de même les motifs de la *musique d'ameublement* seront répétés sans arrêt *et il sera inutile de les écouter.*'

[72] Ornella Volta suggests (private conversation, 2 April 2015) that Milhaud may have been the trombonist.

[73] See Volta, preface to *Musiques d'Ameublement* score. Volta refers to one of the clarinettists as 'Picassou', though this must be Georges Pigassou, who often performed in contemporary music programmes as a bass clarinetist.

[74] Robert Orledge, preface to the SOUNDkiosk edition of the 1920 *Musique d'ameublement* (SKI01).

[75] Auric, preface to Jean Cocteau, *Le coq et l'arlequin*. Paris: Stock, 1979, p. 11.

ambulant' (perhaps a reference to his extensive travels, though more likely a suggestion that he could be a street performer on the barrel organ),[76] and Satie sent the composer, in his capacity as president of the jury, a letter of protest on 17 May 1894 when this unknown young artist failed to be elected to the Institut. (At Ambroise Thomas' death in 1896, Satie, provocatively and inevitably unsuccessfully, also applied for his vacant seat at the Institut.) Satie expressed his contemporary thoughts on Saint-Saëns in a short article for the Communist daily *L'Humanité* in 1919: 'M. Saint-Saëns – that great patriot – was in his time an "advanced" composer. It is true that this "advanced" time was not yesterday, nor even the day before yesterday. We know what M. Saint-Saëns has done for composers of all types. Oh! He's not a "decent sort", that brave M. Saint-Saëns. He certainly knows how to put into practice that nice saying "All for me, nothing for others." What a charming man! There's someone who doesn't like socialists.'[77]

Satie mocks Saint-Saëns in words as a character who is the opposite of the Three Musketeers, foregrounding an alleged characteristic – a lack of solidarity for his fellow composers – which is calculated to repulse the readers of *L'Humanité*. Both Thomas and Saint-Saëns were sworn enemies of Satie, though Satie surely felt at least some connection with *Mignon*, an opera composed in the year of his birth. Satie's insult to these eminent composers is at least threefold: he parodies some of their best-known works; his titles take them out of prestigious Parisian performance venues and place them in popular and domestic spaces; and by locating their music as part of the furniture rather than as the principal focus of attention, Satie asks his audience to direct its attention elsewhere. His toying with standard repertoire by composers at the heart of Parisian cultural life situates his work as a provocative 'other', and as Jacob parodies the drawing-room comedy in his play, Satie parodies drawing-room music in the second entr'acte.

'Chez un bistrot' and 'Un salon' are not background music by virtue of their dynamic levels. The first entr'acte (as Satie labels it) is in 2/4 and has three sections, each eight bars long: in the first, the E♭ clarinet is loud, accompanied by piano duet marked at a lower dynamic level; in the second, the B♭ and A clarinets take on the jaunty tune, again accompanied

---

[76] See Steven Moore Whiting, *Satie the Bohemian: From Cabaret to Concert Hall*. Oxford: Clarendon Press, 1999, p. 96.

[77] Reproduced in Volta (ed.), *Satie Ecrits*, p. 50; original in *L'Humanité*, 11 October 1919, pp. 1–2; 'Monsieur Saint-Saëns – ce grand patriote – a eu son heure « *avancée* ». Il est vrai que cette heure « *avancée* » ne date pas d'hier ni même d'avant-hier. Nous savons ce qu'a fait M. Saint-Saëns pour les musiciens de toutes catégories. Ah! ce n'est pas un « *bon type* », ce brave M. Saint-Saëns. Combien il sait pratiquer la gentille maxime: « *Tout pour moi, rien pour les autres.* » Quel charmant homme! En voilà un qui n'aime pas les socialistes.'

by piano duet. The only loud chords for the piano duet appear at the end of each of these sections. For the final eight-bar section, all instruments (including the trombone) join in very loud, fanfare-like material (Ex. 4.4).

The structure of 'Un salon', which is in 6/8, is slightly more complex: this time, an initial eight-bar phrase for clarinet in A and piano duet is followed by four bars for the whole ensemble. Similar phrase structures are employed for the quieter second half of the piece: 8+4 bars, this time scored for B♭ clarinet, trombone and piano duet. Both entr'actes can be repeated as often as required: the first should end at the final bar of the piece, the second after the first half is almost complete. Here we have yet another example of Satie introducing a deliberate flaw into otherwise mechanistically conceived music: although there is no upbeat at the start of 'Un salon', he indicates 'FIN' after the fifth beat of the six-quaver bar. The mechanism is, despite initial appearances, not perfect.

With the Saint-Saëns extract, Satie gives the macabre chromatic violin tune a jaunty, upbeat character, a stereotypical piano accompaniment and a surprise 'this is the end' gesture in the final bar (Ex. 4.5).

Ex. 4.4 Satie, 'Chez un bistrot': final 4 bars

Repetition and Furniture Music 167

Ex. 4.5 (a) Saint-Saëns, *Danse macabre*: solo violin, second theme, bars 323–411; (b) Satie, 'Un salon': bars 13–20

(a)
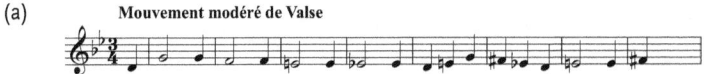

(b)

The mechanical quality of these entr'actes is inherent in their material as well as in their indicated repetitive overall form. The final section of 'Chez un bistrot' illustrates the punchy and deliberately simple nature of the material; note also that the music has no real ending in the form of a cadence (though the first two sections both have emphatic, loud conclusions). There is therefore no musical reason why this piece should end at all. Being in 6/8, 'Un salon' has the barrel organ-like wind-up character which is absolutely typical of Satie's music in this time signature. Again, melodies are mostly conjunct and phrases are symmetrical.

The first, and so far only, performance of *Ruffian toujours, truand jamais* and its associated furniture music took place on 8 March 1920 at the Galerie Barbazanges alongside an exhibition of children's paintings. The Jacob/Satie collaboration was the second half of the programme, the first being devoted to music: Stravinsky's *Berceuse du chat* was performed by Pierre Bertin and the three clarinettists, and Marcelle Meyer played piano works by members of Les Six. Meyer's programme included Auric's 'foxtrot' *Adieu, New York!*, Milhaud's *Printemps* and music by Tailleferre. Children's art was appreciated in avant-garde circles for its freshness and untutored quality: indeed, number 36 (March–June 1924) of the journal *Feuilles libres*, to which Satie contributed, includes drawings and poems by 'Quelques Enfants'. But there is certainly no obvious connection between children's art and the adultery, counterfeit and corruption themes of the play.

Milhaud's well-known account of the performance highlights that 'contrary to our instructions, as soon as the music started, the listeners hurried back to their seats. Satie shouted in vain "Talk! Walk around! Don't listen!" They listened, they were quiet. It was a failure ... Satie hadn't counted on his music's appeal!'[78] Jacob was not present due to illness. On 31 January, while on the way to a Ballets Russes performance of Manuel de Falla's *Three-Cornered Hat*, he was knocked down by a car, taken to hospital and soon contracted pneumonia. He spent two months in a public ward, missing not only *Ruffian toujours, truand jamais* but also his first solo exhibition at Galerie Bernheim-Jeune, which opened on the

---

[78] Milhaud, *Notes sans musique*, p. 138: 'Mais contrairement à nos prévisions, aussitôt que la musique commença, les auditeurs se dirigèrent rapidement vers leurs places. Satie eut beau leur crier: «Mais parlez donc! Circulez! N'écoutez pas!» Ils écoutaient, ils se taisaient. Tout était raté ... Satie n'avait pas compté sur le charme de sa musique!' In his book, Milhaud gives Jacob's play the title *Un figurant au théâtre de Nantes*; he is certainly confusing *Ruffian toujours* with the earlier Jacob play with the title he cites, which was performed at the Galerie Barbazanges on 24 June 1919. This play was given alongside a piece by Poulenc, *Le jongleur*, danced by Caryathis and probably played on the piano; this dancer also commissioned and first performed Satie's *La Belle Excentrique* (1920).

same day as the Galerie Barbazanges premiere.[79] He wrote to a friend in mid-March 1920: 'I wanted to wait until I was well enough before writing a letter worthy of you, but tiredness, a cough, a painful and useless shoulder mean I don't have the strength. I must only thank you briefly for coming to see me in hospital, for all your lovely and precious words, for the unmerited honour of your visit. I'm going to travel south as soon as work commitments allow me to leave.'[80]

Two reviews were published, one by José de Berys in *Comœdia* on 10 March, and another by Jean-Gabriel Lemoine in *Le Crapouillot* on 16 March.[81] Perhaps Lemoine took seriously Satie's request to ignore the entr'acte music, as his review focuses solely on Jacob's play, not mentioning the other elements of the performance at all. The review is largely an overview of the plot, though Lemoine also offers a brief critique of the performance, writing: 'Let's say straight away that the play was superbly performed, notably by Pierre Bertin whose Lucien, whose ambiguous appeal, drawling voice and mixture of jokiness and class make him a completely successful type of modern "ruffian".'[82] Berys, also the author of the preview published in *Comœdia*, mentions the socially select audience and all aspects of the evening's entertainment, starting with Jacob's play:

> It's clear that the dialogue is to be savoured, studded with profound aphorisms, words which are striking and always ironic. The tone is violent humour, with real comic force. A total success. [...] Before

---

[79] Jacob, *Œuvres complètes*, p. 66.

[80] Marcoux and Gompel-Netter (eds), *Max Jacob*, p. 66, addressee unidentified but the editors believe he is le comte de la Garde: 'Je voulais attendre d'être assez bien portant pour vous écrire une lettre digne de vous et la fatigue, la toux, une épaule toute douloureuse et inutile ne m'en laisse [sic] pas la force. Je n'ai que celle de vous remercier brièvement de votre présence si courte près de mon lit d'hôpital, de toutes vos belles et précieuses paroles, de l'honneur immérité de votre visite. Je vais partir au midi aussitôt que mes affaires me permettront un voyage. [...]' Jacob spent April–May 1920 convalescing in the South of France (Jacob, *Œuvres*, p. 66).

[81] A card Satie sent to Jean Lemoine on 12 March 1920 shows him agreeing to meet Lemoine at Graff, a favourite café of his, on 13 March, therefore between the performance and the publication of Lemoine's review in *Le Crapouillot* (card in the private collection of Robert Orledge, to whom I am indebted for this detail).

[82] Jean-Gabriel Lemoine, 'Spectacle d'Avant-garde: Une pièce de M. Max Jacob: *Ruffian toujours, truand jamais* (Représentation unique donnée à la Galerie Barbazanges le 8 mars 1920).' *Le Crapouillot*, 16 March 1920, p. 6: 'La pièce, disons-le tout de suite, a été remarquablement interprétée, et notamment par Pierre Bertin, dont le Lucien avec ses allures ambiguës, sa voix trainante et son mélange de canaillerie et de distinction est un type de «ruffian» moderne tout à fait réussi.'

> Max Jacob's play, Marcelle Meyer was the stylish performer of various works by Igor Stravinsky, Darius Milhaud, Georges Auric and Germaine Tailleferre, and during the intervals we heard a curiosity: 'furniture music' which we were forbidden to listen to, but which gave much pleasure.[83]

The reviews between them list most of the performers: in addition to Pierre Bertin who played Lucien, M. Berley of the Odéon played Ferdinand le bistro, M. Chaumont was Raoul, Mme Thouvenel played the baroness, and MM. Lisflon, Barençay and Daubigny played other roles. It is not clear who played Germaine (a role which may have been acted by one of the two female pianists on the programme) and the real person behind the piano teacher 'Phanérogame' remains an enigma.

■ ■ ■

DANIEL Albright notes that 'Stravinsky had several strategies for objectifying music: one was a preference for the cool sonorities of wind instruments; another was the method of eliminating the human performer (so likely to add expressive phrasing and emphasis) by composing for the pianola – a player piano operated by compressed air and governed by holes punched on paper rolls.'[84] Satie's strategy in his furniture music is different: true, he shows a preference for wind instruments (combined with strings or piano duet and given straightforward dynamic indications), but he paradoxically devised repetitive musical structures to be performed by humans, though the material would most logically and easily be performed by a mechanical instrument. It must be assumed that the flaws inherent in performance by human beings are an essential part of Satie's furniture music, just as the curious cut-off after the fifth beat of the six-quaver bar of 'Un salon' is a deliberate moment of imperfection. But Stravinsky's view that expression is not an intrinsic quality of music is shared by Satie in his *musique d'ameublement*, music which is not intended to be consciously attended to, still less to provoke a more intense emotional response.

---

[83] José de Berys, 'Les petites premières: Ruffian toujours, truand jamais à la Galerie Barbazanges.' *Comœdia*, 10 March 1920, p. 2: 'Sachez que le dialogue en est savoureux, émaillé d'aperçus profonds, de mots cinglants et constamment ironiques. C'est d'un humour violent et d'une grande force comique. Le succès a été complet. [...] Avant la pièce de M. Max Jacob, Mme Marcelle Meyer avait interprété, en pianiste de grand style, diverses œuvres d'Igor Stravinski, de Darius Milhaud, Georges Auric, Germaine Tailleferre, et l'on joua aux entr'actes la curieuse «musique d'ameublement», qu'il était défendu d'écouter, mais qui plut beaucoup.'

[84] Daniel Albright (ed.), *Modernism and Music: An Anthology of Sources* (Chicago: University of Chicago Press, 2004), p. 281.

Tenture de cabinet préfectoral

Satie's 'Wall hanging [or curtain] for a prefect's office' was not, as its title may suggest, composed for a government building. Instead, the client was Agnes Meyer, née Ernst (1887–1980), the wife of Eugene Meyer Jr., who was director of the *Washington Post*. As a journalist, Agnes Ernst was the first woman employed by the New York *Sun*, and she met Alfred Stieglitz in 1908 when she interviewed him at his Photo-Secession gallery at 291 Fifth Avenue, a gallery which became known under its street number. Later that year, she went to Paris to study at the Sorbonne, and in that city she met the Steins and was introduced to Rodin by her future husband.[85] Agnes Ernst married Meyer on 14 February 1910, and they regularly bought art by contemporary artists including Cézanne, Rodin, Renoir, Manet and Toulouse-Lautrec. They were also patrons of Brancusi; the Meyers 'arranged for his first one-man show in New York, held at *291*, from March 12th to April 1st, 1914'.[86]

Agnes Meyer was one of the driving forces behind the founding of the art magazine *291* in 1914, and indeed she was the author of the lead article in the first issue. Many of Satie's Paris contacts and future collaborators contributed to the magazine, not least Francis Picabia and Guillaume Apollinaire. Douglas Hyland writes that 'when Picabia came to New York in the spring of 1915, the spirit of experimentation that had prevailed in Paris before the war was transplanted to New York. The machinist aesthetic, based on forms used in modern technology, is found in his series of portraits in *291* and is typical of the Dada spirit.'[87] While both the gallery and magazine were short-lived, the magazine's European offshoot *391*, founded by Picabia on his return to Europe after the war, was highly influential in avant-garde and Dada circles. The Meyers moved to Washington DC when her husband was appointed to a government position in the Defense Department.

Satie may well have met Agnes Meyer through his friend Henri-Pierre Roché; the author and translator Roché got to know Satie and Georges Auric around 1913, at the time he was working on a translation of Shakespeare's *A Midsummer Night's Dream* (as we saw in Chapter 2, Satie's *Cinq grimaces* were composed for a project based on this play, which may or may not have been the same project as Roché's). In 1919 Roché spent some time in New York where he met the Mexican artist and gallerist Marius de Zayas, co-owner with Alfred Stieglitz of the 291 art gallery. Another factor in this complex web of association was Satie's contribution to the French-based magazine *391*, which was edited by

---

[85] Douglas K. S. Hyland, 'Agnes Ernst Meyer, Patron of American Modernism.' *America Art Journal*, vol. 12 no. 1 (Winter 1980), pp. 64–81, at p. 65.

[86] Ibid., pp. 71 and 73.

[87] Ibid., p. 76.

Picabia. Ornella Volta, for her part, believes that Satie's 'first, and only, [furniture music] client' was introduced to him 'thanks only to Darius Milhaud's American connections'.[88] In the words of Milhaud, *Tenture de cabinet préfectoral* was written to 'furnish this lady's library in Crescent Place for the ear, just as a fine Manet still life furnished it for the eye'.[89]

The score, 'composed specially for Madame Eugène Meyer Jr.', is dated 28 March 1923 and was written on a sheet of paper which is not much larger than A3 size (42×30 cm). *Tenture de cabinet préfectoral* is composed for piccolo, clarinet in B♭, bassoon, horn in F, trumpet in C, percussion (cymbal, bass drum, tambour) and strings, and is twelve bars long. The first four bars are marked 'Pas trop vite'; bar 5 indicated 'Calme et sot' (Calm and stupid); the end is marked 'Se répète à volonté (pas plus)' (To be repeated at will (not more)). The piece is pawky and funny, especially its final bars with their descending E melodic minor scale in all strings plus bassoon, which does not quite span an octave because it lacks its first E. The first section of the work is another 'unappetising chorale': most instruments are in G major, though the bassoon is arguing for B minor, and the viola, for its part, seems unsure whether there is a key at all (Ex. 4.6). The extremely simple trumpet melody in the following phrase is particularly 'sot' ('stupid'), and there is, again, a built-in jerky flaw in this repetitive piece as the last bar is cut off after one and a half quavers.

As Satie never visited the United States and did not compose any other works for American clients, it is remarkable quite how much of a stir he created in fashionable American circles in the last years of his life. In March 1918 Carl van Vechten published an article 'Erik Satie: Master of the Rigolo' in *Vanity Fair*, and Satie himself wrote for the same magazine between 1921 and 1923. Some of these articles were translations of material which had appeared in French ('A Hymn in Praise of the Critics' and 'A Lecture on "The Six"'), though 'A Learned Lecture on Music and Animals' and 'Igor Stravinsky' were commissioned especially for the magazine. *Vanity Fair* also published translations of critiques on Satie by the art gallery owner Paul Rosenfeld and Georges Auric.

This enthusiasm for Satie in *Vanity Fair* can certainly be ascribed to the composer's friend Sybil Harris, the wife of a theatrical agent, William Harris; they were part of the expatriate American contingent in Paris, and like many of this crowd they lived in Montparnasse. Sybil Harris was a close friend of Henri-Pierre Roché and an enthusiast of Les Six as well as Satie. She even looked after Satie during his trip to Brussels in April

---

[88] Ornella Volta, preface to 'Musiques d'Ameublement', pp. VIII–IX: 'sa première, et unique, cliente [...] ne devait se présenter que trois ans plus tard, et grâce seulement aux relations américaines de Darius Milhaud'.

[89] Milhaud, *Notes sans musique*, p. 138: '« Musique pour un Cabinet Préfectoral » [...] meublant ainsi pour l'oreille sa belle bibliothèque de Crescent Place, comme la nature morte de Manet la meublait pour l'œil'.

Ex. 4.6 *Tenture de cabinet préfectoral*: bars 1–4

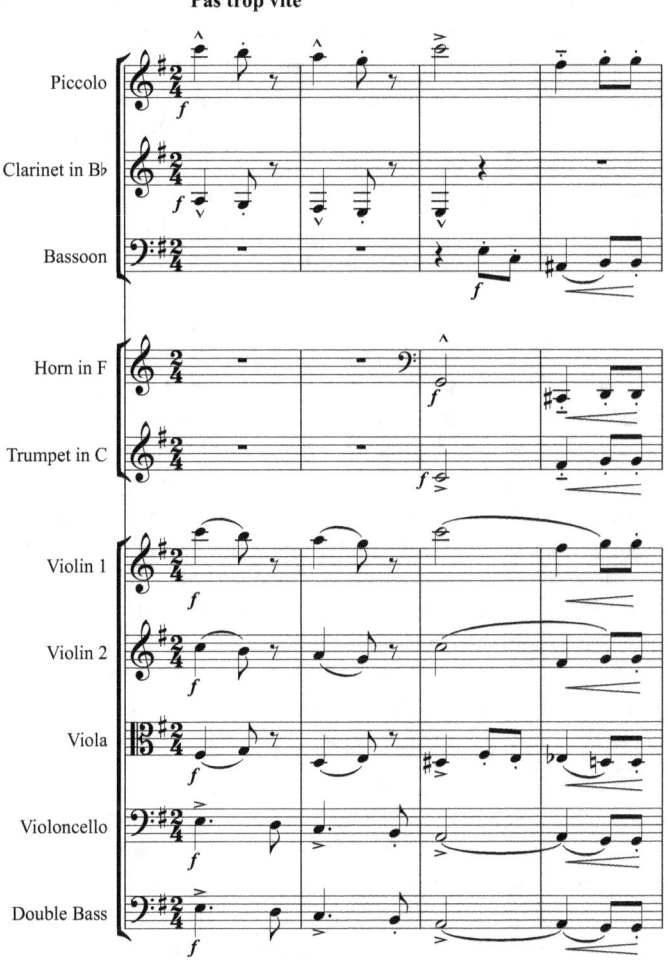

1921,[90] assuming no doubt correctly that the composer would find it difficult to cope away from home on his first foreign excursion as an adult. Harris commissioned and paid for an article 'Igor Stravinsky, a Tribute to the Eminent Russian Composer by a French Confrère' published in *Vanity Fair* in February 1923: it is unsigned, but Satie is the author. An article on Debussy was also written in August 1922 for *Vanity Fair* and paid for by Harris, but was never published in that magazine.[91] Carol Oja is right to stress that

---

[90] Volta (ed.), *Correspondance*, p. 899. Harris donated her collection of Satie scores and manuscripts to the Houghton Library, Harvard University (ibid., p. 900).

[91] Volta (ed.), *Satie Ecrits*, p. 263.

Given Satie's irreverent, ironic style, these articles represented esoteric stuff for mass consumption – the kinds of pieces one might expect to find in 'little magazines' such as *transatlantic*, the *Little Review*, or even the *Dial*. Their appearance in *Vanity Fair* suggests that Satie and issues of modernism in general were of much interest to the smart set as they were to the impoverished intellectuals of Greenwich Village. This is a striking theme in the reception of European modernism in America: not only did it become more commonplace to hear such music by the mid-1920s, but in some circles it became downright fashionable.[92]

Conclusion: furniture music and expression?

It is instructive to view Satie's furniture music in the light of Descartes' theory of dualism: if separated from our intellect, are we merely machines? If we are asked to perform a piece of music 840 times, does this turn us into a machine? Does the thorny notation of *Vexations* make it so difficult to memorise that the performer's powers of concentration are taxed beyond human limits? Carolyn Abbate alludes to Descartes in her article when she writes about 'mechanical' musical works such as Ravel's song *Noël des jouets*: 'As spectacles that portray the clockwork we may harbor inside ourselves, they interrogate the meaning of reproduction, asking what has been stolen by the machine. By extension, they interrogate the humanity in any human musical performance.'[93]

Stravinsky's often misunderstood comment about music and expression is relevant in this context. He wrote in his autobiography:

> For I consider that music is, by its very nature, essentially powerless to *express* anything at all, whether a feeling, an attitude of mind, a psychological mood, a phenomenon of nature, etc. *Expression* has never been an inherent property of music. That is by no means the purpose of its existence. If, as is nearly always the case, music appears to express something, this is only an illusion and not a reality. It is simply an additional attribute which, by tacit and inveterate agreement, we have lent it, thrust upon it, as a label, a convention – in short, an aspect which, unconsciously or by force of habit, we have come to confuse with its essential being.[94]

---

[92] Carol Oja, *Making Music Modern: New York in the 1920s*. New York: Oxford University Press, 2003, p. 54.

[93] Carolyn Abbate, 'Outside Ravel's Tomb.' *Journal of the American Musicological Society*, vol. 52 no. 3 (Autumn 1999): pp. 465–530, at p. 494.

[94] Igor Stravinsky, *An Autobiography*. New York: Simon & Schuster, 1936, pp. 53–4.

For Satie, too, music simply *is*: it can be a means of furnishing a room, of avoiding awkward silences and facilitating social interaction, or of prolonging the mood of a play beyond the stage and into the interval refreshment room.

The importance of Satie's concept of *musique d'ameublement* is recognised by posterity, though in the composer's lifetime the notion was not taken seriously by any publisher and only the furniture music composed for Max Jacob's play was performed in public on a single occasion. Much of Satie's work, even when it is not repetitive, has an automated, mechanical quality: the constant crotchet = 76 beat of *Parade* springs to mind, and it is not surprising that his musical style was the perfect partner to René Clair's film *Entr'acte*, written as an interlude to the ballet *Relâche* in 1924. Pierre-Daniel Templier, Satie's first biographer, believes that 'Furniture music, soon after [1917] found its real purpose in "music for film" – music which is not to be listened to but which must, despite itself, impose itself and contribute to the overall emotional world of the film.'[95] Templier rightly stresses the aesthetic importance of Satie's furniture music and considers it to be an extension of his previous work. Satie's preferred term for background music, 'entr'acte', shows it is something between categories (to use a term favoured by Morton Feldman) – not part of the main show, but an interlude during which our attention can relax.

While Satie is often considered to be a precursor of muzak, his *musique d'ameublement* is quite different in meaning and purpose. Muzak (strictly speaking, this is the trademark of a particular company, though the term has evolved to refer to all commercial background music) is popular music shorn of its words and dynamic variation which is rearranged and juxtaposed with other songs. These sequences are intended to provide an upbeat and pleasant commercial environment, and above all to encourage consumers to purchase products.[96] Only 'Un salon', the second of Satie's entr'actes for Max Jacob's play, is at all similar to muzak in the sense that it is based on two popular pieces of its period which have been arranged for a different instrumental formation, without the original text in the case of the Ambroise Thomas extract. Satie's furniture music was indeed composed in the hope of financial reward in the form of performances and further commissions, but the notion of music used purely as a means of enticing customers and stimulating capitalist behaviour would have been abhorrent to a card-carrying member of the Socialist and later Communist Party.

---

[95] Templier, *Erik Satie*, p. 44: 'La musique d'ameublement trouva, peu de temps après [1917], sa véritable signification dans la «musique de cinéma», qu'il ne faut pas écouter, mais qui doit s'imposer, malgré soi, pour contribuer à l'émotion cinématographique.'

[96] See Lanza, *Elevator Music*.

Satie's music was composed at the start of the era of mechanical sound reproduction, and while he did not himself participate in this technology as a recording artist or composer for new mechanical instruments, his work poses questions about our relationship with technology and with our sonic environment. His furniture music is certainly situated in the machine age, but perhaps most importantly, it has inbuilt flaws compared to machine reproduction because its performers are human. Far from seeing human labour as disposable, Satie composes machine-like music for which human performers are essential.

CHAPTER 5

Science, Society and Politics in Satie's Life

'Everyone will tell you I am not a musician. That's correct,' Satie wrote in 'Ce que je suis', the first section of his *Mémoires d'un amnésique*. Satie includes a reference to this critical judgement: the author cited is Octave Séré, author of a book on contemporary French music and pseudonym of Jean Poueigh, who sued Satie for libel after *Parade*. Satie goes on to say, 'Since the start of my career, I have been classified amongst the phonometrographers. My works are pure phonometrography. Whether one considers *Le Fils des étoiles* or the *Morceaux en forme de poire*, *En habit de cheval* or the *Sarabandes*, one notices that no musical idea presided over the construction of these works. It is scientific thought which is dominant.'[1] It would be easy to dismiss such a statement as a facetious and amusing commentary on the classification habits of musicologists, but in fact it is more fruitful to view Satie in the light of his genuine interest in contemporary scientific discoveries. Satie's lifetime saw enormous changes in Paris, the city in which he lived since the age of ten: scientific knowledge and its application leapt forward hugely.

At the same time Satie was ambivalent about modernity and innovation. His friend Debussy's description of him as a 'gentle medieval musician strayed into this century'[2] implies a rejection of the modern world, but this does not take account of Satie's desire to engage with the new. This engagement might well be playful, could embody a critical or suspicious stance, or conversely could express admiration of the new world.

---

[1] Opening section of 'Mémoires d'un amnésique (fragments).' *Revue musicale S.I.M.*, vol. 8 no. 4 (15 April 1912), p. 69; reprinted in Ornella Volta (ed.), *Erik Satie: Ecrits*. Paris: Editions Champ Libre, 1979, p. 19: 'Tout le monde vous dira que je ne suis pas un musicien.* [*: Voir: O[ctave] Séré, *Musiciens français d'aujourd'hui*, p. 183.] C'est juste. Dès le début de ma carrière, je me suis, de suite, classé parmi les phonométrographes. Mes travaux sont de la pure phonométrique. Que l'on prenne le « Fils des Etoiles », ou les « Morceaux en forme de poire », « En habit de Cheval » ou les « Sarabandes », on perçoit qu'aucune idée musicale n'a présidé à la construction de ces œuvres. C'est la pensée scientifique qui domine.' Séré wrote of Satie: 'Signalons en outre – sans attacher à cela une trop grosse importance – le nom de M. Erik Satie, technicien maladroit mais subtil chercheur de sonorités.'

[2] Cited in Robert Orledge, 'Satie, Koechlin and the Ballet *Uspud*.' *Music and Letters*, vol. 64 no. 1 (1987), p. 27 footnote 4. Debussy wrote these words (in red ink) as a dedication to Satie on a copy of Debussy's own *Cinq poèmes de Baudelaire*.

The composer's description of himself as a phonometrographer has three components: sound, measurement and writing. Satie refers to other forms of musical 'measurement' in this article, examining 'a B♭ of average weight' with a phonoscope (which he found 'disgusting'), and weighing with a 'phono-scale' (*phonopeseur*) an 'ordinary, very common or garden F♯, which weighed 93 kilograms'. He then asks the reader:

> Do you know about the process of cleaning sounds? It's rather dirty. Spinning them is cleaner: knowing how to classify them is an exacting task requiring good eyesight. Here, we are in the realms of photo technique.
>
> As for sonorous explosions, which are often so unpleasant, cotton wool in the ears mitigates the sound conveniently. Here, we are in the realm of pyrophony.
>
> When I wrote my 'Pièces froides', I used a caleidophone recorder. It took seven minutes. I called my servant to listen to them.
>
> I believe I can say that phonology is superior to music. It's more varied. It's more lucrative. I owe my fortune to phonology.
>
> In any event, with the motodynamophone, a phonometer with very little skill can easily notate more sounds than the most able musician can, in the same amount of time and with the same effort. It's thanks to that machine that I have composed so much.
>
> The future therefore belongs to philophony.[3]

Again, Satie is taking on the language of an advertising company or a successful businessman, and as he often does in *Mémoires d'un amnésique*, he evokes a servant who is at his beck and call. So often, Satie uses humour by inversion: his real life, having little money and living in a shabby room with no running water in a working-class suburb of Paris, is precisely the opposite of this description. While it could be considered dangerous to read too much into Satie's amusing tales, perhaps the composer is suggesting that his *Pièces froides* – which last around seven

---

[3] 'Ce que je suis', reprinted in Volta (ed.), *Satie Écrits*, p. 19: 'Connaissez-vous le nettoyage des sons? C'est assez sale. Le filage est plus propre; savoir les classer est très minutieux et demande une bonne vue. Ici nous sommes dans la photo-technique. ¶ Quant aux explosions sonores, souvent si désagréables, le coton, fixé dans les oreilles, les atténue, pour soi, convenablement. Ici, nous sommes dans la pyrophonie. ¶ Pour écrire mes « Pièces Froides », je me suis servi d'un caléidophone-enregistreur. Cela prit sept minutes. J'appelai mon domestique pour les lui faire entendre. ¶ Je crois pouvoir dire que la phonologie est supérieure à la musique. C'est plus varié. Le rendement pécuniaire est plus grand. Je lui dois ma fortune. ¶ En tout cas, au motodynamophone, un phonométreur médiocrement exercé peut, facilement, noter plus de sons que ne le fera le plus habile musicien, dans le même temps, avec le même effort. C'est grâce à cela que j'ai tant écrit. ¶ L'avenir est donc à la philophonie.'

minutes in performance – could have been improvised at the piano and recorded, or indeed improvised and then 'polished up' in the form of music notation. Musical performance in Satie's time could be automated and divorced from a human performer, whether through old technologies such as the barrel organ or the newer phonograph and radio. Was Satie concerned, beneath the facetious surface of his writing, that the job of the composer could be replaced by new technology? Computer-generated composition was not possible until several decades after Satie's death, and notation programs that are able to transcribe live performance accurately are even newer.

Peter Dayan discovered that one of the 'instruments' Satie mentions is not entirely a figment of his imagination. Dayan writes: 'The "caléidophone-enregistreur" was Satie's invention, but the "caléidophone", or kaleidophone, was not. It was a "scientific toy" invented in 1827 by Charles Wheatstone, which turned patterns of vibration, such as those produced in a rod by a violin bow, into visible patterns of light. The purpose of the "caléidophone-enregistreur", then, is double: it records music and it transcribes it in another medium.'[4] Could Satie have read about this scientific toy in the Larousse encyclopedia, so often the source of facts, folksongs and stories he uses in his music? It seems that he took an existing machine and gave it a fantasy extension.

Other nineteenth-century scientists could have inspired Satie's musings on the measurement and preservation of sound. In 1861, Edouard-Léon Scott de Martinville described the 'phonautographe' as 'the movement of a needle set in motion by the breath of human speech, allowing the transcription of sounds on a disc covered with black smoke. But this was an idea which was not put into practice.' Jacques Attali goes on to mention an innovator of whom Satie was surely aware in Montmartre: 'Twenty years later, on 30 April 1877, another self-taught man, Charles Cros, author of *Hareng saur* and founder of the Hydropathe group, deposited at the Académie des sciences the patent for a machine which could reproduce sounds, the paleophone. The sound would be engraved on a wax groove; subsequently, a needle could trace this groove to repeat the sound.'[5] The name of the paleophone stresses that it is an

---

[4] Peter Dayan, *Art as Music, Music as Poetry, Poetry as Art, from Whistler to Stravinsky and Beyond*. Farnham: Ashgate, 2011, p. 41.

[5] Jacques Attali, *Bruits* (revised edition). Paris: Fayard/PUF, 2001, p. 147: 'le mouvement d'une aiguille mise en mouvement par le souffle de la parole permettrait de transcrire les sons entendus sur un disque couvert de noir de fumée. Mais il ne va pas plus loin que l'idée. ¶ Vingt ans plus tard, le 30 avril 1877, un autre autodidacte, Charles Cros, auteur de Hareng saur et créateur du Groupe des hydropathes, dépose à l'Académie des sciences le brevet d'un appareil reproducteur de sons, le paléophone. Le son y serait gravé sur un sillon de cire; il suffirait ensuite de repasser une aiguille sur le sillon pour répéter ce son.'

instrument capable of preserving sounds of the past. But, as Attali notes, Thomas Edison deposited a patent for the phonograph in December 1877, and Edison's greater resources and know-how ensured that it was his invention that was put into production and changed the world of sound and our experience of music.

From the earliest years of his life in Montmartre, Satie was surrounded by people of an eccentric scientific bent. In Satie's Montmartre, science, entertainment and radical politics coexisted and Satie and his contemporaries were comfortable moving between diverse spheres of knowledge which are now usually considered quite distinct. Through men such as Charles Cros and Charles Henry, the artistic avant-garde in Montmartre became aware of current mathematical and scientific thought in a form they could understand: these men were either artistic creators themselves, or were deeply interested in the arts and sought ways to connect science and art in grand overarching theories.

While there is no evidence that Satie's ancestors had particular scientific interests or expertise, the composer's younger brother, Conrad, was an industrial chemist who was a respected authority in perfumery. Conrad Satie (1868–1938) and Paul Jeancard co-authored a book, *Abrégé de la chimie des parfums*, in 1904 and the same men jointly wrote an article 'La chimie des parfums en 1911' which was published in the *Revue générale de chimie pure et appliquée* in 1912. Most intriguingly of all, Conrad also wrote a short article on perfumery for *L'Humanité* in 1936, and he was not the only family member to contribute to the Communist newspaper.

The two Satie brothers' relationship has been compared to that of Vincent and Theo van Gogh: Erik was the impoverished bohemian artist who frequently wrote letters to his younger brother asking for money. These letters reveal details of the composer's life he was unwilling to share with anyone else, though sadly Conrad's letters to Erik have not survived. Conrad even once passed on clothes to Erik in his Montmartre days, as the older brother would otherwise have been unable to work as a piano accompanist as he lacked suitable clothing. The sibling relationship was occasionally troubled, for reasons which are not always clear. Ornella Volta describes Conrad as 'Misanthropic, though a politically active left-winger' and writes that he 'did not escape the mood swings, followed by lengthy breaks in contact, which characterized most of [Satie's] relationships with those close to him'.[6] The brothers did not speak 'from the death of their father (1903) until 1911, then there was a second break during the Great War. The two brothers stopped writing to each other after

---

[6] Ornella Volta (ed.), *Erik Satie: Correspondance presque complète*. Paris: Fayard/IMEC, 2/2003, p. 1105: 'Misanthrope, quoique politiquement engagé à gauche, Conrad Satie n'a pas échappé aux sautes d'humeur, suivies de longues séparations, qui ont caractérisé la plupart des relations de notre compositeur avec ses proches.'

the death of Conrad's wife in January 1924. Alone in his grief, Conrad found out about the death of Erik Satie through a press announcement, his brother not having informed him of his serious illness.'[7] After their father's funeral, Erik was hurt that Conrad did not want to go for a drink with him; one wonders whether this was due to Conrad's misanthropy, or because Conrad was all too aware that his older brother often drank to excess.

The Satie brothers' hometown of Honfleur was also home to the celebrated Montmartre humorist Alphonse Allais (1854–1905). Allais' father was a pharmacist who expected his son to follow in his footsteps (and the family's pharmacy, Passocéan, still exists at 4, place Hamelin, Honfleur) but Alphonse abandoned his studies at the Ecole supérieure de pharmacie to become a writer and the editor of the *Journal du Chat noir* in its heyday. Allais did not completely forget his scientific training as his first published text in the *Journal du Chat noir*, which appeared on 6 May 1882, was a 'Chronique scientifique' which was actually a satirical song published under the name of K. Lomel.[8] Allais' pseudonym here is an allusion to calomel, the chemical compound also known as Mercury(l) chloride which, as he will have known, was used in the nineteenth century as a laxative, a disinfectant and a treatment for syphilis. Allais/K. Lomel introduces the song:

> It is time to stop the absurd farce of gentlemen teaching classes in faculties who are dressed very much in black and are very boring. The Chat Noir journal has on its staff some distinguished professors who can replace these classes with a series of appealing lessons. Today we will start with a chemistry lesson on the well-known tune: 'A la façon de Barbari':
>
>> Oxygen has the density
>> (We have studied it)
>> Of 1.1056
>> Calculated precisely.
>> It facilitates combustion
>> Lalalala, lalala,
>> It supports life
>> Biribi

---

[7] Ibid., p. 1106: 'il semble bien qu'il y eut une première rupture peu après la mort de leur père (1903) et jusqu'en 1911, puis une deuxième interruption pendant la Grande Guerre. Les deux frères ont cessé de s'écrire après la mort de l'épouse de Conrad (janvier 1924). Enfermé dans sa douleur, ce dernier ne devait apprendre que par la presse la disparition d'Erik Satie qui ne l'avait pas informé de sa grave maladie.'

[8] André Velter, preface to *Les poètes du Chat noir*. Paris: Gallimard, 1996, p. 18.

A la façon de Barbari,
My friend.[9]

Two other verses follow. This imaginative form of public engagement with science continued in the *Chat noir* journal on 3 June 1882, when the same K. Lomel wrote an account of the fictitious Faculty of Sciences in Montmartre. Discussing Louis Pasteur's inoculations (which were developed during the 1870s), the author writes: 'A native of Auvergne, just arrived in Paris, was injected with a three-day-old culture taken from M. Manet, and the patient immediately executed a marvellous symphony in violet major.'[10] The following week, the author wrote another song text to the tune of 'A la façon de Barbari'.

Satie and Allais shared more than a sense of absurd humour. They were both artists in the broadest sense of the term, happy to employ whatever media were most appropriate to express their amusing thoughts. Allais was primarily a writer, but one of his works was visual in nature: his *Album primo-avrilesque* published by Paul Ollendorff in 1897. This 'April Fool-ish album' featured seven solid colour 'canvases' including the entirely white *Première communion de jeunes filles chlorotiques par un temps de neige (First Communion of Anaemic Young Girls In The Snow)* and similar red work *Récolte de la tomate par des cardinaux apoplectique au bord de la Mer Rouge (Effet d'Aurore Boréale) (Apoplectic Cardinals Harvesting Tomatoes on the Shore of the Red Sea (Study of the Aurora Borealis))*. This volume concluded with a 'composition', a *Marche funèbre composée pour les funérailles d'un grand homme sourd (March Composed for the Funeral of a Great Deaf Man)* consisting entirely of rest notations – because, as he wrote, 'the great pains are silent'.[11] In the words of Douglas Kahn, 'The avant-garde got quite a bit of mileage from affectionate parodies of the culture of science and technology, and no one got more than the French (Jarry, Roussel, Apollinaire, Duchamp). [...] Jarry satirized the inscriptive impulse within ideas of visual sound; it was left to Erik Satie to take on the ideas of size implicit in acoustical measurement by claiming

---

[9] 'Il est temps de mettre un terme à la fumisterie absurde qui consiste à faire faire des cours dans les facultés par des messieurs très de noir habillés et très-ennuyeux. Le journal le Chat Noir s'est adjoint quelques professeurs distingués qui donneront à cette place une série de leçons attrayante. ¶ Nous commencerons aujourd'hui un cours de chimie sur l'air connu de: A la façon de Barbari. ¶ L'oxygène a pour densité/ On en a fait l'étude,/ 1,1056 calculé/ Avec exactitude./ Il entretient la combustion,/ La faridondaine, la faridondon/ C'est lui qui entretient la vie/ Biribi/ A la façon de Barbari,/ Mon ami.'

[10] 'Un sujet auvergnat fraîchement débarqué est injecté avec un culture de trois jours prise sur M. Manet, et le patient exécute sur-le-champ une symphonie merveilleuse en violet-majeur.'

[11] The album is reproduced in gallica.bnf.fr; 'parce que «les grandes douleurs sont muettes»'.

that he was in fact a phonometrographer, a measurer of sound, not a musician.'[12]

Other Chat Noir authors, particularly the composer and writer Charles de Sivry and the multi-talented poet and inventor Charles Cros, shared Allais' interest in alchemy. Sivry and Cros, according to Steven Moore Whiting, 'both tried (reportedly with success) to fabricate gems on an electric stove, and Alphonse Allais, as a young pharmacy student, frequently joined in Cros's alchemical experiments'.[13] Connections with eccentric scientists are never far from Satie's music and thoughts, well after he had moved away from Montmartre and had lost contact with many of his old friends. As late as 1922, he published an amusing account about Nicolas Flamel, 'A Very Old Man of Letters', who allegedly discovered the Philosopher's Stone which turns base metal into gold. Satie here claims that 'I didn't personally know Nicolas Flamel – for many reasons; but his memory is one I have always cherished.'[14] Satie's acquaintance with Flamel can indeed only have been virtual – the latter was born around 1330 – though their common enthusiasm for calligraphy is only one of their many points of contact. In one published piece of writing, Satie even portrays himself as a character who was part of a circle interested in alchemy. At the beginning of 1913, Satie was toying with ideas about a theatrical work, some of which he employed in his play *Le piège de Méduse* later that year:

> I always had the idea to write a lyric drama on the following and very precise topic: At that time, I was involved in alchemy. Alone in my laboratory, one day I was resting. Outside, the sky was like lead, sinister: a horror!
>
> I was sad, without knowing why; almost fearful, without knowing the reason. An idea took hold of me, to distract myself by counting, slowly on my fingers, from one to two hundred and sixty thousand.[15]

---

[12] Douglas Kahn, *Noise, Water, Meat: A History of Sound in the Arts*. Cambridge, MA: MIT Press, 2001, p. 193.

[13] Steven Moore Whiting, *Satie the Bohemian: From Cabaret to Concert Hall*. Oxford: Clarendon Press, 1999, p. 74 note 33, citing François Caradec, *Alphonse Allais*, Paris: Belfond, 1994, p. 133.

[14] Erik Satie, 'Un très vieil Homme de Lettres', *Catalogue*, 4 (30 June 1922), p. 3, reprinted in Volta (ed.), *Satie Ecrits*, pp. 55–6: 'Comme vous le supposez, je n'ai pas connu personnellement Nicolas Flamel – pour plusieurs raisons; mais son souvenir m'est toujours resté sympathique.'

[15] Erik Satie, 'Choses de théâtre.' *Revue musicale S.I.M.*, vol. 9 no. 1 (15 January 1913), p. 71, reprinted in Volta (ed.), *Satie Ecrits*, pp. 21–2: 'J'ai toujours eu la pensée d'écrire un drame lyrique sur le suivant et particulier sujet: En ce temps-là, je m'occupais d'alchimie. Seul dans mon laboratoire, un jour je me reposais. Dehors, un ciel de plomb, blafard, sinistre: une horreur! ¶ J'étais triste, sans en connaître la raison; presque craintif, sans

The author goes on to say that he was disturbed by someone knocking at the door – who turned out to be his servant (again, we see Satie creating an imaginary world which is the opposite of his real circumstances). Fearful and baffled, the author addresses the servant, asking how he knew he was there; the servant replies 'hiccupping, like a child: "I saw you through the keyhole."' [16] As so often in a fantastical Satie story, one is brought back down to earth at the end by a banal factual statement.

Galerie des Machines

The major event in Paris in 1889 was the Exposition Universelle, a celebration of the 100th anniversary of the French Revolution. The exhibition occupied a substantial city site on the border of the 7th and 15th arrondissements, and its crowning glory was Gustave Eiffel's Tower, an icon of French modernity and construction skill. Sadi Carnot (1837–94) headed the exhibition committee from 1887: he was an engineer and politician, in charge of public works from 1880 and President from 1887.[17] His uncle (also Sadi Carnot) formulated the second law of thermodynamics. While this may not appear to be relevant to our composer, it is surely not a coincidence that one of the nicknames by which he referred to himself was 'Monsieur Sadi'; as late as 1917, Satie wrote a letter and separate drawing to Jean Cocteau on 31 August in which he refers to 'Monsieur Sadi'.[18]

The impact of the various colonial artistic displays on composers is well established: Debussy first encountered the gamelan and Annamite theatre at the Exposition, and the young Satie seems to have been particularly drawn to the Romanian folk music display. Annegret Fauser

---

en savoir la cause. L'idée me prit de me distraire en comptant, lentement sur les doigts, de un à deux cent soixante mille.'

[16] Ibid.; 'en un hoquet, tel un petit enfant; "Je vous ai vu par le trou de la serrure."' The story strongly resembles contemporary accounts of Jules Dépaquit's play *Jack in the Box* (1899), discussed in Chapter 1.

[17] John W. Stamper, 'The Galerie des Machines of the 1889 Paris World's Fair.' *Technology and Culture*, vol. 30 no. 2 (1989): pp. 330–53, at p. 335.

[18] See Volta (ed.), *Satie Ecrits*, p. 218. The drawing is reproduced as the front cover of Robert Orledge, *Satie the Composer*. Cambridge: Cambridge University Press, 1990; it is captioned 'Monsieur Sadi dans sa maison. Il songe.' In her notes to *Correspondances presque complète*, Volta writes on p. 945 that Satie refers to himself as 'Monsieur Sadi' for the first time in a letter to the wife of his childhood friend Louis Le Monnier, written on 1 September 1905. She also states: 'Ce sont ses amis catalans, les peintres Rusiñol et Casas, qui l'appellaient « Sadi » au début des années 1890, on ne sait si pour se moquer de leur propre accent hispanique, ou bien par référence au poète arabe Saâdi, à cause de la musique « orientale » que Satie prétendait composer à cette époque.'

Fig. 5.1 Galerie des Machines

writes that 'the Romanian folk ensemble was echoed in one of Erik Satie's *Gnossiennes* (published as no. 5)'[19] and indeed the date of the manuscript score – '8 July 1889' – bears witness to a likely exhibition visit. The German scholar Grete Wehmeyer published Satie's four-bar *Chanson hongroise*, which, as its title may not suggest, was also inspired by this Romanian folk music display.[20]

The Galerie des Machines, situated directly opposite the Eiffel Tower, was the largest of all the exhibition spaces (Fig. 5.1). Joris-Karl Huysmans compared its form to a modern cathedral: 'The interior of this palace produces a superb effect ... The form of the hall is derived from the Gothic, but it is expanded, magnified, prodigious. It would be impossible to realise in stone.'[21]

The Galerie des Machines opened to the public on 6 May 1889 and was the first of the great exhibition sites to feature novel means of transport as a major draw. The building was equipped with a lift, and cars were

---

[19] Annegret Fauser, *Musical Encounters at the 1889 Paris World's Fair*. Rochester, NY: University of Rochester Press, 2005, p. 205.

[20] Grete Wehmeyer, *Erik Satie*. Regensburg: Gustav Bosse, 1974, p. 32.

[21] Cited in Tim Benton, 'Exhibiting Modernity: The 1889 Universal Exhibition and the Eiffel Tower', in Paul Wood (ed.), *The Challenge of the Avant-garde*. New Haven: Yale University Press, 1999, pp. 156–63, at p. 159.

installed on tracks above the exhibits to carry visitors through the building. But the main attraction in the hall was undoubtedly Edison's phonograph. In the 1889 Exposition, 'for the first time, electroacoustic technology became an integral part of an exhibition project conceived as a gigantic taxonomy of human and industrial achievement'.[22]

Traditional French high culture was present in the Galerie des Machines, though only virtually, as opera extracts were transmitted from the Paris Opéra and Opéra-Comique by 'théâtrophone'. These broadcasts attracted a good deal of press attention, mainly because of the novelty of sound being transmitted without the performers being visible.[23] Another attraction was the 'Fanfare Ader', 'the latest electroacoustic creation of the French telephone pioneer, Clément Ader, especially conceived for the 1889 Exposition. On the front of the tower, above the main entrance and the name plaque of the pavilion, a bank of twenty trumpet-shaped receptors alerted passers-by to the sonic possibilities of electronically transmitted and amplified sound. What they heard was a quartet of musicians who sang fanfares into the mouthpieces of the transmitters in the manner of a kazoo.'[24] The receptors ensured the public had the appropriate visual cue to be able to interpret the sound as a fanfare. It appears, therefore, that the exhibition organisers were sensitive to the audience's potential discomfort at encountering sound without a visible human performer.

But most press attention went to Thomas Edison's exhibits. Despite his American nationality, Edison was feted as a French cultural hero, being made a commander of the Légion d'honneur during his visit to the exhibition, and 'a plaque on the top floor of the Eiffel Tower commemorates the dinner that Gustave Eiffel gave in Edison's honor'.[25] The conservative national daily *Le Figaro* reported in detail on a dinner with entertainment held on 26 August 1889 for which Edison was guest of honour. Their journalist said the event was intended to be a 'summary of what there is in Paris that is typical and indicative of national art, and also, thanks to the Exposition, of exotic art'.[26] Fauser writes that

> The performance started with the Romanian lautari [traditional musicians], followed by performances by Parisian artists from the Comédie-Française, the Opéra, and some variété stages. Then came the 'highlight of the program', 'furnished by Edison himself', of a phonograph performance for the guests. After that, the actor Coquelin improvised a comic scene about Edison, and Jeanne

---

[22] Fauser, *Musical Encounters*, p. 279.

[23] Ibid., p. 286.

[24] Ibid., p. 281.

[25] Ibid., p. 302.

[26] Parisis, *Le Figaro*, 21 August 1889, p. 1; cited in ibid., p. 302.

Granier some 'couplets de circonstance' about the phonograph, set to music by [the operetta composer] Gaston Serpette. The evening ended with performances by the Javanese dancers and the *gitana*, La Maccarona. The composition of the program was itself a reflection not only of Edison's place in the 'brotherhood of letters and science', but even more of the ideology of progress as encapsulated in the structure of the evening.[27]

While the young Satie did not have the status or notoriety to be a guest at this event, it is striking how many of his musical and artistic interests are covered in this programme: popular entertainment, exoticism, opera extracts out of context, interart work and mechanical elements.

Former Hydropathes such as Emile Goudeau (the first editor of the *Chat noir* journal) reviewed the Exposition Universelle. What they thought of this adulation of Edison, rather than their old friend Charles Cros, who died in poverty a year before the exhibition without ever seeing his visionary ideas realised by others, can only be guessed.[28]

Satie and left-wing politics

Satie's sympathy with revolutionary political ideals has been little explored.[29] He consistently sympathised, perhaps empathised, with the downtrodden, to the point of giving away money whenever he was threatened with affluence, and he linked progressivism in art with progressive politics. At the same time, his (limited) discussions of politics tend to evidence the whimsy and comic veneer that are absolutely typical of him. This jokey overlay perhaps represents a fear of being taken seriously, a distaste for pretentious discussion, an essential dislike of straightforward debate or – most likely – a combination of these.

Jane Fulcher states that at the Chat Noir 'A strong influence on [Satie] [...] was D[ynam]-V[ictor] Fumet, a pupil of Franck who had lost his scholarship because of his "advanced" musical and political ideas, which

---

[27] Ibid., pp. 302–3.

[28] Goudeau's article 'Une journée de l'Exposition', published in *La Revue illustrée*, 4 (1889), mentions the Romanian performances. Goudeau also wrote on the construction of the Eiffel Tower.

[29] There are two notable exceptions: Jane F. Fulcher, *French Cultural Politics and Music: From the Dreyfus Affair to the First World War*. New York: Oxford University Press, 1999 and Fulcher, *The Composer as Intellectual: Music and Ideology in France, 1914–1940*. New York: Oxford University Press, 2005. Also see Ann-Marie Hanlon, 'Satie and the French Musical Canon: A Reception Study.' Unpublished PhD thesis, University of Newcastle, 2013.

included Anarchist sympathies.'[30] Fumet (1869–1949) was a student at the Paris Conservatoire who performed at the Chat Noir, meeting Satie in 1887. Robert Orledge believes that 'Fumet almost certainly influenced Satie's early music and ideas: he had an active interest in alchemy and the occult, as well as strong anarchist sympathies, from which his nickname "Dynam[ite]" derived. During the 1880s he was a friend of [Peter] Kropotkin and Louise Michel, and he also contributed to the anarchist journal *La révolte*.'[31] His later career, spent largely as an organist in various Paris churches, was built on his reputation as an improviser and was a good deal more conventional musically than his early years in Montmartre might have suggested.

Satie lived from October 1898 in Arcueil, a working-class suburb south of Paris, in a room with no heating or running water. He moved into a room previously occupied by another Montmartre character, the tramp known as Bibi-la-Purée (who was portrayed by the twenty-year-old Picasso in his *Joker* in 1901).[32] The room was an entirely private place for Satie: he never received visitors and would even insist that anyone giving him a lift home dropped him off a few streets away. Amédée Ozenfant took Satie home after a performance of *Socrate* in 1921, and he recalled, 'At the fortifications at the gates of Arcueil he nervously asked us to stop, and he disappeared into the night, turning round every ten metres to reassure himself that we were not following him.'[33] According to André Veyssière, whose family knew Satie well, 'My father said that the only person who entered Satie's room was the launderer Amblard who helped him move in a piano.'[34] Much of the Parisian banlieue (suburbs) was poorly served by public transport. The Métro, which opened in 1900, had few lines that reached the suburbs, and rail companies focused on

---

[30] Fulcher, *French Cultural Politics and Music*, p. 196.

[31] Robert Orledge, 'Fumet, Dynam-Victor.' *Grove Music Online. Oxford Music Online*, http://www.oxfordmusiconline.com/subscriber/article/grove/music/10383 (accessed 8 January 2015).

[32] According to Léon-Louis Veyssière the name Bibi-la-Purée 'avait ici un double sens. Il caractérisait l'état de misère lamentable du pauvre type et son amour immodéré pour l'absinthe qu'il consommait généralement pure (et qu'on appelait alors «une purée»). See *Réflexions et anecdotes sur Erik Satie par Léon-Louis Veyssière*. Preface by Annette Le Bonhomme-Veyssière. Cachan: Litavis, 2013, p. 10. The tramp's real name was André Salis; he was related to Rodolphe Salis, the proprietor of the Chat Noir.

[33] Amédée Ozenfant, *Mémoires, 1886–1962*. Paris: Seghers, 1968, p. 110: 'Aux fortifications, près de la porte d'Arcueil, nerveusement, il nous le fit arrêter, et il s'enfonça dans la nuit en se retournant tous les dix mètres pour s'assurer que nous ne le suivions pas.'

[34] Veyssière, *Réflexions et anecdotes*, p. 26: 'J'ai entendu dire par mon père que le seul qui était entré chez Satie, c'était le blanchisseur Amblard qui avait donné un coup de main pour entrer un piano.'

profitable long-distance routes. Arcueil was well beyond the southern limit of the Métro network but was unusual in that it was on a commuter line to Paris. However, Satie often missed the last train, which departed around 1 a.m.

By the turn of the twentieth century, the Paris suburbs were a left-wing 'red belt' around the city. Colin Jones notes that working-class living conditions were even worse in the suburbs than in Paris in this period, as 'nine out of ten homes within Paris had piped water; in many banlieue locations the figure was between a fifth and a third'. Poor living conditions, coupled with increasing mechanisation in factories and the resultant deskilling of workers, meant that 'workers in the banlieue were increasingly drawn to left-wing political movements, notably socialism, militant unionism and revolutionary syndicalism'. The bourgeois inhabitants of Paris feared this suburban 'red belt': contemporary newspapers show that moral panics about crime and dissolution in the banlieue were commonplace.[35]

It is in this context that Blaise Cendrars' interesting comments about Satie must be understood. In a radio interview in 1950, the author recalled: 'The thing I found attractive [about Satie] was his suburban side. He lived in the suburbs. He was a Communist at a time when nobody else was. He was the conductor of the local choir in Arcueil-Cachan. He was extremely shy.'[36] Perhaps in Cendrars' Parisian artistic milieu, 'nobody' was a Communist, but in the red belt of Paris suburbs, political engagement well to the left of centre was the mainstream. When he first moved to Arcueil, Satie had little contact with local people, but his interest in social and political life in Arcueil was stimulated by friendship with members of the Templier and Veyssière families. Alexandre Templier was a militant Socialist radical and director of the local newspaper, *L'Avenir d'Arcueil-Cachan,*[37] which was published from 1908 to 1914 and is described on its masthead as an 'organe du parti socialiste et radical-socialiste'. An architect by profession, he was the father of Pierre-Daniel Templier, author of the first substantial biography of Satie which was published in November 1932. Léon-Louis Veyssière (1875–1955), a painter and decorator who later took over his parents-in-law's business selling animal fodder, was a neighbour of Satie in rue Cauchy and a fellow member of the Socialist Party. His memoirs and those of his son

---

[35] Colin Jones, *Paris: Biography of a City*. London: Allen Lane, 2004, pp. 491–2.

[36] Robert Orledge (ed.), *Satie Remembered*. London: Faber, 1995, p. 132 (translated by Roger Nichols). The interview was broadcast on Radio France on 3 July 1950.

[37] Volta (ed.), *Correspondance*, p. 128: 'sa participation, de plus en plus intense, à la vie sociale et politique d'Arcueil, sous l'influence de l'architecte Alexandre Templier, militant radical-socialiste et directeur de l'organe local de ce parti, *L'Avenir d'Arcueil-Cachan.*'

André, published in 2013, give us insights into little-known aspects of the composer's life. Veyssière also had strong interests in local history, founding a history club 'Les Amis du Vieil Arcueil' in 1911 whose president was Alexandre Templier, then the town's mayor.[38]

Léon-Louis Veyssière recalls the first time he and Satie exchanged words:

> At the end of 1899 or very early in 1900, one evening, some friends and I were talking on the pavement on rue Cauchy. Satie, I don't know how, joined in the conversation. I forget the topic we were discussing that evening, but I do remember that he started having a go at religion, at priests which he called Vobiscums, religious services which he called Vobiscrap, and finally, the army and officers whom he called officensors. His diatribe, half-serious and half-joking, amused me very much.

After this conversation, Veyssière 'concluded that Satie was anti-religious, which was not the case, and anti-militarist, which was true and in keeping with his personality'.[39] Satie's attitude to religion is not easy to fathom, but evidence suggests that he combined strong interests in spirituality, church buildings and Gothic paraphernalia with a distrust of organised religion. His childhood experiences may well have influenced him: he was originally baptised into the Protestant denomination, following his Scottish mother's wishes, but after her death when Satie was aged six, his paternal grandparents had him rebaptised a Catholic. Organised religion was therefore, for him, surely associated with family conflict. And there is one revealing remark about his view of military engagement on the front cover of a sketchbook which dates from around World War I as it contains material for *Trois poèmes d'amour* (1914) and *Sonnerie pour réveiller le Bon Gros Roi des Singes* (1921): 'Certainly, the Germans are unpleasant & repeat themselves. So, why would we want to kick them in the backside? What century [are we in]? All this [the war] is just a sort of end of the world, but more stupid than the real one. Let's have indulgence, even for our

---

[38] Veyssière, *Réflexions et anecdotes*, pp. 21–2.

[39] Ibid., p. 12: 'A la fin de 1899 ou tout au début de 1900, un soir que quelques amis et moi bavardions sur le trottoir de la rue Cauchy, Satie, je ne sais trop comment, vint se mêler à notre conversation. J'ai oublié le sujet qui nous occupait ce soir-là, mais je me souviens qu'il partit en une charge à fond contre la religion, les curés qu'il appelait des Vobiscums, les offices religieux qu'il qualifiait de vobisconneries, et enfin, l'armée et les officiers qu'il appelait les officenseurs. Sa charge, mi-sérieuse mi-humoristique, m'avait beaucoup amusé'; 'Je concluais que Satie était anti-religieux, ce qui était inexact, et anti-militariste, ce qui était vrai et conforme à sa caractère.'

enemies; & let's not forget to turn the other cheek, always the other cheek. With this gesture, we will be morally stronger.'[40]

Satie's political and civic engagement moved to another level in 1908 when he became a member of the Comité Radical et Radical-Socialiste d'Arcueil-Cachan. As Fulcher puts it, he joined 'the largest and most important political party in France between 1901 and 1914, the first large party on a national scale. [...] A major component of its doctrine was the strict separation of Church and state, making it all the more ironic that it could recruit a member fresh from the Schola Cantorum.'[41] Satie always ensured that his relationships, whether personal or professional, were kept within boundaries which, as much as possible, were never breached. His increasing participation in community life in Arcueil coincided with his studies at the Schola Cantorum (which he entered in 1905) and it might be argued that this demonstrated a deliberate desire on Satie's part to 'balance' his strict harmony and counterpoint studies at a school renowned as a training ground for church organists and composers with his distinctly secular interests in Arcueil. In 1908 Satie also co-founded the Patronage laïque d'Arcueil-Cachan, whose aim was 'to ensure that children of both sexes are taken away from the dangers of the streets by developing, in groups, a spirit of friendship and solidarity, and by providing them with entertainment which is suited to their age and temperament'. Satie himself organised the opening festivities of this institution on 20 December 1908, which were attended by 150 adults and 200 children.[42]

The composer's contribution to cultural life and youth club activities in Arcueil was twofold: he led music classes and took groups of children for countryside visits. Léon-Louis Veyssière recalls that 'for some years, on Thursdays and Sundays, he took care of children; for adults, too, he

---

[40] Front cover of sketchbook housed in Bibliothèque Nationale de France (Ms 9615(4)): 'Les allemands, certes, sont désagréables & se répètent. Aussi, pourquoi voulons-nous les acculer? Quel siècle? Tout cela n'est qu'une sorte de fin du Monde, mais plus bête que la véritable. Ayons de la mansuétude, même pour nos ennemis; & n'oublions pas de tendre l'autre joue, toujours l'autre joue. Par ce geste nous serons moralement plus fort.'

[41] Fulcher, *French Cultural Politics and Music*, p. 201.

[42] Volta (ed.), *Correspondance*, p. 129: 'Satie contribue également à la fondation du Patronage laïque d'Arcueil-Cachan, qui se propose de «soustraire aux dangers de la rue les enfants des deux sexes, de développer, en les groupant, leur esprit de camaraderie et de solidarité, et de leur procurer les distractions nécessaires à leur âge et à leur tempérament» (novembre). Il organise lui-même la fête d'inauguration de cette institution à laquelle vont participer «cent cinquante personnes et deux cents enfants» (20 décembre).'

conducted a choir'.⁴³ Fulcher is right to emphasise that his solfège (ear training) classes took place on Sunday mornings, 'a time when good Catholic children were in church'.⁴⁴ And the Schola Cantorum student had to apologise in writing to Vincent d'Indy on 3 May 1908 for handing in an analysis exam paper late, the reason being his increasing political engagement. In the words of Ornella Volta, 'On this date, 3 May, the name "M. Satie, music composer" appeared among the signatures of a "Call for voters" – alongside a launderer, a binder, a joiner, a writer and a dyer – published in L'Avenir d'Arcueil-Cachan.'⁴⁵ Whatever Satie's involvement in the local elections, they were not successful for the Socialist Party: L'Humanité reported on 5 May 1908 that 'only M. Veyssière was elected' from the party's list of candidates in this area.⁴⁶

Some of Satie's café-concert friends from Montmartre came to Arcueil to entertain local audiences. Vincent Hyspa and Paulette Darty both performed for the Cercle lyrique et théâtral in Arcueil on 24 October 1909, an event which was promoted in L'Humanité on the same day (though Satie is not mentioned).⁴⁷ On this occasion Darty premiered Satie's song 'La Chemise', to a text by Jules Dépaquit.⁴⁸ The song was successfully reprised in the Scala, the leading Paris café-concert venue, and a critique was published in L'Avenir d'Arcueil-Cachan on 21 November 1909: 'Mlle Paulette Darty, at the Scala, has recently given the first performance of a delightful fantasy by Dépaquit called La Chemise, which our friend Satie has embroidered with lively and graceful tunes which will soon be on everyone's lips. Every evening Performer, Author, and Composer receive deserved acclamation.'⁴⁹ This review appears under a reminder that 'M. Satie's solfège lessons take place every Sunday morning at 9 a.m.' The text is unsigned and one might surmise that Satie himself was the author.

---

[43] Veyssière, Réflexions et anecdotes, p. 7: 'pendant quelques années, jeudis et dimanches, il prendra les enfants en charge; les adultes aussi, qu'il fera chanter en chœur'.

[44] Fulcher, French Cultural Politics and Music, p. 202.

[45] Volta (ed.), Correspondance, p. 913: 'S'il a pris du retard [avec son examen d'analyse] – ce dont il s'excuse ici –, c'est à cause de son tout récent engagement politique. Ce même 3 mai, en effet, le nom de «M. Satie, compositeur de musique», figure – à côté d'un blanchisseur, d'un relieur, d'un menuisier, d'un homme de lettres et d'un coloriste – parmi les signataires d'un «Appel aux électeurs», publié dans L'Avenir d'Arcueil-Cachan, organe de la section arcueillaise du parti radical et radical-socialiste.'

[46] L'Humanité, 5 May 1908, p. 2; 'Liste Veyssière en tête. Seul M. Veyssière est élu.'

[47] Ibid., 24 October 1909, p. 4; see also Volta (ed.), Satie Ecrits, p. 284.

[48] Whiting, Satie the Bohemian, p. 337.

[49] Ibid., p. 340; citing Nigel Wilkins' translation in The Writings of Erik Satie. London: Eulenburg, 1980, p. 161.

According to Ornella Volta, 'When they discovered, much later, that Erik Satie composed another type of music, the Arcueil residents were amazed. He was only known to them as a composer of café-concert music.'[50] Such was Satie's ability to compartmentalise his life.

Léon-Louis Veyssière recalled that 'Satie undertook his tasks with remarkable enthusiasm. Every Thursday and Sunday, he was on duty. He started up an ear training course; he was the pianist for the dance classes, he taught choral singing to families, he rehearsed local amateur performers who were involved in the festivities we organised.'[51] While Satie was happy to propose events and excursions to the Arcueil community, he found membership of the Patronage laïque something of a trial. He tried unsuccessfully to resign from the organisation in January 1909, and the definitive break came on 15 March 1910 when he wrote to Alexandre Templier:

> I must inform you that I am resigning – completely and definitively – from the Patronage laïque d'Arcueil-Cachan.
> Why?
> I no longer want to be a member of a charity whose treasurer disposes of the funds paid to the organisation as he wishes – whatever motives he might have;
> I do not want to be part of an administrative council which accepts that an outsider to the council attends discussions and is allowed, via despicable bribery, to twist facts and turn them against me, I who am the Director named by the General Assembly and sole representative of the administrative council in the interior service.[52]

---

[50] Volta (ed.), *Satie Ecrits*, p. 284: 'En découvrant, beaucoup plus tard, qu'Erik Satie était l'auteur d'un autre genre de musique, les Arcueillais furent bien étonnés. Il ne s'était jamais fait connaître auprès d'eux autrement que comme compositeur de caf'-conc.'

[51] Veyssière, *Réflexions et anecdotes*, p. 13: 'Satie s'acquittait de sa mission avec un zèle remarquable. Tous les jeudis et tous les dimanches, il assura le service de garde. Il avait créé un cours de solfège; il tenait le piano au cours de danse, il apprenait des chœurs aux familles, il faisait répéter les amateurs locaux qui prêtaient leur concours aux fêtes que nous organisions.'

[52] Letter reproduced in Volta (ed.), *Correspondance*, p. 138: 'Je dois vous faire savoir que je me retire – complètement et définitivement – du Patronage laïque d'Arcueil-Cachan. ¶ Le motif? ¶ Je ne veux pas faire partie plus longtemps d'une œuvre dont le trésorier dispose à sa guise – quels qu'en soient les mobiles – des fonds qui lui sont remis; ¶ je ne veux pas faire partie d'un Conseil d'administration qui admet qu'un étranger au Conseil assiste aux délibérations et se permette de dénaturer, par un colportage méprisable, les faits discutés et de les tourner contre moi, moi, Directeur

Satie marked the envelope 'Private' in red ink. Despite his resignation, Satie wrote to the mayor, Louis-Grégoire Veyssière (a cousin of Léon-Louis), on 4 August 1910 proposing another summer outing for a dozen children.[53] Later that decade, Satie struggled with membership of the Nouveaux Jeunes, eventually tendering his resignation although he continued to support many young composers in the group. Satie was never a natural group member.

It was through the Arcueil political-cultural world that, in 1909, Satie received a national decoration: Palmes académiques for 'services civiques', awarded by the Prefect of the Seine for distinguished contributions to education or culture.[54] The distinction was recorded in the *Journal officiel de la République française. Lois et décrets*, though unfortunately his surname in this official record has a typographical error: 'Satié (Eric-Alfred-Leslie), membre du patronage laïque d'Arcueil-Cachan (Seine)'.[55] Veyssière notes Satie's attitude towards this decoration, an attitude that was as contradictory as one might expect:

> Satie had a sovereign disdain for titles, distinctions and prizes, yet he was peculiarly insistent about obtaining the Palmes académiques, nagging anyone who could help him obtain this minor award. When his friends from the patronage organised a celebratory wine reception to hand him the medal in silver set with rubies and the framed diploma, his joy was truly childlike. One day, when for the third or fourth time he had resigned from the patronage, he only agreed to come back on condition that the administrative council conferred on him the title of 'Director of interior services of the patronage laïque'.[56]

Veyssière and his family almost never discussed music with Satie,

---

nommé par l'Assemblée Générale et seul représentant du Conseil d'Administration dans le Service intérieur.'

[53] Ibid., p. 139.

[54] For details about the distinction and images of the award, see http://www.frenchacademicpalms.org/information.html (accessed 6 April 2015).

[55] *Journal officiel de la République française. Lois et décrets*, 1 August 1909, p. 8348.

[56] Veyssière, *Réflexions et anecdotes*, p. 15: 'Satie affichait un souverain dédain à l'égard des titres, des distinctions, des prix, mais il mit cependant une singulière insistance pour obtenir les palmes académiques, harcelant ceux qui pouvaient l'aider à obtenir cette mince décoration. ¶ Quelle joie enfantine fut la sienne lorsque les amis du patronage organisèrent un vin d'honneur pour lui remettre les insignes de cette distinction en argent, sertie de rubis avec le diplôme dûment encadré. ¶ Un jour que pour la troisième ou quatrième fois il avait donné sa démission du patronage, il ne consentit à revenir qu'à la condition que le conseil d'administration lui confère le titre de « Directeur des services intérieurs du patronage laïque. »'

though Satie demonstrated the properties of sound to Léon-Louis by teaching him at night to distinguish musical notes by hitting the gutter with his umbrella.[57] And both Léon-Louis Veyssière and his son André, then aged about seventeen, attended the performance of Max Jacob's play *Ruffian toujours, truand jamais* on 8 March 1920 which featured Satie's furniture music in the entr'actes, one of few moments when his Arcueil and Paris worlds were joined. André Veyssière provides a rare eyewitness account of the evening:

> If it's true that we rarely talked about music in Arcueil, one evening my father was invited to listen to 'furniture music' in Poiret's salon. I was invited too and that evening I accompanied my father on this extraordinary outing. We wandered around Poiret's house and there was music in every room. There was bright lighting and lots of people chatting. People were minding their own business. Impressed, slightly ill at ease among the many guests, we listened and watched with curiosity. Satie then told us not to pay attention to the musicians and not to listen, because it was 'furniture music'.[58]

This was music for use, not music as an artistic experience: the very unpretentiousness of Satie's furniture music in high-society surroundings evinces a political dimension.

From 3 October 1909 until 19 June 1910, Satie (anonymously) contributed a column 'La Quinzaine des Sociétés', a fortnightly roundup of clubs and societies in the town, to *L'Avenir d'Arcueil-Cachan*.[59] His columns promote the many local societies, including a group allegedly devoted to temperance, the 'Rigolos' ('Jokers') and a society of people who, like Satie, hailed from Normandy, though it was clearly a broad-minded organisation as it also welcomed members of Canadian origin. His favourite café, run by Douau, is often mentioned. The newspaper even promoted a 'Groupe Satie' in its number of 2 October 1910; Satie

---

[57] Volta (ed.), *Satie Ecrits*, p. 283.

[58] Veyssière, *Réflexions et anecdotes*, pp. 25–6: 'S'il est vrai que nous parlions peu de musique à Arcueil, un soir quand même, mon père fut invité à écouter de la «musique d'ameublement» dans les salons, chez Poiret, j'avais été invité également et ce soir-là j'accompagnai mon père à cette sortie extraordinaire. On a fait notre petit tour dans la maison de Poiret et ... il y avait de la musique dans toutes les pièces. Il y avait beaucoup de lumière et beaucoup de monde qui bavardait. Les gens s'occupaient de leurs affaires. Impressionné, un peu mal à l'aise parmi ces nombreux invités, nous écoutions et regardions avec curiosité. Satie nous a dit alors de ne pas faire attention aux musiciens et de ne pas écouter, c'était de la «musique d'ameublement».' The couturier Paul Poiret owned several buildings on a corner site, including the Galerie Barbazanges where the performance took place.

[59] These columns are reprinted in Volta (ed.), *Satie Ecrits*, pp. 123–30.

had 'accepted to give his name to a group of twelve children from Arcueil (six boys and six girls) whom he proposed to take on an excursion every summer, thanks to donations from some Parisian ladies of his acquaintance'.[60] Many of his 1910 columns promote then-novel film screenings in a local venue. Although these columns are unsigned, Satie's huckster style combined with his perpetual interest in matters medical is unmistakable:

> *Crazy madman*: Because he can't go to the wonderful and hilarious cinematographic events which take place every Saturday at 8.45 p.m. at M. Ollinger-Jacob's superb salons, an unfortunate gentleman is being locked up. M. Ollinger-Jacob is a philanthropist and also a benefactor of suffering humanity: he cures, through skilful thermo-cinematographic sessions, the most incurable cases of hypochondria and acute depression. Many letters and testimonies. It's good to know.[61]

Satie's political involvement was essentially practical in nature in the sense that he was an active participant in community efforts to improve the lives of young people. His combination of poverty and indifference towards money was genuine: the middle-class virtues of thrift and putting money aside for a rainy day were completely alien to him. This aspect of his practical politics was mentioned in the obituary by Léon-Louis Veyssière published in the *Journal d'Arcueil*: 'Devoid of all mercantile spirit, Satie showed a total indifference towards money, only living for his art, like a real bohemian, of whom he was without doubt, the final representative.'[62] André Veyssière recalls: 'From my window in rue Cauchy, I sometimes saw Monsieur Satie passing by and all the children came to say hello to him. He rummaged in his pouch and handed out

---

[60] Ibid., p. 284: '[Satie] a accepté de donner son nom à un groupe de douze enfants arcueillais (six petits garçons et six petites filles) qu'il se proposer d'emmener, chaque été, en excursion, grâce aux dons de quelques dames parisiennes de ses amies.'

[61] Ibid., p. 129; originally published in *L'Avenir d'Arcueil-Cachan*, 57 (16 January 1910), p. 3: '*Fou furieux* parce qu'il ne peut assister aux magnifiques et hilarantes séances cinématographiques que donne, tous les samedis, à 8h¾, M. Ollinger-Jacob, dans ses superbes salons, on interne un malheureux. ¶ M. Ollinger-Jacob est un philanthrope doublée d'un bienfaiteur de l'Humanité souffrante; il guérit, par d'habiles séances thermo-cinématographiques, les cas les plus incurables d'hypocondrie et de neurasthénie aiguë. Nombreuses lettres et attestations. ¶ C'est bon à savoir.'

[62] Léon-Louis Veyssière, 'Nécrologie', *Journal d'Arcueil*, July 1925, p. 1: 'Débarrassé de tout esprit mercantile, Satie montrait une indifférence totale pour l'argent, ne vivant que pour son art, comme un vrai bohème dont il était sans doute, le dernier représentant.'

all the small coins he might have. Sometimes, he surely didn't have enough left to buy lunch.'[63] He also remembered that Satie had a pupil in Limours and sometimes walked home to Arcueil: 'On many occasions it was suggested that the driver take him back home, but he preferred to return on foot rather than being driven without giving a tip. Certainly, generosity and Satie went together.'[64] This was perhaps not 'generosity' to the driver but a desire not to take a taxi if he did not have any spare change (perhaps because he was in the habit of giving it to children). The approximate distance of Limours to Arcueil is thirty-four kilometres.

While Satie's personal involvement in Arcueil affairs diminished after 1910, a change which coincided with his increasing reputation as a composer and greater involvement in the Montparnasse cultural scene, he retained an interest in left-wing politics. But how seriously did Satie take party politics? Nobody will be surprised to learn that his attitudes were ambiguous and complex. Léon-Louis Veyssière, for one, 'never took Satie's political convictions seriously. When I knew him, he was on the radical and radical-socialist committee. I always thought that he joined that group because he met the main militants of that section at Geng's [bar] and he called them the "zinc committee" although I never knew why.'[65] (The bar would have been made of zinc.) But Satie did not view his political activity simply as an opportunity to socialise with his Arcueil drinking companions. Veyssière recalls that 'after joining the radical socialist committee [Satie] always attended meetings. He even stood at the local elections of November 1919 and then followed the new Communist Party at the creation of the 3rd [*recte*: 2nd] international.'[66]

[63] Veyssière, *Réflexions et anecdotes*, p. 24: 'De ma fenêtre, rue Cauchy, je voyais parfois Monsieur Satie qui passait et tous les enfants venaient lui dire bonjour. Il fouillait dans son gousset et tous les petits sous qu'il pouvait avoir, il les distribuait. Quelquefois même, il n'en avait certainement pas pour aller déjeuner.'

[64] Ibid., p. 25: 'Plusieurs fois on lui a proposé que le chauffeur allait le reconduire et bien, il préférait revenir à pied plutôt que de se faire véhiculer sans donner un pourboire. Certainement la générosité et Satie, ça ne faisait qu'un.'

[65] Ibid., p. 16: 'Je n'ai jamais pris les convictions politiques de Satie au sérieux. Lorsque je l'ai connu, il était au comité radical et radical-socialiste. J'ai toujours pensée qu'il était entré dans cette formation parce qu'il avait côtoyé, chez Geng, les principaux militants de ce groupement qu'il qualifiait de comité de zinc sans d'ailleurs que j'aie jamais su pourquoi.'

[66] Ibid., pp. 7–8: 'après avoir adhéré au comité radical-socialiste, il assiste toutefois aux réunions de la SFIO, à laquelle il adhère. Il se présentera même aux élections municipales de novembre 1919 puis suivra le jeune parti communiste à la création de la 3ème internationale.' Veyssière is mistaken about the World Congress designation (the 2nd World Congress of the Communist International took place in summer 1920 in Moscow, and the 3rd International was in 1921, after Satie joined the Party).

Indeed, astonishing though this may seem, in 1919 Satie was a candidate for office in Arcueil's municipal council. Why he made this decision at a time when he was involved with several projects in Paris is a mystery. Ornella Volta writes: 'For his address to the electorate he spoke – to the Arcueil division of the French Section of the Workers' International, to a mostly working-class audience – of the prejudices one should avoid when making an artistic critique, for instance when visiting the Louvre.' Perhaps Satie thought that one should not patronise an audience by making assumptions about their interests. He was most certainly someone who was happy to mix with people from very different social (and political) backgrounds without finding it necessary to moderate his behaviour or opinions. However, this speech may also show Satie's essential lack of interest in standing for office: was he press-ganged by fellow Party members into adding his name to the list to fulfil a requirement for a certain number of candidates? In any event, 'he only obtained 187 votes, not enough to be elected. Many of his worker comrades considered he was a "reactionary" because he also mixed with Parisian nobility.'[67] Sadly, the electors of Arcueil did not give us the opportunity to find out how Satie would have behaved as a local councillor.

Satie was interested enough in left-wing politics to change his party allegiance more than once. When France was on the brink of World War I 'Satie's response to the assassination of Jean Jaurès on July 31, 1914' was to join 'the internationalist French Socialist party [on 1 August]'.[68] Veyssière provides important clarification on this decision: 'When, a few days before the outbreak of World War I, he joined the socialist section, I believe it was mainly because the party had campaigned against the "three-year law". Satie had served as a volunteer and he was very sincerely antimilitarist.' Indeed, Jaurès was a staunch antimilitarist who opposed Emile Driant's 1913 law about the extension of military service to three years and who sought a peaceful resolution when Europe was on the brink of World War I. But things are never straightforward with Satie, as Veyssière continued: 'I know through friends that he was never a very active militant in the radical party and I was rather surprised to see him ridicule people who, in that period, campaigned in favour of Francisco Ferrer [a Spanish free-thinker who was executed in 1909],

---

[67] Volta (ed.), *Correspondance*, pp. 351–2: 'En guise de discours électoral, il parle – dans la section arcueillaise de la S.F.I.O., devant un auditoire en majorité prolétaire – des préjugés qu'il faut éviter lorsqu'on porte un jugement artistique: en visitant le Louvre, par exemple. Il ne récoltera que 187 voix, insuffisantes pour être élu, plusieurs de ses camarades ouvriers jugeant comme «réactionnaire» le fait qu'il fréquente en même temps la noblesse parisienne.'

[68] Fulcher, *French Cultural Politics and Music*, p. 204.

an affair which greatly concerned people who were passionate about freedom.'[69]

Satie became a member of the Communist Party following the Congrès de Tours of 25–30 December 1920 when the Parti Socialiste split in two. Jean Hugo, a descendant of the great author who married Satie's close friend Valentine Gross in 1919, remembered that Satie 'reproached [Hugo's] grandmother Mme Ménard-Dorien for remaining a socialist. He asked Hugo "So, is your grandmother still on the side of the priests?"'[70] Satie's change of allegiance to the Communist Party was an independent decision which was not mirrored by his Arcueil comrades. A card he wrote to Léon-Louis Veyssière on 8 January 1921 states, 'I am an old Bolshevist and cannot be on your side. But I like you all the same and hope we will not be on bad terms because of this.'[71]

Two of Satie's Party membership cards survive, showing his continuing and evolving political engagement in the last years of his life. His 1920 card, number 4543, is for the Parti Socialiste, Fédération d'Arcueil-Cachan, and has twelve stamps on its inner back cover which prove that Satie paid his membership dues. The first of its declarations notes that 'The Socialist Party is a class-based party whose aim is to socialise the means of production and exchange, that is to transform capitalist society into a collectivist and communist society, by means of the economic and political organisation of the proletariat. [...] The Socialist Party [...] is not a party of reform, but a party of class struggle and of revolution.'[72]

---

[69] Veyssière, *Réflexions et anecdotes*, p. 16: 'Lorsque, quelques jours avant la guerre de 1914, il a donné son adhésion à la section socialiste, c'est surtout, je crois, parce que le parti avait mené campagne contre la «loi des trois ans». Satie avait fait son volontariat et il était très sincèrement antimilitariste. Je sais par des amis qu'il ne fut jamais un militant très actif du parti radical et j'étais assez surpris de le voir ridiculiser ceux qui, à cette époque, menaient campagne en faveur de Francisco Ferrer [libre penseur espagnol, exécuté en 1909], affaire qui passionnait ceux qui étaient épris de liberté.'

[70] François Porcile, *La belle époque de la musique française*. Paris: Fayard, 1999, pp. 120–1; citing Jean Hugo, *Le regard de la mémoire*. Paris: Actes Sud, 1983, p. 157: 'Jean Hugo se souvient qu'il reprochait toujours à sa grand-mère, Mme Ménard-Dorian, d'être restée socialiste. «Alors, votre bonne grand-mère, me demandait-il, toujours dans les curés?»'

[71] Reproduced in facsimile in Veyssière, *Réflexions et anecdotes*, p. 31: 'Je suis un vieux bolcheviste & ne puis être des vôtres. Je vous aime quand même, & j'espère que nous ne seront [sic] pas fâchés pour cela. Bien à vous. Erik Satie.'

[72] The cards are now housed in IMEC, catalogue number SAT 15.36. 'Le Parti socialiste est un parti de classe qui a pour but de socialiser les moyens de production et d'échange, c'est-à-dire de transformer la société capitaliste en une société collectiviste ou communiste, et pour moyen l'organisation

Satie's 1922 Communist Party membership card, number 8756, again includes stamps, with a hammer and sickle design, showing that he was a fully paid-up member. The thirty-two-page text in the red covers of this membership card is twice the length of that in the Parti Socialiste card; pages 23–32 outline the Party rules voted at an extraordinary national congress on 15–17 May 1921. The first of these articles calls for 'Understanding and international action by workers; the political and economic organisation of the proletariat as a class-based party for the conquest of power by fighting against the bourgeoisie; and, through proletarian dictatorship, the socialisation of the means of production and exchange, that is to say the transformation of capitalist society into a communist society.'[73]

While these decisions to adhere to political parties may give the impression that Satie took a serious interest in the background and policies of particular left-wing movements, Veyssière believes that this was not entirely true. In fact, Veyssière himself offered to lend the composer a copy of Marx's *Das Kapital* and was surprised when Satie turned him down: 'He defended himself energetically and added under his breath: "I don't like these boring shits." Satie's language was usually clean. "Boring shits" was one of the few curse words he used.'[74] While *Das Kapital* was surely an overly ambitious choice of primary reading matter on socialism, it is surprising to hear that Satie, who generally showed a wide-ranging intellectual curiosity, rejected Veyssière's offer in such forthright terms.

Satie was a regular attender but not an active participant in Party meetings. Veyssière notes that Satie 'always arrived very late, with a cigar in his mouth and a cane in his hand, because the umbrella is a myth: one saw him far more often with a cane.' He also left early, without voting on the resolutions which had been discussed, and Veyssière said 'I never once heard him say anything' at meetings.[75] And Satie surely mystified his political comrades when he made characteristically quixotic gestures. The Third Republic (1870–1940) was a politically unstable period of

---

économique et politique du prolétariat. [...] le Parti socialiste [...] n'est pas un parti de réforme, mais un parti de lutte de classes et de révolution.'

[73] 'Entente et action internationale des travailleurs; organisation politique et économique du prolétariat en parti de classe pour la conquête du pouvoir de haute lutte sur la bourgeoisie, et la socialisation, par la dictature prolétarienne, des moyens de production et d'échange, c'est-à-dire la transformation de la société capitaliste en une société communiste.'

[74] Veyssière, *Réflexions et anecdotes*, p. 16: 'Il s'en défendit énergiquement en ajoutant sur le ton de la confidence: «je n'aime pas ces emmerdeurs». Satie était en général, correct dans ses propos. «Emmerdeur» était une des rares grossièretés qu'il employait.'

[75] Ibid., pp. 16–17: 'Il arrivait toujours fort tard, le cigare à la bouche et la canne à la main car le parapluie est une légende, on le voyait bien plus souvent avec une canne. [...] Jamais je ne l'ai entendu prendre la parole.'

French history with constantly shifting coalitions and no fewer than eighty-seven prime ministers, some of whom were in office for only a few weeks. Satie thought that he and his comrades could do the job just as well. Veyssière recalls,

> During periods of ministerial crisis, Satie on several occasions proposed to the Head of State that he should form the government. He chose his fellow members from Arcueil residents, naturally without consulting them. [...] During a presidential election, he formed a committee to present me as candidate for this high office, a committee of which he was the head with Douau [owner of Satie's favourite bar in Arcueil] as second in command. There I was, a member-candidate of this committee, without the means of voting or similar. He invested his hopes in a meeting he organised at Douau's bar. He printed out summonses which he sent to several parliamentarians, only some of them because, as he put it, many of these gentlemen were of no importance and besides, Douau didn't have enough chairs for everyone. On the night of the meeting, the three of us awaited everyone in vain before going our separate ways. Satie declared that none of us should pay for drinks – those who were absent should pay the bill. It was certainly Douau who ended up footing the bill for the evening.[76]

Satie wrote one article for the Communist daily newspaper *L'Humanité* (its concluding words suggest it was to be the first of a series, though it stands alone in his writings). The article shows Satie directly addressing a specific audience and is a rare example of him linking music with political engagement:

---

[76] Ibid., pp. 19–20: 'A l'occasion de crises ministérielles, Satie a plusieurs fois proposé ses services au chef de l'Etat pour la formation du gouvernement. Il choisissait ses collaborateurs parmi les habitants d'Arcueil et naturellement, sans les consulter. [...] Lors d'une élection présidentielle, il avait formé un comité pour présenter ma candidature à cette haute fonction, comité dont il s'était octroyé la présidence avec Douau comme suppléant. Moi, j'étais là-dedans, membre-candidat, sans voix consultative ou tout au moins, quelque chose d'approchant. Il avait fondé de grands espoirs sur une réunion qu'il avait organisé chez Douau. Il avait fait imprimer des convocations qu'il avait adressées à quelques parlementaires, à quelques-uns seulement parce que, disait-il, beaucoup de ces messieurs étaient insignifiants et d'autre part, Douau n'avait pas assez de chaises pour les asseoir tous. Au soir dit, nous avons vainement attendu tous les trois, avant de nous séparer. Satie déclara qu'il n'appartenait à aucun d'entre nous de régler les consommations et que c'était aux absents de régler l'addition. C'est très certainement Douau qui a fait les frais de cette soirée.'

When combating an '*advanced*' idea in Politics or Art, all means are good – especially low ones. '*New*' artists – who 'change something' – are well aware that their enemies attacked, and continue to attack, new trends and new visions which they do not understand. Art is like Politics in this sense: Jaurès was attacked, as were Manet, Berlioz, Wagner, Picasso, Verlaine and so many others. [...] In this newspaper I want to defend my composer comrades who belong to 'advanced' music factions. It seems good and useful to do that here, in an environment for which I feel affection and of which I naturally am a part. Isn't it natural that an 'advanced' artist should be 'advanced' in politics? Yes, isn't it? [...]

A radical in music, Debussy was far from being a political and social radical. This artistic revolutionary was very bourgeois in his life. He didn't like the 'eight-hour day' or other social innovations. I can assure you of this. Raises in salary – other than for him – were not very agreeable to him. He had his own 'point of view.' A strange anomaly.

I can tell you – and it's a pleasure to do so – that *young* composers are more likely to share our opinions. They're '*getting there.*' What we want does not frighten them. That's progress – don't you think? They note that there ought to be a connection between their artistic aspirations and social convictions.

At the end of the article, Satie writes that in subsequent pieces he will write about young composers, 'and I will be happy if my efforts can help the development of musical culture in our great Socialist family, an exquisite family which I love with all my heart'.[77] When Satie learned of

---

[77] Erik Satie, 'Notes sur la Musique moderne'; original in *L'Humanité*, 11 October 1919, pp. 1–2, reproduced in Volta (ed.), *Ecrits*, pp. 49–50: "Pour combattre une idée « *avancée* » en Politique ou en Art, tous les moyens sont bons – surtout les moyens bas. Les artistes « *neufs* » – qui « changent quelque chose » – connaissent les attaques que de tous temps leurs ennemis dirigèrent et dirigent contre la nouveauté des tendances – des visions – qu'ils ne comprennent pas. ¶ Il en est en Art comme en Politique: Jaurès a été attaquée comme l'ont été Manet, Berlioz, Wagner, Picasso, Verlaine et tant d'autres. [...] J'ai le désir de défendre dans ce journal ceux de mes camarades musiciens appartenant aux groupements musicaux « avancés ». Il m'a semblé bon et utile de le faire ici, dans un milieu qui a mon affection et dont je fais naturellement partie. N'est-il pas naturel qu'un artiste « avancé » soit « avancé » en Politique? Oui, n'est-ce pas? [...] ¶ Debussy était loin d'avoir politiquement, socialement, les mêmes aspérités de gouts que musicalement. Ce révolutionnaire en Art était très bourgeois dans l'usage de la vie. Il n'aimait pas les « journées de huit heures » ni autres modifications sociales. Je puis vous l'affirmer. L'augmentation des salaires – sauf pour lui, bien entendu – ne lui était pas très agréable. Il avait son « point de vue ». Etrange anomalie. ¶ Je

Lenin's death while travelling on the Metro on 21 January 1924, he could not hold back tears.[78]

Satie's engagement with radical ideas was not confined to politics. Although he could be prudish, he signed a petition in *Le Journal du Peuple* on 25 February 1920 as an act of protest against the refusal of the committee of the Salon des Indépendants to exhibit Brancusi's sculpture *La Princesse X* – a work that, according to the committee, looked like a phallus. Satie had been introduced to Brancusi by Henri-Pierre Roché in November 1919 and they because close friends; Brancusi's sculptures *Platon*, *Socrate* and *Coupe de Socrate* in wood (1922) were inspired by Satie's *Socrate*, and indeed they nicknamed each other Plato (Brancusi) and Socrates (Satie).[79]

■ ■ ■

MARIUS Sidobre's obituary of Satie published in *L'Humanité* (which names the composer 'Eric' throughout) also shows the author linking Satie's political beliefs with his music:

> The major newspapers have written articles on this composer which are more or less convoluted. But, in his works, in his thought, Eric Satie was far from received ideas and officialdom. One fact about him will perhaps amaze the scribblers who are praising him on his death is that he belonged to the Communist Party until 1924, and if he did not continue membership it is because, absorbed by his beloved music, the Party's transformation prevented him from following it actively. But in his heart, he was still with the working-class Party: friends from Arcueil who met him very shortly before his final illness can vouch for that.
>
> Eric Satie joined the Socialist Party about fifteen years ago, in the Arcueil-Cachan section. [...] The charming good humour of our comrade Eric Satie ensured that he was deeply admired by the humble people who knew him. Although his musical works meant that he was acquainted with the upper middle class, he retained extremely simple tastes, and the posh people who followed his funeral procession would perhaps have been surprised when they

---

dois vous dire – et c'est une joie pour moi de le faire – que les «*jeunes*» musiciens partagent mieux nos opinions. Ils «*y viennent*». Ce que nous voulons ne les effraye pas. Ça, c'est un progrès – ne vous semble-t-il pas? Ils aperçoivent qu'il doit y avoir concordance entre leurs aspirations artistiques et leurs vues sociales. [...] et je serai heureux si mes efforts peuvent aider au développement de la culture musicale dans notre grande famille socialiste, famille exquise que j'aime de tout cœur.'

[78] Volta (ed.), *Correspondance*, p. 579: 'En apprenant, dans le métro, la mort de Lénine (21 janvier [1924]), Satie ne peut retenir ses larmes.'

[79] Ibid., p. 701.

passed the old building nicknamed 'The Four Chimneys' on rue Cauchy in Arcueil, if they knew that this building housed both poor families and the person who had entertained them when he was alive.

On 6 July, Eric Satie had a funeral in Arcueil, which he surely would not have wanted, with holy water sprinkled on his bier. The few Communist comrades who had heard of his death and had followed the luxurious hearse, which someone had paid for, knew that Satie's whole life, intellectually and materially, had been a protest against contemporary society which oppresses both peoples' minds and bodies.[80]

Sidobre was a future Communist mayor of Arcueil and the obituary reflects what he thought a staunch Communist should have believed. Fellow Party members such as Veyssière and Templier knew him better, and knew that Satie's political views were far more complex than those portrayed in this obituary. But Sidobre's final point – that Satie's life embodied a protest against conventional society – is worth considering in more detail. In particular, were Satie's political views reflected in his music? It is true that Satie's piano music eschews virtuoso display and is easily accessible to amateur performers. The notion of music that

[80] Marius Sidobre, 'La mort d'un musicien', *L'Humanité*, 11 July 1925, p. 4: 'Les grands journaux d'information on fait sur ce musicien des articles plus ou moins alambiquées. Pourtant par son œuvre, par ses pensées, Eric Satie était éloigné des poncifs et des officiels. Une particularité qui étonnera peut-être les plumitifs qui à l'occasion de sa mort l'ont encensé, c'est que Eric Satie a appartenu au Parti Communiste jusqu'en 1924, et s'il n'a pas continué c'est qu'absorbé par son rat musical, la transformation du Parti l'empêchait d'en suivre la vie active. Mais de cœur il était resté avec le Parti du classe de prolétariat; les camarades d'Arcueil, qui se sont entretenus avec lui très peu avant sa maladie peuvent en certifier. ¶ Eric Satie avait donné son adhésion au Parti Socialiste il y a une quinzaine d'années, à la section d'Arcueil-Cachan. [...] Notre camarade Eric Satie, de par sa bonhomie charmante jouissait auprès des humbles qui le connaissaient, d'une profonde estime. Malgré les relations que ses œuvres musicales lui avait fait avoir avec la haute bourgeoisie, il avait gardé des goûts extrêmement simples et les gens huppés qui ont suivi sa dépouille mortelle auraient peut-être été surpris quand ils ont passés rue Cauchy, à Arcueil, devant la vieille masure surnommé «les 4 cheminées», si on leur avait dit que dans cette immeuble de familles d'ouvriers pauvres habitait celui qui les avait divertis durant son existence. ¶ Eric Satie a eu lundi 6 juillet à Arcueil des funérailles que certes il n'eut pas désirées de son vivant, le goupillon est venu asperger sa bière. Les quelques camarades communistes qui avions appris sa mort et qui avons suivi le luxueux corbillard dont on l'avait gratifié, savions bien que toute sa vie, intellectuellement et matériellement, avait été une protestation contre la société actuelle qui opprime et les cerveaux et les corps des hommes.'

is solely accessible to professionals, which the vast majority of people can approach only as listeners rather than as practising musicians, is anathema to him. This accessibility extends to his employment of popular or popular-type tunes which French listeners of Satie's time would have recognised and which today's listeners can enjoy. Satie sometimes uses academic musical structures such as fugue and the chorale in order to undermine or poke fun at them. He is happy to combine ideas from so-called 'high' and 'low' cultures in one piece: while he was not interested in theorising his musical language, he demonstrated in practice that he saw music of the street and music of the academy as equal. This desire to treat all music on the same terms – as music – without regard to categorisation has a very contemporary resonance and perhaps helps account for his continuing popularity. For Cocteau in *Le coq et l'arlequin* it is Satie, the composer of 'everyday music', who is his model for young composers.[81]

Satie remained in his room in Arcueil, showing no interest in moving to a more comfortable flat or a more bourgeois area. Indeed, whenever he had money after being paid a commission fee, he spent it immediately and gave much of it away. He wrote to the Comtesse de Beaumont, who had organised a festival of Satie's music in June 1920 and had sent him the proceeds: 'This morning I received the accounts for the festival and I have even cashed my cheque. I've given 200 francs to Germaine Tailleferre as a memento, and so she can buy tobacco or something.'[82] No doubt this was his way of showing Tailleferre he cared about her; she could probably have paid her rent for a couple of months with this money, assuming she did not share Satie's contempt for bourgeois values. Whoever he mixed with, Satie remained, both literally and in spirit, Monsieur le Pauvre. Like other radicals of his age such as George Bernard Shaw and Oscar Wilde, Satie hid his political feeling beneath a cover of whimsicality and humour, but unlike most other radical artists, Satie lived his life among the poor with whom he identified.

---

[81] Cocteau, *Le coq et l'arlequin*. Paris: Éditions de La Sirène, 1918, p. 32; 'UNE MUSIQUE DE TOUS LES JOURS.'

[82] Letter dated 14 June 1920; Volta (ed.), *Correspondance*, p. 412: 'J'ai reçu ce matin le compte du «festival» & je l'ai même, à cette heure, «touché». J'ai remis 200 Frcs à Germaine Tailleferre, comme souvenir, & pour qu'elle s'achète du tabac ou autre chose.'

CHAPTER 6

The Provocative Satie and the Dada Connection

SATIE was one of the most multimedia and collaborative of composers. The notion that his music is part of a larger artistic experience – not a self-standing work – is present from his earliest experiments with Montmartre writers. In later life his work increasingly resulted from collaboration, notably with artists he met in Montparnasse cafés and interart events: the most significant works of 1924, his last active year as a composer, are the ballets *Mercure* and *Relâche*. *Mercure* saw Satie rekindling his collaboration with Picasso, while *Relâche*, composed for the Ballets Suédois, was ultimately a Satie/Picabia/René Clair work, though based on a concept by Blaise Cendrars. Satie and André Derain also toyed with a number of ballet scenarios around 1923–4, though none of these resulted in finished works. All these collaborations, like Satie's Galerie Barbazanges furniture music for Max Jacob's play *Ruffian toujours, truand jamais* (1920), saw him moving in experimental artistic and high-society circles and being part of the significant crossover between these groups. Many of Satie's works are inspired by popular entertainment such as the circus, and his last works show an up-to-date interest in mechanical innovations, culminating in his participation in René Clair's film interlude for *Relâche*, a ballet that ended with Satie and Picabia driving onstage in a miniature Citroën car. This chapter tells the story of many of the collaborative works of his last years, exploring the role his music plays as part of a wider artistic context and showing that Satie became increasingly notorious as an avant-garde provocateur.

By World War I we see Satie being an active participant and influence on the contemporary artistic scene, not just as a composer. This scene was characterised by manifestos, art magazines, self-conscious modernity and experimentation. A flurry of short-lived experimental art magazines were venues for artists of all descriptions to bring their work to a small but influential public: Satie was a contributor to many of these magazines, which either implicitly or explicitly aligned him aesthetically with the artistic avant-garde of his day. After the war, Satie was also friendly with members of the Paris Dada circle including Tristan Tzara, though the Dada concept of 'happenings' had already emerged from the tiny Cabaret Voltaire in Zurich in 1916, where multiple performances in different media occurred simultaneously.

Satie's extensive participation in media other than music is unique amongst his contemporaries in that he was not primarily a music critic, like Debussy and Paul Dukas. In fact, some of his writing has little or nothing to do with music, nor can it easily be classified either as journalism or imaginative writing. Rather, he was an experimental creative writer, a *blagueur* who provoked, mystified and amused his readers. We have already seen the advertisements for both real and imaginary products that he wrote during his Montmartre cabaret period, and by the mid-1910s his favourite writing genre of the spoof extended to texts purportedly about himself or his musical style. He grouped some of these writings under the general headings 'Cahiers d'un mammifère' (A Mammal's Notebook) and 'Mémoires d'un amnésique' (Memoirs of an Amnesiac), immediately indicating that these are not autobiographical writings in the conventional manner.

Montmartre publications of the late nineteenth century such as *Journal du Chat noir* featured short stories, poems, aphorisms, cartoons and personal disputes carried out in public, and the ephemeral art magazines of the 1910s and 1920s had a similar style. Satie was at home in this polemical and satirical environment, and many of his texts were published in magazines associated with the international avant-garde. His friend Roland-Manuel co-edited with Gaston Picard the magazine *L'œil de veau*, subtitled 'Revue Encyclopédique à l'usage des Gens d'esprit', for its four numbers published from January to July 1912. In Picard's words, *L'œil de veau* (The Calf's Eye) was 'founded from encounters in cafés', particularly L'Oasis which was close to the Odéon theatre in the 6th arrondissement of Paris. Satie was at the centre of this group of artists, several of whom were invited to dinner at Roland-Manuel's house to discuss plans for the magazine: as well as Satie, the conductor Vladimir Golschmann, the poet Henriette Sauret, Ricciotto Canudo and others were present at a dinner with a dessert course of 'pieces in the shape of a pear' in Satie's honour.[1] For *L'œil de veau*, whose editorial address was also the home of Roland-Manuel's parents, Satie wrote a text which is purportedly about Ambroise Thomas but which focuses more on his fruitless search for an umbrella ('My umbrella will be most concerned to have lost me'),[2] and for its final number he contributed a short piece on the topic of jokes, 'Observations d'un imbécile (Moi)' subtitled 'Juste remarque' and dedicated to Henriette Sauret.[3]

---

[1] Gaston Picard, 'L'écrivain chez Erik Satie', *Le Figaro* (supplément littéraire), 11 July 1925, p. 2: 'La revue naquit des rencontres que le café favorisait. [...] En l'honneur d'Erik Satie, notre malicieuse mais affectueuse jeunesse n'avait eu garde d'omettre, pour les desserts, d'inévitables morceaux en forme de poire.'

[2] *L'œil de veau*, 2, février 1912, p. 33: 'Mon parapluie doit être très inquiet de m'avoir perdu.'

[3] Ornella Volta has suggested that Satie and Sauret may have been involved in a romantic relationship, though there is no evidence to prove or disprove this tantalising suggestion. See Caroline Potter, 'Satie as Poet, Playwright and Composer', in Caroline Potter (ed.), *Erik Satie: Music, Art and Literature*. Farnham: Ashgate, 2013, pp. 67–84, at p. 69. Sauret

This crowd of writers, musicians and artists of all types met both socially and professionally, often in venues which were not traditionally associated with artistic performance. The outbreak of World War I is relevant here, as artists sought refuges, support and professional opportunities at a time when many theatres and concert halls were open only sporadically. Unconventional performance venues included the artist's studio 6 rue Huyghens, the Galerie Barbazanges, other art galleries and couture houses, many of which were the venues of Satie premieres. This was a small world: the Jove couture house was run by Germaine Bongard, sister of the couturier Paul Poiret who also owned the Barbazanges site, and Bongard's lover, the artist and impresario Amédée Ozenfant, ran the art magazine *L'Elan* from the same address. *L'Elan* was one of the many small artistic and literary publications intended to foster communication between avant-gardists at home and on the front during World War I. Germaine Bongard's salon concerts at Jove included a Satie and Granados evening in May 1916.[4] *L'Elan* featured polemics, poetry and original artwork, and its connections with Satie's circle are obvious as contributors included Guillaume Apollinaire, Max Jacob and Ricciotto Canudo, while featured artists included Ozenfant himself, his first wife Zina and Albert Gleizes.

Satie also contributed to the New York magazine *The Blind Man*, edited by his friend Henri-Pierre Roché; *391*, edited by Francis Picabia, whose final number, published in June 1924, features extensive material on their collaboration *Relâche*; and Tristan Tzara's magazine *Le Cœur à barbe* (1922). Sometimes Satie wrote material aimed at an audience of musicians and music lovers, though he did not change his writing style for this more specialist public. For the premier music journal in Paris, *Revue musicale S.I.M.*, he provided a number of fragments of *Mémoires d'un amnésique*: 'fragments' according to their author, though no completed version exists. Satie's contributions were 'Ce que je suis' (15 April 1912); 'Parfait entourage' (July–August 1912); 'Mes trois candidatures' (November 1912); 'Choses de théâtre' (15 January 1913); 'La journée du musicien' (15 February 1913); 'L'intelligence et la Musicalité chez les Animaux' (1 February 1914). At this point Satie's contribution ceased, mainly because he was angry when nine fake 'Commandements du Catéchisme du Conservatoire' appeared anonymously in the journal on 15 February 1914. It was assumed incorrectly that Satie was the author; the composer told the editor Jules Ecorcheville that he always signed what he wrote and he insisted on an apology. The critic Michel-Dimitri Calvocoressi revealed that this text, which aimed to provoke a split

---

contributed a prose poem, 'Le Froid', to the March–April number of *L'œil de veau*.

[4] See Ornella Volta (ed.), *Erik Satie: Ecrits*. Paris: Editions Champ Libre, 1979, p. 259.

between Satie and Debussy, was the joint work of Willy and the editor of the *Revue musicale S.I.M.* Emile Vuillermoz.[5] After the war, Satie preferred the generic title 'Cahiers d'un mammifère' (rather than 'Mémoires d'un amnésique') for his thoughts, using this new title in *L'Esprit nouveau* (1921), *Le Cœur à barbe* (1922), *391*, *Création* and *Le Mouvement accéléré* (1924).

Satie's changing relationship with Cocteau and Les Six can be traced through his writings in the 1920s. His contribution of acerbic aphorisms to the four numbers of Cocteau's magazine *Le Coq* (1920) show him being part of the gang, but by 1924 he was dismissing Auric and Poulenc in *Paris-Journal* in a critique replete with untranslatable puns and plays on words. Following a performance of their ballets *Les Fâcheux* and *Les Biches* in Monte Carlo, Satie referred to their work as 'musical fizzy pop' (du limonade musical) and as 'mélanges sexuels, insexuels et vomitifs'.[6] Robert Orledge has described Satie as 'hyper-moral' and has drawn attention to his disapproval of Auric and Poulenc's drug taking and distaste for Cocteau's homosexual circle (though Auric was straight).[7] But in the *Paris-Journal* article, Satie was surely using sexual insults as a cheap and tasteless way of attacking his former friends. Satie was, after all, happy to work with Picabia and other artists whose work uses explicit sexual material to shock the bourgeoisie, but the composer himself remained apparently unmoved and it is perhaps more accurate to describe him as amoral. We do know that Satie disliked the physical contact of 'footsie' under the table, as he wrote in *391* 'Contradiction: Cocteau adores me ... I know he does (*too much, even*) ... But why does he kick me under the table?'[8]

One of Satie's most characteristic verbal tics was his habit of 'finir les mots' (in Jean Cocteau's words) – twisting a verbal expression by adding a word at the end which provides a new meaning. The title of his *Trois petites pièces montées* (1919) is a simple example of this: here, the unremarkable musical title 'Trois petites pièces' is seamlessly combined with 'pièces montées', a term referring to a large decorative cake of architectural form such as a wedding cake (I suggest it could be translated 'Three little pieces of cake'). Suzanne Peignot recalled that this type of play on words was constantly used at the Saturday get-togethers of Cocteau,

---

[5] See Ornella Volta (ed.), *Erik Satie: Correspondance presque complète*. Paris: Fayard/IMEC, 2/2003, p. 831.

[6] 'Ballets Russes à Monte Carlo (Souvenirs de Voyage)', *Paris-Journal*, 15 February 1924; reprinted in Volta (ed.), *Satie Ecrits*, pp. 70–1.

[7] Robert Orledge, *Satie the Composer*. Cambridge: Cambridge University Press, 1990, p. 254.

[8] *391* no. 10 (July 1924), p. 2: 'Contradiction: Cocteau m'adore ... Je le sais (*trop, même*) ... Mais pourquoi me donne-t-il des coups de pied sous la table? ...'

Les Six and their friends,[9] a private joke which helped to bond the group. And in the last decade of his life, Satie's notoriety as an author and humorist spread beyond his French circle of friends across the Atlantic.

Satie and the New York experimental art scene

Satie never visited the United States, though he created a stir in artistic circles there thanks to friends such as Edgard Varèse and Henri-Pierre Roché who criss-crossed the Atlantic in the 1910s. Varèse was of partly Italian origin (though his relationship with his Italian father was always strained), and perhaps for this reason, as well as for his interest in new sounds and instruments, he was often mentioned in the same breath as the Italian Futurist school. But his approach to sound and music was quite different from that of Marinetti and Russolo: he had no interest in sound for its own sake, but only insofar as it could be used for creative purposes. Similarly, Paul Griffiths wrote that Varèse 'was less interested in science as an investigation of causes than in science as a generation of new images, ideas and phenomena. [...] His interest in science [...] was poetic rather than analytic.'[10] This reflected Varèse's fundamentally interdisciplinary outlook; when he arrived in New York in 1915, Varèse 'went straight to [the art gallery] 291 at the suggestion of Marcel Duchamp. It became the only place in New York in which he felt at home.'[11] In New York he was close to Satie's friend Henri-Pierre Roché and future collaborator Francis Picabia, who all shared an experimental aesthetic that crossed traditional artistic boundaries. Indeed, Varèse's friend Beatrice Wood claimed that in 1916 he wanted 'to make music of the streets, the sounds of the street cars, the bells on horses'.[12]

The 291 gallery founded an experimental art magazine, named after the gallery, to which artists including Picabia contributed. The magazine was financed by Agnes Meyer, the first woman hired by the New York *Sun* as a journalist; she had met Alfred Stieglitz, the owner of the Photo-Secession gallery at 291 Fifth Avenue, in 1908 when she interviewed him. Later that year, she met her future husband, a banker, in Paris, and they became patrons of the arts after their marriage in 1910.[13] The

---

[9] Volta (ed.), *Satie Ecrits*, p. 246: 'Selon Suzanne Peignot, aux «diners de samedi» qui réunissaient régulièrement les Six et leurs amis dans le quartier de la Madeleine, tout le monde faisait ce genre de gag introduit par ES. Cocteau appelait cela «finir les mots».'

[10] Cited in Olivia Mattis, 'Varèse and Dada', in James Leggio (ed.), *Music and Modern Art*. New York: Routledge, 2002, pp. 129–61, at p. 138.

[11] Ibid., p. 147.

[12] Ibid., p. 145.

[13] See Douglas K. S. Hyland. 'Agnes Ernst Meyer, Patron of American Modernism.' *America Art Journal*, vol. 12 no. 1 (Winter 1980): pp. 64–81.

first edition of *291* magazine includes a text by Agnes Meyer on science and art (p. 3), and the second features Picabia and Alberto Savinio. This was one of the first of a number of similar small-circulation magazines: Marcel Duchamp, Beatrice Wood and Henri-Pierre Roché produced *The Blind Man* in 1917, whose second and final issue (confusingly called *The Blindman*)[14] featured a short text by Satie which the Trinitarian-obsessed composer insisted was positioned on page 3. This text, in English, appears under a surreal drawing of multiple eyes by Robert Carlton Brown.[15] The 'Tale By Erik Satie' reads: 'I once had a marble staircase that was beautiful, so beautiful, that I had it stuffed and used only my window for getting out.' Satie must have been fond of the idea of a uselessly beautiful staircase, as an even more rare and elaborate version had appeared in 'Marche du grand escalier', the third of his *Enfantillages pittoresques* (1913).[16]

A line is drawn under this tale, and below this line appears a text in French credited to 'S.T., E.K.':

> Elle avait des yeux sans tain
> Et pour que ça n'se voie pas
> Elle avait mis par-dessus
> Des lunettes à verres d'écaille.

The presentation of this text under the English-language miniature tale might lead the reader to assume that this is a French translation, but it is not. Perhaps the author – who may well be Satie – was deliberately making a connection with the surreal eye imagery when he wrote: 'Her eyes were not silvered/ And so that could not be seen/ She placed over them/ Glasses with tortoiseshell lenses.' The surrealism is thus extended

---

Agnes Meyer later commissioned Satie's 1923 furniture music piece, *Tenture de cabinet préfectoral*; see Chapter 4 of this book.

[14] In addition to *The Blind Man*, Duchamp launched another short-lived magazine, *Rongwrong*: he had intended the title of the magazine to be Wrongwrong, but a printing error transformed it into Rongwrong. Only one issue was published, in July 1917.

[15] Carlton Brown (1886–1959) was a native of Chicago. His eclectic literary output included poetry, popular fiction and cookbooks; in the 1910s he contributed frequently to art magazines and his circle included Man Ray, later a friend of Satie. *The Blind Man* also featured a text about Duchamp's infamous urinal artwork by Louise Norton (later Varèse).

[16] The in-score text of this children's piano piece reads: 'C'est un grand escalier, très grand. Il a plus de mille marches, toutes en ivoire. Il est très beau. Personne n'ose s'en servir de peur de l'abîmer. Le Roi lui-même ne s'en est jamais servi. Pour sortir de sa chambre, il saute par la fenêtre.' ('It's a big staircase, very big. It has more than a thousand stairs, all ivory. It is beautiful. No one dares use it; they fear they might damage it. The King himself has never used it. To get out of his bedroom, he jumps out of the window.')

to the tortoiseshell being shifted from its commonplace function as a frame for glasses to the material of the lenses. Many commentators surmise that Satie is also the author of this miniature story because the cryptic signature features letters from Satie's name. More pertinently, the eyes/glasses theme recurs frequently in Satie's texts, whether written for publication in magazines or as part of a texted piano work.

On his return to Europe in 1915, Picabia founded the magazine *391*, whose name was an obvious homage to the New York magazine. Indeed, the magazine moved to New York in 1917: Dawn Adès states that 'numbers 5, 6 and 7 of *391* appeared monthly from June, taking over from *The Blind Man*. A chess game had apparently decided which of the two reviews was to function as the organ of the group of American and European artists gathered around W. C. Arensberg.'[17] Contributors to the New York *391* included Varèse, who wished to emphasise in 1917 that he should not be confused with the Italian futurists:

> LET MUSIC RESOUND. Our alphabet is inadequate and illogical. Music, which should pulsate with life, needs new means of expression, and science alone can infuse it with youthful vigour.
>
> Italian futurists: why do you slavishly reproduce the fears of everyday life, looking only at the superficial and embarrassing side?
>
> I dream of instruments obedient to my thought, which with their contribution of a flourishing new world of unsuspected sounds, will lend themselves to the exigencies of my inner rhythm.[18]

Like its New York counterpart, *391* was a bilingual magazine; the same number features a poem by Varèse in French. *391* was later used as a promotional vehicle for the Satie/Picabia collaboration, *Relâche*, which will be discussed later in this chapter. Its last number appeared in October 1924, and here 'Picabia introduces an entirely new movement, "Instantaneism". As a movement it was never more than a red herring, but as an attack on Breton's Surrealism specifically and on all movements in general (the only real anti-movement, perhaps) Picabia was quite

---

[17] Dawn Adès, *Dada and Surrealism Reviewed*. London: Arts Council of Great Britain, 1978, p. 140.

[18] *391*, no. 5 (June 1917), p. 2: 'QUE LA MUSIQUE SONNE. Notre alphabet est pauvre et illogique. La musique qui doit vivre et vibrer a besoin de nouveaux moyens d'expression et la science seule peut lui infuser une sève adolescente. ¶ Pourquoi futuristes italiens reproduisez-vous servilement la trépidation de notre vie quotidienne en ce qu'elle n'a que de superficiel et de gênant? ¶ Je rêve des instruments obéissants à la pensée – et qui avec l'apport d'une floraison de timbres insoupçonnés se prêtent aux combinaisons qu'il me plaira de leur imposer et se plient à l'exigence de mon rythme intérieur.'

serious.'[19] Elsewhere in the magazine, Picabia showed broader tastes. Satie himself contributed bawdy aphorisms to *Le Pilhaou-Thibaou*, a 'supplément illustré' to *391* published on 10 July 1921: 'J'aimerais jouer avec un piano qui aurait une grosse queue' ('I'd like to play with a piano that has a big knob', a 'piano à queue' being a grand piano); 'Ce n'est pas beau de parler du nœud de la question ...' ('It isn't the done thing to talk about the crux of the question' – though 'le nœud' can also mean the glans of the penis). These aphorisms decorated the top left-hand corner of the first page. Picabia and Satie shared some tastes in humour, as this type of boys' school sexual banter was a regular feature of the magazine. This number also included a letter from Auric and a couple of short articles on Cocteau's collaborative work for the Ballets Suédois with music by five of Les Six, *Les mariés de la Tour Eiffel* (1921).

Satie and the origins of Dada and surrealism

As a notorious figure on the Parisian scene and regular contributor to magazines, Satie was a familiar name in avant-garde circles, and his collaboration with Cocteau and status as figurehead of Les Six meant that he tended to be associated with Cocteau's aesthetic whether he liked it or not. While it is not easy to unravel all the threads which entangle one avant-garde movement with another, and while it is true that the wider public was generally unaware of the marginal aesthetic differences between artists who considered themselves enemies, it is clear that Satie was a figure to be reckoned with in the complex cultural debates surrounding the nascent surrealist and Dada movements.

The origins of Dada are generally traced to Zurich in 1916, where Tristan Tzara, Jean Arp and others wrote manifestos and put on mixed-media performances in the Cabaret Voltaire. New York was a second location of Dada activities, focused around the 291 gallery. Tzara was in contact with various Paris avant-garde artists and writers, including Max Jacob, Cocteau, Breton and Apollinaire. A letter addressed to Tzara by Francis Picabia on 28 March 1919 shows that he was being fed a partial view of the Paris scene: 'Jean Cocteau is in everyone's bad books: Erik Satie declares he's an idiot and everyone else calls him a brat, so you can imagine the delightful life to be had here.'[20]

When Tzara arrived in Paris in 1920 he issued more manifestos, contributed to magazines such as *Littérature* and met Satie. *Littérature*, edited by Philippe Soupault (who financed the magazine), André Breton and Louis Aragon, was published regularly from 1919 to 1921 and as special numbers only until 1924. Although its title suggests a sole focus

---

[19] Adès, *Dada and Surrealism Reviewed*, p. 149.
[20] Michel Sanouillet, *Dada in Paris*, trans. Sharmila Ganguly. Cambridge, MA: MIT Press, 2012, p. 402.

on the written word, contemporary music was also a topic of interest: Cocteau, in the words of Michel Sanouillet, 'offered [his tract on music] *Le Coq et l'Arlequin* [...] but Satie read the text, which was highly flattering to him, at Adrienne Monnier's bookshop and would hear nothing of it. Cocteau had to withdraw his article at the last minute. This was the first of the quarrels between Cocteau and Dada.' However, Satie's quixotic behaviour did not dissuade the editors of *Littérature* from promoting his work, as the second number, published in April 1919, featured a review of *Socrate* by Auric.[21] And in 1920, the magazine put on a performance in the Palais des Fêtes, in the central Halles district of Paris, which featured poetry readings and music by Auric, Milhaud, Poulenc and Henri Cliquet-Pleyel.

Initially a showcase for the work of the editors and their friends, *Littérature* changed direction when Tzara was added to the team in May 1920: 'this issue published the entire "Vingt-trois manifestes du mouvement dada", which had been previously unveiled at a reading on 27 March during the Soirée Dada, organized at the Maison de l'Œuvre theater'.[22] Picabia, always at the centre of avant-garde events in this period, organised his own exhibition featuring music at the Galerie Povalowsky in December 1920. Members of Les Six, Satie and Cocteau participated; the event 'gave Cocteau the opportunity to flow with the current of fashion by being at the head of a little group which he called a "jazz band". The orchestrations by Auric and Milhaud of jazz numbers which had been played at Dada and avant-garde Paris events shows the appropriation of this genre by Les Six.'[23] Cocteau also enjoyed banging a drum alongside musician friends who performed at the bar named after his collaboration with Milhaud, *Le bœuf sur le toit*. Presumably Sébastien Arfouilloux is here referring to Auric's then-popular 'fox-trot' *Adieu! New York* and Milhaud's 'shimmy' *Caramel mou*, which are original works rather than

---

[21] Ibid., pp. 75 and 77.

[22] Didier Schulmann, 'Littérature' (translator not credited), http://www.dada-companion.com/journals/per_litterature.php (accessed 7 April 2015).

[23] Sébastien Arfouilloux, *Que la nuit tombe sur l'orchestre. Surréalisme et musique*. Paris: Fayard, 2009, p. 107: 'L'exposition donne à Cocteau l'occasion de se couler dans le courant de la mode en se montrant à la tête d'une petite formation qu'il nomme jazz-band. L'orchestration par Auric et Milhaud de musique jazz interprétée notamment dans les soirées de Dada et de l'avant-garde parisienne montre l'appropriation de cette musique par Les Six.' Jann Pasler discovered a passage headed 'Pourquoi je joue du jazz' in Cocteau's notebooks: he pointed out that 'The two principal "advantages" of such music are that first, "it makes so much noise that it suppresses any literary conversation", and second "it prevents people from taking me seriously."' See Pasler, 'New Music as Confrontation: The Musical Sources of Jean Cocteau's Identity.' *Musical Quarterly*, vol. 75 no. 3 (1991): pp. 255–78, at p. 269 (her translation).

orchestrations of authentic jazz, which was then little known in Paris. These same pieces were performed at the public premiere on 24 May 1921 of Satie's own absurd short play, *Le piège de Méduse*.

The first Dada art exhibition was held at the Galerie Montaigne on 6 June 1921, on which occasion Tzara's play *Le Cœur à gaz* was performed. It is immediately obvious that this play is close in spirit to the Montmartre avant-garde of the late nineteenth century: Tzara parodies classical drama, creating absurd dialogue within the frame of a very short three-act play, and he gives each character the name of a body part (Tzara performed the role of the Eyebrow). In this sense, it has much in common with Satie's *Le piège de Méduse* and, more broadly, with Satie's textual obsession with isolated parts of the body. Tzara published a similarly titled magazine, *Le Cœur à barbe* (which he described as a 'journal transparent') in April 1922. Satie, who surely enjoyed the paradoxical description, contributed two items to this unique number: an extract of his *Mémoires d'un amnésique* and 'L'Office de la Domesticité', both of which feature attacks on his former friend Amédée Ozenfant.[24] Ozenfant and Satie broke acrimoniously early in 1922 during the Congrès de Paris affair in which Ozenfant had attempted to mediate in a falling out between the surrealist pioneers André Breton and Tristan Tzara.[25]

Satie was a willing participant in the polemics and personal slights which culminated in the Congrès de Paris 'affair' of 1922. This affair was provoked by André Breton, who

> took the initiative to organize a group representing the different artistic trends under the broad banner of 'l'esprit moderne'. He invited painters, writers and composers, notably Auric who acted as intermediary with Les Six. Tzara refused to participate in the group, considering that this mix of different trends would be 'harmful to the search for newness'. Breton reacted in a letter, accusing Tzara of being the 'promoter of a "movement" coming from Zurich'. This was a poor choice of expression considering the meeting was promoted as being an 'international congress'. Satie led the protest meeting on 17 February which called for a vote of no confidence in the steering committee and in Breton himself; this was so successful that the congress failed.[26]

---

[24] See Volta (ed.), *Satie Ecrits*, p. 52.

[25] Sanouillet, *Dada in Paris*, pp. 240–1.

[26] Arfouilloux, *Que la nuit tombe sur l'orchestre*, p. 115: 'Breton a pris l'initiative d'organiser un congrès regroupant les différentes tendances de l'art dans le concept très large de « l'esprit moderne ». Il s'adresse à des peintres, des écrivains et des musiciens, notamment Auric qui [...] joue le rôle de contact avec les Six. Tzara renonce à participer au congrès, considérant que le mélange de tendances très diverses sera « nuisible à cette recherche du nouveau ». Breton réagit dans un communiqué traitant

Indeed, Satie had been a signatory (with Eluard, Ribemont-Dessaignes and Tzara) of the letter to Breton demanding a meeting at the Closerie des Lilas café on 17 February; this letter was published in *Comœdia* on 14 February 1922.[27] The upshot of these events was Breton's split from Dada and the birth of surrealism.

A second performance of Tzara's *Le Cœur à gaz*, at the Théâtre Michel on 6 July 1923, was another evening featuring performances in different media; musical items included Satie's *Trois Morceaux en forme de poire* and works by Auric, Milhaud and Stravinsky. Short films and a play by Georges Ribemont-Dessaignes were also on the eclectic programme.[28] At this performance, known as the 'soirée *Cœur à barbe*', Breton insulted the performers, triggering yet another Parisian riot which ultimately led to the demise of Dada. Satie had tried to withdraw from this performance, claiming that performers were not going to be available so late in the season and the musical element was not central to the event.[29] Although evidence of his continuing contact with Tzara after this performance is scanty, a letter to Roger Désormière on 16 February 1924 mentions that he is planning to write 'two little things in collaboration with Tzara'.[30] We will never know whether these 'little things' would have been the final fling of Dada or something completely new, as sadly they were never written.

■ ■ ■

SATIE's last works are often described as surreal or Dada, more because of the composer's connections with other artists associated with these movements than for any particular musical reason. While it is hard to pin specific characteristics on the Dada movement, its manifestations often feature seemingly random juxtapositions and recognisable objects put in unexpected contexts. The creativity, sheer provocation and essential amorality of the movement are all strongly aligned with Satie's last two ballets. These late works are inherently interdisciplinary, written in collaboration with many of the artists with whom he interacted in the

---

Tzara de « promoteur d'un 'mouvement' venu de Zurich ». Les termes sont mal choisis pour une réunion dont on met en avant le caractère de « congrès international ». Satie dirige la réunion de protestation du 17 février qui retire sa confiance au comité directeur en même temps qu'à Breton, si bien que le congrès échoue.'

[27] Sanouillet, *Dada in Paris*, p. 243. A copy of the letter is housed in the Bibliothèque Kandinsky, Centre Pompidou, Paris (Fonds Brancusi).

[28] See Georges Ribemont-Dessaignes, *Déjà Jadis; ou, du movement Dada à l'espace abstrait*. Paris: René Julliard, 1958.

[29] In a letter written to Tzara on 29 June 1923; Volta (ed.), *Correspondance*, p. 545.

[30] Arfouilloux, *Que la nuit tombe sur l'orchestre*, p. 117: 'Satie envisage d'écrire « deux petites choses en collaboration avec Tzara ».'

Dada and experimental art scenes. The ballets *Mercure*, supported by Comte Etienne de Beaumont, and *Relâche*, a Ballets Suédois commission, were both first performed in 1924 and marked Satie's farewell to the Paris stage. But in 1922–4 he had several other ideas for projects that were ultimately not realised. One of these was a project for a work based on *Alice in Wonderland*, a proposed collaboration between Louise Norton (later Varèse's wife) and Satie. The writer and composer had appeared side by side in the pages of the *Blind Man* magazine, and Satie got on well with Norton when she visited Paris in 1921; she recalls him saying 'I am the only Frenchman who understands English humour and the only composer whose music "understands" Alice.'[31] He was surely right, but sadly the project did not come to fruition. In 1922, Satie was much occupied with a three-act opera based on Bernardin de Saint-Pierre's *Paul & Virginie* adapted by Cocteau and Raymond Radiguet. Satie signed a contract with Jacques Hébertot for a production at the Théâtre des Champs-Elysées – and Cocteau proposed the project simultaneously to Diaghilev's Ballets Russes – but only a small number of sketches survive. As 1922 is otherwise a lean year compositionally speaking for Satie, Robert Orledge speculates that more of this opera was written and has perhaps yet to surface.[32]

There is far more intriguing documentary evidence about Satie's projected collaborations with André Derain, and the two men were unusually close. Derain had already collaborated with Diaghilev as the set and costume designer of *La boutique fantasque* (1919), a ballet based on Rossini orchestrated by Respighi, and he and Satie came up with various projects for either Diaghilev's troupe or the Ballets Suédois. Satie and Derain met in 1921 and the artist was to have designed sets and costumes for *Paul & Virginie* and for various ballets. Their work appeared on the same bill when Derain provided scenery for *Gigue*, choreographed by Massine for Etienne de Beaumont's Soirée de Paris season in 1924. Satie and Picasso's ballet *Mercure* was on the same programme, as were pieces by Bach, Handel and Scarlatti, played by Satie's favourite pianist Marcelle Meyer.[33]

Supercinéma was a proposal for the Ballets Suédois about which Satie and Derain corresponded in 1921. The project was supposedly postponed until the following year, though no scenario or music survives; the title

---

[31] Cited in Volta (ed.), *Correspondance*, p. 1147: 'Je suis le seul Français qui comprenne l'humour anglais et le seul compositeur dont la musique «comprenne» Alice.' (Louise Varèse, *Varèse: A Looking Glass Diary*, vol. 1, 1973, p. 161).

[32] See Robert Orledge, 'Chronological Catalogue of Satie's Compositions and Research Guide to the Manuscripts', in Caroline Potter (ed.), *Erik Satie: Music, Art and Literature*. Farnham: Ashgate, 2013, pp. 311–12.

[33] Steven Moore Whiting, *Satie the Bohemian*. Oxford: Clarendon Press, 1999, p. 521 note 29.

is suggestive given Satie's cinematic collaboration with the Ballets Suédois in *Relâche*. *Les Archidanses* was another of their projects, this time conceived in winter 1922–3 for Diaghilev as a ballet lasting '20 minutes or 200 seconds' in two parts plus an interlude. This must have progressed slightly more, as Orledge states that 'some of Derain's designs [for *Les Archidanses*] were used for Comte Etienne de Beaumont's production of *Jack in the Box* in May 1926'.[34] *Couleurs* (1923) was an idea for Diaghilev's Monte Carlo season in 1923–4, and *Concurrence* (1924) was proposed for the same troupe the following year.[35] Satie always put a lot of effort into devising imaginative titles, and it appears that most of these projects exist solely in this form. Although the Satie/Derain collaboration was not ultimately very fruitful, the artist told Robert Caby that it was important to him at a difficult period in his life: 'I have only had two or three great friends in my life, but I had the good fortune to have Erik Satie. Without him, I don't know what I would have become. I owe everything to him. When I came back [to Paris] after the war ... I was lost. It was Satie who helped me stick with it, find a style. Without him, I would have been nothing at that moment.'[36]

A Satie/Derain project for which more extensive sketches survive is *La Naissance de Vénus*, which was intended to appear alongside Stravinsky's *Les noces* in the 1922 Ballets Russes season. While this sounds like it would have had a classical theme, Ornella Volta notes that 'another friend of Satie's, Raymond Radiguet, often used the expression "the birth of Venus" to evoke the adolescent sexual awakening which must not, according to him, be confused with "the birth of love"'.[37] Radiguet's lover Cocteau appears to have known about the ballet, which was to have

---

[34] Orledge, 'Chronological Catalogue of Satie's Works', p. 314.

[35] Orledge (ibid., p. 318) writes: 'A ballet titled *Concurrence* with scenery and costumes by Derain, music by Auric and choreography by Balanchine was performed by the Ballets de Monte Carlo at the Théâtre des Champs-Elysées, Paris on 12 April 1932, and the two may share a common basis in a humorous song about two tailors performed by Xanrof at the Chat Noir cabaret.'

[36] Cited in Volta (ed.), *Correspondance*, pp. 794–5 (original testimony in IMEC): 'Je n'ai eu que deux ou trois grands amis dans ma vie, mais j'ai eu le bonheur et la chance d'avoir Erik Satie. Sans lui, je ne sais pas ce que je serai devenu. Je lui dois tout. Quand je suis rentré, après la guerre ... j'étais désemparé. C'est Satie qui m'a aidé à tenir, à trouver un style. Sans lui, je n'aurais rien été, à ce moment-là ...'

[37] Ornella Volta, *Satie et la danse*. Paris: Plume, 1992, p. 114: 'un autre ami de Satie, Raymond Radiguet, utilisait couramment l'expression "la naissance de Vénus" pour évoquer, chez l'adolescent, l'éveil de la sexualité qu'il ne fallait surtout pas confondre, recommandait-il, "avec la naissance de l'amour".'

featured 'a Venus of mature years, surrounded by green backs, kiss-curls, soda siphons, cancan frills and beer glasses'.[38]

While no music survives for *La Naissance de Vénus*, Derain's scenario ideas, now housed in IMEC, suggest a ballet which is highly reminiscent of Ravel's *Daphnis et Chloé* or a similar mythical story with nymphs and naiads. The scenario describes a 'very white' central female figure in a setting which somehow combines countryside and a seascape. This central figure is surrounded by a Satiean trinity of cortèges: 'As the curtain rises in darkness, a young woman dressed in a tunic which looks about to fall off and to which she modestly clings, dances on the front of the stage in the middle of a graceful and pleasant dance, filled with naïve playfulness. [...] There is a cortège of nymphs who dance preceding the goddess Flore.' A second version of the opening features the only specific reference to music in the scenario: 'As the curtain rises in darkness, a young woman dressed in a tunic to which she chastely clings appears naked at the front of the stage and starts a threading dance filled with grace and sweetness. (Do not forget that as an act of worship to this goddess, women dance night and day to the sound of the trumpet.)'[39] At this stage, there is no reference to Venus being a mature lady. The Grecian tropes of whiteness and nudity are common evocations in Satie's work from the three *Gymnopédies* to *Socrate* and beyond, and the female figure struggling to cling to a flimsy tunic that is falling off suggests a statue coming to life. Derain's ideas include many specific effects of light and atmosphere (especially clouds), suggesting his imagination was running riot, way beyond a practical, easy-to-realise stage design.

Another document now in the IMEC collection suggests that Derain, and surely Satie too, given their extensive discussion about various projects, had a bigger idea in mind: no less than the formation of a ballet troupe and the renovation of the art of dance. This thirty-four-page document is dated 'Rome MIMXXI', and on the cover Derain has drawn

---

[38] Ibid., p. 114: 'une Vénus d'âge mûr, entourée de dos verts, d'accroche-cœurs, de jets de siphons, de mousse de cancan et de bocks'. Volta claims that this extract was deleted from Cocteau's *Lettre à Jacques Maritain*, published in 1926.

[39] 'Projet d'un ballet intitulé La Naissance de Vénus (André Derain)', IMEC, SAT 15.12: 'Au lever du rideau la scène et dans l'obscurité une jeune femme vêtue d'une tunique qui parait prête à la quitter et qu'elle retient avec pudeur vient danser sur le devant de la scène au milieu une danse pleine de grâce d'amabilité et d'enjouement naïfs [...] Le cortège est composée de Nymphes qui dansent en précédant la déesse Flore.' 'Au lever du rideau la scène et dans l'obscurité une jeune femme vêtue d'une tunique qu'elle retient chastement apparaît nu le devant de la scène et commence une danse enfileuse [?] de grâces et de suavité. ¶ (Ne pas oublier que pour célébrer cette déesse les femmes dansaient nuit et jour au son de la trompette.)'

a rather chubby Venus below a lyre from which a violin fingerboard, two trumpet bells and a bass drum are sprouting.[40] Some specific detail in the text perhaps refers to plans for *La Naissance de Vénus*:

> The orchestra will be comprised of 10 instruments. No changes to this number will be possible because each instrument corresponds to an action. In principle, later changes that may happen can only apply to the nature [of the instrument].
>
> Voice: 3 instruments [2 violins, 1 flute]
> accompaniment: 4 instruments [1 bassoon, 1 oboe, 2 clarinets]
> percussion: 3 instruments [1 tambour, 1 tambourine, 2 timpani][41]

Derain adds: 'In every branch of expression, one should get as far as possible from imitation when constructing pieces. It would not be possible to ban it entirely; the general principle would be to exclude it, which means it could be employed as an exceptional measure. [...] This should be applied to dance, music, costumes, gestures, but not to décor which would retain a very classical character.'[42] Décor was, of course, Derain's principal theatrical concern as a creative artist; it would appear that he did not want to be restricted by the self-imposed regulations to be applied to other elements of the performance. Perhaps the most important ideas are first, that the troupe should consist of ten carefully selected dancers and ten instrumentalists, though the plan does not explicitly state that each dancer is somehow linked to a corresponding instrument. (Derain also mentions that 'non-dancing walk-on parts' could be included in this troupe.)[43] Second, the author mentions, tantalisingly: 'On choreography/ Dances in themselves and music which is added to them'.[44] Here, we

---

[40] André Derain, *Mémoire pour servir à la constitution d'une troupe de ballet et la rénovation de l'art de la danse*, IMEC, SAT 15.13.

[41] Ibid., p. 5: 'L'orchestre sera composé de 10 instruments aucune modification ne sera possible quant au nombre car chaque instrument correspond à un action. En principe les modifications postérieures capables d'en être apporté ne pourraient toucher qu'à leur nature propre. ¶ chant 3 instruments ¶ accompagnements 4 instruments ¶ batterie 3 instruments ¶ 1o 2 violons, une flûte ¶ 2o 1 basson, un hautbois, deux clarinettes ¶ 3o 1 tambour, 1 tambourine, 2 timbales'.

[42] Ibid., p. 6: 'Dans toutes les branches de l'expression on devra s'éloigner le plus possible de l'imitation dans la construction générale des pièces cependant on ne saurait la bannir entièrement puisque le principe général est sa proscription cela revient dans certains cas à l'employer exceptionnellement. [...] Ceci s'applique à la danse et la musique et aux costumes gestes musique mais pas aux décors qui restent une [caractère ?] très classique.'

[43] Ibid., p. 9: 'Des figurants non dansants'.

[44] Ibid., p. 9: 'De la Chorégraphie/Des Danses en elles même et de la musique qui s'y ajoute'.

see Satie and Derain anticipating John Cage and Merce Cunningham's experimental work of the 1950s, though the American couple could not possibly have known about Satie and Derain's sketched ideas.

Other notes, under the heading 'Ballet. Satie', are written in very pale blue ink and not all of these are legible. The material which can be deciphered gives intriguing hints of various aspects of the project, from costumes to characters to design: 'Corps de ballet costume – tough ice/ Paste/ Metal ring to support buttons/ ostrich feathers/ Curtain with Montparnasse wooden horses/ Barrel organ and Gavioli [a well-known barrel organ manufacturer]/ Monkey/ Lady with barrel organ/ Sky blue/ Shells/ Cutout trees'.[45] All this suggests that the ancient Greek theme would be combined with contemporary images and sounds drawn from popular street entertainment and the music hall. It sounds like a very Satiean project, with *Parade*-like popular references and an instrumental ensemble reminiscent of *Trois petites pièces montées*. But this particular notion of 'the renovation of the art of dance' was quite new, though Satie had previously collaborated with Valentine de Saint-Point, whose concept of Métachorie was an attempted fusion of words, dance and music. Robert Orledge notes that Satie was so enthusiastic about Derain's idea that he broke a lifelong habit of never using the telephone to discuss it with the Comtesse de Beaumont: 'He [Satie] asked friends to take the phone off the hook when he visited them, and presumably he only rang the Comtesse because she was a wealthy patron and because he was excited about the new concept of choreography he had devised with André Derain, in which the movements were to come before the music rather than deriving from it. But this logical concept was sadly never put into practice.'[46]

Comte Etienne de Beaumont (1883–1956) and his wife Edith (1876–1952) were the most important supporters of Satie in his final years. The couple had met Cocteau during World War I and in February 1920 they supported Cocteau's 'Premier spectacle-concert' at the Comédie des Champs-Elysées, an event which featured Satie's *Trois petites pièces montées* and Milhaud's *Le bœuf sur le toit*. They also backed the first Festival Erik Satie, held at the Salle Erard on 7 June 1920. Etienne de Beaumont was a forward-thinking and daring patron, who in 1918 had staged Paris' first jazz performances using black American soldiers.[47] He and his wife were also great party-givers who held memorable costume balls at their home on rue Duroc in the 7th arrondissement; Satie's songs to texts by

---

[45] Ibid., p. 13: 'Costume des corps de ballet – glaces coriaces/ Strass/ Métal à cercle faire support à boutons/ plumes d'autruches/ Tenture des chevaux de bois de Montparnasse/ Limonaire et Gavioli/ Le Singe/ La dame de l'orgue de barbarie/ Le bleu du ciel/ Les coquillages/ Les arbres écorchés'.

[46] Robert Orledge, 'Satie's Personal and Musical Logic', in Caroline Potter (ed.), *Erik Satie: Music, Art and Literature*. Farnham: Ashgate, 2013, pp. 6–7.

[47] http://nga.gov.au/Exhibition/BalletsRusses/Default.cfm?MnuID=4&GALID=15179&viewID=3 (accessed 7 April 2015).

Léon-Paul Fargue, *Ludions*, and his tiny 'divertissement' for organ and trumpet, *La Statue retrouvée*, were composed for their 1923 Bal baroque. The following year, Etienne de Beaumont decided to promote a French rival to the Ballets Russes and Ballets Suédois, mounting a series of shows given the distinctly local title 'Soirée de Paris'. These were held at the Théâtre de la Cigale on the fringe of Montmartre (120 boulevard de Rochechouart), a venue which was until then associated with music hall performances. Like their Russian and Swedish rivals, these shows featured the leading artists, composers, designers and choreographers of the day in collaboration.[48] When Satie composed the ballet *Mercure* for a 'Soirée de Paris' event, it was as if his musical life had gone full circle back to Montmartre.

Mercure, 'poses plastiques'

This ballet was a collaboration with Picasso and Massine for the 'Soirée de Paris', which Orledge describes as 'a series of chic but ill-organised spectacles that borrowed their title from the review founded in 1912 as a vehicle for Apollinaire's talents'[49] (see Fig. 6.1).

Although the Comte de Beaumont himself wrote a three-page typescript scenario for *Mercure*,[50] Picasso is generally considered to be the main catalyst in the production. As Satie described, this is not a text-based work:

> Though it has a subject, this ballet has no plot. It is a purely decorative spectacle and you can imagine the marvellous contribution of Picasso which I have attempted to translate musically. My aim has been to make my music an integral part, so to speak, with the actions and gestures of the people who move about in this simple exercise. You can see poses like them in any fairground. The spectacle is related quite simply to the music hall, without stylization, or any rapport with things artistic. In other respects, I always return to the subtitle 'Poses plastiques', which I find magnificent.[51]

---

[48] For biographical details about the Beaumonts, see Volta (ed.), *Correspondance*, pp. 668–9.

[49] Orledge, *Satie the Composer*, p. 230.

[50] Pietro Dossena, 'Collaborative Works in Satie's Last Years', in Caroline Potter (ed.), *Erik Satie: Music, Art and Literature*. Farnham: Ashgate, 2013, pp. 161–82, at p. 174.

[51] Cited in Robert Orledge, 'Erik Satie's Ballet "Mercure" (1924): From Mount Etna to Montmartre.' *Journal of the Royal Musical Association*, vol. 123 no. 2 (1998): p. 232 n. 17. Original published in *Paris-Journal* on 30 May 1924, p. 2. 'S'il a un sujet, ce ballet n'a pas d'intrigue. Il est purement décoratif, et vous devinez le merveilleux apport de Picasso que j'ai essayé

Fig. 6.1 Photo of Satie by René Clair (1924) in front of 'Soirée de Paris' poster, dedicated by René Clair to his future wife Bronja Perlmutter (Archives de la Fondation Erik Satie, Paris)

de traduire musicalement. J'ai voulu que la musique fasse corps, pour ainsi dire, avec les faits et gestes des gens qui se meuvent dans ce simple problème. Ces poses sont exactement semblables à celles que l'on peut voir dans toutes les foires; le spectacle s'apparente au music-hall tout bêtement, sans stylisation, et par aucun côté n'a pas de rapport avec les choses de l'art. J'en reviendrai, d'ailleurs, au sous-titre de poses plastiques que je trouve magnifique.'

The subtitle recalls the composer's sketches for *Socrate*, a work originally conceived as background music to a series of poses or dances. Again, we see Satie's music being part of a multimedia spectacle: there is no sense in which music is the superior partner in this ballet. The relationship of the work to the fairground and music hall immediately calls to mind *Parade*, and the subtitle that Satie liked so much harks back to the static conception which lies behind his work as far back as the *Gymnopédies*.

Mercure was premiered on 15 June 1924 at the Théâtre de la Cigale. The programme states that the show ran from 17 to 30 June and the proceeds went to charities supporting war widows and – showing their concerns were not narrowly chauvinistic – Russian refugees.[52] An exhibition of art inspired by the music hall, theatre and circus was shown alongside the ballet programmes.[53] Orledge believes that 'the count's choice of subject [in *Mercure*] was almost certainly a dig at Cocteau, who often turned up at masked balls dressed as Mercury'.[54] Elsewhere, Orledge has demonstrated that Satie planned the number of bars in each number to fit precisely with the timings proposed by Picasso,[55] common practice for a ballet score: for instance, Marius Petipa gave Tchaikovsky detailed instructions for the length of each section of *The Nutcracker* (1892).

If we are to believe Satie that the score has no 'rapport with things artistic', we can equally argue that there is a numerical and probably symbolic basis to the music. The art historian Kenneth Allan sees connections between *Mercure* and a poem written by Man Ray for *391* magazine. An extract of Satie's 'Cahiers d'un mammifère', which was essentially an attack on Auric and Cocteau, was first published in the seventeenth number of *391* in June 1924. These words are published alongside a drawing by Picabia, *Savon*, which features Satie in merman guise with a one-footed Venus on his back, and an eloquent 'text' by Man Ray which looks like a series of words which have all been blanked out.[56] Kenneth Allan discovered that 'this seemingly resistant, non-signifying

---

[52] Soirées de Paris programme in IMEC, SAT 25.55: 'Programme complet avec dessins et textes des Soirées de Paris organisées par le Comte Etienne de Beaumont au Théâtre de la Cigale du 17 mai au 30 juin 1924 au bénéfice de l'Œuvre d'Assistance aux Veuves de la Guerre et du Comité de Secours aux Réfugiés Russes'.

[53] The catalogue of the exhibition notes that the artists involved were Andrieux, Cézanne, Daumier, Degas, Delacroix, Deveria, Constantin-Guys, Gavarni, Grévin, H. Lamy, Manet, Seurat and Toulouse-Lautrec. The latter was represented by twenty-five paintings, more than any other artist.

[54] Orledge, 'Erik Satie's Ballet "Mercure" (1924), p. 234.

[55] Orledge, *Satie the Composer*, p. 231.

[56] A digital copy of this number of *391* is accessible via the Digital Dada Library, a valuable repository of primary sources: http://sdrc.lib.uiowa.edu/dada/collection.html (accessed 7 April 2015).

work may, in fact, be deciphered by means of the Morse code. All three works [Satie's 'Cahiers' extract, Man Ray's text and Picabia's *Savon*] employ codes of different sorts, and recognition of the appearance of the Morse code allows for a closer relation to develop between Man Ray's poem and Satie's text, as well as to the other forms of encoding that Picabia seems to employ on the *391* page.'[57] More precisely, the poem features the two dash symbol – 'M' in Morse code, pronounced 'da-da'. This situates *Mercure* in the context of the ferocious artistic arguments of the period between Dada, the surrealists and Cocteau. Allan continues: 'The letter "M" pronounced as "dah-dah" is of additional interest when considering that Satie's ballet was entitled *Mercure*, and that his writing, "Cahiers d'un mammifère", is an attack on Jean Cocteau. [...] In Act 3 of the ballet, the god Mercury advertises a ball with the "Polka of the Letters", which partly involves presentations of invented letters belonging to a universal alphabet.'[58]

Satie's music tends to be foursquare, sectional in construction and built on sequential repetition. A 'Marche-Ouverture' is followed by three tableaux divided into twelve numbers. The fourth number, 'Signes de Zodiaque', is almost identical to part of the 'Petite fille américaine' in *Parade*, surely a deliberate recollection of Satie's previous collaboration with Picasso (Ex. 6.1).

The music for *Mercure* was criticised for being excessively simple, not least by Satie's former friends Auric and Poulenc. Auric sent Satie a baby's rattle with a beard drawn on it, intended to represent him, which deeply offended Satie. Breton led an attempt to disrupt the second performance on 15 June, which Allan believes 'would suggest that Breton, Auric and the others may have been reacting in part against Satie's provocative criticism in this June issue of *391*'.[59] But all these bitchy polemics reflect only one side of *Mercure*. While much of the music has a 'wind-up' mechanical feel – the 'Danse des Grâces', a waltz which opens the second tableau, is a good example of this – 'Bain des Grâces' is a striking example of how neoclassicism can sit alongside mechanically conceived music. This scene, featuring Three Graces (who are men in drag) bathing, is marked 'très calme sans aucune nuance' and is, like many numbers in the ballet, essentially comprised of descending sequences (Ex. 6.1a is another example). Constant Lambert believed that in *Mercure*, 'Satie achieved a more complete objectivity than any other composer has done' though he also wondered whether 'to obtain the static abstraction of Satie's best work, it is worth while throwing over the dynamic movement and

---

[57] Kenneth R. Allan, 'Metamorphosis in *391*: A Cryptographic Collaboration by Francis Picabia, Man Ray, and Erik Satie.' *Art History* (February 2011): pp. 102–25, at p. 116.

[58] Ibid., p. 122.

[59] Ibid., p. 124 note 27.

Ex. 6.1 (a) Satie, *Mercure*, 4 ('Signes du Zodiaque'): bars 1–8; (b) Satie, *Parade*, 'Petite fille américaine': bars 59–62

expressiveness which has hitherto always been considered an essential part of music'.[60]

Relâche

Satie's final work, *Relâche* ('no performance'; *relâche* is the term employed on French theatre bills when there is no performance on a particular night), was a collaborative work written for the Ballets Suédois which was his most controversial public performance. Satie and Derain's projected collaboration with this ballet company in 1921, *Supercinéma*, had not come to fruition, and the idea for *Relâche* (then titled *Après-dîner*) went through several stages. Blaise Cendrars, who had just worked with Milhaud and the Ballets Suédois on the jazz-influenced ballet *La création du monde*, had

[60] Constant Lambert, *Music Ho! A Study of Music in Decline*. London: Faber, 1937, p. 133.

the initial idea for *Relâche* late in 1923. While both Cendrars and Satie attended *Montjoie!* gatherings at Canudo and Saint-Point's salon around 1912–13, they recalled meeting in 1916 over a plate of bouillabaisse.[61] From that year, their names appeared jointly on several programmes, for instance at 6 rue Huyghens or the Théâtre du Vieux-Colombier, and Satie's music was published by La Sirène following Cendrars' suggestion that the imprint bring out music scores as well as books. Several years after this memorable dinner, their potential ballet collaboration was scuppered, as Cendrars recalled in 1950: 'I wrote the libretto for old Satie. Francis Picabia ripped off my idea for the plot and the cinematic interlude of *Entr'acte*, thanks to which René Clair was able to make his debut as a director. Picabia had taken advantage of my departure for Brazil.'[62] Picabia's ideas for the work took over, abetted by Cendrars' absence, and Rolf de Maré, the director of the Ballets Suédois, commissioned Satie to write the music and Picabia to design the sets.

The Ballets Suédois were active in Paris from 1920 to 1925 and were direct competitors to the Ballets Russes. Rolf de Maré was an art collector and (unlike Diaghilev) wealthy; he secured the Théâtre des Champs-Elysées as the venue for his company's performances by buying it. Both the Ballets Russes and Ballets Suédois brought together cutting-edge composers, writers, set and costume designers and choreographers, and there was some overlap in their list of collaborators. The Ballets Suédois worked with members of Les Six and other contemporary composers based in Paris, including Prokofiev, though sadly no attempts were made to revive the company or their commissions after its dissolution in 1925. One of their most successful ballets was *Le marchand d'oiseaux* (1923), by the all-female team of the designer Hélène Perdriat and composer Germaine Tailleferre, which was performed ninety-three times. And Steven Moore Whiting points out that 'Since de Maré also owned the magazines *La Danse, Théâtre et Comœdia illustré, Paris-Journal* and *Le Monsieur*, he had little difficulty generating the necessary publicity.'[63]

Picabia was particularly close to Satie in the last years of the composer's life. The artist was active in several media and published a poem 'Auric-Satie à la noix de Cocteau' in yet another small art magazine, *Z*.[64] The title is a complex play on words: 'noix de coco' ('coconut') is used in the slang phrase 'à la noix de coco', meaning lousy or crummy – the

---

[61] Blaise Cendrars, 'Les affinités électives: Blaise Cendrars parle d'Erik Satie'. Interview broadcast on 3 July 1950 by Radio-France, now accessible via www.ina.fr. They met at the home of the Marseillaise journalist Valentine Mas (Volta (ed.), *Correspondance*, p. 713).

[62] Cendrars, *Œuvres complètes*, vol. 13, p. 148; cited in Mikhail Iampolski, *The Memory of Tiresias: Intertextuality and Film*. Berkeley: University of California Press, 1998, p. 266.

[63] Whiting, *Satie the Bohemian*, p. 533 note 57.

[64] Edited by Paul Dermée, this magazine survived for only one issue.

insinuation being that the two composers were caught up in Cocteau's lousy ideas. Dedicated to Georges Ribemont-Dessaignes, whose work appeared on the same programmes as Satie on several occasions, the short poem is both surreal and pornographic.[65] Its stream of consciousness ends:

> La verge verte le lait des femmes
> dans l'arsenic
> sans indiquer le lieu précis
> firent claquer la porte pâmée.
> On les surveille.

[The green verge women's milk/ in arsenic/ without indicating the precise place/ make the faded door slam./ We are watching them. 'Verge' is also a slang term for the penis.]

On the same page, Picabia comments, in italics in the text: '*Si vous lisez André Gide tout haut pendant dix minutes, vous sentirez mauvais de la bouche.*' [If you read André Gide out loud for ten minutes, you will get a nasty taste in the mouth.] Picabia's printed attacks on his enemies did not reflect well on Satie, though the composer never found it easy to maintain good relations with people. André Gide had acted as narrator in *Socrate* and regularly met Satie at Adrienne Monnier's bookshop, but it appears that their cordial relationship had soured by 1924.

Picabia was editor of *391* from 1917 to 1924, and the multi-talented artist joined with René Clair to create the film *Entr'acte* (a highly Satiean title) which formed the central part of *Relâche*. The final number of *391* is headed 'Dadaism, Instantaneism/Journal of Instantaneism FOR A WHILE/ INSTANTANEISM IS AN EXCEPTIONAL BEING, CYNICAL AND INDECENT'.[66] Clearly, the authors were happy to align themselves with Dada, although its obituary had been written by Tzara himself – he delivered a 'Conférence sur la fin de Dada' in Weimar in May 1923 – and by its enemies including Breton, Aragon and Eluard when they stormed the stage at the 'Soirée du Cœur à gaz' in July that year. Picabia's neologism 'instantaneism' is a unique distinguishing feature of his work which sidesteps the issue of Dada's continuing relevance to the avant-garde. This term is explained in a manner strikingly reminiscent of Satie's description of furniture music: 'Instantaneism' is defined successively

---

[65] Ribemont-Dessaignes was a writer and artist who also produced some musical works for Dada events; see Michael Boerner's thesis 'Intermedial and Aesthetic Influences on Erik Satie's Late Compositional Practices' (unpublished MA thesis, Penn State University, 2013) for details of his musical activities.

[66] 'Dadaisme, Instantanéisme/Journal de l'Instantanéisme POUR QUELQUE TEMPS/L'INSTANTANEISME EST UN ETRE EXCEPTIONNEL CYNIQUE ET INDECENT'.

as something which 'is not interested in yesterday/ is not interested in tomorrow/ does entrechats/ makes pigeon wings/ is not interested in great men/ only believes in today/ wants freedom for all/ only believes in life/ only believes in perpetual motion'.[67] No doubt the apparent allusion to Poulenc's recent set of three piano pieces entitled *Mouvements perpétuels* (1919) was unintentional. The connection between the 'instantanéisme' descriptions and *Relâche* is all the more clear because the final item on the back cover is an advertisement for the ballet, described by its creators as a 'ballet instantanéiste'. The audience is here advised to 'bring dark glasses and earplugs'. Picabia never missed an opportunity to provoke his artistic and literary enemies, who are addressed at the bottom of the page as 'former Dada gentlemen' and are 'asked to come and demonstrate, especially to shriek "DOWN WITH SATIE! DOWN WITH PICABIA! LONG LIVE THE NOUVELLE REVUE FRANCAISE!"' This, the house magazine of Picabia's enemies, proved far more durable than *391*, which ceased publication after this nineteenth number.

Another influence on *Relâche* was Marcel Duchamp. He had begun a work entitled *La Mariée mise à nu par ses Célibataires, même* (The Bride stripped bare by her Bachelors, even) in 1912, finally abandoning it unfinished in 1923.[68] The generic character names are shared by both works, and the suggestion of a stripping episode is fully realised in the ballet. Duchamp and Picabia had encountered each other in New York and both contributed to *291*, and Picabia, as Blaise Cendrars knew to his cost, had no scruples about 'borrowing' ideas from his acquaintances. By 1923, Duchamp was focusing on chess more than art, and he appears in the filmed entr'acte to *Relâche* playing the game with Man Ray. He also had a cameo role in a revue, *Cinésketch*, which was orchestrated by Picabia and René Clair for a New Year's Eve 1924 gala night at the Théâtre des Champs-Elysées. Here, Duchamp appeared naked alongside the model Bronia Perlmutter in a tableau based on Lucas Cranach's painting *Adam and Eve* (1526).[69]

---

[67] *391*, no. 19, p. 1 (the anonymous author is presumably Picabia): 'L'Instantanéisme: ne veut pas d'hier. L'Instantanéisme: ne veut pas de demain. L'Instantanéisme: fait des entrechats. L'Instantanéisme: fait des ailes de pigeons. L'Instantanéisme: ne veut pas de grands hommes. L'Instantanéisme: ne croit qu'à aujourd'hui. L'Instantanéisme: veut la liberté pour tous. L'Instantanéisme: ne croit qu'à la vie. L'Instantanéisme: ne croit qu'au mouvement perpétuel.'

[68] See Frank Claustrat, 'La danse pour infini: Jean Börlin, Etoile des Ballets Suédois', in Mathias Auclair, Frank Claustrat and Inès Piovesan (eds), *Les Ballets Suédois: Une compagnie d'avant-garde (1920–1925)*. Paris: Bibliothèque Nationale de France, 2014, pp. 23–37, at pp. 32–3. The title of Duchamp's work was borrowed by Calvin Tomkins for his classic critical assessment *The Bride and the Bachelors*, first published in 1965.

[69] Claustrat, 'La danse pour infini', p. 36. Perlmutter later married René Clair.

The twenty-two short numbers of *Relâche* are divided into two acts of eleven numbers each, with the filmed 'entr'acte' between them. Music for the filmed section, which is divided into ten parts, was composed from 26 October to 10 November 1924: it was Satie's final work. The overall structure is therefore symmetrical, though the film entr'acte is anticipated at the start of the ballet as its first two numbers, which feature Satie and Picabia inspecting a cannon on the roof of the Théâtre des Champs-Elysées, should be accompanied by the first two numbers of Act I, 'Ouverturette' and 'Projectionnette', before the curtain rises for the third number, simply titled 'Rideau'.[70]

Satie's description of *Relâche* as an 'obscene' or 'pornographic' ballet makes sense in the context of Picabia's love of explicit puns, and more particularly in relation to the stage action. Almost all the numbers are dances specifically for men or for women, and anyone with a slightly dirty mind will read a sexually explicit programme behind the titles which follow the innocent first three numbers, 'Little Overture', 'Little Projection' and 'Curtain':

ACT I

4. *Entrée de la Femme* (Entrance of the Woman)
5. *'Musique' entre l'entrée de la Femme et sa 'Danse sans musique'* ('Music' between the entrance of the Woman and her 'Dance without music')
6. *Entrée de l'Homme* (Entrance of the Man)
7. *Danse de la Porte tournante (l'Homme et la Femme)* (Dance of the Revolving Door (the Man and the Woman))
8. *Entrée des Hommes* (Entry of the Men)
9. *Danse des Hommes* (Dance of the Men)
10. *Danse de la Femme* (Dance of the Woman)
11. *Final* (Finale)

ACT 2

12. *Musique de Rentrée* (Music for the Return)
13. *Rentrée des Hommes* (Return of the Men)
14. *Rentrée de la Femme* (Return of the Woman)
15. *Les Hommes se dévêtissent (La Femme se rhabille)* (The Men remove their clothing (The Woman puts hers back on))

---

[70] See Orledge, 'Catalogue of Satie's Compositions', pp. 319–22. The timings of the first two numbers of the ballet and the film's introduction are, however, not synchronous: presumably Satie intended some phrases to be repeated to fit in with the film.

16. *Danse de Börlin et de la Femme* [*Danse de l'Homme et de la Femme*] (Danse for [Jean] Börlin and the Woman)
17. *Les Hommes regagnent leur place et retrouvent leurs pardessus* (The Men go back and collect their coats)
18. *Danse de la Brouette (La Femme et le Danseur)* (Wheelbarrow dance (The Woman and the Male Dancer))
19. *Danse de la Couronne (La Femme seule)* (Crown dance (The Woman alone))
20. *La Danseur dépose la Couronne sur la tête d'une spectatrice* (The Dancer places the Crown on the head of a lady member of the audience)
21. *La femme rejoint son fauteuil* (The lady goes back to her seat)
22. *La 'Queue' du Chien (Chanson Mimée)* [*Petite danse finale*] (The 'Tail' of the Dog (Mimed Song) [Little final dance])

So, this is a scenario featuring one woman and multiple men; clothes being taken off and put back on again; positions which are the opposite of elegant when performed on stage, particularly the wheelbarrow dance and the finale with its allusion to the male member; and audience participation. Pietro Dossena points out that 'men and women were presented in their double dimension: as elegantly dressed bourgeois, but also as apparently naked bodies (actually covered with body tights) deprived of any social characterisation'. While the dance of the revolving door may suggest changing partners, perhaps a lightning-quick relationship, this number instead features, in Ornella Volta's words, 'a short bellboy dressed in a red and gold uniform who dances with the revolving door of a nightclub'.[71] The title is Blaise Cendrars', but the scenario is a later addition. It is typical of Satie's literal-mindedness that the dance is not a metaphor for changing partners, or even for two people going through a revolving door, but for a person and the door itself (which has to be imagined, as it is not one of the props on stage).

Satie's score quotes liberally from popular songs which the audience would have recognised, such as the children's songs *Savez-vous planter les choux?* and *Cadet Rousselle*, and *Flagrant délit* which was made famous by the cabaret performer Xanrof. Some of these are explicitly obscene, while others, as Steven Moore Whiting has pointed out, are songs 'with alternate lyrics, both children's rhymes and barracks songs'[72] (the nursery song *Cadet Rousselle* has a vulgar counterpart in *Le Père Dupanloup*). The clothed/naked bodies of the dancers are thus paralleled by the quotation

---

[71] Ornella Volta, 'Une relation peu explorée: Blaise Cendrars et Erik Satie.' *Cahiers Blaise Cendrars*, 3. Neuchâtel: Editions de la Baconnière, pp. 87–105, at p. 91: 'un petit chasseur vêtu d'un uniforme rouge et or, en train de danser avec la porte tournante d'une boîte de nuit'.

[72] Whiting, *Satie the Bohemian*, p. 539.

of songs with nursery/ribald lyrics. Dossena's analysis of *Relâche* focuses on its 'subtle interpenetration of "high" and "low" artistic categories, where each could be transformed into (or mistaken for) the other in a disorienting (and authentically Dada) aesthetic experience'.[73] The work's riotous combination of popular song and counterpoint, of people who appear on film and on stage in the flesh, of ancient and modern means of transport (a camel and a Citroën car), is underpinned by a symmetrical arrangement of numbers and the frequent employment of mechanical musical figures.

While the premiere was scheduled for 24 November 1924 at the Théâtre des Champs-Elysées, in a supreme irony the lead male dancer Jean Börlin was ill and unable to perform; there was, indeed, *relâche* that night at the theatre. Happily Börlin soon recovered and the rearranged public dress rehearsal on 4 December was followed by the official premiere three days later. Henry Malherbe, writing in *Le Temps*, refers aptly to the 'aesthetic factory' of the Ballets Suédois, though the crux of his review is a schoolmasterly ticking off of the main protagonists: 'Note that the authors of *Relâche* possess a sort of intelligence. They only lack a gift, study and a taste for work. In order to attract the public's attention, they find it more convenient to create a scandal.'[74]

A far more interesting and highly detailed critique of the premiere by Jane Catulle-Mendès was published in *Presse et Patrie* on 6 December (she must have attended the dress rehearsal). Catulle-Mendès vividly describes her combination of admiration and despair at the modern world:

> There is newness in this enormous farce, governed by a sort of rhythm relating to cosmogony and ataxia and, all in all, fairly representative of this age of ours which Francis Picabia is seeking to render instantaneous ... First of all, we have some cinema – very funny, thanks to the opposition of slow and super-fast motion – in which we see two men, one moving in a methodical fashion, the other frantically shooting a cannonball at us: a symbol that is not difficult to interpret. Then, the curtain rises on a strange, glittering décor, clearly intended to symbolise the wings of a theatre by presenting a magnified image of the lighting panel, seen in terms of enormous coloured discs. The backdrop is made up of several hundred motorcar headlights – a salute to [the Italian Futurist] Balla! – directed towards the auditorium. When these are lit, the

---

[73] Dossena, 'Collaborative Works in Satie's Last Years', pp. 180–1.

[74] Henry Malherbe, 'Chronique musicale', *Le Temps* (10 December 1924), p. 3: 'Remarquez que les auteurs de *Relâche* ont une sorte d'intelligence. Il ne leur manque que le don, l'étude et le gout du travail. Pour s'imposer à l'attention du public, ils trouvent plus commode de faire scandale. [...] l'usine d'esthétique de M. Rolf de Maré.'

spectators, blinded, can no longer see what is happening on stage.⁷⁵

The two men who appear in the first scene of the film are Picabia and Satie. On the roof of the Théâtre des Champs-Elysées a cannon moves, apparently unaided, and Picabia and Satie leap in slow motion towards it. Satie, always clutching an umbrella, inspects a pencil-like piece of cannon fodder with Picabia and loads it into the barrel. Picabia and Satie leap away from the cannon before it fires, a cue for the start of the ballet. Catulle-Mendès links the staging with the Italian futurist movement and underlines the overwhelming power of the backdrop, a truly in-your-face modernist gesture. 'Entr'acte' is described as 'A highly bizarre sequence of film [which] acts as a filler here, pushing to the limit the "chases" typical of American cinema; it's a sort of convulsive bacchanal, giving frantic expression to the current material and moral disorder.'⁷⁶ The 'plot' of 'Entr'acte', such as it is, jumps from inflating and deflating balloons which have heads painted on them, to a female ballet dancer filmed from below (1924 predates the invention of Lycra and her tights are baggy and wrinkled), to a funeral procession with the hearse pulled by a camel. Many characters associated with the Montparnasse artistic scene have a walk-on part in the funeral procession, including Germaine Tailleferre whose ballet *Le marchand d'oiseaux* was one of the major successes of the Ballets Suédois' short life. The hearse breaks free of the camel, triggering a hilarious chase sequence when the coffin hurtles along countryside roads and is pursued by frantic funeral attenders – though the older members of the party, including Satie, do not join in the chase.

To return to Catulle-Mendès' valuable first-hand account in *Presse et Patrie*, she recognises the mechanical qualities of Satie's score: 'The music of Erik Satie, the great patron of the noisy young school, is based on themes from children's round games, in which I thought I recognised, among others, *A mon beau château, ma tante Tirelire*, and uses rhythms imitating modern machinery.' Either she did not recognise, or was unaware of, the salacious alternate lyrics of many of these tunes. She continues:

> All the cinematographic comings and goings follow the triple time of a locomotive engine puffing out steam at full pelt, repeated to the point at which it produces a kind of oppression. First Erik Satie was cheered, the audience clamouring for him to be hauled back on stage; then Picabia, who came out, bowing, in a motorcar, with Erik Satie at his side, and the latter's many followers applauded him a second time. For hardly anyone was shocked, or jeered ... there

---

⁷⁵ Reproduced in Bengt Häger, *Ballets Suédois*, trans. Ruth Sharman. London: Thames and Hudson, 1990, p. 53.
⁷⁶ Ibid.

wasn't a hint of a whistle. Was Francis Picabia – who claimed: 'I prefer to hear them shouting than clapping' – not going to be disappointed by his success?[77]

While critical reception to *Relâche* was mixed, writers who focused more on the music than on the multimedia extravaganza were disappointed by Satie's contribution. Writing in London, the critic Georges Jean-Aubry, who had been one of Satie's earliest supporters in print in his 1916 book *La musique française d'aujourd'hui*, published an article in *The Chesterian* which was significantly titled 'The End of a Legend'. Jean-Aubry claimed the audience of *Relâche* was 'disillusioned' and they were 'forced to confess [...] that they were listening to nothing'. He continued:

> Erik Satie is a shadow which has lost its substance, a fate that we had long since foreseen. With that ferocity not uncommon to youth, especially to our post-war youth, Satie is now thrown to the dogs. After giving him too much, he is now given too little. One would forget all his work: one would make him pay for his desire to appear so much younger than his age and for throwing stones in larger and richer gardens than his own, instead of cultivating his own which, though very small, was not without charm.[78]

Jean-Aubry was also the editor of *The Chesterian*, the house magazine of the music publisher Chester whose stable of composers in this period included Stravinsky, Poulenc and Milhaud. While Stravinsky was too established a name to bother about these polemics, Jean-Aubry was surely reflecting the views of many of the younger French composers published by Chester, perhaps including Poulenc.

Parisian journalists were, on the whole, unsupportive of Satie in the latter part of his life. The adverse critical reception Satie experienced in 1924 was not only prompted by a dislike of his Ballets Suédois collaborations, which were considered trivial and shocking for the sake of being shocking; these critics also viewed him as a noxious influence on other composers. Whether he liked it or not, Satie was considered a figurehead of both Les Six, such as it still existed in 1924, and of L'Ecole d'Arcueil. The latter group (Henri Sauguet, Henri Cliquet-Pleyel, Maxime Jacob and Roger Désormière) named themselves after Satie's suburban home: Désormière was to become eminent as a conductor, and only Sauguet made any impact on the musical world as a composer.

Paul Bertrand, one of the principal music critics in *Le Ménestrel*, published an article on 27 June 1924 on the Ballets Russes season at the Théâtre des Champs-Elysées, a season which saw premieres by Poulenc

---

[77] Ibid., pp. 53–4.

[78] G[eorges] Jean-Aubry, 'The End of a Legend', *The Chesterian*, 46 (May 1925): pp. 191–3.

(*Les biches*), Auric (*Les fâcheux*) and Milhaud (*Le train bleu*). Bertrand notes the influence of Stravinsky on these composers – today's term 'neo-classical' was not then current, but it is clear this is the Stravinsky style he is discussing – and adds, 'To be honest, another, less happy, influence is still active on these young composers: Erik Satie, whose true musical intuition is combined with an overtly abstruse turn of mind, an affectation of youthful spirits which can easily be confused with puerility. Such trends, when taken to extremes by his followers, exacerbate their already well-developed sense of irony, as if music were not something which should for the most part be taken seriously.'[79] The shock value of Satie's late ballets therefore affected his reputation, even though the music is not notably different from his previous works. And in these ballets, the music is, of course, part of a wider artistic context and should be considered as such. That being so, it is ironic that the ballets are only known today through Satie's music, as sadly, stage performances are exceptionally rare events. But Satie did not respond to his journalist critics as he did to Jean Poueigh, perhaps because around this time he fell seriously ill and was diagnosed with cirrhosis of the liver.

---

[79] Paul Bertrand, 'Saison Olympique du Théâtre des Champs-Elysées: Ballets russes', *Le Ménestrel*, 27 June 1924, pp. 288–9, at p. 289 (Paris was the Olympic Games host city in 1924): 'A vrai dire, une autre influence, moins heureuse, agit encore puissamment sur nos jeunes musiciens: c'est celle de M. Erik Satie, chez lequel se mêle à une intuition réelle un étalage d'esprit abscons, une affectation de jeunesse de pensée qui confine aisément à la puérilité: tendances propres à exaspérer à l'excès, chez ses adeptes, leurs sens déjà vif de l'ironie, comme si la musique n'était pas tout de même une chose qui mérite le plus souvent d'être prise au sérieux.'

CHAPTER 7
Satie's Death and Musical Legacy

RELÂCHE was Satie's last work. Composers who had supported him in the past, including Auric and Roland-Manuel, were critical of this ballet, and as a result Satie wrote to both terminating their friendship. Roland-Manuel's trenchant dismissal of the work, and indeed of the composer as his article is entitled 'Adieu Satie', was published in December 1924: 'Farewell *Relâche*, farewell Satie. May you be dragged to the abyss with your love of wrong spellings and your cult of bad taste, this supposed classicism which is but an absence of grace and this appalling romanticism which even distrusts sincerity.' This article leaves an unpleasant taste in the mouth, not only because Satie could never be accused of romanticism (or, indeed, wrong spellings), but also because Roland-Manuel would have been aware that Satie was by then terminally ill. Nine months after Satie's death, Roland-Manuel published a belated apology in the same magazine.[1] Another singularly ill-timed article was published in Belgium: written in spring 1925, the musical satire *Tombeau de Socrate* was published at the end of July following Satie's death on the first day of that month. Paul Hooreman and André Souris decided they would try to out-parody Satie, composing a piece which featured no bar lines, key signature or clefs at the start of lines, whose musical language combined pseudo-Gregorian chant and pseudo-'mazurka java'.[2]

Darius Milhaud was one of very few people with whom Satie never fell out. His memoir, *Notes sans musique*, first published in 1949, includes vivid descriptions of Satie's last year and death. Milhaud and his wife Madeleine were the composer's principal carers, together with Brancusi, Derain and the young composer Robert Caby (1905–92), who met Satie at the dress rehearsal of *Relâche*. Brancusi brought Satie chicken broth

---

[1] Roland-Manuel's 'Adieu Satie' was published in *Revue Pleyel*, 15 (December 1924), pp. 21–2; 'Adieu Relâche, Adieu Satie. Puissiez-vous entraîner dans l'abîme, avec l'amour de la faute d'orthographe et le culte de la faute de goût, ce prétendu classicisme qui n'est qu'absence de grâce et cet abominable romantisme qui méconnaît jusqu'à la sincérité.' Cited in Malou Haine, 'Jean Cocteau et ses compositeurs en Belgique', talk given on 6 March 2004, available at http://www.arllfb.be/ebibliotheque/seancespubliques/06032004/haine.pdf. 'Excuses à Satie' was published in *Revue Pleyel*, 30 (March 1926), pp. 8–9.

[2] See David Gullentops and Malou Haine, *Jean Cocteau: Textes et musique*. Liège: Mardaga, 2005, p. 280 and Haine, 'Jean Cocteau et ses compositeurs en Belgique'.

which he had made himself.[3] Picasso was another regular visitor to the composer's bedside, somehow managing to overcome his fear of illness and death to pay homage to his friend and collaborator. John Richardson, in the third volume of his magisterial biography of Picasso, notes that the great painter even changed Satie's sheets.[4]

Milhaud wrote that in the last year of his life, Satie 'got into the habit of coming to Paris every day, having lunch in turn with Derain, Braque or me. He ate little, sitting right up against the chimney with his raincoat on, his hat pulled down to his eyes, holding his umbrella: he stayed like that, still and silent, until he left to get the train back to Arcueil. We were not happy with this routine and nagged Satie so much that he ended up deciding to live in Paris.'[5] Satie first stayed in the Grand Hotel, where 'Still wearing his hat and coat and holding his umbrella, sitting in a large armchair, he passed the time contemplating himself in the mirror facing him, operating the latch on the door with a very complicated string mechanism which he devised himself.'[6] He moved to the Hôtel Istria in Montparnasse, which he much preferred, either because or in spite of its noisy location surrounded by students and artists.[7]

Milhaud continues the story at the point Satie was hospitalised:

When the doctor insisted he be transferred to hospital, the Comte de Beaumont, who had endowed a ward in the Hôpital Saint-Joseph, helped us put things in place and obtained a private room for him. [...] The nun who arranged his personal affairs quickly realised that she was not dealing with an ordinary patient; Satie's only toiletries were a brush and a pumice stone with which he must have exfoliated his skin. Despite his intolerable suffering, he kept his most original character: when [Jacques] Maritain brought a priest to

---

[3] See Ornella Volta (ed.), *Erik Satie: Correspondance presque complète*. Paris: Fayard/IMEC, 2/2003, p. 702.

[4] John Richardson, *A Life of Picasso*, vol. 3: *The Triumphant Years, 1917–1932*. London: Jonathan Cape, 2007, p. 275.

[5] Darius Milhaud, *Notes sans musique*. Paris: Julliard, 1949, p. 194: 'Il prit alors l'habitude de venir tous les jours à Paris déjeuner à tour de rôle chez Derain, chez Braque ou chez moi. Il mangeait très légèrement et il s'asseyait tout contre la cheminée avec son pardessus, son chapeau enfoncé jusqu'aux yeux, son parapluie à la main; il restait ainsi immobile et silencieux jusqu'au moment de reprendre son train pour Arcueil. Ces déplacements quotidiens nous déplaisaient et nous insistâmes tellement auprès de Satie qu'il finit par se décider à s'installer à Paris.'

[6] Ibid.: 'Toujours avec son chapeau, son manteau et son parapluie, assis dans un large fauteuil, il passait ses journées à se contempler dans la glace qui lui faisait face, actionnant le verrou de la porte grâce à un jeu de ficelles très compliqué qu'il avait élaboré.'

[7] Ibid., p. 195.

see him, he described him to us the following day: 'He looked like a black Modigliani on a blue background.'[8]

Satie died in this hospital on 1 July 1925.

Did this institution prompt Satie to reconsider his religious beliefs in his last months? Stravinsky in conversation with Robert Craft tantalisingly hints this may have happened: 'He had been turned towards religion near the end of his life and he started going to Communion. I saw him after church one morning, and he said in that extraordinary manner of his: «Alors, j'ai un peu communiqué ce matin.» He became ill very suddenly and died quickly and quietly.'[9] 'I have communicated a bit this morning' certainly sounds like a typical Satie play on words, though one wonders how much Stravinsky knew about Satie's last months spent in hotels and then hospital if he believes that the composer 'died quickly and quietly'. We do know that a priest visited Satie in hospital, the wonderfully named abbé Saint (Satie was naturally 'happy to finally see a saint with my own eyes').[10] And the Catholic writer and society habitué Jacques Maritain claims to have attended a 'sort of conversion' on Satie's deathbed.[11]

■ ■ ■

WHEN the news media learned of Satie's death, journalists and musicians mostly needed to perform a delicate pirouette to pay appropriately respectful homage to the composer they had recently been criticising. The obituary in *L'Humanité* by Marius Sidobre, cited in Chapter 5, inevitably focused on Satie's left-wing sympathies; most of the other death announcements stressed Satie's links with young composers, collaborations and friendship with Debussy. One obituary writer avoided controversy by highlighting a very early work – the three

---

[8] Ibid.: 'Lorsque le Docteur exigea qu'il fût transporté à l'hôpital, le Comte de Beaumont, qui avait fondé une salle à l'hôpital Saint-Joseph, nous facilita les démarches et lui obtint une chambre privée. [...] La religieuse qui rangea ses objets personnels put vite juger qu'elle n'aurait pas à faire à un malade ordinaire: Satie ne possédait pour tout objet de toilette qu'une brosse de chiendent et une pierre ponce avec lesquelles il devait sans doute se frotter la peau. ¶ Malgré ses souffrances intolérables, il conserva son esprit si particulier; quand Maritain lui amena un prêtre, il nous le décrivit le lendemain: «Il avait l'air d'un Modigliani noir sur fond bleu».'

[9] Igor Stravinsky and Robert Craft, *Conversations with Igor Stravinsky*. London and New York: Faber, 1959, p. 68.

[10] Volta (ed.), *Correspondance*, pp. 642–3: 'Je suis heureux, dit Satie, de voir enfin un saint de mes yeux.'

[11] Ibid., p. 656. Maritain specialised in artistic conversions: Satie's friend Jean Hugo, the composer Maxime Jacob (of L'Ecole d'Arcueil), Roland-Manuel and (briefly) Jean Cocteau were all turned to the Catholic faith by him. (See ibid., pp. 906, 918 and 1094.)

Gymnopédies – rather than Satie's recent work with the Ballets Suédois.[12] Some mentioned *Paul & Virginie*, the projected opera collaboration with Cocteau and Radiguet. The *Revue musicale* published Auric's 'La leçon d'Erik Satie' in its number dated 1 August 1925; Auric, who had known Satie since he was a young teenage writer and composer, was able to move beyond the insults Satie threw at him in Monte Carlo in 1924 to pay tribute to a composer whose 'great strength was only to use what is *essential*'. Auric draws attention to one of many paradoxical sides of Satie: 'It may seem an astonishing virtue for someone who passed for a "humorist", but for us, he truly was a wise counsellor.'[13] It is Auric who first drew attention in print to Satie as a musical humorist in one of the first extensive articles published on the composer. But at the end of his life and after his death, Auric and other obituary writers hint that Satie and Socrates have become one: the eccentric teacher, accused of leading young minds astray, is portrayed by Plato as a wise man. Socrates' death, by his own hand, was illustrated by Satie in music of unforgettable simplicity and dignity (Ex. 7.1).

Milhaud recalls the administrative problems he had to deal with after Satie's death. Satie had not seen his nearest relative, his brother Conrad, during his final illness, and Milhaud had to commission a news agency to place advertisements in the French local press in order to locate Satie's family. Conrad 'was very upset that he had not been able to care for his brother; he loved him tenderly and had stopped talking to him for family reasons of no real importance'.[14] Conrad proved extremely accommodating after his brother's death, authorising Milhaud and the other close friends who helped clear the Arcueil room to remove any musical manuscripts and publish anything they considered worthy of dissemination.

Milhaud, Conrad Satie, Roger Désormière, Jean Wiéner and Robert Caby took on the job of clearing out Satie's room in Arcueil. Milhaud's horrified description of Satie's room is worth quoting in full:

> A narrow corridor with a washbasin led to the room which Satie had never allowed anyone to enter, not even the concierge. The idea of entering it was overwhelming. What a shock we had when we opened the door! It was inconceivable that Satie had lived in such poverty. He, whose impeccable dress resembled that of the

---

[12] Anonymous, 'Nécrologie: Erik Satie', *Le Ménestrel*, 10 July 1925, p. 312.

[13] Georges Auric, 'La leçon d'Erik Satie', *Revue musicale*, 1 August 1925, pp. 98–9, at p. 98: 'Sa force, c'est en effet de n'user toujours que de l'essentiel. [...] Etonnante vertu de qui passe pour un «humoriste», il fut pour nous, vraiment, un conseiller de sagesse.'

[14] Milhaud, *Notes sans musique*, p. 197: '[Conrad] était très peiné de n'avoir pu soigner son frère qu'il aimait tendrement et avec lequel il s'était brouillé pour des raisons de famille sans importance véritable ...'

Ex. 7.1 Satie, 'La mort de Socrate': bars 278–end

most strict civil servant in its conservatism and cleanliness, owned next to nothing: a miserable bed, a table covered with various things, a chair, a half-empty wardrobe on which a dozen identical old-fashioned new velvet suits were piled up; in every corner were walking canes, old hats, newspapers. On the rattly old piano, whose pedals were connected with string, there was a parcel whose postmark showed that Satie had received it several years before; he had torn a small corner of the packaging to see what it contained: it was a small painting, perhaps a New Year present. On the piano we found a token of a dear friendship, a luxury edition of Debussy's Baudelaire settings, his *Estampes* and *Images* with affectionate dedications: 'To Erik Satie, gentle and medieval musician', and 'To Erik Satie, the celebrated contrapuntist'. Behind the piano, we found a notebook which Satie thought he had lost on a bus containing *Jack in the Box* and *Geneviève de Brabant*. With the meticulousness which was typical of him, he had put more than four thousand little pieces of paper the size of a visiting card in an old cigar box; on these he had made odd drawings and extravagant calligraphed inscriptions.[15]

---

[15] Ibid., pp. 198–9: 'un étroit couloir avec un lavabo conduisait à la chambre où Satie n'avait jamais laissé pénétrer qui que ce fût, même la concierge.

Some of these rediscovered works were performed less than a year after Satie's death. Comte Etienne de Beaumont organised a tribute festival to Satie with the intention of raising money to erect a monument to the composer, though the monument project did not come to fruition. As Volta reports, 'Brancusi would have liked to sculpt a monument for Satie, or at least engrave his tomb as he had done for the Douanier Rousseau. A misunderstanding with the composer's family prevented him from realising this project.'[16] Beaumont's festival took place in the Théâtre des Champs-Elysées on 17 May 1926 and featured the premiere of *Geneviève de Brabant* (without Contamine de Latour's text, which did not resurface until the early 1980s) in Roger Désormière's orchestration. For this festival, Milhaud orchestrated *Cinq grimaces* and Derain produced costumes for *Jack in the Box*, at Beaumont's request.[17] Poulenc provided a measured review for *Le Ménestrel* on 4 June, promoting the forthcoming performance of *Jack in the Box* by the Ballets Russes and stating, 'Isn't order the secret weapon of Satie's work?'

The brief *Journal des débats* announcement of Satie's death concludes by mentioning his projected opera based on *Paul & Virginie*, though

> L'idée d'y entrer nous bouleversait. Quel choc nous éprouvâmes en ouvrant la porte! Il était inconcevable que Satie eût vécu dans un tel dénuement. Lui, dont la mise impeccable se rapprochait par sa correction et sa propreté de celle du plus rigoureux fonctionnaire, ne possédait pour ainsi dire rien: un misérable lit, une table recouverte d'objets disparates, une chaise, une armoire à moitié vide sur laquelle s'empilaient une douzaine de costumes de velours neufs et démodés, tous pareils; dans tous les coins, des cannes, de vieux chapeaux, des journaux. Sur le vieux piano-crécelle, dont les pédales étaient retenues avec des ficelles, il y avait un paquet, dont le cachet de la poste prouvait que Satie l'avait reçu plusieurs années auparavant, il avait déchiré un petit coin du papier pour voir ce qu'il contenait; un petit tableau, cadeau de jour de l'an, sans doute. Sur le piano, nous avons trouvé, témoignage d'une amitié précieuse, l'édition de luxe des *Poèmes de Baudelaire* de Debussy, les *Estampes*, les *Images* avec d'affectueuses dédicaces: «A Erik Satie, musicien médiéval et doux», et «A Erik Satie, le célèbre contrapuntiste». Derrière le piano, nous retrouvâmes un cahier contenant *Jack in the Box* et *Geneviève de Brabant* que Satie croyait avoir perdus dans un autobus. Avec l'ordre méticuleux qui le caractérisait, il avait rangé dans une vieille boîte à cigares plus de quatre mille petits bouts de papier de la grandeur d'une carte de visite, sur lesquels il avait fait des dessins étranges et calligraphié d'extravagantes inscriptions.'

[16] Volta (ed.), *Correspondance*, p. 702: 'Brancusi aurait voulu élever un monument funéraire à Erik Satie, ou tout au moins graver sa tombe, ainsi qu'il l'avait fait pour Henri Rousseau, le Douanier. Un malentendu avec la famille du compositeur l'empêcha de réaliser ce projet.'

[17] Lynn Garafola, *Diaghilev's Ballets Russes*. New York: Oxford University Press, 1989, pp. 459–60 note 59.

its focus is on a provisional assessment of Satie's reputation: 'He was a highly original composer whose reputation never reached beyond avant-garde circles, though he did considerably influence modern music. Although some overly enthusiastic young disciples made extravagant claims for him, Erik Satie continued his work in a modest manner. As with his friend Debussy, the importance of his work will surely be recognised far into the future.'[18] The view that Satie's reputation is confined to specialist circles is mirrored in the *Ménestrel* report of his death, which also gives an overview of Satie's educational background at the Conservatoire and Schola Cantorum. Like other obituaries, this article highlights Satie's friendship with Debussy (exaggerating Debussy's contribution: he did not 'orchestrate a certain number of his compositions', just the first and third *Gynmopédies*) and support of younger composers.[19] More interestingly, a later issue of the same journal reported that there had been a significant Italian reaction to Satie's death, mentioning that *Socrate* was singled out as his major work.[20] It appears that the Italian press were, like most of their French colleagues, more comfortable with the serious, larger-scale side of Satie's production. And from the Swiss perspective, the *Semaine littéraire de Genève* drew attention to the humorous titles of several Satie works and again mentioned the *Paul & Virginie* project.[21]

Satie's old friend, the experimental composer and writer Carol-Bérard (whose work is discussed in Chapter 2), published a tribute to the composer in *La Semaine à Paris* in November 1925. Illustrating the article with his own photo of Satie, he drew attention to Marcelle Meyer's concert series devoted to the composer and 'works by composers whose spirit is in sympathy with Satie's: Chabrier, Debussy, Stravinsky and those young composers he always supported, Poulenc, Auric, Sauguet and Darius Milhaud'.[22] Carol-Bérard is therefore situating Satie within a broader

---

[18] Anonymous, 'Deuil: Erik Satie', *Journal des débats*, 4 July 1925, p. 4: 'C'est un compositeur d'une grande originalité, dont la réputation ne se haussa jamais au-dessus des cénacles d'avant-garde, mais qui eut une influence considérable sur la musique moderne. Malgré le bruit fait autour de son nom par des jeunes disciples trop zélés, Erik Satie poursuivit avec modestie son œuvre dont l'importance ne sera sans doute, comme celle de Debussy, dont il fut l'ami, évaluée que beaucoup plus tard.'

[19] Anonymous, 'Nécrologie: Erik Satie', *Le Ménestrel*, 10 July 1925, p. 312: 'qui orchestra un certain nombre de ses productions'.

[20] G.-L. Garnier, 'L'Italie', *Le Ménestrel*, 31 July 1925, p. 335: 'La mort d'Erik Satie a trouvé dans la presse italienne un écho ému. Les moins fervents de sa musique rendent hommage à l'originalité de sa nature et saluent dans son *Socrate* une œuvre durable.'

[21] Anonymous, *La Semaine littéraire de Genève*, 11 July 1925, p. 333.

[22] Carol-Bérard, 'A la mémoire d'Erik Satie', *La Semaine à Paris*, 13 November 1925, pp. 75–6, at p. 75: 'des œuvres de compositeurs dont l'esprit va de

musical context, placing the composer at the centre of a French musical tradition that combined humour with a return to classicism (and ignoring the fallings-out which scarred Satie's last year).

Robert Caby wrote music criticism for *L'Humanité*, including a series of articles in 1928, which kept Satie's name before the Communist-sympathising public. Caby shared Satie's political outlook: indeed, he visited the Soviet Union in 1933 and 'a few years later, welcomed the exiled Leon Trotsky into his home in Paris'.[23] He pays extravagant tribute to Satie in an article published to commemorate the third anniversary of his death: 'A born musician, Satie wrote works before 1900 which were novel in their harmonic system, simple in construction, of admirable purity.' More importantly, Caby points out that 'Most of [Satie's] music is based on popular themes which he dressed up wonderfully; in his last work, *Relâche*, he thus strikingly achieved a buffoonish grandeur. [...] The same artistry which we admire in his music hall waltzes can also be admired in *Socrate* in which, with restricted means, he attains something as grand as any antique art.'[24] And in an article on music and film, Caby draws attention to 'old Satie's great success with René Clair's *Entr'acte*'.[25] Caby edited Satie's piano works for Salabert, an edition first published in 1968 which was in its day one of the most important sources for performers. It is a shame that misprints and dubiously attributed works are included in this volume; Robert Orledge's 2016 revised edition happily corrects these errors.

Satie's memory was also sustained by *Le Populaire*, a newspaper which billed itself 'the only daily socialist newspaper in Paris'. Ravel is less readily associated with left-wing politics than Satie, but he was a reader

---

compagnie avec celle de Satie: Chabrier, Debussy, Stravinsky et ces jeunes pour qui il garda toujours une si bienfaisant sympathie, Poulenc, Auric, Sauguet et Darius Milhaud'.

[23] Christopher Moore, 'Socialist Realism and the Music of the French Popular Front.' *Journal of Musicology*, vol. 25 no. 4 (Fall 2008): pp. 473–502, at p. 480.

[24] Robert Caby, 'Anniversaire de la mort d'Erik Satie', *L'Humanité*, 9 July 1928, p. 4: 'Satie, musicien né, écrivit avant 1900 des pages nouvelles par leur système harmonique, élémentaires de construction, et d'une pureté admirable'; 'La majeure partie de sa musique est faite de thèmes populaires qu'il savait travestir adorablement, et qui dans sa dernière œuvre *Relâche* atteignit, avec un incomparable éclat, une grandeur bouffonne. [...] Le même art que nous admirons dans ses valses de music-hall, nous l'admirons dans son *Socrate* où, avec des moyens restreints, il atteint à ce que l'humanité antique a produit de plus grand.'

[25] Robert Caby, *L'Humanité*, 1 March 1928, p. 4: 'la prodigieuse réussite du vieux Satie, avec le film *Entr'acte*, de René Clair'.

of this newspaper.²⁶ *Le Populaire* published a tribute to Satie four years after his death: 'Last Sunday, on 30 June, a plaque was affixed to the house in Cachan [sic] where one of the great composers of our time, Erik Satie, lived. Friends of the late composer recalled the simple and generous life of this innovative and modest artist [...] such a noble and lofty character.' The author unsurprisingly focuses not only on Satie's musical reputation, but also on his membership of the Socialist Party and friendship with the political activist Léon-Louis Veyssière. The article concludes: 'As a composer, Satie had much influence on the new generation. His work changed the traditional modes of sensitivity and expression. His work, so simple, stripped-back and charming, did more for the glory of French music and of music in general than those great "machines" who are crowned by the Institut and performed in certain concert halls.'²⁷

Satie's political views were shared by some composers of his generation and the next, some of whom went further than him in writing 'engaged' art. In the wake of the Popular Front's election victory in May 1936, 'Many French composers drew close to pro-Soviet cultural organizations such as the Maison de la Culture and the Association des Ecrivains et Artistes Révolutionnaires (AEAR) and engaged in artistic projects with manifest left-wing political themes.'²⁸ Many former members of Les Six were involved in this organisation, notably Milhaud, Honegger, Auric and Durey, and Albert Roussel, Jean Wiéner and Charles Koechlin were other composers allied to the movement. But again, Satie's influence was strongest on the friend of his last year, Robert Caby, who 'believed that the revolutionary spirit of Communism could only be expressed if modern composers broke with the formal and semantic conventions of so-called bourgeois music'.²⁹

A major posthumous premiere was presented in the context of an evening dedicated to 'L'Humour d'Erik Satie', ensuring that the popular view of the composer as essentially a humorist has persisted. At this 1937

---

²⁶ Roger Nichols, *Ravel*. New Haven and London: Yale University Press, 2011, p. 356.
²⁷ R.L., writing in *Le Populaire*, 4 July 1929, pp. 1–2, at p. 1; 'Dimanche dernier, 30 juin, une plaque a été apposé sur la maison qu'habita à Cachan Erik Satie, un des plus grands musiciens de notre temps. Des amis du disparu ont rappelé la vie simple et généreuse, d'artiste novateur et modeste [...] une si noble et si haute personnalité. [...] Satie, compositeur, a eu une grande influence sur la nouvelle génération de musiciens. Son œuvre a modifié les modes de sensibilité et d'expression. Son art attirant, simple, dépouillé et charmant a plus fait pour l'honneur de la musique française et de la musique en général que ces grandes « machines » couronnées par l'Institut ou exécutées dans certains concerts.'
²⁸ Moore, 'Socialist Realism and the Music of the French Popular Front', p. 475.
²⁹ Ibid., p. 480.

event, the complete *Jack in the Box* – a staged performance with Jules Dépaquit's text as well as Satie's music – was presented by the troupe Rideau de Paris. Most unfortunately, this was the only performance of *Jack in the Box* with Dépaquit's text, as its present location is unknown. The performance was previewed in *Le Figaro* on 23 November by Marcel Herrand, the director of Rideau de Paris. Herrand recalls first meeting Satie at a rehearsal of Apollinaire's play *Les mamelles de Tirésias* in 1917, describing him as 'an extraordinary creative artist' whose Montmartre-style humour is no longer part of the culture. Herrand writes: 'It is undeniable that, well before the first silent films by the great Charlie Chaplin, the Mack Sennet comedies, the Marx Brothers and cartoon films, the good master of Arcueil invented this burlesque mixture of screwball naivety and unbuttoned, sharp-edged humour which has since spread across the world.' Herrand also mentions that Marcelle Meyer would play piano works including *Les trois valses distingués du précieux dégoûté* and *Sonatine bureaucratique*, and that she would be joined by Ida Jankélévitch for a piano duet performance of *La Belle excentrique*. Jane Bathori was also involved, singing Satie's *Trois poèmes d'amour*. Madeleine Milhaud was both actress (playing the role of Frisette in *Le piège de Méduse*) and reader of texts by Satie. Other performers named include Henri Sauguet, who played Méduse and, in *Jack in the Box*, 'little "Gribisches" who saw furniture in half, put goldfish in the stew, put shoes on to roast, sit on the pendulum, etc.'.[30]

It was Robert Caby's view that great revolutionary music is 'most likely to be produced by the musical autodidacts among France's workers – "naïve" composers like himself and his erstwhile mentor Satie, who had developed at the margins of France's academic and institutionalized musical traditions'.[31] Instead, the most prominent composers in France from the mid-twentieth century were revolutionary in their music rather than their politics. It was left to popular singers to claim the popular territory, and to American and British experimentalists to take up Caby's call to break 'with the formal and semantic conventions' of the classical music tradition. I will briefly assess Satie's importance to these

---

[30] Marcel Herrand, 'L'humour d'Erik Satie', *Le Figaro*, 22 November 1937, p. 5: 'il est indéniable que bien avant les premiers films muets du grand Charlie Chaplin, les Mac-Sennet [sic] comédies, les Marx Brothers et les dessins animés, le bon maître d'Arcueil avait inventé ce burlesque mélange de naïveté loufoque et d'humour décousu et amer qui, depuis, a fait le tour du monde'; 'les petits « Gribisches » qui scieront les meubles, mettront les poissons rouges dans le pot-au-feu, feront rôtir les souliers, s'assiéront sur la pendule, etc.'. 'Gribische' is a Norman dialect word meaning 'wicked woman'.

[31] Moore, 'Socialist Realism and the Music of the French Popular Front', p. 483.

experimental artists after considering the attitudes of the French musical establishment to Satie.

France's most important music journal, *Revue musicale*, published tribute numbers – *tombeaux* – to Debussy (1920) and Dukas (1936) not long after their deaths. Satie was not honoured with a complete *tombeau* edition, perhaps because the number published on 1 March 1924, fifteen months before his death, had featured three articles on him and fragments of Satie's own writings.[32] The journal ceased publication in 1940, restarting sporadically after World War II and regularly from 1952. One of its first productions in this new era was a number devoted to Satie's memory (though not labelled a *tombeau*), edited by the British musicologist Rollo Myers and published in June 1952[33] – twenty-seven years after the composer's death. This was, naturally, largely a tribute to Satie by those who admired him, many of whom had known the composer. Cocteau, René Chalupt, Valentine Hugo, E. L. T. Mesens, Robert Caby and others contributed their memories, and Poulenc wrote on Satie's piano music. Most of the other contributors were British or American composers or musicologists, continuing an Anglophone interest in Satie's music that started with authors such as Carl van Vechten and Constant Lambert and continues to the present day. Virgil Thomson's 'La place de Satie dans la musique du XXe siècle' opens: 'I agree with Darius Milhaud and some other contemporary French composers that Satie's work should be considered one of the supreme musical productions of our century.'[34] Wilfrid Mellers' contribution, 'Satie et la musique «fonctionnelle»', focuses on film music and was first published in his *Studies in Contemporary Music* in 1947, and Roger Shattuck's thought-provoking article 'Satie et la musique de placard' anticipates his highly influential 1955 book *The Banquet Years*, in which Satie is considered alongside Apollinaire, the Douanier Rousseau and Alfred Jarry. French musicology is represented by Jean Roy, whose article on Satie as a writer precedes a selection of Satie's texts, some of which were intended for piano works and previously unpublished, plus others including 'Mémoires d'un amnésique' which were published in the composer's lifetime.

The final article is a surprise in this context. 'Chien flasque' ('Flabby Dog') is written by Pierre Boulez, who refuses to join the general

---

[32] However, Henri Cliquet-Pleyel's piano work titled *Le tombeau de Satie*, composed in 1926, was published as the musical supplement to the *Revue musicale* number of 1 April 1928.

[33] Rollo Myers (ed.), 'Erik Satie, son temps et ses amis.' *Revue musicale* no. 214 (June 1952).

[34] Virgil Thomson, 'La place de Satie dans la musique du XXe siècle.' *Revue musicale* no. 214 (June 1952), p. 13: 'Je suis d'accord avec Darius Milhaud et quelques autres musiciens français contemporains pour placer l'œuvre de Satie parmi les plus hautes valeurs musicales de notre siècle.'

approbation of Satie. Written the same year as 'Schönberg est mort' (several months after the actual event on 13 July 1951) and seven years after he booed Stravinsky's *Danses concertantes* at the Théâtre des Champs-Elysées, Boulez satirises Satie by adapting his title *Préludes flasques (pour un chien)* and adopting his telegraphic 'causerie' style: pauses noted in the text, plays on words and lists. An extract gives the flavour of his writing:

> Description of glandular atrophy: Satie's styles; Satie's discoveries – or inventions; Satie's humour.
>
> Some of Satie's inventions:
>
> – ninth chords which resolve unconventionally
>
> – lack of bar lines
>
> – 'returns to'
>
> – his disciples.
>
> The only thing he could have done to enhance his reputation would have been to found the concours Lépine (minor inventor section).[35]

The concours Lépine is a competition for inventions run by the city of Paris. It is hardly surprising that the young composer of *Structures I*, an integral serial work composed the same year as this article, is no admirer of Satie's music, though as a provocateur he lacked only Satie's sense of humour. Boulez's dogmatic assertions (pun intended) that in music, his way was the only way, were part of his compositional persona in the early 1950s. Satie's piano music, though, has ultimately proved far more appealing to performers, audiences and even scholars than *Structures*; once considered a major musical landmark, Boulez's work is now almost completely forgotten.

A less-known French composer paid a high price for criticising Satie. Jean Barraqué (1928–73) wrote only a handful of works and suffered all his adult life from physical and mental health problems, alcoholism and sheer bad luck (for instance, his flat and manuscripts were destroyed in a gas explosion late in 1969).[36] While he was struggling to complete a series of ambitious works based on Hermann Broch's novel *The Death of Virgil*, Barraqué wrote a short book on Debussy for the publisher

---

[35] Pierre Boulez, 'Chien flasque.' *Revue musicale* no. 214 (June 1952), pp. 153–4, at p. 153: 'Description d'une atrophie glandulaire: les styles de Satie; les découvertes – ou inventions – de Satie; l'humour de Satie.' 'Quelques inventions de Satie: ¶ – les accords de neuvième à résolutions exceptionnelles ¶ – la suppression de la barre de mesure ¶ – les 'retours à' ¶ – ses disciples. ¶ Il ne manque à sa gloire que d'être fondateur du concours Lépine (rayon des petits inventeurs).'

[36] See Laurent Feneyrou (ed.), *Jean Barraqué: Ecrits*. Paris: Publications de la Sorbonne, 2001 and Paul Griffiths, *The Sea on Fire: Jean Barraqué*. Rochester, NY: University of Rochester Press, 2003.

Seuil to commemorate the centenary of the composer's birth in 1962. Sadly for this troubled man, his many insightful passages on Debussy's music were overshadowed by a reference to Satie as an 'accomplished musical illiterate [...] who found that his friendship with Debussy was an unhoped-for opportunity to loiter in the corridors of history'.[37] For this remark he was taken to court ten years after the book's publication. In France it is possible to sue for defamation of a deceased relative, and it is on these grounds that Satie's only surviving blood relation, Pierre Joseph-Lafosse Satie, successfully sued Barraqué.

Joseph-Lafosse was the grandson of Satie's sister Olga. She had fled France for Argentina in 1902 following the death of her husband, a doctor also named Pierre Joseph-Lafosse. Her late husband's relatives had made her life intolerable and she ceded guardianship of her son, who was born after his father's death, to her in-laws. Her son in turn had a son who informally added the surname 'Satie' to his own name. Pierre Joseph-Lafosse Satie never knew his great-uncle but he was his only heir and he proved a tenacious defender of the composer's rights. In addition to the Barraqué affair, he launched a long series of legal actions against the unauthorised publication or performance of Satie's works. The esteemed British scholar Nigel Wilkins, who had himself been obliged to withdraw his proposed English-language edition of Satie's letters in the face of Joseph-Lafosse's objections, described the Barraqué case as 'an astounding adverse judgement said by some to have hastened the composer's sad and premature death'.[38] Barraqué appealed in 1973 against the fine of 3000 francs which was imposed the previous year but he was unsuccessful.[39] Neither Barraqué nor Boulez was aware of the broad intellectual culture which informed Satie's work, nor of the systematic basis of many Satie pieces which has since been uncovered by scholars including Orledge and Whiting. But these deeply serious composers were evidently uncomfortable with the simplicity, irony and humour at the heart of Satie's music. The eclecticism of Satie's sources – musical and extramusical, popular and artistic – was also something very far from the aesthetic of both Boulez and Barraqué.

Since his death, Satie has appealed more to American and British composers and artists than to their French contemporaries. The American enthusiasm for the composer started in Montparnasse in the 1910s and early 1920s and immediately showed Satie's appeal to a constituency beyond contemporary music. Peter Dickinson notes that 'As early as 1914,

---

[37] 'un analphabète musical accompli[...]ayant trouvé dans ses relations avec Debussy une occasion inespérée de faufiler dans les coulisses de l'histoire'. This passage was removed from later editions of the book.

[38] Nigel Wilkins, 'Erik Satie's Letters to Milhaud and Others.' *Musical Quarterly*, vol. 66 no. 3 (July 1980): pp. 404–28, at p. 404.

[39] Feneyrou (ed.), *Jean Barraqué: Ecrits*, p. 30.

[the poet and amateur composer S. Foster] Damon was apparently the author of an unsigned article on Satie in *The Harvard Musical Review*.'[40] The same university hosted the poet e.e. cummings in 1915, who said in an address: 'Erik Satie is, in many respects, the most interesting of all modern composers. Nearly a quarter of a century ago he was writing what is now considered modern music.'[41] Again, the notion of Satie as a precursor appealed to artists in search of novelty. Performances followed: Virgil Thomson, another admirer of the stripped-down quality of Satie's music, ensured *Socrate* was given an American premiere in Cambridge, Massachusetts and New York in 1923, and the pianist Jane Mortier toured Satie's works in the last years of the composer's life.

It is fair to say that Satie's reception in the USA immediately after the composer's death was mixed. Late in 1925, Walter V. Anderson reviewed a concert in New York and showed particular interest in Satie's Scottish heritage:

> The wily Scot and untravelled Frank, the late Eric Satie [sic], was represented by seven dances from the ballet-comedy, 'Le Piège de Méduse', in which some of the more important of his piano works are made use of. It is characteristic Satie: wilfully banal melody, a boom on the big drum, impromptu cessation after a dozen bars ... in a word, music of no intrinsic value. One whose Scotch intellect pawned his French heart, Satie can ultimately receive – in truth rather than in charity – only the benediction of that French proverb: 'He had the defects of his virtues,' an irony none appreciated better than he.[42]

Anderson is mistaken about the dances from *Le piège de Méduse*, which were composed specifically for Satie's own play rather than being chippings of earlier pieces, and these barrel organ-like miniatures are designed to be played as often as required to fit in with Jonas the monkey's dance. The author does raise an interesting question, however, about Satie performance practice: do these miniatures work in concert performance, separated from their original context as accompaniment to dance?

A leading American experimentalist of the twentieth century understood Satie as a composer whose music is part of a bigger artistic picture: John Cage's discovery of Satie proved decisive and durable. Cage and his lifelong collaborator and partner Merce Cunningham promoted

---

[40] Peter Dickinson, 'Stein Satie Cummings Thomson Berners Cage: Toward a Context for the Music of Virgil Thomson.' *Musical Quarterly*, vol. 72 no. 3 (1986): pp. 394–409, at p. 399.

[41] Cited in ibid., p. 398.

[42] Walter V. Anderson, 'Reflections from New York', *The Chesterian*, 50 (November 1925): pp. 54–5, at p. 55.

Satie as early as 1948 when, at Black Mountain College, Cage gave lectures on Satie and they jointly put on the US premiere of *Le piège de Méduse* on 14 August (Cunningham played Jonas the monkey and Cage was the pianist). William Fetterman summarises Satie's appeal to Cage as 'compositions that may often irritate middle-class taste and sensibilities; an irrelevant (and sometimes irreverent) sense of humor; an interest in structure; a seemingly innocent yet mature insight into the significance of mundane or trivial events; a restrained although passionately engaged emotional content beneath the veneer of impersonality; and the inherent calligraphic beauty of their hand-written scores'.[43] A year before their residency at Black Mountain, Cunningham had choreographed the first movement of *Socrate*, Cage having transcribed the work for two pianos, but the publisher Eschig refused permission to use Satie's original in this performance. Cage decided therefore to create a new work for solo piano based on *Socrate*. As the choreography was based on the rhythm of Satie's work, Cage retained this and used I Ching-derived chance procedures to obtain the rest of the musical material. *Socrate* was a work which obsessed Cage: in 1969 he made a version for solo violin titled *Cheap Imitation* which again subjects Satie's piece to modifications based on processes selected by chance. Cage's final dance composition for Cunningham, written a year before his death, was *FOUR³* (1991) 'which includes chance determined variations of the cantus firmus and the counterpoints of Satie's *Vexations*'.[44]

Cage had been involved in the first complete public performance of *Vexations* in New York on 8–9 September 1963, and Satie's influence is one of few continuing threads in his art. But rather than producing music that sounds like Satie, it is Satie's attitude which was a model for Cage. As an iconoclast who, magpie-like, drew on whatever sources from whatever art form were most suitable for his ideas, Satie was refreshingly different from the mainstream European classical music tradition. The enigmatic, ironic, is-he-being-serious-or-not? quality of Satie's thought has a level of ambiguity which allows room for personal interpretation, and the deadpan quality of much of his music facilitates its perception as a blank canvas on which others can project their own creativity.

The composer and critic Peter Dickinson believes that 'Satie provided a European blessing for the idea of drawing upon popular music as well as an example of how to strip music to its barest essential.'[45] Indeed, many of Dickinson's own works pay sensitive tribute to Satie. The 'stripped-

---

[43] William Fetterman, *John Cage's Theatre Pieces*. London: Routledge, 1997, p. 16.

[44] Ibid., p. 16. See also Matthew Mendez, 'History, Homeopathy and the Spiritual Impulse in the Post-war Reception of Satie: Cage, Higgins, Beuys', Caroline Potter (ed.), *Erik Satie: Music, Art and Literature*. Farnham: Ashgate, 2013, pp. 183–228.

[45] Dickinson, 'Stein Satie Cummings Thomson Berners Cage', p. 409.

down' aspect of Satie particularly appealed to composers of the English experimental school, most notably Howard Skempton. In Skempton's case, the homespun quality, simplicity (again) and brevity of Satie are centrally important. Skempton's charming and naïve piano miniatures echo his description of Satie's piano music: 'the brevity of course suggests communication on an intimate level – that's the way I see it. These aren't grand, pretentious statements – he's very quick to prick that particular bubble, and I think that if you're looking for something really central about Satie, I think it's the intimacy of the music.'[46]

For Skempton as for so many others, it is Satie's early piano music which proved most inspiring. John Adams' piano concerto *Century Rolls* (1996), composed for Emanuel Ax and the Cleveland Orchestra, includes an explicit homage to Satie. While the outer movements of this concerto feature, in the composer's words, 'a kind of automatic re-writing of the pianola music of the [twentieth] century', the central slow movement has a different mood and influence: Adams wanted both to showcase Ax's 'timbre and lyrical warmth that sets his performances apart from all other pianists'[47] and pay tribute to Satie. The movement's elliptical title, 'Manny's Gym', does not refer to Ax's supposed exercise schedule but to Satie's *Gymnopédies*. The unmistakeable rhythm and texture of these pieces had already inspired Satie's contemporaries Ravel and Roland-Manuel: Adams shows that the *Gymnopédies* still resonated late into the twentieth century. He starts the movement by using the basic 'gymnopédie' rhythm, often in the piano, and gives a Satiean melody to wind soloists, though the movement soon moves away from this texture into complex rhythmic and pianistic figurations which are worlds apart from Satie's directness, brevity and simplicity.

Indeed, it is this simplicity which appealed most to American composers. Virgil Thomson encapsulated this quality of Satie's in a letter of 3 February 1981 to Thomas Dilworth: 'Satie used very few notes but they were all in the right place.'[48] In many ways, Satie has more in common with popular music composers than with the classical tradition. His works are almost all very short, simple in texture, repetitive and accessible to amateur performers, and he prizes melody above harmonic complexity. Satie's music rarely modulates – another feature in common with pop tracks – and he uses repetition or juxtaposition of ideas rather than classical development to create larger-scale structures. It is therefore

---

[46] Howard Skempton, 'After Satie', Caroline Potter (ed.), *Erik Satie: Music, Art and Literature*. Farnham: Ashgate, 2013, pp. 229–42, at p. 231.

[47] John Adams, programme note for *Century Rolls* cited in http://www.earbox.com/orchestra/century-rolls (accessed 7 April 2015).

[48] Thomas Dilworth and Susan Holbrook (eds), *The Letters of Gertrude Stein and Virgil Thomson: Composition as Conversation*. New York: Oxford University Press, 2010, p. 7.

hardly surprising that his music has appealed to pop musicians in quest of easy-listening instrumentals.

This popular legacy includes the former member of Genesis Steve Hackett's album *Sketches of Satie* (2000, reissued 2014), featuring Hackett on acoustic guitar with his brother John playing the flute on some of his performances of the three *Gymnopédies*, six *Gnossiennes*, *Avant-dernières pensées*, *Pièces froides* and five *Nocturnes*. These are respectful transcriptions of Satie which add no additional material to the originals, though they do show that Satie can have a surprising affinity with the guitar. Hackett recalls 'around 1969 I was haunted by a piano melody I'd heard in the distance. I often used to sing it to people and asked if they recognised it. At that time it wasn't quite as well known as it is today.'[49] This piece was Satie's first *Gymnopédie*. Perhaps Hackett was inspired by Blood, Sweat and Tears' *Variations on a Theme of Erik Satie*, released on Columbia in 1968, which subjects the first *Gymnopédie* to arrangements for two different combinations of instruments: flute and acoustic guitar, and syncopated and synthesised horns and drumkit. The haunting melody of the first *Gymnopédie* is a stalwart of 'relaxing' and 'chillout' classics compilations, the ideal antidote to a frenetic, plugged-in world. What Satie would have thought of this marketisation of his very early work can only be imagined. When Stravinsky rejected the *Sports et divertissements* project, allegedly because the money offered was insufficient, Satie allegedly rejected it because the fee was too large. But would 'Monsieur le Pauvre' have rejected the considerable royalties that today's recording industry would have brought him? He would probably have spent the money immediately or given it away.

Satie is a mass of contradictions. He is a popular composer, though many of his works are rarely heard; his persona continues to intrigue people, though the 'real' person remains an enigma. Let us leave the last word to John Cage, who pithily summarised his importance to experimental artists: 'he's indispensable'.[50]

---

[49] http://www.hackettsongs.com/blog/steve130.html (accessed 7 April 2015).
[50] John Cage, 'Erik Satie', in *Silence*. Westport, CT: Wesleyan University Press, 1976, p. 82. First appeared in the 1958 *Art News Annual*.

Select Bibliography

Abbate, Carolyn. 'Outside Ravel's Tomb'. *Journal of the American Musicological Society*, vol. 52 no. 3 (Autumn 1999): pp. 465–530.

Abbott, Helen. *Between Baudelaire and Mallarmé: Voice, Conversation and Music*. Farnham: Ashgate, 2009.

Adès, Dawn. *Dada and Surrealism Reviewed*. London: Arts Council of Great Britain, 1978.

Albrecht, Florent. 'Verlaine l'anti-théoricien: contre la poétique, la musique?' *Revue silène*, 2010, http://www.revue-silene.com/f/index.php?sp=liv&livre_id=140.

Albright, Daniel. *Stravinsky: The Music Box and the Nightingale*. Amsterdam: Gordon & Breach, 1989.

——. *Untwisting the Serpent*. Chicago: University of Chicago Press, 2000.

—— (ed.). *Modernism and Music: An Anthology of Sources*. Chicago: University of Chicago Press, 2004.

Allan, Kenneth R. 'Metamorphosis in *391*: A Cryptographic Collaboration by Francis Picabia, Man Ray, and Erik Satie'. *Art History* (February 2011): pp. 102–25.

[Anonymous]. *Paris Exposition, 1900: Guide pratique du visiteur de Paris et de l'exposition*. Paris: Hachette, 1900.

[Anonymous]. 'Un type populaire qui disparaît: Le joueur d'orgue de Barbarie'. *Le Petit Journal*, 26 April 1908: p. 2.

Antheil, George. *Bad Boy of Music*. New York: Da Capo Press, 1981 (originally published in 1945).

Antliff, Mark, and Patricia Leighten (eds). *A Cubism Reader*. Chicago: University of Chicago Press, 2008.

Appignanesi, Lisa. *The Cabaret*. New York: Universe Books, 1976.

Arfouilloux, Sébastien. *Que la nuit tombe sur l'orchestre. Surréalisme et musique*. Paris: Fayard, 2009.

Armengaud, Jean-Pierre. *Erik Satie*. Paris: Fayard, 2009.

Attali, Jacques. *Bruits* (revised edition). Paris: Fayard/PUF, 2001.

Auclair, Mathias, Frank Claustrat and Inès Piovesan (eds), *Les Ballets Suédois: Une compagnie d'avant-garde (1920–1925)*. Paris: Bibliothèque Nationale de France, 2014.

Battier, Marc. 'Des unanimistes à l'art sonore: Quand la littérature, l'art et la musique recréent la technologie', in Sylvain Caron, François de Médicis and Michel Duchesneau (eds), *Musique et modernité en France*. Montréal: Presses Universitaires de Montréal, 2006, pp. 389–416.

Berys, José de. 'Chez Orphée: La musique d'ameublement. Une idée de M. Erik Satie. «Comme la tapisserie!» «Inutile d'écouter!»' *Comœdia*, 5 March 1920, p. 2.

——. 'Les petites premières: Ruffian toujours, truand jamais à la Galerie Barbazanges'. *Comœdia*, 10 March 1920, p. 2.

Borsaro, Brigitte. 'Cocteau, le cirque et le music-hall'. *Cahiers Jean Cocteau*, nouvelle série, 2 (2003), pp. 9–132.

Brigstocke, Julian. 'Defiant Laughter: Humour and the Aesthetics of Place in Late 19th Century Montmartre'. *Cultural Geographies*, vol. 19 no. 2 (April 2012): pp. 217–35.

Cate, Philip Dennis, and Mary Shaw (eds). *The Spirit of Montmartre*. New Brunswick, NJ: Rutgers University Press, 1996.

Chou Wen-Chung. 'Varèse: A Sketch of the Man and his Music'. *Musical Quarterly*, vol. 52 no. 2 (April 1966): pp. 151–70.

Classen, Roxanne. 'Satie as Flâneur and Trois morceaux en forme de poire'. http://academic.macewan.ca/classenr/2012/02/19/satie-as-flaneur-and-trois-morceaux-en-forme-de-poire/, accessed 4 April 2015.

Claude-Lafontaine, Lucien. 'Erik Satie'. *Le Quadrige*, 3 (January 1913): pp. 10–12.

Cocteau, Jean. *Le rappel à l'ordre*. Paris: Stock, 1926.

——. *Le coq et l'arlequin*. Paris: Editions de la Sirène ('Collection des Tracts no 1'), 1918. New edition Paris: Stock, 1979.

Cœuroy, André, and Theodore Baker. 'Further Aspects of Contemporary Music'. *Musical Quarterly*, vol. 15 no. 4 (October 1929): pp. 547–73.

Corvin, Michel. *Le théâtre de recherche entre les deux guerres: Le laboratoire art et action*. Lausanne: La Cité – L'Age d'Homme, 1976.

Craft, Robert. 'Stravinsky Pre-Centenary'. *Perspectives of New Music*, vol. 19 nos. 1–2 (1980–1): pp. 464–77.

Crespelle, Jean-Paul. *A Montmartre au temps de Picasso*. Paris: Hachette, 1991.

Davis, Mary E. 'Modernity à la mode: Popular Culture and Avant-Gardism in Erik Satie's "Sports et divertissements"'. *Musical Quarterly*, vol. 83 no. 3 (Autumn 1999): pp. 430–73.

——. *Classic Chic: Music, Fashion, and Modernism*. Berkeley: University of California Press, 2006.

——. *Erik Satie*. London: Reaktion, 2007.

Dawson, Christopher. 'Erik Satie Viewed as a Writer: With Special Reference to his Texts from 1900 to 1925'. Unpublished DPhil thesis, University of Oxford, 1993.

——. 'Erik Satie's *Vexations* – an Exercise in Immobility'. *Canadian Music Review*, vol. 21 no. 2 (2001): pp. 29–40.

——. 'Erik Satie's Sententious Writings'. *A.U.M.L.A.: Journal of the Australasian Universities Modern Language Association*, vol. 95 (2001): pp. 55–74.

——. 'Menus propos modernistes: Absurdity in Erik Satie's "La Journée du Musicien"'. *Nottingham French Studies*, vol. 44 no. 2 (2005): pp. 55–62.

Dayan, Peter. 'Truth in Art, and Erik Satie's Judgement'. *Nineteenth-Century Music Review*, 6 (2009): pp. 91–107.

——. 'Apollinaire's Music'. *Forum for Modern Language Studies*, vol. 47 no. 1 (2011): pp. 36–48.

De Groote, Pascale. *Ballets Suédois*. Ghent: Academia Press, 2002.

Dorf, Samuel N. '"Etrange, n'est-ce pas?" The Princesse Edmond de Polignac, Erik Satie's Socrate, and a Lesbian Aesthetic of Music?', in James Day (ed.), *Queer Sexualities in French and Francophone Literature and Film*. French Literature Series, vol. 34. London: Rodopi, 2007, pp. 87–99.

Drew, David. 'The Savage Parade – from Satie, Cocteau and Picasso to the Britten of *Les Illuminations* and beyond'. *Tempo*, 207 (2001): pp. 7–21.

Fermigier, André. 'Jean Cocteau et Paris 1920'. *Annales. Economies, Sociétés, Civilisations*. 22e année, no. 3 (1967): pp. 495–513.

Fortassier, Pierre. 'Verlaine, la musique et les musiciens'. *Cahiers de l'Association internationale des études françaises*, vol. 12 (1960): pp. 143–59.

Fouché, Pascal. *La Sirène*. Paris: Bibliothèque de littérature française contemporaine de l'Université Paris 7, 1984.

Fulcher, Jane F. *French Cultural Politics and Music: From the Dreyfus Affair to the First World War*. New York: Oxford University Press, 1999.

———. *The Composer as Intellectual: Music and Ideology in France, 1914–1940*. New York: Oxford University Press, 2005.

Fung, Catherine H. M., 'Asperger's and Musical Creativity: The Case of Erik Satie'. *Personality and Individual Differences*, vol. 46 no. 8 (2009): pp. 775–83.

Gillmor, Alan. 'Erik Satie and the Concept of the Avant-Garde'. *Musical Quarterly*, vol. 69 no. 1 (Winter 1983): pp. 104–19.

———. 'Musico-poetic Form in Satie's 'Humoristic' Piano Suites (1913–14)'. *Canadian University Music Review*, vol. 8 (1987): pp. 1–44.

———. *Erik Satie*. Boston: Twayne, 1988.

Guichard, Léon. 'A propos d'Erik Satie: Notules incohérentes'. *Université de Grenoble, U.E.R. de Lettres, Recherches et travaux Bulletin no. 7*, pp. 63–80.

Häger, Bengt. *Ballets Suédois*, trans. Ruth Sharman. London: Thames & Hudson, 1990.

Haine, Malou. 'Jean Cocteau et ses compositeurs en Belgique'. Talk given on 6 March 2004, available at http://www.arllfb.be/ebibliotheque/seancespubliques/06032004/haine.pdf.

———. 'Jean Cocteau, impresario musical à la croisée des arts', in Sylvain Caron, François de Médicis and Michel Duchesneau (eds), *Musique et modernité en France*. Montréal: Presses Universitaires de Montréal, 2006, pp. 69–134.

Halbreich, Harry. *Arthur Honegger: Un musicien dans la cité des hommes*. Paris: Fayard, 1992. Translated by Roger Nichols, Portland, OR: Amadeus Press, 1999.

Hanlon, Ann-Marie. 'Satie and the French Musical Canon: A Reception Study'. Unpublished PhD thesis, University of Newcastle, 2013.

Honegger, Arthur. *Lettres à ses parents, 1914–1922*. Geneva: Editions Papillon, 2005 (with preface and annotations by Harry Halbreich).

Howat, Roy. *Debussy in Proportion*. Cambridge: Cambridge University Press, 1983.

Hyland, Douglas K. S. 'Agnes Ernst Meyer, Patron of American Modernism'. *America Art Journal*, vol. 12 no. 1 (Winter 1980): pp. 64–81.

Inglis, Katherine. 'Becoming Automatous: Automata in *The Old Curiosity Shop* and *Our Mutual Friend*'. *Interdisciplinary Studies in the Long Nineteenth Century*, 6 (2008), www.19.bbk.ac.uk.

Jankélévitch, Vladimir. 'Le symbolisme et la musique: Satie le simulateur'. *Europe*, 15 June 1936, pp. 249–56.

——. 'Satie et le matin', in *La musique et les heures*. Paris: Seuil, 1988.

Jeanne, Paul. *Les théâtres d'ombres à Montmartre de 1887 à 1923*. Paris: Les Editions des Presses Modernes au Palais-Royal, 1937.

Kahn, Douglas. *Noise, Water, Meat: A History of Sound in the Arts*. Cambridge, MA: MIT Press, 2001.

Klüver, Billy. *A Day with Picasso*. Cambridge, MA: MIT Press, 1999.

Lambert, Constant. *Music Ho! A Study of Music in Decline*. London: Faber, 1937.

Langwill, Lyndesay G. and Arthur W. J. G. Ord-Hume. 'Barrel Organ'. *Grove Music Online*. *Oxford Music Online*. Oxford University Press, accessed 4 April 2015, http://www.oxfordmusiconline.com/subscriber/article/grove/music/02111.

Lawson, Rex. 'Maurice Ravel: *Frontispice* for Pianola'. *The Pianola Journal*, no. 2 (1989).

Leggio, James (ed.). *Music and Modern Art*. New York: Routledge, 2002.

Lejeune, Emile. 'Montparnasse à l'époque héroïque, 7: 1re exposition (du 19 Novembre au 5 Décembre 1916, Kisling, Matisse, Modigliani, Ortiz de Zarate, Picasso)'. *Tribune de Genève* no. 33/6, 8–9 février 1964, p. 1.

Lemoine, Jean-Gabriel. 'Spectacle d'Avant-garde: Une pièce de M. Max Jacob: *Ruffian toujours, truand jamais* (Représentation unique donnée à la Galerie Barbazanges le 8 mars 1920)'. *Le Crapouillot*, 16 March 1920, p. 6.

Marcoux, Annie, and Didier Gompel-Netter (eds). *Max Jacob: Les propos et les jours. Lettres 1904–1944*. Paris: Zodiaque, 1989.

Martens, Frederick H. 'Music Mirrors of the Second Empire – Part II'. *The Musical Quarterly*, vol. 16 no. 4 (October 1930): pp. 563–87.

Mattis, Olivia. 'Theater as Circus: "A Midsummer Night's Dream"'. *The Library Chronicle of the University of Texas at Austin*, vol. 23 no. 4 (1993): pp. 43–77.

Mawer, Deborah. 'Musical Objects and Machines', in Deborah Mawer (ed.), *The Cambridge Companion to Ravel*. Cambridge: Cambridge University Press, 2000: pp. 47–70.

Meyer, Felix, and Heidy Zimmermann (eds). *Edgard Varèse: Composer, Sound Sculptor, Visionary*. Woodbridge: The Boydell Press, 2006.

Milhaud, Darius. *Notes sans musique*. Paris: Julliard, 1949.

Milorad. 'Jean Cocteau avec les musiciens'. *Cahiers Jean Cocteau*, 7 (1978): pp. 13–106.

Moore, C. H. 'Verlaine's "opéra bouffe"'. *Proceedings of the Modern Language Association*, vol. 83 no. 2 (May 1968): pp. 305–11.

Moore, Christopher. 'Socialist Realism and the Music of the French Popular Front'. *Journal of Musicology*, vol. 25 no. 4 (Fall 2008): pp. 473–502.

Myers, Rollo. *Erik Satie*. London: Dennis Dobson, 1948.

Oberthür, Mariel. *Le Cabaret du Chat Noir à Montmartre (1881–1897)*. Geneva: Slatkine, 2007.

Oja, Carol J. *Making Music Modern: New York in the 1920s*. New York: Oxford University Press, 2003.

Olivier, Philippe (ed.). *Aimer Satie*. Paris: Hermann, 2005.

Orledge, Robert. *Satie the Composer*. Cambridge: Cambridge University Press, 1990.

——. 'Satie at Sea, and the Mysteries of "La Belle Cubaine"'. *Music & Letters*, vol. 71 no. 3 (1990): pp. 361–73.

——. 'The Musical Activities of Alfred Satie and Eugénie Satie-Barnetche, and Their Effect on the Career of Erik Satie'. *Journal of the Royal Musical Association*, vol. 117 no. 2 (1992): pp. 270–97.

—— (ed.), *Satie Remembered*. London: Faber, 1995.

——. 'Satie's Sarabandes and their Importance to his Composing Career'. *Music & Letters*, vol. 77 no. 4 (November 1996): pp. 555–65.

——. 'Erik Satie's Ballet "Mercure" (1924): From Mount Etna to Montmartre'. *Journal of the Royal Musical Association*, vol. 123 no. 2 (1998): pp. 229–49.

——. 'Erik Satie's Ballet *uspud*: Prime Numbers and the Creation of a New Language with Only Half the Alphabet'. *Musical Times*, vol. 150 no. 1908 (Autumn 2009): pp. 31–41.

Ouellette, Fernand. *Edgard Varèse*, trans. Derek Coltman. New York: Orion, 1968.

Ozenfant, Amédée. *Mémoires, 1886–1962*. Paris: Seghers, 1968.

Parrino, Francesco. 'Alfredo Casella and "The *Montjoie!* Affair"'. *repercussions*, vol. 10 no. 1 (Spring 2007): pp. 96–123.

Pasler, Jann. 'New Music as Confrontation: The Musical Sources of Jean Cocteau's Identity'. *Musical Quarterly*, vol. 75 no. 3 (Autumn 1991): pp. 255–78.

Perloff, Nancy. *Art and the Everyday: Popular Entertainment and the Circle of Erik Satie*. Oxford: Clarendon Press, 1991.

Peyser, Joan. 'The Phonograph and Our Musical Life'. *Musical Quarterly*, vol. 64 no. 2 (April 1978): pp. 250–4.

Potter, Caroline. 'Erik Satie's "Obstacles venimeux"'. *Ars Lyrica*, 20 (2011): pp. 99–114.

—— (ed.). *Erik Satie: Music, Art and Literature*. Farnham: Ashgate, 2013.

Rašin, Vera. 'Les Six and Jean Cocteau'. *Music & Letters*, vol. 38 no. 2 (April 1957): pp. 164–9.

Read, Peter. *Apollinaire et Les mamelles de Tirésias: La revanche d'Eros*. Rennes: Presses Universitaires de Rennes, 2000.
Reilly, Kara. *Automata and Mimesis on the Stage of Theatre History*. Basingstoke: Palgrave Macmillan, 2011.
Richardson, John. *A Life of Picasso*, vol. 2. London: Pimlico, 1996.
Rothschild, Deborah Menaker. *Picasso's 'Parade'*. New York: Sotheby's Publications/The Drawing Center, 1991.
Rozaitis, William. 'The Joke at the Heart of Things: Francis Picabia's Machine Drawings and the Little Magazine *291*'. *American Art*, vol. 8 nos. 3–4 (Autumn 1994): pp. 42–59.
Sanouillet, Michel. *Dada in Paris*, trans. Sharmila Ganguly. Cambridge, MA: MIT Press, 2009.
Schmidt, Carl B. (ed.). *Ecrits sur la musique de Georges Auric* (4 vols). Lewiston: Edwin Mellen, 2009.
Shattuck, Roger. *The Banquet Years*. London: Jonathan Cape, 1969.
Stamper, John W. 'The Galerie des Machines of the 1889 Paris World's Fair'. *Technology and Culture*, vol. 30 no. 2 (1989): pp. 330–53.
Taruskin, Richard. 'Stravinsky's *Petrushka*', in Andrew Baruch Wachtel (ed.), *Petrushka: Sources and Contexts*. Evanston, IL: Northwestern University Press: pp. 67–114.
Templier, Pierre-Daniel. *Erik Satie*. Paris: Editions Rieder, 1932.
Townsend, Christopher. 'The Art I Love is the Art of Cowards': Francis Picabia and René Clair's Entr'acte and the Politics of Death and Remembrance in France after World War I'. *Science as Culture*, vol. 18 no. 3 (2009): pp. 281–96.
——. 'The Last Hope of Intuition: Francis Picabia, Erik Satie and René Clair's Intermedial Project *Relâche*'. *Nottingham French Studies*, vol. 50 no. 3 (2011): pp. 43–66.
Vanel, Hervé. *Triple Entendre: Furniture Music, Muzak, Muzak-Plus*. Urbana, Chicago and Springfield: University of Illinois Press, 2013.
Vechten, Carl van. 'Erik Satie: Master of the Rigolo'. *Vanity Fair*, 10 (March 1918): p. 57.
Veyssière, Léon-Louis. *Réflexions et anecdotes sur Erik Satie par Léon-Louis Veyssière*. Preface by Annette Le Bonhomme-Veyssière. Cachan: Litavis, 2013.
Volta, Ornella (ed.). *Satie Ecrits*. Paris: Champ-Libre, 1979.
—— (ed.). *L'ymagier d'Erik Satie*. Paris: Van de Velde, 1979.
——. 'Une relation peu explorée: Blaise Cendrars et Erik Satie'. *Cahiers Blaise Cendrars*, 3. Neuchâtel: Editions de la Baconnière, 1981, pp. 87–105.
—— (ed.). 'Erik Satie – L'os à moelle'. *Revue internationale de musique française*, 23 (June 1987): pp. 5–98.
——. *Erik Satie et la tradition populaire*. Paris: Fondation Erik Satie/ Musée des Arts et des Traditions populaires, 1988 (Catalogue de l'exposition 10–30 mai 1988).
——. *Satie et la danse*. Paris: Plume, 1992.

———. *Erik Satie*. Paris: Hazan, 1997.
———. Preface to score *Erik Satie: Musiques d'ameublement pour petit ensemble*. Paris: Salabert, EAS 17141X, 1998.
——— (ed.). *Erik Satie: Correspondance presque complète*. Paris: Fayard/IMEC, 2/2003.
Warren, Rosanna. *'Live Like a Poet!': At Home in the Bateau Lavoir*, http://littlestarjournal.com/blog/2011/12/"live-like-a-poet-at-home-in-the-bateau-lavoir"-by-rosanna-warren/ (accessed 4 April 2015).
Weiss, Jeffrey. *The Popular Culture of Modern Art: Picasso, Duchamp, and Avant-Gardism*. New Haven: Yale University Press, 1994.
Whitesitt, Linda, Charles Amirkhanian and Susan C. Cook. 'Antheil, George'. *Grove Music Online. Oxford Music Online*. Oxford University Press, accessed April 4, 2015, http://www.oxfordmusiconline.com/subscriber/article/grove/music/00997.
Whiting, Steven Moore. 'Musical Parody and Two "Œuvres posthumes" of Erik Satie: The *Rêverie du pauvre* and the *Petite musique de clown triste*'. *Revue de musicologie*, vol. 81 no. 2 (1995): pp. 215–34.
———. 'Erik Satie and Vincent Hyspa: Notes on a Collaboration'. *Music & Letters*, vol. 77 no. 1 (1996): pp. 64–91.
———. *Satie the Bohemian: From Cabaret to Concert Hall*. Oxford: Clarendon Press, 1999.
Wilkins, Nigel. 'Erik Satie's Letters to Milhaud and Others'. *The Musical Quarterly*, vol. 66 no. 3 (July 1980): pp. 404–28.
———. *The Writings of Erik Satie*. London: Eulenburg, 1980.

Index of Names

6 rue Huyghens, 47–8, 73–4, 84–8, 151–2, 154, 156, 208, 227
291 (magazine), 171, 210–11, 229
391 (magazine), 171–2, 208, 209, 212, 213, 224–6, 228–9

Abbate, Carolyn, 16, 35, 63, 174
Abbott, Helen, 16
Adams, John: *Century Rolls*, 252
Adès, Dawn, 212
Albéniz, Isaac, 60
Albert-Birot, Germaine, 72
Albert-Birot, Pierre, 72
Albrecht, Florent, 13
Albright, Daniel, 50, 143, 170
Allais, Alphonse, 3, 5, 22, 23, 34, 181–3
   Album primo-avrilesque, 182
   Marche Funèbre composée pour les Funérailles d'un grand homme sourd, 34
Allan, Kenneth, 224–5
Andersen, Hans Christian, 58
Antheil, George, 19, 95–7
   Airplane Sonata, 95
   Ballet mécanique, 61, 96–7
   Mechanisms, 95
   Sonata Sauvage, 95
Apollinaire, Guillaume, 2, 42, 48, 49, 60, 66–9, 71–3, 86, 89, 103, 156, 171, 208, 213, 222, 247
   Alcools, 69
   Antitradition Futuriste, L', 66, 68
   Calligrammes, 48, 69
   Couleur du temps, 61–2
   Fantôme de nuées, Un, 67–8
   Mamelles de Tirésias, Les, 71–2, 245
   Roi Lune, Le, 48
Aragon, Louis, 213, 228
Arcueil, 18, 30, 115, 188–201
Arfouilloux, Sébastien, 214
Armengaud, Jean-Pierre, 126, 130
Art et Liberté, 51, 61
Astruc, Gabriel (a.k.a. Surtac), 63
Attali, Jacques, 11, 179–80

Auberge du Clou, 22, 26, 27
Auric, Georges, 64, 71, 79–80, 83, 88, 89, 101, 103, 164, 171, 209, 213, 214, 215, 216, 225, 227–8, 236, 243, 245
   as writer: 'Erik Satie: Musicien Humoriste', 42, 58–9, 101–2
   'La leçon d'Erik Satie', 239
   as composer: *Adieu, New York!*, 168, 214
   Fâcheux, Les, 209, 235
   Huit poèmes de Jean Cocteau, 87–8
   Pièces en trio, 86
   'Prélude' (*L'Album des Six*), 88
Auriol, Georges, 22, 23
Ax, Emanuel, 252

Bakst, Léon, 54
Balanchine, George, 32
Ballets Russes, 32, 42, 63, 80, 97, 217, 218, 222, 234–5
Ballets Suédois, 26, 54, 90, 97, 213, 217, 218, 222, 226–7, 232–4, 239
Barbazanges, Galerie, 157, 168, 208
Barbier, Jean-Joël, 106
Barraqué, Jean, 248–9
barrel organ (orgue de Barbarie), 8–18, 35, 45–6, 93
Bathori, Jane, 79, 152, 246
Battier, Marc, 48, 61
Baudelaire, Charles, 2, 13, 14
   Morale du joujou, 16
Bazaillas, Albert, 58–9
Beaumont, Edith de (Comtesse), 205, 221–2
Beaumont, Etienne de (Comte), 217, 218, 221–2, 224, 237, 242
Beethoven, Ludwig van: Symphony no. 5, 102
Bergson, Henri, 43, 102
Bertelin, Albert, 100
Bertin, Pierre, 87, 151, 152, 153, 157, 158, 160, 162, 164, 168
Bertrand, Paul, 90, 234–5
Berys, José de, 163, 169

Bibi-la-Purée (pseudonym of André Salis), 188
Blémont, Emile, 3
Blind Man, The, 208, 211, 212, 217
Blood, Sweat and Tears: *Variations on a Theme of Erik Satie*, 253
Bongard, Germaine, 208
Börlin, Jean, 231, 232
Boulanger, General Georges, 24
Boulanger, Lili, 116
Boulez, Pierre, 249
   Chien flasque, 247–8
Brancusi (Brâncuși), Constantin, 144, 171, 203, 236, 242
Braque, Georges, 152, 237
Breton, André, 212, 213, 215, 216, 225, 228
Buffet, Gabrielle (later Picabia), 136
Busoni, Ferruccio, 61

Caby, Robert, 139, 218, 236, 239, 244, 245, 246
Cage, John, 18, 221, 250–1, 253
   Cheap Imitation, 251
   $FOUR^3$, 251
Calvocoressi, Michel-Dimitri, 99, 100, 208
Canudo, Ricciotto, 53–5, 62, 93–4, 95, 207, 208, 227
Caran d'Ache, 23–4, 25
   L'épopée, 23
Carnot, Sadi, 24, 184
Carol-Bérard, [Louis], 60–2, 80, 243
   Symphonie des forces mécaniques, 61
Carroll, Lewis, 108
Casella, Alfredo, 51–2, 54, 93
Catulle-Mendès, Jane, 232–4
Cendrars, Blaise, 48, 103, 151, 156, 189, 206, 226–7, 229, 231
   'Musickissme, Le', 151
   Prose du Transsibérien et de la petite Jehanne de France, La, 48
Chabrier, Emmanuel, 1, 74, 243
   Etoile, L', 74
   Fisch-Ton-Kan, 74
   'Idylle' (*Pièces pittoresques* no. 6), 122
   Vaucochard et fils 1er, 74
Chalupt, René, 108, 130, 247

Chat Noir
   cabaret, 2, 21–6, 187–8
   journal, 5, 7, 14, 18–19, 22, 25, 33–4, 105, 107, 110, 116, 164–5, 181–2, 187, 207
Chopin, Frédéric
   Berceuse, 154–5
   Funeral March (Sonata in B flat minor), 103, 143
Cinésketch, 229
Clair, René, 26, 27, 96, 206, 222, 227, 229
   Entr'acte, 227–9, 232–4, 244
Cliquet-Pleyel, Henri, 214, 234
Cocteau, Jean, 31–2, 42, 44, 50, 60, 73, 75–7, 80, 83–9, 129, 145, 150, 151–3, 156, 157, 158, 184, 209, 213, 214, 217, 218, 221, 224, 225, 227–8, 239, 247
   Coq et l'Arlequin, Le, 42, 79, 83, 104, 205, 214
   'Hommage à Erik Satie', 88, 151
   Mariés de la Tour Eiffel, Les, 88, 213
   Midsummer Night's Dream (project), 63, 84
Cœur à barbe, Le, 208, 209, 215
Collet, Henri, 88
Comœdia, 158, 163, 169–70, 216
Contamine de Latour, Patrice (a.k.a. Lord Cheminot), 3, 5, 24, 56, 100, 242
Copeau, Jacques, 152
Coq, Le, 209
Corvin, Michel, 79
Cousin, Victor, 145
Cowley, Earl of (Henry Wellesley), 10
Craft, Robert, 93
Cros, Charles, 183, 187
   as author, 2, 33–4
   inventor of phonautograph (paleophone), 2, 179, 180
Cunningham, Merce, 221, 250–1

Dada, 206, 213–17, 225, 228–9, 232
Dandelot, Arthur, 85
Darty, Paulette, 21, 31, 192
Davis, Mary E., 83, 106
Davies, Hugh, 52–3
Dawson, Christopher, 114, 139–40, 142
Dayan, Peter, 68, 179

Index of Names

Debussy, Claude, 7, 28, 47, 50, 63, 90, 98, 100, 101, 103–4, 115, 116, 121, 123, 128, 129, 136, 173, 177, 202, 209, 238, 243, 247, 248–9
  Ariettes oubliées, 133
  Boîte à joujoux, La, 103
  'Cathédrale engloutie, La' (*Préludes* book 1), 104
  Cinq Poèmes de Baudelaire, 241
  Diable dans le beffroi, Le, 131
  Estampes, 241
  Etudes, 123
  Gymnopédies (Satie orch. Debussy), 243
  'Hommage à S. S. Pickwick' (*Préludes* book 2), 37, 102–3
  Images (piano), 143, 241
  Marche écossaise, 38–9
  Mer, La, 123, 127, 131
  'Mouvement' (*Images* book 1), 143
  Pelléas et Mélisande, 129
  Sonata for flute, viola and harp, 100
Delaunay, Sonia: *Prose du Transsibérien et de la petite Jehanne de France, La*, 48
Delgrange, Félix, 151–2, 162, 164
Demets, Eugène, 101
Dépaquit, Jules, 28–31, 34, 38–40, 44, 56, 192, 246
  L'Eponge en porcelaine, 31
Derain, André, 32, 206, 217–21, 226, 236, 237, 242
Dermée, Paul, 156
Descombes, Emile, 1
Désormière, Roger, 216, 234, 239, 242
Diaghilev, Serge, 60, 73, 76, 218, 227
Dickens, Charles, 12
  Our Mutual Friend, 35–7
  Pickwick Papers, The, 37
Dickinson, Peter, 249–50, 251
Divan japonais, Le, 3
Dossena, Pietro, 231, 232
Drew, David, 74–5
Duchamp, Marcel, 210, 211, 229
Dukas, Paul, 60, 123, 206, 247
Duncan, Isadora, 54
Durey, Louis, 87, 88, 89, 90, 152, 245
  Carillons, 86, 87, 90
  Images à Crusoé, 87
  Neige, 90

Ecorcheville, Jules, 208
Ecole d'Arcueil, 234
Edison, Thomas, 2, 180, 186–7
Edwards, Misia, *see* Sert, Misia
Eiffel Tower, 184
Elan, L', 208
Eluard, Paul, 216, 228
Exposition Universelle (1889), 184–7

Falla, Manuel de, 54, 168
Fargue, Léon-Paul, 221–2
Fauré, Gabriel, 52, 154–5
Faure-Favier, Louise, 156
Fauser, Annegret, 184–6
Feldman, Morton, 142–3, 175
Flamel, Nicolas, 183
Flaubert, Gustave, 1
  La Tentation de saint Antoine, 24–5
Fragerolle, Georges, 27
  La marche à l'étoile, 27–8
Fratellini brothers, 40, 44, 63
Fulcher, Jane, 108, 187–8, 191, 192
Fuller, Loïe, 54
Fumet, Dynam-Victor, 187–8
Fung, Catherine, 141–2

Ganne, Louis: *Les Saltimbanques*, 75
Gavioli (barrel organ manufacturer), 78, 221
Gide, André, 147n18, 154, 228
Gillmor, Alan, 103, 104, 108, 125
Gleizes, Albert, 54, 64, 208
Godard, Benjamin, 154–5
Golschmann, Vladimir, 207
Goudeau, Emile, 2, 28, 187
Gounod, Charles: 'Chanson de Magali' (*Mireille*), 108
Granados, Enrique, 208
Gross, Valentine (later Hugo), 55, 73, 84, 199, 247
Guichard, Léon, 102, 109

Hackett, Steve: *Sketches of Satie*, 253
Haine, Malou, 153
Halbreich, Harry, 154
Hanlon, Ann-Marie, 43, 107, 136
Harris, Sybil, 172–3
Hébertot, Jacques, 217
Henry, Charles, 180
Herrand, Marcel, 34, 246

Hocquet, Vital ('Narcisse Lebeau'), 7
Honegger, Arthur, 86, 87, 88, 89, 152, 153–5, 245
  Dit des jeux du monde, Le, 79
  Musique d'ameublement (Entrée, Nocturne et Berceuse), 87, 153–5
  Skating Rink, 54
  Pacific 231, 153
  Trois Couleurs, 153–4
  Violin Sonata no. 2, 88
Honfleur, 115–17, 181
Hooreman, Paul, 236
Hugill, Andrew, 24–5
Hugo, Jean, 199
Hugo, Valentine, *see* Gross, Valentine
Hugo, Victor, 124
  Dieu, 128–9
Humanité, L' (Communist newspaper), 165, 180, 192, 201–2, 203–4, 244
Huysmans, Joris-Karl, 184
  A rebours, 114
Hydropathes, 2–3, 28, 187
Hyspa, Vincent, 21, 26, 29, 31, 39, 107, 137, 192
  Noël, 26

Indy, Vincent d', 62, 192
Inglis, Katherine, 35

Jacob, Max, 31, 66, 155–62, 168–9, 208, 213
  Cabinet noir, Le, 149
  Matorel en province, 31
  Phanérogame, 159
  Ruffian toujours, truand jamais, 149, 155, 157–62, 168–70, 195, 206
  Trois nouveaux figurants du théâtre, 157
Jacob, Maxime, 155n45, 234
Jankélévitch, Vladimir, 16, 95, 103–4, 105, 136
Jarry, Alfred, 182, 247
Jaurès, Jean, 198, 202
Jean-Aubry, Georges, 234
Jordan-Morhange, Hélène, 131n60
Joseph-Lafosse Satie, Pierre (great-nephew of Satie), 249
Jourdain, Francis, 33

Kahn, Douglas, 182
Klüver, Billy, 157, 159
Koechlin, Charles, 87, 152, 245

Laforgue, Jules, 13, 15–16
  Les complaintes, 15
Lamartine, Alphonse de, 58
Lambert, Constant, 225–6, 247
Lanterne japonaise, La, 3, 7; *see also Divan japonais, Le*
Lara, Louise, 79
Latude, Jean-Henri, 3–4
Lawson, Rex, 93–4
Le Flem, Paul, 161
'Lebeau, Narcisse', 7–8; *see also* Vital Hocquet
'Lebeau, Virginie' (pseudonym of Satie), 8
Leblanc, Georgette, 96
Léger, Fernand, 96, 144–5
L'Herbier, Marcel: *L'inhumaine*, 95–6
Lejeune, Emile, 85, 151
Lemoine, Jean-Gabriel, 169
Lenin, Vladimir Ilyich, 203
Levadé, Charles, 3–4
Lhote, André, 64

Malipiero, Gian Francesco, 93
Mallarmé, Stéphane, 2, 3
  Coup de dés, Un, 48
  Plainte d'automne, 15–16
Man Ray (Emmanuel Radnitzky), 30, 96, 224–5, 229
Maré, Rolf de, 90, 227
Marinetti, Filippo Tommaso, 26–7, 48, 49–50, 210
  Futurisme mondial, Le, 51
  Futurist Manifesto, 49
  Futurist synthetic theatre manifesto, 49–50
Maritain, Jacques, 237–8
Martin, Charles, 69, 106
Marx, Karl: *Das Kapital*, 200
Massine, Léonide, 44, 60, 67, 73, 145, 217, 222
Mattis, Olivia, 64–5
Médrano, Cirque, 40, 42, 43–4, 63
Méerovitch, Juliette, 86
Melchers, Henrik, 85
Mellers, Wilfrid, 247

Menaker Rothschild, Deborah, 42, 45, 67, 69
Méral, Paul, 79, 154
Mesens, E. L. T., 247
Meyer, Agnes (Mrs Eugene, née Ernst), 171, 210–11
Meyer, Marcelle, 93, 158, 164, 168, 217, 243, 246
Milhaud, Darius, 32, 43–4, 66, 86, 89, 90, 95–6, 141, 152, 162–4, 168, 172, 214, 216, 226, 234, 236–7, 239, 241, 242, 243, 245
   Bœuf sur le toit, Le, 221
   Caramel mou, 214
   Création du monde, La, 234
   Opéras-minute, 90
   Printemps, 163, 168
   String Quartet no. 4, 87
   Symphonies de chambre, 90
   Train bleu, Le, 235
Milhaud, Madeleine, 236, 246
Minors, Helen Julia, 106
Monnier, Adrienne, 228
Monteux, Pierre, 54
Montjoie!, 54–6, 227
Montmartre, 1–8, 13, 17–18, 21–3, 26, 28–9, 39, 41–4, 46, 47, 53, 115, 179–83, 206–7, 215, 222
Montparnasse, 47–8, 83–5, 150–1, 206, 233, 237, 249
Mortier, Jane, 104–5, 250
Myers, Rollo, 247

Napoleon III, 10
Nichols, Roger, 105, 123
Norton, Louise (later Varèse), 217

Oberthür, Mariel, 17
orgue de Barbarie, *see* barrel organ
Orledge, Robert, 26, 39, 55–6, 72, 76, 86, 110, 116, 125, 164, 188, 209, 217, 218, 221, 222, 224, 244, 249
Ozenfant, Amédée, 106–7, 150, 188, 208, 215

Peignot, Suzanne, 209
Péladan, Sâr Joséphin, 62
   Le Fils des étoiles, 62, 138–9
Perdriat, Hélène, 227
Perlmutter, Bronia, 229

Perloff, Nancy, 5, 44
Piatti, Ugo, 52
Picabia, Francis, 27, 67, 171–2, 206, 208, 209, 210, 211, 212, 213, 224–5, 227–34
Picard, Gaston, 207
Picasso, Pablo, 11, 41–2, 44, 60, 66, 67, 73, 85, 90, 145, 152, 188, 206, 217, 222, 224, 225, 237
Pickford, Mary, 73
Plato, 145–6
Player piano, 18–19
Poiré, Emmanuel, *see* Caran d'Ache
Poiret, Paul, 156–7, 208
Polignac, Princesse Edmond de, 82, 153
Populaire, Le (Socialist newspaper), 244–5
Poueigh, Jean, 80–3, 86, 158, 235; *see also* Séré, Octave
Poulenc, Francis, 71, 72, 86, 88, 89, 115, 122, 209, 214, 225, 234, 242, 247
   Biches, Les, 209, 235
   Mouvements perpétuels, 90, 229
   Sonata for two clarinets, 87
Pratella, Francesco Balilla, 52
   Manifesto of Futurist Musicians, 51
   Musica futurista, 52
Prokofiev, Serge, 227
Puvis de Chavannes, Pierre, 138

Radiguet, Raymond, 89, 217, 218, 239
Ravel, Maurice, 22, 42, 47, 53, 54, 63–4, 87, 91, 93–5, 98, 99, 100, 101, 103, 116, 252
   as reader of *Le Populaire*, 244–5
   Boléro, 94
   Daphnis et Chloé, 219
   Frontispice, 93–4
   Noël des jouets, 174
   Sainte, 95
   Tombeau de Couperin, Le, 16
Read, General Meredith, 38–9
Reverdy, Pierre, 156
Ribemont-Dessaignes, Georges, 216, 228
Richardson, John, 76, 237
Rimsky-Korsakov, Andrei, 93
Rivière, Henri, 23

Roché, Henri-Pierre, 64, 171, 172, 208, 210, 211
Roland-Manuel (Alexis Lévy), 42–3, 86, 87, 98, 101, 207, 236, 252
Rousseau, Henri (Le Douanier), 88, 242, 247
   Charmeuse de serpents, La, 125
   Rêve, Le, 125
Roussel, Albert, 60, 62, 87, 123–4, 245
Roy, Jean, 247
Rubinstein, Ida, 54
Rusiñol, Santiago, 26
   Portrait of Eric Satie at the harmonium, 27
   Romanza, Una, 26, 139–40
Russolo, Luigi, 52–3, 60, 210
   L'Arte dei Rumori (The Art of Noises), 52, 67

Saint-Point, Valentine de, 51, 53–60, 62, 67, 94, 221, 227
   Manifesto of the Futurist Woman, 53
   Poèmes ironiques, 58
Saint-Saëns, Camille, 164–5
   Danse macabre, 129, 131, 164, 166–7
Salis, Rodolphe, 5, 22, 23, 28
Salmon, André, 156
Sanouillet, Michel, 214
Sarcey, Francisque, 4
Satie, Adrien ('Sea Bird') (uncle), 115
Satie, Alfred (father), 6, 30
Satie, Conrad (brother), 29, 30, 70, 110, 115, 127, 180–1, 239
Satie, Jane (née Anton, mother), 30, 38, 125
Satie, Olga (sister), 73n72, 249
Savinio, Alberto, 68, 211
Sauguet, Henri, 141, 234, 243, 246
Sauret, Henriette, 207
Schmitt, Florent, 53, 54, 63–4
Schola Cantorum, Satie studies at, 1, 32, 47, 62, 124, 191, 243
Schubert, Franz, alleged author of 'Mazurka', 103
Scott de Martinville, Edouard-Léon, 179
Séré, Octave (pseudonym of Jean Poueigh), 177
Sert, Misia, 82
Shattuck, Roger, 18, 146, 247

Skempton, Howard, 252
Sidobre, Marius, 203–4, 238
Sirène, La (music and book publisher), 31–2, 227
Sivry, Charles de, 14, 27–8, 183
   Ailleurs, 28
Soirée de Paris (Etienne de Beaumont's ballet season), 217, 222
Soirées de Paris, Les (magazine), 66
Soupault, Philippe, 213
Souris, André, 236
Stieglitz, Alfred, 171, 210
Stravinsky, Igor, 19, 54, 63–4, 66, 91–3, 170, 173, 174, 216, 234, 235, 238, 243, 253
   Berceuse du chat, 164, 168
   Etude pour pianola, 19, 91–2
   Noces, Les, 93, 97, 218
   Petrushka, 58, 77, 93
   Rite of Spring, The (Le Sacre du printemps), 55

Tailleferre, Germaine, 86, 88, 89, 90, 152, 168, 205, 233
   Jeux de plein air, 90
   Image, 87
   Marchand d'oiseaux, Le, 227, 233
Templier, (Pierre-)Alexandre, 115, 189, 193, 204
Templier, Pierre-Daniel, 175, 189
Thomas, Ambroise, 164–5, 175, 207
   Mignon, 164–5
Thomson, Virgil, 247, 250, 252
Tinchant, Albert, 22
Townsend, Christopher, 26
Tzara, Tristan, 125, 206, 208, 213, 215, 216, 228
   Le Cœur à gaz, 215, 216

Utrillo, Maurice, 26
Utrillo, Miguel (Utrillo y Molins, Miquel), 26

Valadon, Suzanne, 26
   relationship with Satie, 26, 139–40
Varèse, Edgard, 60, 62–4, 210, 212
   Rapsodie romane, 62–3
Varèse, Louise, *see* Norton, Louise
Vaurabourg, Andrée, 88, 164
Vechten, Carl van, 54, 105, 172, 247

Verlaine, Paul, 2, 3, 5, 13, 14–15, 28, 74, 116, 127, 133
  'Echelonnement des haies, L'', 128
  Epigrammes, 14
  'Heure du berger, L'', 128, 133
  'Mon rêve familier', 116
  'Nocturne parisien', 14–15
  'Ombre des arbres, L'', 133
Veyssière, André, 188, 190, 195, 196–7
Veyssière, Léon-Louis, 189, 191–2, 193–5, 196, 197, 198–9, 200–1, 204, 245
Villiers de l'Isle-Adam, Jean-Marie-Mathias-Philippe-Auguste de, 3
Viñes, Ricardo, 60, 73, 82, 93, 101, 115
Volta, Ornella, 26, 29, 31, 32, 38, 62, 73, 138, 149, 172, 180, 192, 193, 198, 218, 231, 242
Vuillermoz, Emile, 209

Wagner, Richard, 50
Whiting, Steven Moore, 2, 4, 21, 22, 23, 24, 33, 39–40, 63, 65, 98, 107, 126, 133, 136–7, 183, 227, 231, 249
Wiéner, Jean, 239, 245
Wilde, Oscar, 205
  Salomé, 31
Wilkins, Nigel, 249
Willy (Henri Gauthier-Villars), 209
Wood, Beatrice, 210, 211

Index of Works by Satie
(including projects and sketches)

Airs à faire fuir, see *Pièces froides*
Alice au Pays de Merveilles, 217
Aperçus désagréables, 58
Archidanses, Les, 218
Avant-dernières pensées, 71, 110, 111, 112, 113, 114, 118, 121–4

Belle Excentrique, La, 246

Carrelage phonique, 147, 149–50, 152, 155
Carrelage pour cabinet noir de luxe, 148–9
Chanson hongroise, 184
Chapitres tournés en tous sens, 112, 113, 114
 'Celle qui parle trop', 118–21
Chemise, La, 192
Chez le docteur, 21
Choses vues à droite et à gauche (sans lunettes), 110, 111, 112
Cinéma, see *Relâche*
Cinq Grimaces pour 'Le Songe d'une nuit d'été', 63–6, 171, 242
Concurrence, 218
Corcleru, 99
Couleurs, 218
Croquis et agaceries d'un gros bonhomme en bois, 111, 114

Danses de travers, see *Pièces froides*
Descriptions automatiques, 58, 112, 113
Dîner à l'Elysée, Un, 31
Diva de 'l'Empire', La, 21

Embryons desséchés, 101–3, 107, 112, 113, 114, 143, 159
En Habit de cheval, 177
Enfantillages pittoresques, 211

Fantaisie-valse, 7
Fils des étoiles, Le, 138–9, 177

Geneviève de Brabant, 25, 241, 242
Globules ennuyeux, Les, 116

Gnossiennes, 26, 68, 98, 146
Gymnopédies, 3–4, 6–7, 17, 18, 41, 50, 98, 109, 138, 139, 146, 219, 224, 239, 252

Heures séculaires et instantanées, 104, 111, 112, 113, 114, 119, 124–36

Irnebizolle, 99

Jack in the Box, 29–41, 43, 69, 104, 138, 218, 241, 242, 246
Je te veux, 21

Ludions, 222

Menus propos enfantins, 111, 112, 113
Mercure, 156, 206, 217, 222–6
Messe des pauvres, 63, 139
Motifs lumineux, 31
Musique d'ameublement, 25, 31, 49, 137, 144–76
 1920 set (*Sons industriels*), 163–8

Naissance de Vénus, La, 218–20

Ogives, 6, 7, 116
Ontrotance, 99

Pantins dansent, Les, 54–60
Papier phonique, 148
Parade, 39, 41–2, 44, 50, 60, 67, 73–83, 86, 152, 175, 177, 221, 224, 225–6
Paul & Virginie, 217, 239, 242, 243
Peccadilles importunes, 111, 112, 113
Pièces froides, 99, 100, 107, 111, 178
Piège de Méduse, Le, 5, 29–30, 38, 56, 58, 73, 83, 98, 125, 183, 215, 246, 250, 251
Prélude de la Porte héroïque du ciel, 98, 104
Préludes flasques (pour un chien), 58, 248

Relâche, 26, 50, 97, 156, 175, 206, 208, 212, 217, 218, 226–34, 236, 244

Sarabandes, 1, 7, 99, 164, 177
Socrate, 61, 109, 146–7, 148, 188, 214, 219, 224, 228, 239–41, 243, 244, 250, 251
Sonatine bureaucratique, 110, 111, 112, 113, 246
Sonnerie pour réveiller le bon gros Roi des Singes (lequel ne dort toujours que d'un œil), 110, 111, 113, 190
Sonneries de la Rose+Croix, 139
Sports et divertissements, 140, 253
  'Bain de mer, Le', 112, 113
  'Balançoire, La', 111
  'Carnaval, Le', 112
  'Chasse, La', 113
  'Colin-Maillard', 111, 112
  'Comédie Italienne, La', 112
  'Courses, Les', 113
  'Feu d'Artifice, Le', 112, 113
  'Flirt, Le', 112, 113
  'Golf, Le', 69–71, 106, 112, 113
  'Pêche, La', 112, 113
  'Picnic, Le', 111, 113
  'Pieuvre, La', 111, 113
  'Quatre Coins, Les', 112, 113
  'Réveil de la Mariée, Le', 113, 114
  'Tango, Le', 113
  'Tennis, Le', 111, 112
  'Traineau, Le', 113
  'Water-chute, Le', 111, 112, 113
  'Yachting, Le', 112, 113

Statue retrouvée, La (Divertissement), 222
Supercinéma, 217–18, 226

Tapisserie en fer forgé, 147–50, 152, 155
Tenture de Cabinet préfectoral, 171–3
Tenture sonore, 148
Trépied à deux pieds, 107, 148
Trois mélodies: 'Chapelier, Le', 108
Trois morceaux en forme de poire, 53, 73–4, 88, 177, 216
Trois petites pièces montées, 209, 221
Trois poèmes d'amour, 5, 98, 190, 246
Trois Valses distinguées du Précieux dégoûté, Les, 111, 112, 114, 246

uspud, 24–5, 100

Valse-ballet, 7
Véritables Préludes flasques (pour un chien), 101, 111, 113, 114, 137
Vexations, 93, 135, 139–42, 174, 251
Vieux sequins et vieilles cuirasses, 110, 112, 114, 143–4

www.ingramcontent.com/pod-product-compliance
Lightning Source LLC
Chambersburg PA
CBHW050208240426
43671CB00013B/2261